HOHOKAM ARCHAEOLOGY ALONG PHASE B OF THE TUCSON AQUEDUCT
CENTRAL ARIZONA PROJECT

Volume 3: Excavations at Water World (AZ AA:16:94)
A Rillito Phase Ballcourt Village in the Avra Valley

Edited by

Jon S. Czaplicki and John C. Ravesloot

Contributions by

Jon S. Czaplicki
William L. Deaver
R. Thomas Euler
Suzanne K. Fish
Sherry C. Fox
Robert E. Gasser
William B. Gillespie

Ronald Gardiner
Carl D. Halbirt
Bruce B. Huckell
Martha Hueglin
Scott Kwiatkowski
John C. Ravesloot
Arthur W. Vokes

Prepared for

United States Bureau of Reclamation
Contract No. 6-CS-30-03500

Cultural Resource Management Division
Arizona State Museum
University of Arizona

1989

Archaeological Series 178, Volume 3

CONTENTS

FIGURES

TABLES

PREFACE

This is the third of five volumes that report results of the Tucson Aqueduct Phase B Project. The excavation was funded by the United States Bureau of Reclamation under Contract No. 6-CS-30-03500 from December 1985 to December 1988. In this volume the results of excavations at Water World (AZ AA:16:94), a Rillito phase Hohokam ballcourt village located at the southern end of the Avra Valley west of Tucson, Arizona, are described.

The Tucson Aqueduct Phase B project involved excavation or surface collection and mapping of 13 sites including Water World. Other sites investigated during the 1986 field season included Fastimes (AZ AA:12:384 ASM), a collection of at least five Hohokam farmsteads; two farmstead-field house sites (AZ AA:16:97 and AZ AA:16:161); a probable protohistoric site (AZ AA:11:26); four limited-activity sites (AZ AA:12:383, AZ AA:12:465, AZ AA:12:481, and AZ AA:12:484, better known as Hawk's Nest); and four quarry sites (AZ AA:16:95, AZ AA:16:96, AZ AA:16:157, and AZ AA:16:175). Data recovery at these sites is described and discussed in other volumes that have been arranged in the following manner.

Volume 1. Interpretation and Synthesis

This volume provides synthetic discussions of the various specialized studies as well as chapters on the project research design, geomorphological assessment of the project area and sites, excavation strategy and methods, and an evaluation of the Phase B data recovery project.

Volume 2. Excavations at Fastimes (AZ AA:12:384)

Volume 2 provides detailed descriptions of the excavation results from a Rillito phase site located near the northern end of the Avra Valley. In addition to a background discussion of the site, there are chapters on site chronology, excavated and unexcavated features, material culture, and concluding thoughts and interpretations.

Volume 4.   Small Sites and Specialized Studies

This volume contains the results of investigations conducted at
11 small sites, including the late Pioneer-early Colonial period site of
Hawk's Nest (AZ AA:12:484).   Also included are reports on the
archaeomagnetic dating of Phase B sites, turquoise source analysis, and
supplemental survey of some 4,000 acres along the Phase B corridor.

Volume 5.   Data Appendixes

A fifth volume provides specific provenience data for ceramic,
flaked stone, ground stone, shell, and faunal remains recovered during
the Phase B excavations.

Successful completion of the excavations at Water World was the
result of the cooperation and perseverance of a number of people.   In
the field, excavation during the 1986 and 1987 field seasons was
supervised by Tom Euler; in 1986, Tom was ably assisted by Carl Halbirt.
Crew members for the 1986 season were Martha Hueglin, Terry Miskell,
Joan Lloyd, Robin Poague, Kathleen Green, Ruben Vasquez, Fred Ortega,
Ron Beckwith, Gerri Antone, Deni Seymour, Rick Anduze, Holly De Maagd,
and Brenda Randolph.   During the brief 1987 season, Ron Gardiner and
Rick Anduze worked with Tom Euler.   Ed Brooks and Georgina Boyor
provided valuable volunteer assistance during the excavation.

Greg Thompson served as backhoe operator in 1986, and in 1987
Dan Arntt provided backhoe services.   General site mapping and gridding
were done by Charles Sternberg.   General field and public relations
photography were done by Arizona State Museum photographer Helga Teiwes
and Cultural Resource Management Division photographer Jannelle Weakley.
The Bureau of Reclamation provided aerial photographs of the site.
Michael Waters provided a geomorphological assessment of the site area.
Archaeomagnetic samples were collected by Barbara Murphy and Bill
Deaver.   Sharon Urban, staff archaeologist for the Arizona State Museum,
served as tour guide for three public tours of the site that were
offered as part of a public information program.   Another facet of this
important program was the development and installation at the Arizona-
Sonora Desert Museum (ASDM) of two exhibits on the excavation project.
Rex Clausen developed the 1986 exhibit, and Ron Gardiner and Dave
Klanderman teamed up to do the 1987 exhibit.   These exhibits could not
have been possible without the cooperation of David Beals, Assistant
Director of the ASDM, and Mitch Basefsky, Exhibits Curator at the ASDM;
both deserve special thanks for their assistance.

Material from the Water World excavation was processed at the
Arizona State Museum archaeological laboratory.   Under the supervision
of Arthur W. Vokes, laboratory personnel washed, labeled, and cataloged
the thousands of artifacts recovered.   Several people deserve mention

for their work during the course of the project: Lisa Zimmerman, Susan Crawford, Jannelle Weakley, Priscilla Molinari, Nadine Oftedahl, and John Leonard.

Producing the final report on the results of the Water World excavations was a major undertaking that required the cooperation of many people. Specialists who contributed to the research and report writing include: William L. Deaver, ceramics; Bruce B. Huckell, flaked stone; Carl D. Halbirt, ground stone; Arthur W. Vokes, shell and architecture; William B. Gillespie, nonhuman vertebrate remains; Sherry C. Fox, human remains; Suzanne K. Fish, pollen; and Robert E. Gasser and Scott Kwiatkowski, macrofloral (flotation) remains. Archaeomagnetic samples were analyzed by Jeffrey Eighmy and J. Holly Hathaway of the Colorado State University Archaeomagnetic Laboratory. Carbon-14 dating was done at the University of Arizona Tandem Accelerator Facility, and wood charcoal identifications were made by Richard Warren of the University of Arizona Tree-Ring Laboratory.

Special thanks go to Ron Gardiner who proofed drafts, checked and rechecked tables, and compiled data for other tables. Charles Sternberg drafted the maps, graphs, charts, and feature plans and profiles. Ron Beckwith and Helga Teiwes photographed the artifacts; Ron also helped to correct errors in some of the drafted figures during final editing of the volume. Word processing was done by Jeanne Witt, Alice Prochnow, and Barbara Murphy. Carol Heathington and C. A. Gualtieri edited the volume. Heathington supervised manuscript preparation prior to printing and worked with the printers during the production stage. Lynn S. Teague served as co-principal investigator for the Phase B project and, as Head of the Cultural Resource Management Division, provided support and guidance during the project. Tom Lincoln of the Bureau of Reclamation also deserves thanks for his continued support since the first days of the project. Undoubtedly, there are people we forgot to mention. To these unnamed, but not unimportant people, we apologize and thank you.

Jon S. Czaplicki
John C. Ravesloot

ABSTRACT

During 1986 and 1987 archaeologists from the Cultural Resource Management Division, Arizona State Museum, University of Arizona, excavated a Rillito phase Hohokam settlement that lay in the right-of-way for the Tucson Aqueduct Phase B, Central Arizona Project. Known as Water World (AZ AA:16:94 ASM), the site is located at the southern end of the Avra Valley on the distal end of a lower bajada of the Tucson Mountains.

One hundred and forty-seven features were identified by backhoe trenching and surface stripping, including 45 structures. Fifty-nine features were investigated: 21 structures, a ballcourt, 14 pits or hearths, 21 cremations, a midden deposit, and potbreak. The features were divided into seven house groups, a ballcourt area, and a possible central plaza.

The artifactual, nonartifactual, and site structure data suggest that Water World was a formalized ballcourt village that was probably occupied permanently for a relatively short period of time during the Rillito phase (A.D. 700 to 900) of the Colonial period. It is also possible that the site's population increased during the winter months, when residents subsisted on stored food supplies.

Water World is located in a nonriverine environment where flood-water farming potential should have been very good. There are, however, tentative hints that agriculture may not have been as intensively practiced as expected. Furthermore, the apparent paucity of the ritual and ceremonial objects that were also expected at a ballcourt site brings into question how the site may have functioned in local Hohokam economic organization.

Chapter 1

BACKGROUND INFORMATION ON THE EXCAVATION

Jon S. Czaplicki
Ronald Gardiner
and
Martha Hueglin

Research Objectives and Volume Organization

The Tucson Aqueduct Phase B data recovery project represents the first substantial archaeological excavations to be conducted in the Avra Valley. Prior to the 1983 intensive survey of the Phase B alignment by archaeologists from the Arizona State Museum, archaeological investigation of the Avra Valley had been limited primarily to occasional archaeological clearance surveys and test excavations. The identification of 47 prehistoric sites during the 1983 survey (Downum and others 1986) and the investigation of 13 of these sites during the 1986 data recovery project mark the beginning of intensive archaeological studies of this previously little-studied area west of Tucson.

As stated in the research design (Volume 1, Chapter 2), data recovery at the 13 Phase B sites selected for investigation had two broad objectives. The first was to focus research on themes relevant to the larger objectives of Central Arizona Project research and to other investigations underway in southern Arizona (Teague and Crown 1983-1984; Doelle 1985a, 1985b; Doelle and Wallace 1986; Doelle and others 1985; Rice and others 1984; Dart and others 1985; Rice 1987; Henderson 1987; Dart 1987). The other objective was to contribute to a better understanding of the pre-Classic period, specifically the Rillito phase, in the Tucson Basin area. This was to be accomplished by compiling a data base that could be used to begin to address questions of chronology, organization, and economy. Research efforts were geared toward acquiring a broadly defined data base that could be compared with data and interpretations from other studies along Phase A of the Tucson Aqueduct (Weaver and others 1986; Ciolek-Torrello 1987; Rice 1985, 1987; Henderson 1987), from along the Salt-Gila Aqueduct (Teague and Crown 1983-1984), from ANAMAX-Rosemont (Ferg and others 1984), from the San Xavier Bridge Site (Ravesloot 1987), and from the Hodges Ruin (Kelly 1978; Layhe 1986).

1

The primary data recovery effort was focused on Fastimes (AZ AA:12:384) and Water World (AZ AA:16:94), two large Rillito phase settlements that offered the best potential for recovering data on material culture, architecture, internal site organization, and chronology for this relatively unstudied phase. Proportionately less effort was to be given to two farmstead-field house sites (AZ AA:16:97 and AA:16:161), which were believed to have been occupied from the late Colonial period into the Sedentary and early Classic periods and which offered data on subsistence and settlement patterning. One possible protohistoric site (AZ AA:11:26) was investigated to obtain information on chronology, ceramics, and nonriverine subsistence during this little-studied period that has been the subject of considerable speculation. Finally, considerably less effort was spent on eight limited-activity sites (AZ AA:12:383, AA:12:465, AA:12:481, AA:12:484, AA:16:95, AA:16:96, AA:16:157, and AA:16:175). One of these sites, AZ AA:12:484 (or Hawk's Nest), required substantially more effort than expected (see Volume 4, Part 1). Data recovery efforts at these sites are described in other volumes.

This report is divided into 11 chapters. Background information including previous research, research objectives, data recovery strategy, and excavation methods is provided in Chapter 1. Chronological information and site structure are summarized in Chapter 2; in Chapter 3, architecture, trash deposits, and cremations are discussed, and excavated features are discussed in detail. Chapters 4 through 10 include detailed descriptive reports on ceramics, flaked-stone artifacts, ground-stone artifacts, shell artifacts, vertebrate (nonhuman) remains, pollen, and macroplant (flotation) remains, respectively. These data are discussed and site interpretation offered in Chapter 11.

Location and Environmental Setting

AZ AA:16:94 covers about 208,000 square meters and is located about 4 km southwest of Brown Mountain (Fig. 1.1). It was christened Water World by the survey crew after a nearby recreational vehicle park whose hallmark is a large water slide. The site name is somewhat of a misnomer, however, because the nearest naturally occurring water is a spring about 6 km away in the Tucson Mountains. The site is situated on an alluvial fan on the lower bajada of the Tucson Mountains, and the surface of the fan in the vicinity of Water World is composed of silty sand, gravel, and cobbles. Portions of the site have been affected by sheetwash, deflation, and gullying, which gave the impression at the time the site was recorded of potentially serious erosional disturbance to buried features (Rankin and Downum 1986: 68-72).

The alluvial fan deposit on which Water World rests is Holocene in age and is part of a discontinuous gully system; as a result, it is an area of active deposition and erosion (Waters and Field 1986; Waters, Volume 1, Chapter 3; also Schuster and Brackenridge 1986). Alternating

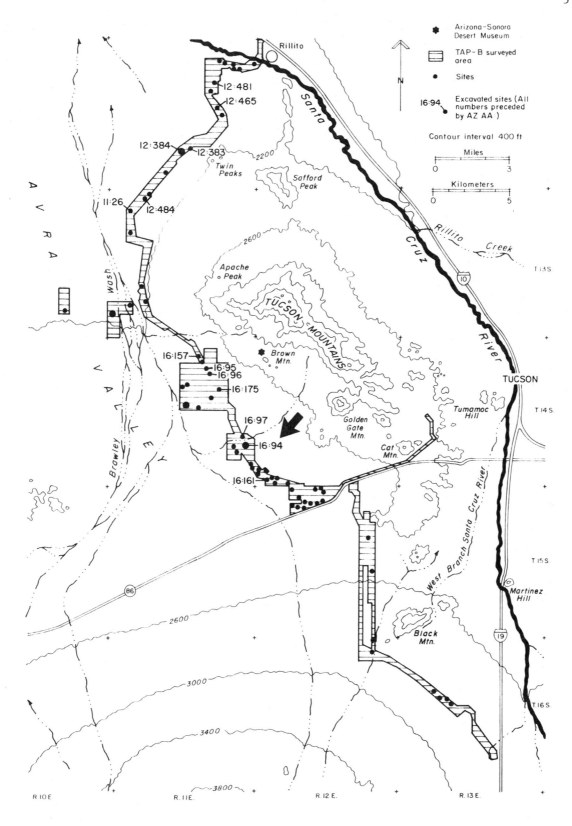

Figure 1.1. Map of Tucson Aqueduct Phase B showing location of the sites excavated during 1986. Water World (AZ AA:16:94) is located in the middle of the Phase B survey area (arrow).

sequences of deposition and erosion have not only affected the condition
of the site relative to preservation of features and artifacts (Downum
and others 1986), but also have provided at least one rationale for why
the Hohokam selected the area for occupation. The terminus of a
discontinuous gully fan provides an ideal situation for floodwater
farming because it is here that runoff spreads out over the desert
surface, depositing silt and providing moisture. Such a terminus is
located just west of Water World; the site itself is located in an area
where channelization would have limited, if not prevented, agricultural
pursuits (see Waters, Volume 1, Chapter 3).

A large wash cuts across the southern side of the site from the
northeast to the southwest, and two smaller washes cut across the
northern part of the site from the same direction. These larger washes,
along with numerous smaller washes that run across the site, flow
westward off the bajada and drain into Brawley Wash, the primary
tributary in the Avra Valley.

The dominant vegetation covering is creosote and bur sage, with
mesquite and cat claw acacia present along the larger washes. Saguaro
and barrel cacti also are scattered across the site (Rankin and Downum
1986: 68-73).

Previous Research

Water World was transect recorded and limited testing was
carried out as part of the 1983 Phase B survey (Downum and others 1986).
Systematic and random surface collections were made at this time (Fig.
1.2). Ten meter square collection units, placed in the northeast corner
of each of the 50-m by 50-m grid units that had been laid out over the
site, were completely surface collected. Random collection units of the
same size were placed in multiple artifact class (MAC) areas once these
had been defined by intensive transect recording (ITR; Czaplicki and
Heathington 1986: 33-40; also Volume 1, Chapter 4). ITR delineated
33,450 square meters of MAC area divided among 11 loci (Fig. 1.2).
Additionally, all decorated sherds, shell, and flaked-stone tools had
been provenienced and collected as they were encountered elsewhere on
the site. Analysis of the decorated sherds collected from the sample
units indicated that Water World was occupied primarily during the
Rillito phase (A.D. 700 to 900; Kelly 1978). The presence and surface
distribution of the few Snaketown/Cañada del Oro Red-on-buff/brown,
Cañada del Oro Red-on-brown, and Cañada del Oro/Rillito Red-on-brown
sherds collected suggested that site occupation may have begun near the
southern end of Locus 1 in the late Pioneer period (Downum 1986: 199,
201, Fig. 4.21).

Eleven series of trenches, totaling 529 m, were excavated with a
backhoe within and outside of MAC areas (Fig. 1.2). These trenches were
judgmentally placed to provide general information on the depth,
density, form, and preservation of buried features, as well as data on

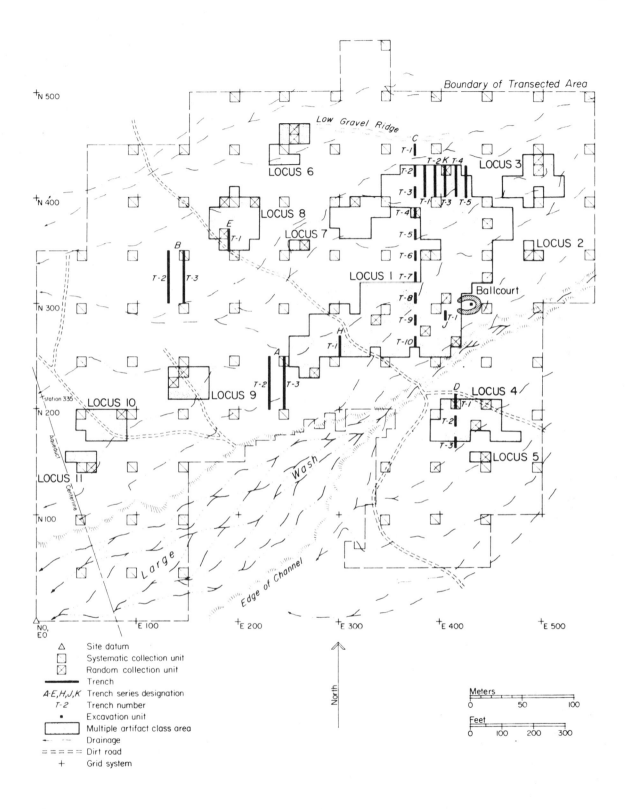

Figure 1.2. Map of Water World showing area that was transect recorded and location of backhoe trenches excavated during 1983 testing. Direct impact zone from aqueduct construction extends about 91 meters (300 feet) either side of centerline.

the predictive utility of the MAC area concept (Czaplicki and
Heathington 1986; Czaplicki and Ravesloot 1987; Volume 1, Chapter 4).

Six pit houses, one cremation, and several roasting pits and
trash deposits were identified by trenching; specific information on
the testing results can be found in Downum and others (1986). The
impression of Water World at the conclusion of testing was that the site
most likely contained abundant subsurface remains, especially in low-
lying or otherwise protected areas. Exposed high points, such as ridge
tops, were thought to have been badly damaged by erosion. Based on the
decorated ceramics recovered during testing, Water World appeared to
date primarily to the Rillito phase of the Colonial period (A.D. 700 to
900), with the possibility of earlier occupation during the early
Colonial period (Cañada del Oro phase, A.D. 500 to 700) and perhaps the
late Pioneer period (A.D. 300 to 500). Of particular interest was the
presence of a depression in the southern part of the site that was
tentatively identified as a ballcourt, the first such feature to be
reported in the Avra Valley (Fig. 1.2). The excavation of a test unit
in the ballcourt located a possible floor as well as a possible basin-
shaped pit (Rankin and Downum 1986: 90-91; Downum 1986: 198-210).

Research Objectives

Research efforts focused on chronology, site organization,
economy, and subsistence. The establishment and abandonment of the
site, as well as specific aspects of the Rillito phase such as ceramic
styles and architectural features, were to be dated by radiocarbon and
archaeomagnetic methods. Whenever possible, radiocarbon samples were to
be selected from features where archaeomagnetic samples also were
available. Local and regional relationships were to be studied using
intrusive ceramic types, shell artifacts, and other artifact types
recovered from the site. Analysis of the arrangement of pit houses and
extramural features was to provide information on Rillito phase
architecture and site structure. Environment and subsistence were to be
assessed using geomorphological, macrofloral, pollen, and faunal data.
Finally, the MAC area concept and intensive transect recording strategy
were to be evaluated through intensive mechanical trenching. Some of
the questions posed by Downum (1986: 198-212) that were considered
relevant for the data recovery project included:

1. Is it possible to construct a sequence of decorated ceramic
   styles within the Rillito phase, in essence a subphase
   chronology?

2. Do the faunal remains show significant differences in either
   the range or relative proportions of animal species?

3. Do the floral remains show significant differences in the relative abundance of maize remains between Fastimes and Water World? What is the importance of wild plant foods relative to domesticates like maize?

4. Are houses arranged in clusters of contemporaneous dwellings? If so, what is the function of the houses within a cluster?

5. Is there evidence for the production of ceramic or other crafts at the household level? Do some houses contain artifacts indicative of specialized subsistence or other pursuits?

Additional information on the Phase B research objectives is presented in Volume 1, Chapter 2. A discussion of the questions above can be found in Volume 1 of the Phase B final report.

Data Recovery Strategy

The excavation at Water World was centered primarily outside the direct construction impact zone (Fig. 1.2). The area of intensive investigation was in a secondary impact zone that would be flooded by water backed up behind a retention dike on the up-slope side of the canal. Although the majority of the site lay beyond the direct impact zone, Reclamation approved the data recovery project because of the significance of the site, the opportunity to acquire comparative data on a second Rillito phase site (Fastimes was the other Rillito phase site; see Volume 2), and the potential for damage from flooding and vandalism.

The original 50-m by 50-m grid units were reestablished, and MAC areas and previously excavated trenches were relocated. Because the surface artifact collections taken during the testing phase were considered representative, no additional collections were made. Backhoe trenching focused on MAC areas (Loci) 1, 3, 4, 6, and 8 because testing indicated that these areas had the best potential for buried features, and because it was necessary to concentrate excavation efforts during the eight-week field season. A systematic and judgmental trenching pattern was designed (Fig. 1.3), using 50-m and 10-m intervals, the latter to be used in MAC areas. A 5-m interval also was to be used in some cases. Trenching was continuous through MAC areas, unless burials were encountered. The previous limited trenching indicated that only after trenches had been faced and left open to dry did features become readily apparent.

Trenching was concentrated in MAC areas, although non-MAC areas also were trenched at 50-m intervals. Because not all features that were found could be excavated or even tested during the eight-week field season, the decision to excavate or test particular features was reviewed continually as new areas were exposed and a tentative pattern

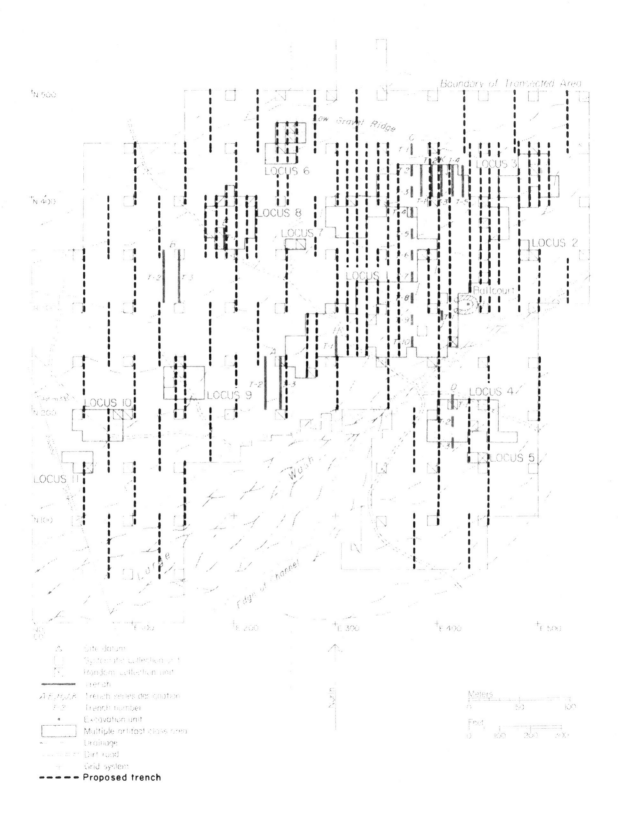

Figure 1.3. Proposed trenching strategy for Water World; solid lines are trenches excavated during 1983 testing.

of feature layout became apparent. Areas were selected, mostly on the basis of potential feature and artifact preservation, for surface stripping and intensive excavation. Other areas and features received varying degrees of attention ranging from complete excavation to limited testing to profiling of trenches.

The eight-week field season did not permit excavation of every identified feature, and consequently certain areas received more attention than others. Three of the 11 MAC areas or loci delineated by intensive transect recording (Fig. 1.2) were investigated relatively intensively by mechanical trenching and excavation: Loci 1 (including the ballcourt), 3, and 8. Portions of these areas were stripped mechanically and by hand, and a variety of features were completely or partially excavated. Locus 4 was trenched with a backhoe at 10-m intervals, but no stripping or excavation was carried out. The remaining MAC areas were trenched to some extent by a backhoe.

Excavation Methods

Backhoe trenching (Fig. 1.4) began during the last week in March, 1986, with a partial field crew present. As soon as a number of features had been exposed, the crew was increased to 10 archaeologists. During the course of the eight-week excavation period occasional volunteers or additional crew members briefly increased crew size. Excavations ended on May 23, 1986, although several more days were spent completing mapping and recording before the site was backfilled; 340 person-days were spent on the 1986 excavations.

From January 14 to March 27, 1987, additional excavation and backhoe trenching were conducted at Water World. This work focused on three specific goals: (1) to complete excavation of the cremation area located in Locus 8 at the end of the 1986 field season; (2) to determine by excavation whether Feature 13 was a ballcourt; and (3) to complete backhoe trenching in Locus 4 in the southeastern part of the site. Seventy-four person-days were required to achieve these three goals.

Excavation procedures followed those described in the ASM Cultural Resource Management Division Data Recovery Manual (Teague and others 1982). All overburden was removed with a front-end loader, except in certain areas such as the cremation area; overburden usually was not screened. Stripping around some features was done either by hand or with a front-end loader.

In each of the 21 structures investigated a 2-m by 2-m control unit was excavated in arbitrary 10-cm or 20-cm levels, or in natural levels, and screened through quarter-inch mesh. In nine cases, this control unit (and in several instances, one or two other similar units) was the only excavation done in the structure. These screened control units provided the only true comparable samples from structures. When a structure was excavated, overburden was removed in 2-m by 2-m units and

10

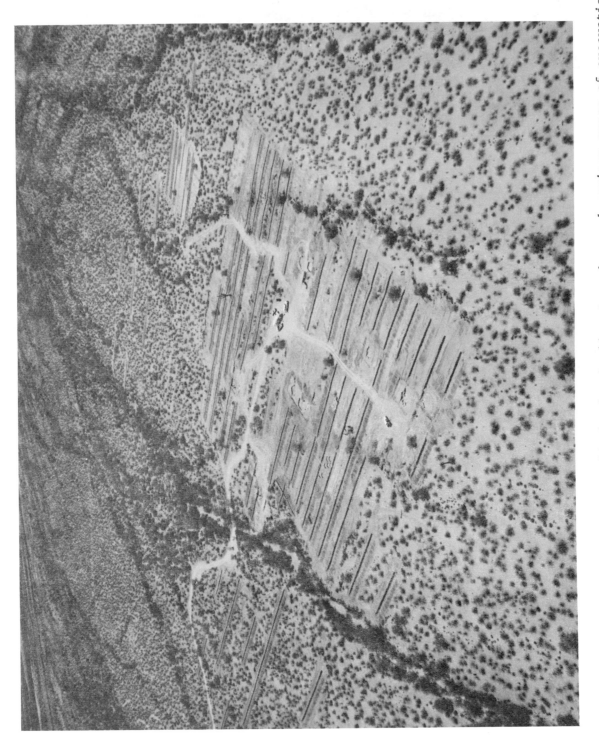

Figure 1.4. Aerial view of Water World showing backhoe trenches and various areas of excavation. Ballcourt is located to left of center where two trenches form a cross. (Bureau of Reclamation photograph.)

arbitrary 10-cm to 20-cm levels until the top of the feature was located. In the absence of natural stratigraphy, fill from within features was removed in arbitrary levels using grid units 1 m or 2 m square for control. Fill (Stratum 1) from structures usually was not screened, with only a grab sample af artifacts taken during excavation. Floor fill (Stratum 2, or occasionally Stratum 3) was screened through quarter-inch mesh. Plan views and profiles of all excavated pit houses and other features were drawn, and floor artifacts were point provenienced. A site map of the excavated areas was drafted at a scale of 1 inch to 1 meter, and all trenches, stripped areas, and excavated and unexcavated features were mapped using a transit. Fill from cremations was sifted through window screen. Table 1.1 lists the natural and cultural strata assigned for recording features.

Table 1.1

NATURAL AND CULTURAL STRATA DEFINED AT WATER WORLD

Stratum	Description
Natural	
Stratum 50	Loose, sandy silt with small pebbles; overburden
Stratum 60	Sterile, tan-orange sandy silt with gravels
Cultural	
Stratum 1	Feature fill
Stratum 2	Feature fill, usually floor fill
Stratum 3	Floor fill when used
Stratum 10	Occupation surface
Stratum 20	Pit house floor
Stratum 21	Lower of two pit house floors
Stratum 30	Organic material (ash or charcoal, or both) with artifacts in sandy silty soil; midden deposit

The excavation methods used for extramural features followed a standard procedure. For those excavated features identified in backhoe trenches, a profile was drawn and the overburden was removed by hand or by machine stripping to expose the feature in plan view. The feature fill was excavated in arbitrary 20-cm levels in the absence of cultural strata; features that exhibited multiple strata were dug accordingly. This strategy differed slightly for extramural features that were exposed in plan view during stripping activities. Ideally the larger features were bisected and one half was excavated in arbitrary 20-cm levels. If the remaining unexcavated feature fill displayed stratigraphy, a profile was drawn and the remainder of the feature fill

was excavated according to the cultural strata. Where no stratigraphy
was present, the remaining fill was excavated in the same arbitrary
levels. Smaller features were not bisected and were dug as one
horizontal unit in arbitrary 20-cm levels. If multiple strata were
recognized, excavation followed the cultural strata. All feature fill
was screened through quarter-inch mesh, and a small portion of it was
retained for pollen and flotation samples. Upon completion of the
excavation, plans and cross sections of each feature were drawn.

Ash lenses occasionally were exposed in trench profiles. These
were generally amorphous and could not be identified as distinct
features, but might have been associated with the cleaning out of other
features. Whereas at Fastimes (AZ AA:12:384) only one such feature was
assigned a feature number and only the location and approximate size of
these lenses were recorded, at Water World nearly all ash lenses that
were found were profiled and assigned a feature number.

Excavation Results

During the two field seasons at Water World, backhoe trenches
totaling 6,284 m were excavated (about 2% of the site) and 1,870 square
meters were stripped by front-end loader or by hand. Although trenching
was concentrated in several MAC areas, only 694 m (14%) of the trenches
were excavated in or immediately adjacent to (that is, on the edge of)
MAC areas, whereas 4,288 m (86%) were excavated in non-MAC areas or just
outside MAC areas (Fig. 1.5). Of the area that was stripped, 1,401
square meters (75%) were within and 469 square meters (25%) were outside
MAC areas. Stripping between structures was not a major focus of the
excavation as it was at Fastimes.

At the end of the 1987 field season, 147 features had been
identified. Of these, 111 (75%) were found in MAC areas; most of these
(85, or 77%) were located by trenching (Fig. 1.6). The correspondence
between a locus and the features in a house group was very good: House
Group 1 = Locus 3; House Groups 2, 3, 4, and 6 = Loci 1 and 2; House
Group 5 = Locus 8; and House Group 7 = Locus 4 (see Figs. 1.3 and 1.6).
Thirty-six features were located in non-MAC areas, almost three-quarters
(26) of which were found by trenching. A more in-depth evaluation of
the trenching effort and the MAC area concept is provided in the
discussion of Intensive Transect Recording in Volume 1, Chapter 4.

Figure 1.6 shows the location of all identified features, and
Tables 1.2 and 1.3 provide specific information on excavated and
unexcavated features by type and provenience. Fifty-nine features were
investigated; 21 of these were structures, of which 12 were either
completely or partially excavated, and 9 were tested with one 2-m by 2-m
excavation unit each. A wide but typical range of artifacts was
recovered, as were data on pit house architecture, site organization,
and chronology. The following chapters provide specific descriptions
and an interpretive discussion of these materials and data. More

comprehensive and comparative interpretive discussions of Water World in relation to the other Phase B sites can be found in Volume 1 of this report series.

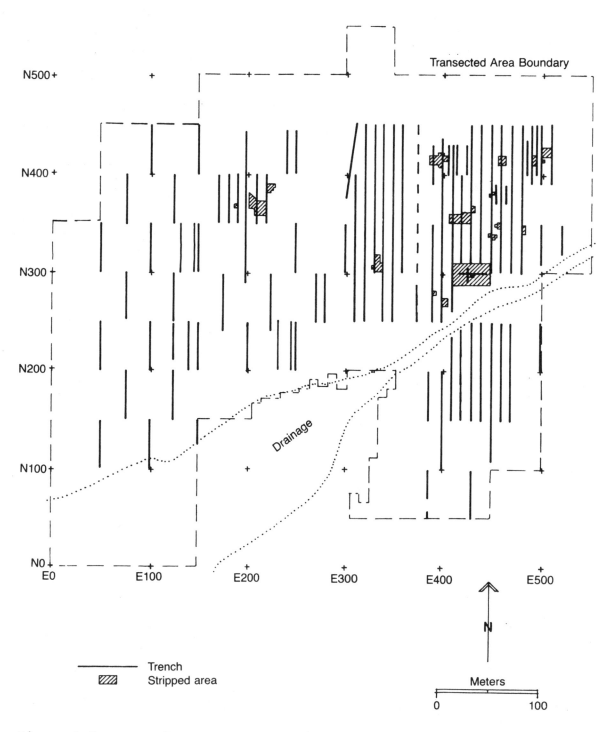

Figure 1.5. Map of Water World showing backhoe trenches excavated and areas stripped during 1986 and 1987 excavations.

14

Figure 1.6. Map of Water World showing location of house groups, features, and plaza area.

Table 1.2

EXCAVATED FEATURES

No.	Type	Provenience
7	Pit house	N408.10-412.80 E394.65-396.70
13**	Ballcourt	N293.40-302.00 E416.60-436.00
18	Borrow pit	N412.90-414.75 E498.50-499.90
19	Pit house	N418.95-425.10 E498.65-503.20
20	Pit house	N411.35-415.85 E457.55-461.80
25	Pit house	N411.24-417.23 E486.64-492.20
26	Pit house	N412.05-417.10 E385.65-391.10
27	Pit house	N351.70-357.55 E406.50-411.95
29	Pit house	N414.90-419.90 E394.20-398.40
33	Pit house	N363.10-368.00 E428.80-431.85
35	Pit house	N379.35-382.00 E448.31-451.50
36	Pit house	N371.70-374.50 E458.95-460.90
40	Cremation	N339.36-339.92 E448.30-448.75
44	Pit house/structure	N348.00-349.52 E478.95-480.50
46	Cremation	N348.22-348.56 E457.69-457.90
53	Pit house	N350.85-355.90 E416.00-421.60
54	Roasting pit (Type A*; intrusive)	N414.14-414.71 E491.44-491.95
55	Pit house	N411.65-416.98 E486.75-492.00
56	Roasting pit (Type A*; intrusive)	N413.46-413.94 E488.58-489.07
57	Miscellaneous pit	N417.30-418.10 E396.94-398.10
58	Pit house	N302.60-309.35 E338.25-343.95
59	Midden deposit	N413.10-415.85 E386.05-389.95
60	Cremation	N289.90-290.34 E409.69-409.86
61	Pit house	N312.85-318.00 E339.60-342.25
66	Specialized work area/ramada?	N272.00-274.00 E406.85-408.85
67	Specialized work area?	N278.00-282.00 E390.00-392.00
68	Specialized work area?	N269.15-272.98 E399.30-403.90
76	Extramural hearth	N305.56-306.10 E342.00-342.72
78	Pit house	N367.00-369.00 E186.00-188.30
79	Pit house	N388.70-392.15 E198.00-200.50
80	Cremation	N366.20-366.66 E209.80-210.11
81	Cremation	N363.60-364.92 E209.90-210.27
82	Cremation	N365.27-365.65 E208.97-209.15
83	Cremation	N362.76-363.30 E208.45-209.20
85	Cremation	N385.00-385.53 E217.98-218.45
86	Roasting pit (Type A*)	N360.28-361.23 E424.39-425.29
87	Miscellaneous pit (secondary cremation pit)	N365.10-365.47 E211.06-211.34
87.1	Cremation	N365.10-365.47 E211.06-211.34
88	Cremation	N364.30-364.57 E210.67-210.90
89	Cremation	N364.02-364.30 E210.95-211.08
90	Animal bone	N363.91-364.20 E211.33-211.61
94	Cremation	N371.62-372.04 E208.07-208.50

Table 1.2, continued

EXCAVATED FEATURES

No.	Type	Provenience
95	Possible roasting pit	N371.60-372.20 E200.45-201.10
96	Miscellaneous pit	N365.70-366.08 E212.73-213.12
104	Cremation	N367.05-367.23 E213.25-213.43
105	Cremation (primary?)	N366.10-366.48 E211.45-211.84
106	Cremation	N364.84-365.22 E212.58-213.00
107**	Potbreak	N371.40-371.70 E210.77-211.15
108	Cremation (primary?)	N365.76-366.07 E211.29-211.65
109**	Cremation	N370.95-371.40 E212.40-212.96
110**	Pit house	N374.50-379.80 E199.70-204.50
118**	Cremation	N368.89-369.30 E211.52-212.01
119**	Cremation with vessels	N387.85-388.07 E220.60-220.82
137**	Cremation with vessels	N291.23-291.50 E411.17-411.43
138**	Roasting pit	N301.05-302.07 E415.35-416.48
139**	Roasting pit	N294.88-295.48 E441.76-442.30
143**	Roasting pit?	N293.02-293.40 E430.30-430.76
144**	Roasting pit?	N295.00-295.28 E431.48-431.83
147**	Hearth?	N300.70-301.70 E436.80-437.65
148**	Roasting pit?	N291.00-291.68 E443.93-444.56

* Type A roasting pits are well-formed pits with extensive in situ
  burning on sides and base.
**Features excavated during 1987 field season.

Table 1.3

UNEXCAVATED FEATURES

No.	Type	Provenience	
1	Possible pit house	N243.80-249.10 E245.70	TT54
2	Probable pit house	N403.85-408.95 E375.00	TT23
3	Probable pit house	N407.60-411.50 E385.00	TT22
4	Roasting pit	N267.00-267.75 E300.00	TT82
5	Cremation with vessels	N293.00-293.00 E405.00	TT83
6	Probable pit house	N400.00-402.75 E405.00	TT17
8	Roasting pit	N417.95-419.90 E404.30	TT17

Table 1.3, continued

UNEXCAVATED FEATURES

No.	Type	Provenience	
9	Roasting pit	N413.70-415.30 E405.00	TT17
10	Hearth	N403.80-404.45 E394.30	TT19
11	Undetermined	N414.25-414.85 E424.30	TT14
12	Roasting pit	N402.75-403.70 E405.00	TT17
14	Possible pit house	N265.15-267.15 E375.00	TT23
15	Cobble-filled pit	Within Feature 13 (excavated)	
16	Possible pit house	N404.45-405.90 E414.30	TT15
17	Pit	N426.60-427.00 E498.80	TT4
21	Pit	N416.24-416.94 E458.20	TT9
22	Ash lens	N424.90-425.80 E458.30	TT9
23	Ash lens	N435.90-436.17 E448.30	TT10
24	Probable pit house	N422.80-424.60 E489.75	TT6
28	Ash lens	N435.83-436.13 E358.70	TT24
30	Ash lens	N380.53-380.85 E349.50	TT25
31	Ash lens	N357.60-357.90 E428.60	TT12
32	Roasting pit	N358.70-359.30 E428.60	TT12
34	Possible pit house	N360.20-361.00 E440.25	TT11
37	Roasting pit	N327.59-328.17 E389.00	TT21
38	Roasting pit	N311.58-312.06 E389.70	TT21
39	Roasting pit?	N332.42-333.42 E418.70	TT26
41	Possible pit house	N319.25-321.75 E418.70	TT26
42	Charcoal lens	N318.55-318.73 E418.70	TT26
43	Pit	N313.60-314.60 E429.00	TT12
45	Burial?	N338.90-341.40 E518.50	TT2
47	Pit	N334.70-335.38 E478.90	TT7
48	Pit	N336.25-336.82 E478.90	TT7
49	Pit	N337.37-337.57 E478.90	TT7
50	Ash lens	N346.50-347.65 E498.50	TT5
51	Ash lens	N358.70-360.00 E448.80	TT10
52	Pit	N448.90-449.40 E358.50	TT24
62	Roasting pit	N280.75-281.60 E349.40	TT25
63	Ash lens	N299.45-301.75 E409.60	TT16
64	Roasting pit	N323.90-324.80 E319.40	TT31
65	Ash lens	N407.45-407.80 E339.50	TT18
69	Pit house	N337.20-341.20 E318.60	TT31
70	Roasting pit	N234.90-235.75 E498.40	TT35
71	Roasting pit	N195.23-196.00 E448.50	TT36
72	Roasting pit	N 66.33- 67.30 E425.04	TT40
73	Roasting pit	N189.87-190.64 E429.70	TT37
74	Roasting pit	N197.05-196.26 E449.20	TT36
75	Ash lens	N174.46-175.15 E400.75	TT38
77	Possible pit house	N390.50-394.90 E188.40	TT45
84	Roasting pit	N390.22-390.86 E208.70	TT43

Table 1.3, continued

UNEXCAVATED FEATURES

No.	Type	Provenience
91	Nonfeature	
92	Probable pit house	N275.80-278.10 E339.50 TT29
93	Probable pit house	N281.00-285.65 E339.50 TT29
97	Ash lens	N266.80-268.60 E302.00 TT33
98	Roasting pit	N244.40-245.90 E 99.60 TT68
99	Roasting pit	N212.36-214.58 E100.25 TT68
100	Probable pit house	N219.65-223.00 E140.40 TT59
101	Pit house	N198.95-204.00 E149.00 TT58
102	Probable pit house	N230.65-233.55 E151.00 TT58
103	Possible pit house	N398.45-402.55 E409.20 TT16
111	Roasting pit	N381.10-381.80 E216.20-216.70
112	Ash lens	N145.55-145.75 E 99.65 TT57
113	Roasting pit	N269.60-270.80 E280.00 TT51
114	Pit	N413.85-414.17 E484.60 TT80
115	Pit house	N240.10-242.55 E249.60 TT53
116	Ash lens	N416.44-418.19 E250.24 TT48
117	Ash lens	N439.00-440.70 E249.69 TT48
120*	Roasting pit ?	N250.00-250.60 E225.00 TT87
121*	Possible pit house	N196.85-199.80 E408.95 TT88
122*	Pit ?	N187.65-188.60 E408.95 TT88
123*	Pit house	N184.00-187.50 E408.95 TT88
124*	Possible pit house	N172.70-176.50 E409.70 TT88
125*	Pit house	N167.30-171.00 E408.95 TT88
126*	Trash deposit ?	N160.00-164.00 E408.95 TT88
127*	Possible pit house	N197.12-200.45 E418.90 TT89
128*	Pit	N190.45-191.29 E418.90 TT89
129*	Cremation w vessel	N179.00-181.00 E419.00 TT89
130*	Pit ?	N162.58-163.05 E439.85 TT90
131*	Trash deposit ?	N183.20-187.40 E459.40 TT91
132*	Borrow pit ?	N237.60-243.90 E459.40 TT91
133*	Possible pit house	N156.20-157.75 E470.00 TT92
134*	Roasting pit	N177.75-178.10 E470.00 TT92
135*	Roasting pit	N179.20-179.70 E470.00 TT92
136*	Roasting pit	N189.60-189.98 E470.00 TT92
140*	Roasting pit ?	N305.00-306.10 E415.70-416.90
141*	Ash stain	N306.00-306.60 E302.90-303.50
142*	Roasting pit ?	N306.00-306.70 E424.45-425.15
145*	Ash stain	N291.30-291.60 E432.60-432.90
146*	Roasting pit ?	N296.45-296.95 E438.95-439.45

*Found during 1987 field season.

Chapter 2

DATING AND SITE DEVELOPMENT

John C. Ravesloot
and
Jon S. Czaplicki

Seven groups of pit houses and extramural features were identified at Water World (Fig. 1.6). These groups appear to be spatially discrete and may or may not have been occupied at the same time. It is equally possible, however, that these house groups represent temporally distinct building episodes that resulted over time from the process of "village drift." Village drift has been defined by Ezell (1961: 110) and Spier (1970) as the process by which the center of a settlement shifts through space as old house groups are abandoned and new ones constructed (see Crown 1983: 9 for additional discussion of this process regarding Hohokam settlements along the Salt-Gila Aqueduct). Assuming that a pit house had an average use-life of no more than and probably much less than 25 years, a settlement such as Water World may have evolved over a very short period of time (that is, 100 years or less). Obviously the length of time this developmental process took is dependent on how many, if any, of the house groups were constructed and occupied contemporaneously. The presence of a large plaza and a ballcourt at Water World suggests that, at least to some extent, the structure of this settlement was planned. This chapter provides a developmental sequence for Water World that takes both possibilities into consideration. That work in several of the house groups was limited primarily to locating and profiling features makes this objective more difficult to achieve.

The same relative and chronometric dating techniques used to reconstruct the developmental sequence at Fastimes (Volume 2, Chapter 2) were used to study Water World. These techniques included stratigraphy, ceramic cross-dating, refitting of artifacts, sherd densities in pit house fills, and archaeomagnetic and radiocarbon dating.

Stratigraphic Relationships

The stratigraphic relationships of all excavated features, by house group, are illustrated in Figure 2.1, which shows an exaggerated view of the stratigraphic relationship among all excavated features with

20

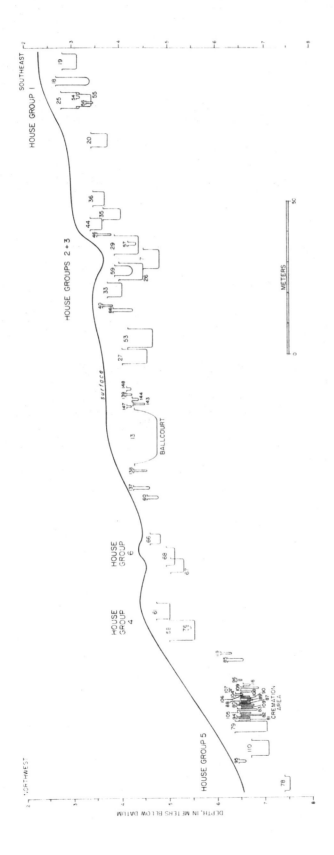

Figure 2.1. Stratigraphic relationships of all excavated features (horizontal and vertical scales are exaggerated).

reference to the site datum. Features identified in House Group 7 are
not included because none of these were excavated. Feature depth below
the present ground surface ranged from 8 cm (Feature 80) to 85 cm
(Feature 78) with a range of 32.9 cm. Figure 2.1 reveals that some
stratigraphic differences are present within and between house groups at
Water World. Within House Group 1, one pit house, Feature 25, is
clearly superimposed over another, Feature 55. This case, however,
represents the only structure superpositioning encountered. In House
Groups 1, 2, 4, and 6, at least one pit house is stratigraphically lower
and apparently was constructed earlier than the others. The
stratigraphic position of Feature 13, the ballcourt, suggests that it
was constructed during the initial occupation of the site. A few
intrusive features such as roasting pits, hearths, and pits in the fill
of pit houses were the only other examples of stratigraphic
superpositioning identified. In general, with the exception of House
Group 1, the stratigraphic evidence suggests that the occupation of
Water World was short lived.

Decorated Pottery

The distribution of ceramic types by feature is provided in
Table 2.1. Decorated pottery makes up less than 10 percent of the
ceramic assemblage recovered from Water World. Tucson Basin red-on-
brown types dominate this assemblage, accounting for approximately 92
percent of the decorated pottery. Over 50 percent of the red-on-brown
was typed as Rillito; 42 percent could not be typed, but most closely
resembled Colonial period styles. Less frequently occurring types
include Cañada del Oro (N=21), indeterminate Snaketown-Cañada del Oro
(N=1), and indeterminate Rillito-Rincon (N=4).

One hundred and seven sherds, almost 8 percent of the decorated
assemblage, were recovered from floor contexts (Table 2.2). Not
unexpectedly, Rillito Red-on-brown (including the white-slipped variety)
(N=86, or about 80%) was the most prevalent decorated type; however,
none of these sherds represented reconstructible vessels. A partial
reconstructible Cañada del Oro Red-on-brown flare-rimmed bowl found on
the floor of Feature 25 was the only decorated vessel recovered from
floor context.

The decorated ceramic assemblage suggests that Water World was a
single-component site occupied primarily during the Rillito phase. The
low frequency of earlier Colonial period types, as well as the extensive
program of subsurface trenching, suggests that earlier features would
have been located if they were present. Some of the unexcavated pit
houses and features might predate the Rillito phase, but the lack of
superpositioning suggests that they do not. Alternatively, the presence
of some Cañada del Oro pottery in contexts considered to date to the
Rillito phase may indicate that these types were produced for at least a
short time during the Rillito phase. The correlation of a single

Table 2.1

CERAMIC ASSEMBLAGE FROM EXCAVATED FEATURES, TUCSON BASIN BROWN WARES

Feature Number	Indeterminate Colonial/Sedentary	Indeterminate Red-on-brown	Indeterminate Snaketown/Cañada del Oro	Cañada del Oro	Indeterminate Colonial	Indeterminate Colonial White Slipped	Rillito Red-on-brown	Rillito/White Slipped	Indeterminate Rillito/Rincon	"Crude" Red-on-brown	Indeterminate Buff	Indeterminate Red-on-Buff	Gila Butte Red-on-buff	Santa Cruz Red-on-buff	Indeterminate Santa Cruz (Cruz/Sahuaro)	San Simon/Dos Cabezas Red-on-brown	Possible Red Ware	Plain Ware Bowl	Plain Ware Jar	Plain Ware Indeterminate	Plain Ware Unidentified	Subtotal Bowl	Subtotal Jar	Subtotal Indeterminate	Total
7	0-0-3																	4	7	51	0-0-8	4	7	63	67
13		0-0-1*		1-0-0	2-0-11		5-0-18		0-0-1									3	2	216	0-0-9	11	7	261	279
18				1-0-0	0-0-1		0-0-1		0-0-1											55	0-0-2	1	2	68	71
19					4-0-23	0-0-2	9-0-2								0-0-6			21	23	1,118	0-0-167	38	23	1,382	1,443
20					0-0-2		0-0-2	0-0-6						3-0-7				2	2	64	0-0-4	2		72	76
25		0-0-2		0-0-1	8-0-27		5-0-24			0-2-0				0-0-2	0-0-2			35	24	1,040	1-0-140	49	26	1,244	1,319
26		0-0-1		4-0-1	6-0-19		7-1-8											7	12	237	0-0-19	20	13	287	320
27					1-0-2		4-0-11											5	1	117	0-0-4	11	1	128	140
29	0-0-3	0-0-6		2-0-3	6-0-6	2-0-0	7-0-42					0-0-1		0-0-1	0-0-1			12	8	272	0-0-15	22	8	306	336
33					3-0-10		2-0-3											8	9	438	0-0-34	20	9	541	570
35					1-0-13		2-0-2											2	2	174	0-0-31	7	2	219	228
36																		5		114	0-0-6	8		135	143
40																				6	0-0-1			9	9
44		0-0-1			3-0-5		0-0-6							0-0-2	0-0-1	0-0-1		3	2	84	0-0-6	6	2	106	114
53					1-0-9		1-0-9							0-0-4				5	2	472	0-0-41	7	2	548	557
55				1-0-1	1-0-26	0-0-2	9-0-18										0-0-1	17	15	589	0-0-90	27	15	725	767
56		1-0-0																		30	0-0-1			31	31
57			0-0-1	1-0-1	1-0-4		5-0-14	1-0-1			0-0-1							1		14	0-0-1	2		16	18
58					0-0-11		0-0-1											2	8	184	0-0-8	10	8	212	230
59		0-0-1			1-0-14		2-0-19											6		55	0-0-3	6		60	66
61					10-2-52		2-0-11						1-0-5					3	4	203	0-0-18	6	4	257	267
66					1-0-26		7-4-34							0-0-1				1	2	124	0-0-10	4	2	159	170
67				0-0-4	2-0-6		11-1-44				0-0-1							6	6	391	0-2-115	23	17	603	643
68					2-1-16		4-1-24											5	9	173	0-0-21	17	9	269	295
78							0-0-1													54	0-0-15	2		75	77
79					0-0-1													3	6	330	0-0-77	9	8	447	464
80																								1	1
82																								1	1
83																				3			1	3	4
85																			1	3				3	4
86																				8				9	9
87							1-0-1		0-0-1		0-0-1								1	16	0-0-1	1		17	18
94	0-0-2						0-0-1													2				17	18
107																				3				2	2
108																								6	6
109					0-0-1		0-0-1													2				2	2
110		3-0-14					0-0-6	1-0-8	0-0-1											86	0-0-8	3		115	118
119																				61	0-0-2			63	63
137																				7				7	8
158							0-0-3												1	45	0-0-7		1	58	59
Total	0-0-3	4-0-29	0-0-1	9-0-12	54-3-306	2-0-9	84-7-369	1-0-8	0-0-4	0-2-0	0-0-13	0-0-9	0-0-1	4-0-28	0-0-3	0-0-1	0-0-3	157	154	6,842	1-2-871	316	168	8,512	8,996

Includes only ceramics recovered from fill, floor fill, and floor contexts.
Strata 50 and 30 not included.
* Bowl-Jar-Indeterminate

Table 2.2

DECORATED POTTERY RECOVERED FROM PIT HOUSE FLOOR CONTEXT

Ceramic Type	Pit House													Total
	19	20	25	27	29	33	35	44	53	55	58	68	78	
Indeterminate Gila Basin Buff	2													2
Indeterminate Gila Basin Red-on-buff			1											1
Santa Cruz Red-on-buff		1												1
Indeterminate Santa Cruz-Sacaton			1											1
Indeterminate Tucson Basin Colonial	2		2		1			3					2	10
Tucson Basin Colonial, White Slipped						1				1				2
Indeterminate Tucson Basin Red-on-brown						2								2
Indeterminate Gila Butte Red-on-buff						1								1
Cañada del Oro Red-on-brown				1										1
Rillito Red-on-brown			4			27	1	3	13	1		8		57
Rillito Red-on-brown, White Slipped	1										28			29
Total	5	1	8	1	1	31	1	6	13	2	28	8	2	107

ceramic type with a single phase upon which Hohokam chronology is based may not be as clear cut as traditionally believed (Plog 1980; Dean 1988).

Other Artifact Classes

The recovery of diagnostic nonceramic artifacts lends support to the temporal placement of Water World in the Colonial period. Five styles were recognized in the 27 projectile points recovered. These styles have been recovered from Colonial period contexts in the Tucson Basin and surrounding areas (see Huckell, Chapter 5, for a detailed discussion of the temporal sensitivity of these styles). All but two of the Water World points were recovered from contexts other than house floors (see Volume 5, Appendix B-7 for their provenience).

The presence of stone palettes and bowls similar to those recovered from Colonial period contexts at other Hohokam sites provides additional supporting evidence.

Artifact Refitting

Refitting of fragmented artifacts was one of the methods used to delineate temporal differences between features within and between house groups. Not unexpectedly, most instances where adjoining artifacts could be fitted back together were observed in the ceramic assemblage (see Deaver, Chapter 4). Ceramic matches were identified between House Groups 2 and 3, 2 and 6, 3 and 6, and 4 and 6. With the exception of the three mends observed between House Groups 4 and 6, all of the others were single occurrences. This pattern contrasts with Fastimes where no mends between house groups were noted. The presence of these cross-mends provides some limited evidence to support the assumption that these house groups were contemporaneous.

On the other hand, attempts to refit fragmentary artifacts in other classes were for the most part unsuccessful. Only one such case, two metate fragments recovered from House Group 1 (fill of Feature 20) and House Group 2 (fill of Feature 29), was found.

Structure Contemporaneity

One approach in establishing the relative contemporaneity of pit houses at Hohokam sites has used the density of sherds in fill to define trash-filled structures (Deaver 1983; Elson 1986; Gregory 1984). For example, this problem was approached at the Hodges Ruin by Whittlesey (1986: 120-123) using a relative measure of abandonment formulated by Reid (1973, 1978) to define the building sequence at Grasshopper Pueblo, a late Mogollon site located on the White Mountain Apache Reservation. Reid's measure of room abandonment is based on the number of sherds observed in the fill. Sherd totals are used to calculate relative densities of sherds per square meter of fill (see Reid 1973 and 1978 for a detailed summary of this measure and the assumptions upon which it is based). Rooms in use late in the occupational sequence were found to have low densities of sherds in their fill whereas the opposite was found to be true for rooms abandoned early in the sequence.

Whittlesey (1986: 122) found the use of this measure at the Hodges Ruin "to be a valid estimation of the earliest and latest structures to have been abandoned." Because of these promising results she suggested that this measure of abandonment warranted further use at Hohokam sites. For this reason, this approach was used to assess structure contemporaneity at Fastimes (Volume 2, Chapter 2). The results of the Fastimes study suggest that this technique also should be used to investigate feature contemporaneity at Water World.

Sherd counts and densities are provided in Table 2.3. This table also includes distributional data for reconstructible ceramic vessels, whole ground-stone artifacts, and sherds recovered from floor contexts. It was impossible to calculate densities for those structures where excavation was restricted to 2-m by 2-m units and floor area was not determined. Only House Groups 1 and 2 provided the level of information necessary to apply this measure. The number of sherds per square meter of pit house fill ranged from 2.6 to 46.8. On the basis of these densities it appears that Feature 20 may have been the last house occupied in House Group 1. Apparently the occupants of this house deposited their trash in one of the other three structures. The temporal relationships of the remaining three structures are not entirely clear, although Feature 55 definitely postdates Feature 25 on the basis of stratigraphic evidence. Feature 25 had the second highest density of sherds, and its floor assemblage also included approximately one-half of a Cañada del Oro Red-on-brown jar and two ground-stone artifacts. This floor material is considered to represent trash, although solid evidence to support this interpretation cannot be offered.

In House Group 2 sherd densities calculated for Features 26 and 29 are almost identical. Stratigraphic evidence suggests that these two structures were constructed and occupied at about the same time, whereas Feature 7 was constructed earlier.

Archaeomagnetic Dating

Seventeen features were sufficiently burned to sample for archaeomagnetic dating. Samples collected from these features were submitted for analysis to the Archaeomagnetic Laboratory at Colorado State University. A report summarizing the dating results for the Tucson Aqueduct Phase B project including Water World can be found in

Table 2.3

SHERD DENSITIES FROM PIT HOUSES

House Group	Pit House	Area (m²)	Sherds[a] in Fill	Sherds per m²	Restorable Vessels	Floor[b] Sherds	Whole Ground Stone
1	19	19.6	918	46.8	–	54	1
	20	13.4	35	2.6	–	8	2
	25	20.4	628	30.8	1	116	2
	55	15.3	322	21.0	–	33	–
2	7*		29		–	–	2
	26	20.7	94	4.5	–	9	–
	29	18.2	78	4.3	–	28	1
3	27	18.5	87	4.7	–	2	–
	33*		191		–	90	–
	35*		174		–	5	–
	36*		143		–	–	–
	44*		95		–	16	1
	53		79		–	37	2
4	58	22.2	93	23.8	1	5	3
	61*		70		–	1	–
5	78*		68		–	7	–
	79*		143		–	--	–
	110*						

[a] Sherd frequency based on 2-m by 2-m control units.
[b] Does not include worked sherds.
*Partially excavated or tested; floor area was not calculated.

Note: The structures in House Group 6 were not considered to be pit houses and are not included.

Volume 4, Chapter 21. Table 2.4 provides provenience data for all of
the samples and a synthesis of dating results. As with some of the
features at Fastimes (Volume 2, Chapter 2), the other Colonial period
site excavated by the project, several of the sampled features did not
yield dates. These poor dating results may be attributed to a multitude
of factors (Volume 4, Chapter 21).

Table 2.4

ARCHAEOMAGNETIC DATES

Sample Number	Feature Number	Feature Type	Date Statistical Method	Visual Inspection
1	54	Roasting pit		
2	54	Roasting pit		
3	19.1	Hearth	A.D. 680-795, 840-865	A.D. 715-775, 850-875
4	20.1	Hearth	A.D. 700-725, 925-1000	A.D. 925-940
5	76	Hearth	A.D. 680-950	pre-A.D. 700-925
6	56	Roasting pit		
7	55.1	Firepit	A.D. 680-950	pre-A.D. 700-935
8	53.3	Hearth	A.D. 680-800, 835-915	A.D. 840-900
9	86	Roasting pit		
10	27.1	Hearth	A.D. 680-1000	A.D. 700-920
11	29.1	Hearth	A.D. 680-790	A.D. 715-775, 850-900
12	7.1	Hearth	A.D. 680-730, 900-950	A.D. 920-930
13	36	Burned floor of pit house	A.D. 720-770	A.D. 725-780
14	35.3	Pit	A.D. 725-765, 780-855	A.D. 750-840
15	58.1	Hearth		
16	67.1	Hearth		
17	79	Burned floor of pit house	A.D. 680-815, 830-1025, 1375-1450	pre-A.D. 700-790, A.D. 835-1000, A.D. 1350--post-1425

The dated samples ranged from A.D. 680 to 1000, and fit the calendar date range proposed by Kelly (1978: 4) for the Rillito phase. These dates, however, are difficult, if not impossible, to interpret because 6 of the 10 features produced alternative date options. For example, hearths (Features 19.1, 20.1, and 55.1) from three of the pit houses in House Group 1 yielded six different mean dates, and the sample collected from Feature 20.1 encompassed the range of mean dates (A.D. 712 to 962) for this house group. Contemporaneity of House Groups 1, 2, and 3 could be suggested by the fact that at least one feature from each of these groups produced a mean date of A.D. 745 or earlier.

Radiocarbon Dating

Two radiocarbon samples were submitted to the Tandem Accelerator Mass Spectrometer (TAMS) Facility at the University of Arizona. Several factors account for the small sample size. First and foremost, the decision to use only single-year annuals such as corn (Zea mays) greatly reduced the pool of potential samples. In the case of Water World, carbonized corn cupules were obtained from only 4 of the 47 macrofloral samples analyzed. Of the four features (25.1, 27.1, 53.3, and 56) represented, two (27.1 and 53.3) were either associated with features or were themselves sufficiently oxidized for archaeomagnetic sampling. Second, mesquite charcoal samples from two roasting pits (Features 4 and 9) had been dated by Beta Analytic of Florida using conventional radiocarbon dating and published in the Phase B survey and testing report (Rankin and Downum 1986: 83-88; see also Table 2.5).

Table 2.5 provides the radiocarbon B.P. dates and dendrocalibrated ranges for all of the dates. The calibrated means (A.D. 789 and 809) for the dates from the two corn cupules are within a range of 20 years, not surprising because these two adjacent structures in House Group 3 appeared to be contemporaneous based on ceramic and stratigraphic evidence. The two remaining radiocarbon dates are from wood charcoal collected during the testing phase. The date from Feature 9, a roasting pit, agrees with the corn dates, but the other, from Feature 4, produced a calibrated mean date of A.D. 1063. This date is several hundred years later than expected, if Kelly's (1978) traditional dating of the Rillito phase (A.D. 700 to 900) is correct. Overall, the radiocarbon dates agree with the archaeomagnetic dates and with previously reported dates for the Rillito phase.

Site Structure

This discussion is based on Wilcox's investigation of site structure at Snaketown, where he identified house clusters consisting of two or more pit houses that opened onto a common courtyard or work area (Wilcox and others 1981: 157). Although not necessarily absolutely contemporaneous, the houses reflected a class of space used for domestic

Table 2.5

RADIOCARBON DATES

Lab Number	Field Number	C-14 Age (Years B.P.)	Calibrated Range 95% C	Mean	Provenience	Depth (MBD)	Material
Beta 9257		1020 ± 60	980-1146	1063	Feature 4, roasting pit	Lower fill	Mesquite charcoal
Beta 9237		1130 ± 60	781-984	882	Feature 9, roasting pit	Lower fill	Mesquite charcoal
AA-2885	534	1214 ± 57	A.D. 691-888	789	Feature 27, structure; sample recovered from residue of flotation sample	Floor fill 4.45-4.57	Corn cupule
AA-2886	943	1205 ± 48	A.D. 730-888	809	Feature 53.3, hearth; sample recovered from residue of flotation sample	Fill 4.70-4.80	Corn cupule

MBD = meters below datum

activities by a family group. Wilcox referred to the family or extended family as the primary group, the basic unit of production and consumption (Wilcox and others 1981: 154). The space used by the primary group included pit house interiors and various exterior areas where extramural features were located. Houses defined interior living space; exterior work areas were defined by pits, roasting pits, rock clusters, and ash deposits, and burial areas were defined by the presence of cremations or inhumations, or both.

Three aspects of site structure at Water World were examined: patterning of pit houses and extramural features, temporal trends, and comparisons of Water World site structure with other Colonial period sites in southern Arizona (Downum 1986: 208-209; Volume 1, Chapter 2). Patterning and temporal trends are analyzed here; site structure comparisons are discussed in Volume 1.

House Groups

The seven house groups identified at Water World (Fig. 1.6) were defined on the basis of how the houses appeared to cluster. House Group 7 was the only group that was not excavated although all of the features were profiled. Other house groups probably existed. Five probable pit houses that were identified in the southwest corner of the site may represent two other house groups, but due to a lack of data they have been excluded from the developmental reconstruction presented here.

Features labeled "probable pit houses" or "possible pit houses" were identified in trenches and were classified on the basis of the limited information visible in the trench profile. "Probable pit houses" usually were represented in profile by a corner of a pit house wall, a good or at least reasonable example of a pit house floor, or some other typical characteristic. When the evidence was more tenuous and its interpretation less certain, the feature was classified as a "possible pit house".

House Group 1

Four definite pit houses (Features 19, 20, 25, and 55) and one possible pit house (Feature 24) were identified in this group (Fig. 2.2). Extramural features associated with those houses consist of two ash lenses, three pits, two intrusive roasting pits, and a borrow pit.

There is one probable house cluster consisting of Features 25/55 and 19; Feature 24 also may have been part of this cluster, but its entryway orientation is unknown. Because Feature 25 is superimposed over Feature 55, it follows that the latter structure was built first. Prior to construction of Feature 25, a roasting pit (Feature 56) was dug into the fill of Feature 55, indicating that its space was temporarily reclaimed for a work area after the earlier house had been abandoned.

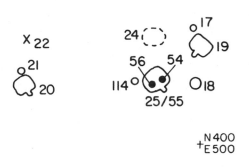

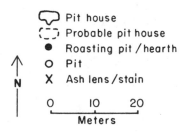

Figure 2.2.   House Group 1.

        Feature 25 was built on the fill of Feature 55, using the same
general entry orientation.   After it was abandoned the superstructure
collapsed, partially filling the house depression, which was then used
as a trash dump.   The recovery of ceremonial objects such as figurines
suggests that ritual disposal may have occurred as well (Chapter 11).
The house space was eventually reclaimed as a work area when a roasting
pit (Feature 54) was dug into the trash fill.

        Another pit house, Feature 19, may have been a contemporary of
either Features 25 or 55, or perhaps both.   Decorated sherds from all
three structures support a Rillito phase occupation for the houses.
Archaeomagnetic dates from hearths, Features 19.1 and 55.1, provide
additional support for this temporal placement.   Feature 19 was trash
filled, indicating that after it was abandoned, it was used as a dump,
perhaps by the occupants of Feature 20 or Feature 24.   Features 19 and
55 contained a hearth and two firepits, respectively, and were probably
used primarily for habitation, although they certainly could have been
used for other activities.   Feature 25 had no firepit or hearth and was
probably used for storage and food processing; ground stone and pollen
data tend to support this interpretation (Chapters 6 and 9).

        One pit house in this group, Feature 20, does not appear to be
part of any house cluster.   The paucity of floor artifacts suggests that
it burned after being abandoned, and it apparently was not used as a

trash dump; its fill contained very few artifacts, and most of these may have washed into the house depression. Feature 20 may have been one of the last structures occupied in House Group 1. Among the few sherds present in the fill and overburden were four Rillito Red-on-brown sherds, indicating at least relative contemporaneity with the other structures. The presence of a single firepit within it suggests that it probably was used for habitation.

The four extramural pit features and the two ash lenses present in this area indicate outside work areas (Fig. 2.2). The ash lenses probably represent the discarded remains of roasting pits, hearths, and other domestic trash that were dumped away from inhabited structures. The borrow pit (Feature 18) showed at least four episodes of trash deposition, so it apparently was used for limited trash dumping, probably by the residents of Features 25/55 and 19. As noted above, a roasting pit (Feature 56) was dug into the fill of Feature 55 and predates both Feature 25 and the roasting pit (Feature 54) that postdates it; however, the extent of time between the construction of each of these features cannot be determined.

The pairing of one large and one small house has been noted at other late Colonial period sites such as Siphon Draw (AZ U:10:6; Gregory 1984) in the Queen Creek area and Fastimes (AZ AA:12:384; see Volume 2, Chapter 2). Feature 19 (19.6 square meters) and Feature 55 (15.3 square meters) may represent such a pair, although the difference in area between the two houses is not great. Feature 25 is only slightly larger (20.4 square meters) than Feature 19 and would not have been paired with it in this way. Feature 20 is the smallest house at 13.4 square meters, but apparently was not paired with another structure.

House Group 1 may represent a discrete group of structures. During analysis sherds from Features 25 and 55 (Chapter 4) were refitted. This is not particularly significant, however, because of the superpositioning of the two houses and the probability of mixing of their fills with the building of Feature 25 and the later intrusive roasting pits. Two metate fragments, one from the fill of Feature 20 and another from the fill of Feature 29 in House Group 2, were refitted, indicating that some contact occurred between the two house groups.

House Group 2

There are at least three and perhaps eight or more pit houses in this house group (Fig. 2.3). Excavated pit houses include Features 7, 26, and 29; unexcavated, probable houses include Features 2, 3, and 6. Features 16 and 103 were identified as possible houses. Extramural features include three roasting pits (Features 8, 9, and 12), a hearth (Feature 10), a pit (Feature 57), a trash midden (Feature 59), and on the periphery of the house group, three ash lenses (Features 28, 30, and 65), and one pit (Feature 52).

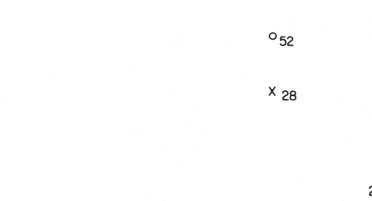

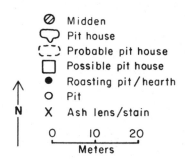

	Midden
	Pit house
	Probable pit house
	Possible pit house
	Roasting pit / hearth
	Pit
	Ash lens/stain

0   10   20
Meters

Figure 2.3.   House Group 2.

Houses 26 and 29 appear to form a house cluster. Upon abandonment they were used as trash dumps, and eventually the house depressions were reclaimed as work areas with the excavation of pit Feature 57 and trash midden Feature 59. These two houses probably were among the first structures built in the house group, and were most likely contemporary habitation structures.

The stratigraphic position of another pit house, Feature 7, suggests that it was constructed before Features 26 and 29. It may have formed a house cluster with one or more of the possible or probable pit houses (Features 3, 6, 16, or 103) shown in Figure 2.3. Pit Feature 57 and trash midden Feature 59, which clearly postdate Features 26 and 29, were perhaps dug by the inhabitants of these unexcavated pit houses, but the construction sequence of the other extramural features cannot be determined. Features 8, 9, 10, and 12 are located in the work area of the house cluster formed by Features 26 and 29; however, some or all of these features also could be associated with Feature 7 and its possible house cluster.

There is no apparent large house-small house pairing, although additional excavation might have provided evidence of such pairings. Houses 26 and 29 are similar in size, 20.7 square meters and 18.2 square meters, respectively. Feature 7, however, is estimated to be a little less than 12 square meters in area and may have been paired with one of the unexcavated houses.

Ceramic evidence from the excavated houses consists primarily of Rillito Red-on-brown sherds from the fill of these structures, indicating that the structures were relatively contemporaneous with each other and with the structures in House Group 1.

On the periphery of House Group 2 are three ash lenses (Features 28, 30, and 65) and one pit, Feature 52; their association with the house group is not definite. The ash lenses may represent areas of ash and trash deposition from House Group 2 or from other house groups, or both. Inspection of their profiles revealed no evidence to suggest that the features were anything other than deposits of ash and charcoal.

House Group 3

More structures were excavated or tested in this house group than in any other house group at Water World. Pit house Features 27, 33, and 53 were completely excavated, one-half of Feature 36 was excavated, and 2-m by 2-m test units were excavated in Features 35 and 44. In addition to these six structures, a seventh (Feature 34) may represent a pit house. Extramural features included three ash lenses (Features 31, 50, and 51), two roasting pits (Features 32 and 86), three pits (Features 47, 48, and 49), two cremations (Features 40 and 46), and one inhumation (Feature 45; Fig. 2.4).

Features 33 and 53 were not considered to be trash filled, although their fills did contain artifacts derived from both natural erosion and probably occasional light dumping. Neither feature is capped by a Stratum 30 trash deposit. Feature 27, on the other hand, is overlain by a Stratum 30 deposit as much as 33 cm thick. This structure was burned and had no floor artifacts, suggesting that it had been abandoned before it burned. On the basis of this evidence, Feature 27 may have been one of the earlier structures in House Group 3.

Features 33 and 53 may represent contemporary pit houses that formed a house cluster. Their common work area contained two roasting pits (Features 32 and 86) and an ash lens (Feature 31), which may have been produced when the two roasting pits were cleaned of ash and

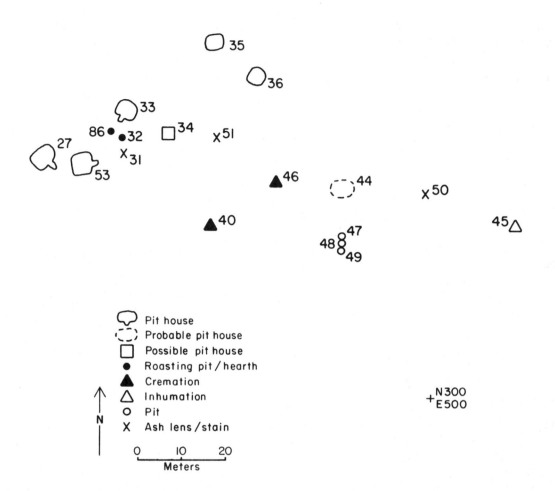

Figure 2.4. House Group 3.

charcoal. Feature 34 may have been part of this cluster, or may have formed a house cluster with Features 35 and 36 (Fig. 2.4). The trash deposit covering Feature 27 probably represents trash dumped by the occupants of Features 53 and 33.

The limited excavation data available for Features 35, 36, and 44 provide some information about these houses. Features 35 and 36 appeared to contain considerable trash, although neither structure was covered by a Stratum 30 deposit. Feature 44 was overlain by a Stratum 30 midden deposit that was at least 38 cm thick. These structures were probably some of the first to be built and abandoned, and subsequently were used for trash disposal, perhaps by the occupants of Features 33 and 53. The lack of trash fill in the latter indicates that these houses may represent the latest occupation of House Group 3.

Features 33 and 53 may have formed a large house-small house pair. Feature 53 had a floor area of 21.7 square meters. The excavation of only 60 percent of Feature 33 revealed a floor area of 10.6 square meters; completely excavated, its floor area would have been about 17 square meters. Feature 27 had a floor area of 18.5 square meters, but does not appear to have been paired with another house.

The two cremations and the one inhumation may be isolated burials, or they may be part of a larger, undefined cemetery area similar to the one located on the western portion of the site in House Group 6. Limited stripping in the area did not reveal additional cremations.

Ceramic evidence indicates a Rillito phase occupation for this house group. Rillito Red-on-brown sherds were the dominant decorated ceramic type, although the fills of Features 27 and 33 each yielded Ca~ada del Oro Red-on-brown sherds, and another was found on the floor of Feature 27. These sherds probably do not indicate an early Colonial period occupation for these features; they are more likely isolated sherds that became incorporated in the fill. Ceramics from Features 33 and 53 were refitted; nine sherds from Feature 33, seven from floor context, fit together and joined with a single sherd from the floor fill of Feature 53. This association strengthens the proposed contemporaneity of the two structures (Chapter 4).

House Group 4

Included in this house group are three pit houses, Features 58, 61, and 69, and two probable structures, Features 92 and 93 (Fig. 2.5). Only Features 58 and 61 were excavated, the latter only partially. There are three roasting pits (Features 62, 64, and 76) and an ash stain (Feature 141) associated with the structures. Some distance to the southwest are two more roasting pits (Features 4 and 113) and an ash lens (Feature 97) that may be associated with the house group.

There is no apparent house cluster; the orientation of the excavated houses, Features 58 and 61, suggests that they did not share a common courtyard, and stratigraphic evidence suggests that they were occupied at different times. Because Features 92 and 93 were not excavated, the possibility that one or both may have formed part of a house cluster cannot be evaluated. The presence of an intrusive roasting pit (Feature 78) in the fill of Feature 58 indicates that this house had been abandoned for some undetermined period before the pit was excavated, but the sequence of construction and abandonment for the other features cannot be determined. Because three of the five houses were not excavated, it is impossible to determine whether this group included a large house-small house pair. Feature 58 had a floor area of 22.2 square meters; the excavated area of Feature 61 (roughly 60%) was 19+ square meters. Its projected size is about 31 square meters, making it the largest excavated pit house at Water World. Feature 58 is the next largest house. Both structures may have been used for more than

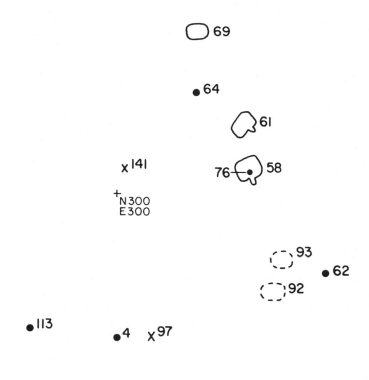

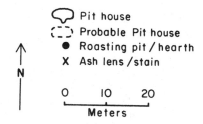

Figure 2.5.   House Group 4.

habitation. Their size and the presence of a variety of different
artifacts in Feature 58 suggest that one or the other, or both, may have
served some special purpose, possibly related to the ballcourt (Chapter
11).

House Group 5

A single 2-m by 2-m test unit was excavated in three of the four
structures included in this house group (Features 78, 79, and 110; Fig.
2.6). A possible pit house (Feature 77) was identified in a trench
profile. It is impossible to describe or discuss any of these features,
the relationships between them, or construction and abandonment

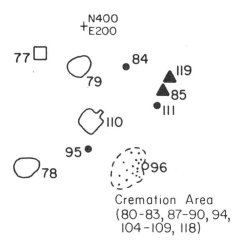

HOUSE GROUP 5

Figure 2.6. House Group 5.

sequences, because data on structure size and orientation are almost entirely absent. Few artifacts were recovered. One example of ceramic refitting was identified from Houses 78 and 79. This may indicate some degree of contemporaneity for these structures, although one sherd was found in the Stratum 50 overburden of Feature 78, and the other sherd came from the Stratum 1 fill of Feature 79. Three extramural roasting pits (Features 84, 95, and 111) may be located in a work area associated with a possible house cluster comprised of Features 110 and 79. Decorated ceramics indicated that the structures belonged to the Rillito phase and were relatively contemporaneous with the other house groups.

Eighteen cremations were located in House Group 5. All but two (Features 85 and 119) were found in an area south and east of the pit houses, which has been identified as a cremation area (Fig. 2.6). It is unlikely that all 18 cremations represent only the occupants of House Group 5; it is more likely that the cremation area served as a cemetery for other house groups and was intentionally located at some distance from these habitations. Given the closeness of the cremation area to the structures in House Group 5, it is also likely that all or most of these structures were abandoned when the cremation area was in use. At Snaketown, Haury (1976: 164) noted that residence areas and human ash disposal areas seemed to have been differentiated by the Hohokam.

House Group 6

House Group 6 consisted of four structures (Features 66, 67, 68, and 14; Fig. 2.7). Features 66 and 67 were tested and Feature 68 was partially excavated. None can be positively identified as a pit house. Only Feature 68 had evidence of a pit wall and its maximum height was 15 cm. No evidence of roof support posts was found in any of the

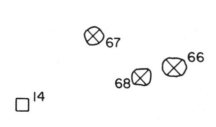

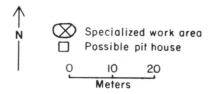

Figure 2.7. House Group 6.

structures, and only Feature 66 contained burned daub that could be interpreted as roof fall. The three features may have been specialized work areas that, with the possible exception of Feature 66, probably were not roofed. Feature 14 was identified in a trench profile as a compacted "floor" surface. No walls were noted in the profile, however, and it is likely that this feature was similar to the other features.

Because none of the features were completely excavated, their "floor" areas were not determined. Feature 67 was overlain by a Stratum 30 midden deposit, and both it and Feature 68 contained large numbers of artifacts in the fill indicating they were trash filled. Although the fill of Feature 66 contained some artifacts, it apparently was not trash filled like the two nearby structures.

Decorated ceramics were primarily Rillito Red-on-brown, indicating relative contemporaneity with the rest of the features at Water World. Because at least two of the structures were trash filled, it would appear that these structures were occupied at an earlier date and then abandoned and used for trash disposal.

House Group 7

This group of features was identified during limited backhoe trenching in 1987 (Fig. 2.8). The features were only recorded and profiles drawn; because none were excavated, there are no data on house clusters or the sequence of construction and abandonment. Three pit houses were identified (Features 123, 125, and 127) and three possible houses were located (Features 121, 124, and 133). Extramural features, including at least one small trash midden (Feature 131), an ash lens (Feature 75), and one cremation (Feature 129), also were present (Fig. 2.8).

No decorated ceramics were recovered during the testing of House Group 7, but surface collections made during the 1983 survey (Rankin and Downum 1986, Fig. 4.21, Table 4.5) show that Rillito Red-on-brown was the dominant decorated ceramic type. Based on that evidence, House Group 7 was probably more or less contemporaneous with the rest of Water World, but its exact place in the sequence of construction and abandonment cannot be determined.

Ballcourt Area

The ballcourt and the numerous extramural features surrounding it (Fig. 2.9) were not included in any house group. Only one of the various extramural features, Feature 41, may have been a pit house; however, it was seen only in profile, and this interpretation is by no means certain. There were eight roasting pits in the immediate vicinity of the ballcourt (Features 138, 139, 140, 142, 143, 144, 146, and 148) and three more at some distance north and west of the court (Features

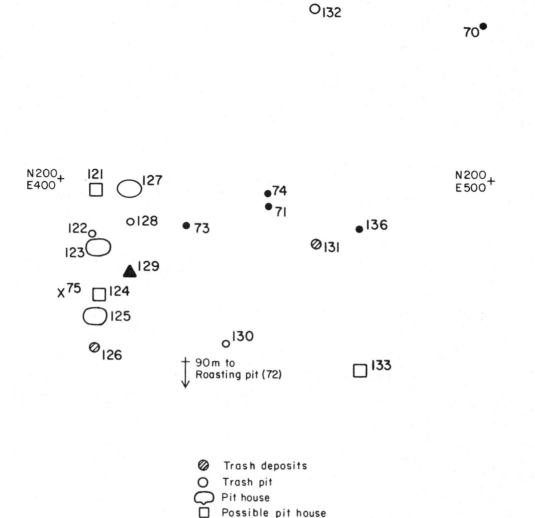

Figure 2.8.   House Group 7.

37, 38, and 39; Fig. 2.9).   Because of its proximity Feature 39 could just as easily be associated with House Group 3.   In front of the plastered entryway on the east end of the court was a large, circular, oxidized area that may be a hearth (Feature 147), and near the western entry were three cremations (Features 5, 60, 137).   Two ash lenses (Features 42 and 63) were located near the court and probably represented areas where debris from the roasting pits was deposited when the pits were cleaned out.

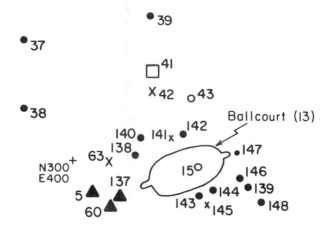

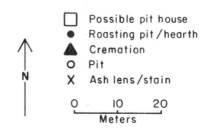

Figure 2.9. Ballcourt area.

The apparent absence of pit houses in the vicinity of the
ballcourt suggests that this area was intentionally kept clear of
habitation or storage structures. The possible specialized activity
areas southwest of the court in House Group 6 (Features 66, 67, and 68)
may be associated with the ballcourt, but also could predate or postdate
it. In addition, the two unusually large pit houses in House Group 4
(Features 58 and 61) may be associated with the ballcourt; both their
size and the unusual artifact assemblage from Feature 58 suggest this
possibility, despite their distance from it (over 80 m).

The ballcourt fill contained a relatively light amount of
ceramic material (Chapter 3). Some may represent trash dumped into the
depression, but most of these artifacts most likely eroded into the
court from the berms that bordered the depression on the north and
south.

The artifact content of the associated roasting pits varied.
Feature 138 was excavated and contained, among other artifacts, a
restorable Rillito Red-on-brown bowl, indicating general contemporaneity
with the other excavated features. Feature 143 was located under the

berm that bordered the southern side of the ballcourt; its position beneath the berm implies that the roasting pit was in use before the berm, and therefore the ballcourt, was constructed. Feature 144, on the other hand, intruded on the southern edge of the court, indicating that this small hearth or roasting pit was used after the court had been built and perhaps after it no longer functioned in its special capacity. Three other excavated roasting pits or hearths (Features 139, 147, and 148) contained no artifacts. The other features in the vicinity of the ballcourt (Features 42, 63, 43, 140, 145, 37, 38, and 39) were not excavated. All these features and the ballcourt itself are assumed to date to the Rillito phase.

With the few exceptions noted above, evidence is scant of the construction and abandonment sequence for the ballcourt and the extramural features surrounding it. There is limited evidence (Feature 143) to suggest that this area of Water World was used both before the ballcourt was constructed and after it ceased to function as such. Exact relationships between the ramada features of House Group 6, the ballcourt, and the extramural features around the court cannot be determined with the available data. It appears likely that the ballcourt and some of the roasting pits around it were in use simultaneously; whether the ramada features were contemporaneous with the ballcourt is not known.

Probable Central Plaza

Downum (1986: 209) defined a crescent-shaped distribution of surface artifacts at Water World as a result of intensive transect recording. He proposed that the cleared area it outlined represented a plaza around which houses were located. Doelle (1987: 358) also has mentioned the possibility of a central plaza at other Colonial period sites in the Tucson Basin. Although trenching on the western edge of this plaza area (near House Group 5) was less extensive than at the eastern end (Fig. 1.5; N300-N400 and E200-E300), the resulting data support the idea of a central plaza bordered on the west by House Group 5, on the north by House Group 2, on the east by House Group 3 and the ballcourt area, and on the south by House Group 4 (Fig. 1.6). The solitary ash lens (Feature 30) located in the plaza area could have been deposited before or after the plaza area was formed. There was no obvious hard-packed surface or other direct physical evidence of a plaza; only the distribution of houses and extramural features around an area free of features suggests it. Whether this patterning is intentional or fortuitous, this area of Water World apparently was not used for habitation, work space, or burial; instead, it probably served as a plazalike area if not an actual well-defined plaza.

Isolated Cremations

In addition to the cremations discussed with House Group 5, five cremations and one possible inhumation were found during the excavations. Three cremations (Features 5, 60, and 137) were located about 10 m southwest of the ballcourt, and two cremations (Features 40 and 46) and the possible inhumation (Feature 45) were found near House Group 3. The age of the cremations near the southwest entrance to the ballcourt relative to the use of the ballcourt cannot be determined. Features 40, 45, and 46 may represent either isolated burials associated with one of the surrounding house groups or a cremation area that was not defined during the excavation.

Comments

Unlike the house groups identified at Fastimes, the other Rillito phase site excavated during the Phase B Project, all of the house groups at Water World may not be the discrete, separate groups of structures that have been defined for purposes of analysis and discussion. Only House Groups 1, 2, and 5 appear to be easily defined units, and only House Groups 1 and 5 may represent discrete units. With the exception of House Groups 1 and 5, refitted sherds indicate that artifact disposal was not confined to the immediate vicinity of a particular house group (Chapter 4) as was the case at Fastimes. The one refitted ground-stone artifact also may provide evidence for contact between house groups.

Because chronometric data from Water World cannot provide the fine-scale measurements to indicate absolute contemporaneity or provide the temporal data to unequivocally illustrate construction and abandonment sequences, an accurate model of site development cannot be advanced. Undoubtedly many of the houses and extramural features, including the ballcourt, were in use at the same time.

Chapter 3

ARCHITECTURE, TRASH DEPOSITS, CREMATIONS,
AND FEATURE DESCRIPTIONS

Architecture

Arthur W. Vokes

Forty-five of the features located at Water World have been interpreted as pit houses or other structures. Most of these were located during the initial trenching; from this set, a sample of 21 structures was chosen for investigation. Eight houses were excavated completely, four additional structures were partially excavated, and nine were tested with one or more 2-m by 2-m grid units. Whenever possible, these 2-m by 2-m units were excavated over the projected location of the hearth, in front of the pit house entryway. The structures were generally well defined, having been excavated into a sterile sandy silt mixed with numerous small gravels. Deposits of larger gravels in some areas probably indicate old stream channels, which are characteristic of this geological deposit.

The structures are divided into at least six discrete house groups on the basis of their spatial location; a seventh house group includes unexcavated features profiled in 1987 (Fig. 1.6). House Groups 1, 2, and 3 were the focus of the greatest effort, and were located in the northeastern portion of the site area. Pit house architectural data are summarized in Table 3.1.

Preservation

A factor that may have affected the preservation of the structural features is the relatively low incidence of burned structures in the sample. Four structures (Features 20, 27, 53, and 58) had been burned, at least one during occupation (Feature 58). Two additional structures (Features 33 and 78) may have suffered the same fate. Feature 33 is part of House Group 3, as are Features 27 and 53, two of the other burned structures. Burning may contribute to the preservation of floor and wall plaster; evidence of wall plaster was noted in three of the burned structures and in only one of the unburned structures.

45

Table 3.1

SUMMARY OF ARCHITECTURAL DATA

Feature Number	House Group	Burned	Floor Shape	Area (m²)	Wall Form	Height (cm)	Plaster	Entry Form	Step Height	Orientation (degrees east of north)	Postulated Roof Support	Pits	As Pit	Bench	Hearth/Firepit
7 (70%)	2	No	Subrectangular	14*	Vertical S. Wall adobe	25 (mean)	No	Ramped	–	163	Unknown	0	–	–	1 Hearth (P) / 1 Firepit
19	1	No	Subrectangular	19.6	Vertical	20–30	No	Ramped	–	218	4 Post?	3	1	–	1 Hearth (P)
20	1	Yes	Square	13.4	Vertical	30–40	No	Ramp-Step	10 cm	115	4 Post	1	1	–	1 Firepit
25	1	No	Subrectangular	20.4	Vertical	25–35	No	Ramp-Step	?	139	4 Post	2	–	?	None
26	2	No	Near square	20.75	Near Vertical	25	No	Ramp	–	106	4 Post	1	–	–	1 Unknown
27	3	Yes	Subrectangular	18.5	Vertical	50–60	Yes	Ramp-Step	25 cm	130	4 Post	1	–	–	1 Firepit
29 (80%)	2	No	Subrectangular	18.2	Vertical	40–50	No	Stepped	30 cm	172	4 Post	0	–	–	1 Hearth (P)
33 (60%)	3	Yes	Subrectangular	10.6+*	Vertical	20–35	No	Ramped	–	195	4 Post?	1	–	–	2 Firepits
35**	3	No	Unknown	Unk.	Unknown	Unknown	No	Unknown	–	Unk.	Unknown	2	–	–	Unknown
36**	3	No	Subrectangular	Unk.	Sloped	18–23	No	Unknown	–	Unk.	Unknown	3	–	–	None
44**	3	No	Subrectangular	Very Small	Near Vertical	20–25	No	Unknown	–	Unk.	Unknown	0	–	–	None
53	3	Yes	Square	21.7	Vertical	40–55	Yes	Ramped-2 Steps	12/20? cm	93	4 Post	0	–	–	1 Hearth (P)
55	1	No	Square	15.3	Vertical	25	Yes	Ramp-Step	15 cm	144	4 Post	1	–	–	2 Firepits
58	4	Yes	Subrectangular	22.2	Vertical	50–60	Yes	Ramp-Step-Grooved	30 cm	159	4 Post	3+	1 (1?)	–	1 Hearth (P)
61 (60%)	4	No	Subrectangular?	9.16+	Unknown	Unknown	No	Ramp-Step	–	112	Unknown	0	–	–	1 Firepit
66**	6	No	Unknown	Unk.	Unknown	Unknown	Unk.	Unknown	–	Unk.	Unknown	Unk.	–	–	None
67**	6	No	Unknown	Unk.	Unknown	Unknown	Unk.	Unknown	–	Unk.	Unknown	Unk.	–	–	1 Firepit
68**	6	No	Unknown	Unk.	Unknown	10–15?	Unk.	Unknown	–	Unk.	Unknown	1	–	–	None
78**	6	No	Unknown	Unk.	Unknown	Unknown	Unk.	Unknown	–	Unk.	Unknown	0	–	–	1 Hearth (P)
79**	6	No	Unknown	Unk.	Unknown	Unknown	No	Unknown	–	Unk.	Unknown	0	–	–	None
110**	6	No	Square	Unk.	Slope?	Unknown	No	Unknown	–	39	Unknown	0	–	–	None

% = Percent excavated

* = Estimated

** = Sampled by test units

(P) = Plastered

Although this is suggestive, the near absence of preserved plaster in structures cannot be positively attributed to the low incidence of burning in the sample.

House Form

There is comparatively little variation in the form of the structures at Water World. Among excavated structures, where the form was identifiable, all were subrectangular or square; there were no examples of oval-shaped floors. Further, these forms tended to grade into one another so that the two designations, subrectangular and square, probably represent a continuum of form rather than two discrete types. Structure size varies considerably, ranging from small (unexcavated) structures estimated at roughly 10 square meters (Features 44, 36, and 61) to a large structure with a floor area in excess of 22 square meters (Feature 58).

House Floors

The majority of houses at Water World were constructed by excavating into the sterile substrate. Only one example of superimposed houses was noted: Feature 25 was built over the fill of Feature 55. The majority of floors do not appear to have been further modified by the application of a "plaster" or a prepared surface. Plastered floors were identified in six of the 21 structures investigated, and two of these (Features 29 and 35) appear to have been plastered only in the area near the hearth. In Feature 29, the floor plaster differed from the plaster used on the hearth. The plaster used at Water World was generally a silty clay mixture that apparently did not include caliche.

The presence of a prepared floor may be correlated with the nature of the substrate. In the case of the superimposed structures, the overlapping portion of the upper floor had a thick layer of plaster; this layer did not extend beyond the boundaries of the earlier pit house. Other structures with plastered floors, Features 26, 55, and 61, were excavated into a soil matrix with higher than normal amounts of gravels. This was not always the case, however, for Feature 7, which was partially constructed over what appears to be an old stream channel, and which lacked evidence of floor plaster except for a thin layer restricted to the entry. Nonetheless, surface preparation was apparently a response to the conditions of the substrata.

Walls

The walls of all structures, with one possible exception, were constructed with a near vertical face (Fig. 3.1). The walls of Feature

Figure 3.1. House construction at Water World involved digging a pit, the sides of which were used as the lower part of the walls. The pit walls, and the earthen floor, were occasionally plastered with a silty clay material (ASM photograph).

26 may have been sloped slightly; however, the loose nature of the substrata made it difficult to define the exact nature of the wall. There is considerable variation in the height of the pit walls, which range from a minimum of 10 cm to a maximum of 60 cm; the majority seem to fall between 20 cm and 40+ cm in height. In only four structures (Features 27, 53, 55, and 58) was there evidence of wall plaster. Three of these structures had greater-than-average wall heights; the walls in Features 27 and 58 were between 50 cm and 60 cm high, making these the deepest house pits excavated. There is no correlation between the presence of wall plaster and prepared floors. One wall of Feature 7 was unusual in that it was made of a clayey silt adobe and was constructed over and against a substrate of loosely compacted gravels, probably the remains of an old stream channel. This wall may have served to keep this matrix from slumping into the house.

In the majority of cases it is difficult to determine whether the base of the wall frame originated in the pit or rested outside on the prehistoric ground surface. The absence of wall grooves and peripheral postholes supports the latter interpretation; however, the side walls could have been constructed without such features. The apparent absence of wall plaster in the majority of structures also is inconclusive. Its presence in four structures supports the concept of a structure in which the walls of the pit were incorporated into the overall superstructure. It is possible that all of the excavated structures were constructed in this manner.

Entryways

The 12 identifiable entryways represented three different forms: a simple ramped entry, a stepped entry, and a combination of these types. Examples of ramped entries were found in Features 7, 19, 26, and 33. The ramps originated from the floor level between the hearth and the opening of the entry in the structure wall. The ramp then extended in a relatively even slope up to the prehistoric ground surface.

Only Feature 29 had a simple stepped entry. The structure had a level entry floor that terminated with a step 30 cm high. This was one of only two entries at the site that incorporated a step this high; the other was in Feature 58.

The most common form of entryway combined ramps and steps. Most were composed of a ramp with a single step located near the midpoint of the entryway. In one case (Feature 53), a second step was located at the outer end of the entryway. The degree of inclination of the ramp varied from a slight to a relatively steep slope. The most complex of these entries was in Feature 58. It was a ramp-step combination with a series of associated grooves that paralleled the sides and bisected the entry. The presence of two postholes at the ends of these side grooves suggests that a superstructure probably extended out from the front wall of the structure. The groove that divided the entry was located immediately in front of the step and was probably the result of a sill of wood or stone being placed there. Feature 27 also exhibited evidence of a superstructure over the entry. Although the entry was not grooved, it did include two postholes that flanked the entryway just beyond the step, at some distance from the front wall. These were the only structures that produced evidence of a sheltered entry.

Orientation

All of the entryways identified had parallel sides and extended straight out from the front walls of the structures. The majority opened to the southeast, between 93 and 172 degrees east of true north (Table 3.1; Fig. 3.2). This orientation is roughly aligned with the main pass between the body of the Tucson Mountains to the east and Black

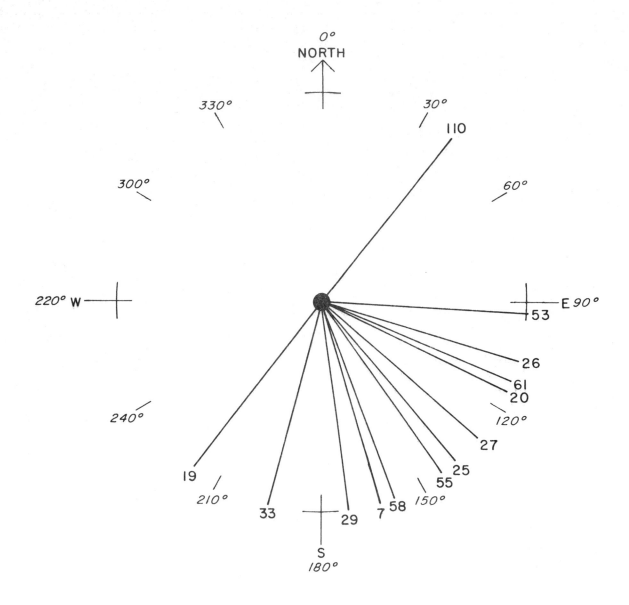

Figure 3.2. Pit house entryway orientations (true north).

Mountain to the southeast; however, there is no way to determine if this
was a factor in establishing this pattern or merely a coincidence.
Multiple structures within house groups exhibited this southeast
orientation; the structures with alternative orientations occur with
lower incidence throughout the groups. The orientation could be
determined for only 13 structures, making any generalizations tentative.

Roof Construction

The nature of the roof construction is inferred from indirect
evidence (Fig. 3.3). There is little direct evidence of the form and

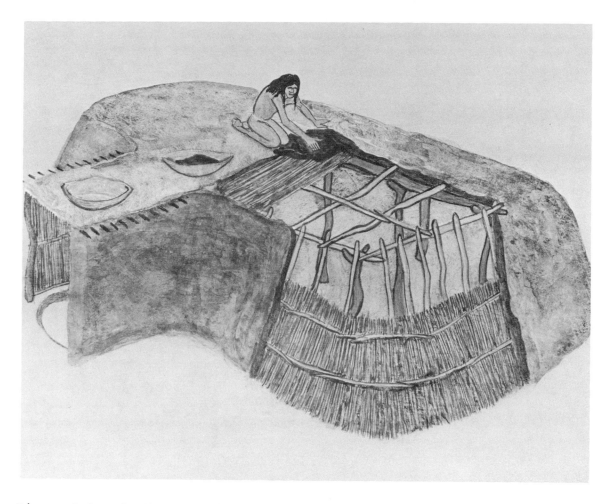

Figure 3.3. At Water World a four-post primary roof support was used in house construction. These posts and other major roof and wall beams were made of mesquite wood. Saguaro ribs probably were used as lattice to cover the main structural frame.

techniques involved. Some amorphous daub fragments were found in the lower levels of structure fill and probably represent debris from upper collapsed walls and roofs (Fig. 3.4). Most of the information concerning the roof structure comes from posthole patterns exposed in the floor and from other attributes discussed above.

Evidence of the roof support system, in the form of postholes in the floor, was found in nine structures. In most of these, the evidence indicates a four-post system in the approximate center of the floor. Postholes ranged in diameter from a minimum of 7 cm in Feature 19 to a maximum of 40 cm in Feature 26. The locations of the posts represented by the lower end of the size range suggest that these posts may not have functioned as primary roof supports, but as supports for other internal features. The smallest of the postholes in Feature 19 occurred toward

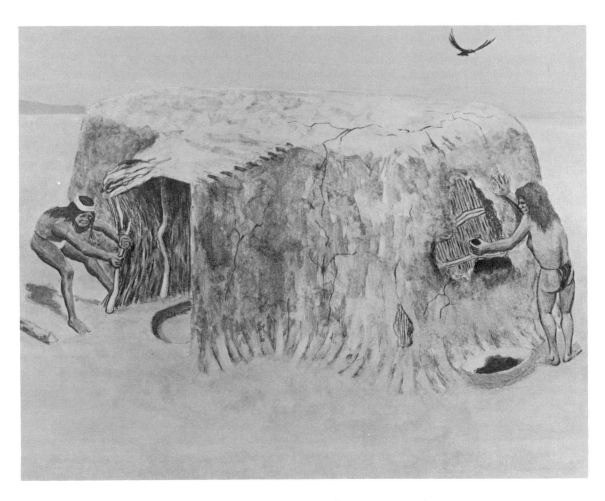

Figure 3.4. The pit house was covered with mud, which undoubtedly required frequent maintenance. Several pit houses at Water World had covered entryways into which a person had to step down when going into a house. Burned mud, or daub, was found in the fill of some houses.

the side and rear of the house. Postholes representing primary vertical support beams range in size from about 15 cm to 40 cm; one posthole in Feature 27 was 12 cm in diameter. In several instances there are additional postholes that may represent secondary support posts or additional vertical supports. One example, Feature 55, included an alignment of four large postholes and one small, shallow posthole along the east side of the floor. It is impossible to determine from the available evidence whether this arrangement was established at the time of initial construction. It may represent an attempt to bolster the superstructure subsequent to the initial construction. Nine structures produced sufficient evidence to permit interpretation of the vertical support system; only one of these, Feature 19, did not have a four-post system. The presence of the two postholes in the central area of the floor in an alignment paralleling the front wall suggests a two-post support system; however, the rather short distance between these features calls into question the stability of such a structure.

Structural Wood Identification

Additional information concerning the nature of roof construction is available from the charcoal samples recovered from roof fall material and postholes. Sixteen wood charcoal samples were submitted for identification to the Laboratory of Tree-Ring Research at the University of Arizona (Volume 5, Appendix H). Both mesquite and saguaro ribs were identified. One of the postholes in Structure 19 (Feature 19.4) produced a sample of mesquite, suggesting that vertical supports may have been made from this desert wood. Fifteen samples were recovered from floor and floor fill contexts; the remaining sample came from a pit. Saguaro wood was recovered from two structures, Features 20 and 58. Due to the relatively fragile nature of saguaro wood, it is improbable that this material was part of the primary support system of the superstructure. Saguaro ribs were most likely used in the construction of the upper walls and roof lattice (Fig. 3.3; Haury 1976: 113).

Internal Features

Hearths and Firepits

Structures at Water World exhibited two kinds of hearths: prepared basins and unplastered firepits. The basic form of both types of features was a shallow basin located just inside the door of the structure, often at the base of the entry ramp. Only one of the plastered hearths had a collar around it; the rest appear to have been plastered only up to the floor level. There is apparently no correlation between the presence of prepared floor and the nature of the hearth; only two hearths occurred in structures with prepared floors. No hearth or firepit was located in Feature 25, the structure that was superimposed over Feature 55. The area where a hearth probably would have been located was within the plastered area, and such a feature should have been identified if it was present. The absence of a hearth or firepit in one of the larger structures is unusual and may indicate that the primary function of the structure was other than habitation.

Ash Pits

Three structures--Features 19, 20, and 58--included features identified as ash pits. This functional designation was assigned on the basis of the fill of these features, a fine white ash, and their location within the house. Two of the ash pits were associated with plastered hearths, the other with a firepit.

Floor Pits

Eleven of the 21 structures in the sample contained floor pits. Five structures (Features 19, 25, 35, 36, and 58) had multiple pits, with a maximum of five possible pits occurring in Feature 58. Excavation of Structures 35 and 36 was limited to a series of 2-m by 2-m units, so these features may have included additional pit features that were not found. Most subfloor pits probably were used for storage, although at least one (Feature 19.8) contained fire-cracked rock and ash and may have had a different function, perhaps associated with cooking.

Most floor pits were located along one side of the structure, either to the right of the entry, or along the back of the structure, clustering near the left corner. Two pits (Features 25.3 and 27.2) were located just inside the entries of their respective structures. The nature of their fills suggests that they were intentionally filled before the structures were abandoned. Feature 25.1, one of the three centrally located pits (Features 19.5, 25.1, and 36.1), was apparently a recess for holding a mortar. Corn pollen was found in soil samples taken from this pit (Chapter 9). Interestingly, Feature 25 did not contain a hearth or firepit. The function of the other two pits (Features 19.5 and 36.1) is unclear, but they are possibly storage pits. Features 35 and 58 produced multiple pit features. No hearth or entry was defined for Feature 35; however, it was not entirely excavated so any possible relationships between the pits within it and other types of features cannot be ascertained. This structure is thought to have been quite small and may have had a function other than habitation.

Floor pits range from a maximum of 85 cm to a minimum of 22 cm in diameter, with the majority between 30 cm and 50 cm. The relationship between the largest pit in the sample (Feature 35.2) and its associated structure is unclear due to the limited testing of the structure and the amorphous nature of its fill. The pit may represent the lower portion of an intrusive pit rather than a floor pit.

Nonstructural Postholes

Evidence of floor features other than pits is limited. A shallow depression in the floor of Feature 55 might have functioned as a potrest. The presence of probable nonstructural postholes suggests the possibility of some form of internal "furniture" such as small platforms. Two postholes in Structure 25 (Features 25.4 and 25.6) were aligned parallel to the front wall and might have supported a shelf that extended out from the wall.

Structure Function

The architectural features of Water World are consistent in form. The structures were constructed with a basic rectangular or square floor plan with nearly vertical walls. Most entryways were oriented toward the southeast. Most structures contained a firepit or hearth, suggesting that internal space was probably used for habitation. Several structures (Features 25, 35, 36, and 44), however, exhibited evidence suggesting that they may have been the focus of some nonhabitation activities. Feature 25 is the largest of these. It did not have a hearth or firepit, but did have a number of other floor features including a mortar that had been mounted in a small pit in the center of the floor. A variety of economic pollen types was recovered from this pit house, suggesting that it may have functioned as a food processing and storage locus for House Group 1 (see Chapter 9). Structures 35, 36, and 44 are probably storage features; all were located on the periphery of House Group 3. These features were only tested and functional data are therefore limited. All are comparatively small and shallow, and the tested portions lacked hearths or entryways. Two of the structures had a series of interior pits associated with them. These data do not conclusively demonstrate the use of these structures as storage facilities, but they are suggestive.

Another group of features that deviate from the apparent pattern is clustered to the south of the ballcourt and includes Features 66, 67, and 68. These features, which make up House Group 6, were sampled by a series of 2-m by 2-m excavation units. They appear to be areas of compacted soil with little or no evidence of a defined boundary. No true walls could be defined, nor was there any evidence of an entry or roof structure. Feature 67 had a possible firepit, whereas Feature 68 had a shallow depression that may have been a pit associated with it. Overall, these features may well have been specialized activity areas. Feature 66 may have been covered by a ramada. Their location away from the main habitation areas and near the ballcourt suggests a possible specialized function. This isolation is more pronounced if one views the ballcourt and its immediate environs as a specialized activity area. It is also possible that they were associated with the plaza area (see Chapter 2), perhaps as a formal activity area.

The closest pit houses to House Group 6 are the structures in House Group 4. One of these, Feature 58, also exhibited some unusual characteristics. It was by far the most complex of the structures, with a relatively elaborate covered entry and a complex set of internal features. It is also the largest structure in the sample. The unusual floor assemblage from Feature 58 included deer crania and mandibles and a bighorn sheep horn core. This may be evidence that this structure had a ceremonial function or was used to store ceremonial paraphernalia. Its location directly west of the ballcourt may support this interpretation. Generally, the structures that appear to have been habitation structures are located in the northern portion of the site.

Trash Deposits

Jon S. Czaplicki

Feature Types

Trash Middens

Trash middens are rare at Water World in contrast to Fastimes (Volume 2), where seven midden deposits were identified. Only two trash middens were positively identified at Water World (Features 59 and 131), and one other deposit (Feature 126) was tentatively called a midden. Features 126 and 131 were located in abandoned stream channels in House Group 7. The tentative identification of Feature 126 was based on the presence of sherds, one flake, and some charcoal in the profile of a trench wall. This material might have washed into the channel from elsewhere in the house group, as was noted at the time the feature was recorded. Feature 131 apparently contained considerably more cultural debris than Feature 126; it also was identified in a trench profile and was not tested. Feature 59, recorded as a trash-filled pit, was a midden deposit that covered almost 11 square meters, and its gray, ashy fill contained 13 animal bones and some 80 artifacts. It was situated above pit house Feature 29 in House Group 2 and appeared to be distinct from the pit house.

Four structures were covered by Stratum 30 midden deposits: Features 27, 29, 44, and 67. At Fastimes, six structures were identified with overlying Stratum 30 deposits. The Stratum 30 deposit above Feature 27 was from 28 cm to 33 cm thick and covered a layer of roof and wall fall. The trash deposit located above Feature 29 varied from 15 cm to 35 cm thick and was confined to a basin-shaped depression similar to the Feature 59 deposit above the adjacent Feature 26. The midden deposit that overlay Feature 44 was 38 cm thick. The trash identified as Stratum 30 above Feature 67 may instead be part of the Stratum 1 trash fill of this feature. In none of these cases did the Stratum 30 deposits appear to extend beyond the limits of the underlying structures, suggesting that the deposits were probably formed in a relatively short period of time and that the occupation responsible for them was not of a sufficient duration to create extensive midden deposits.

Trash-Filled Pit Houses

Upon abandonment, a pit house that had not burned or been cannibalized for wood eventually decayed; the roof and walls collapsed into the pit, leaving a partially filled depression. Often the abandoned structure or pit depression was used as a convenient trash dump by occupants of surrounding houses, as indicated by the sometimes dense amounts of charcoal and ash and the many discarded animal bones and artifacts intermixed in the dirt fill. Some pit house depressions were filled more gradually with water- and wind-borne deposits of silt and sand, which also contained some artifacts (for example, Features 7 and 20). Eventually the depression was filled with these naturally deposited sediments (Haury 1976; Seymour and Schiffer 1987).

All of the 21 structures that were excavated or tested contained some cultural material and debris, which was labeled Stratum 1 and in some cases, Stratum 2. The basic artifact counts for fill levels in these structures (see below, Excavated Pit Houses, and also Chapter 11) show some variation in the amount of cultural material present. Structures with large amounts of sherds, animal bones, and lithic material in the fill were probably intentionally trash filled (Features 25, 26, 29, 35, 36, 55, 67, 68, and 79). Other structures whose fill contained lesser quantities of cultural material and debris (most of the remaining structures) probably reflect episodes of both intentional trash dumping and natural deposition of basically sterile sediment. These too can be considered trash filled, although they were not subjected to intensive or continuous refuse disposal.

Extramural Pits with Trash

Of 17 extramural features investigated, 8 contained no artifacts in their fill (Features 54, 76, 95, 139, 143, 144, 147, and 148). Features 56, 57, 86, 87, and 96 contained from several to 30 or more sherds, pieces of flaked stone, or animal bones; these fills probably represent a mixture of both naturally deposited sediment containing occasional sherds, bones, or lithics, and some intentionally deposited trash. Four features (Features 18, 59, 138, and 13, the ballcourt) contained sufficiently large amounts of cultural material and debris to suggest at least occasional intentional dumping of trash. When no longer needed some of the pit features may have been purposefully filled to prevent accidents, and some cultural material may have found its way into these pits in this manner.

Content of Trash Fill

Sherds, animal bones, stone, and shell are the artifact types represented in the screened and "grab sample" collections. In many of the pit houses, architectural debris such as roof and wall daub, ash, and charcoal were present in the fill, especially in structures that had burned. The presence of ash and charcoal may be attributed to both the disposal of unwanted deposits in hearths or roasting pits and the burning of the structure itself. Fire-cracked rocks, plant remains, ash, and charcoal were common in many of the extramural pit features, particularly those identified as roasting pits. Macrofloral and pollen remains also were found in many of the dirt samples collected from features.

The Scarcity of Trash Deposits

What is interesting about the trash deposits at Water World is their apparent paucity. There are no midden features comparable to the seven midden deposits at Fastimes, which were both surface trash deposits and also possibly overflow from trash-filled pit houses that had spread laterally as material was added to the deposit (Volume 2, Chapter 3). Only one of the deposits at Water World can be considered a definite, albeit not particularly extensive or rich, midden (Feature 59), whereas Feature 131 probably is a trash midden. Feature 59 is only about 11 square meters in area and does not exceed the area of the structure it overlies, and the extent of Feature 131 is not known.

The Stratum 30 deposits that overlay four structures (Features 27, 29, 44, and 67), do not spread laterally away from the features, in fact, they do not even completely cover these features. In the case of Feature 67, the Stratum 30 deposit may be part of the Stratum 1 trash fill.

Almost one-half (8 of 17) of the extramural pit features contained no artifacts, and only four of the remaining nine features contained relatively substantial amounts of intentionally deposited trash (Features 18, 59, 138, and 13).

Erosion may have affected midden deposits, but some trace could be expected to remain even if the deposits were few in number and small in size. Feature 131, located in an abandoned stream channel, was readily discernible in profile. The degree of erosional disturbance was questioned during the 1983 survey (Rankin and Downum 1986: 77), but subsequent excavations indicated that erosion had had a negligible effect on the vast majority of features. It seems more likely that the lack of evidence for midden deposits is due not to erosion, but to their never having been created by the inhabitants of Water World.

Although the occupants of Water World did use abandoned structures as trash dumps, some more intensively than others, it appears that occupation may have been unintensive and perhaps of limited duration, with the result that no large surface trash middens were created. Abandoned structures provided adequate disposal space while the site was occupied. Alternatively, the lack of surface middens might reflect the sampling design; other, less intensively investigated areas of the site may contain such features. The core of the site appears to be centered around the ballcourt, however, and it is in this area, where the excavations were concentrated, that occupation would be expected to be heaviest. Yet there are virtually no large trash deposits outside the pit houses that were used for dumps.

Excavated Pit Houses

R. Thomas Euler, Ronald Gardiner
and Jon S. Czaplicki

The pit house descriptions are organized by house groups; House Group 7 is omitted because no features in it were excavated. Pit house floor areas were measured using a computer digitizer.

House Group 1

Feature 19

Feature Type:	Pit house (Figs. 3.5 and 3.6)
Provenience:	Test Trench (TT)4; N418.95-425.10 E498.65-503.20
Stratigraphic Location:	Originates in Stratum 60 at 2.80 meters below datum (MBD) Terminates in Stratum 60 at 3.12 MBD
Shape-Dimensions:	Subrectangular; 5.5 m northwest-southeast, 4.2 m northeast-southwest
Entry:	The entry for this structure opened to the southwest (218 degrees west of north) and measured approximately 0.8 m by 0.8 m. It was slightly ramped and showed no evidence of a prepared surface.
Walls:	The pit walls were fairly well defined and varied from nearly vertical to slightly sloping to meet the floor. They consisted of unprepared sterile Stratum 60 and were from 20 cm to 30 cm in height. The presence of some possible burned and unburned wall fall in the fill was the only evidence of upper wall construction.
Roof:	No evidence
Fill:	The fill of the feature was divided into two distinct strata. Stratum 1 was a light brown sandy silt with small- to medium-sized gravels intermixed with charcoal flecks and artifacts. Stratum 2, which varied from 5 cm to 15 cm above the floor, consisted of gray-brown sandy silt with chunks of hard-packed orangish soil mixed with small gravels.

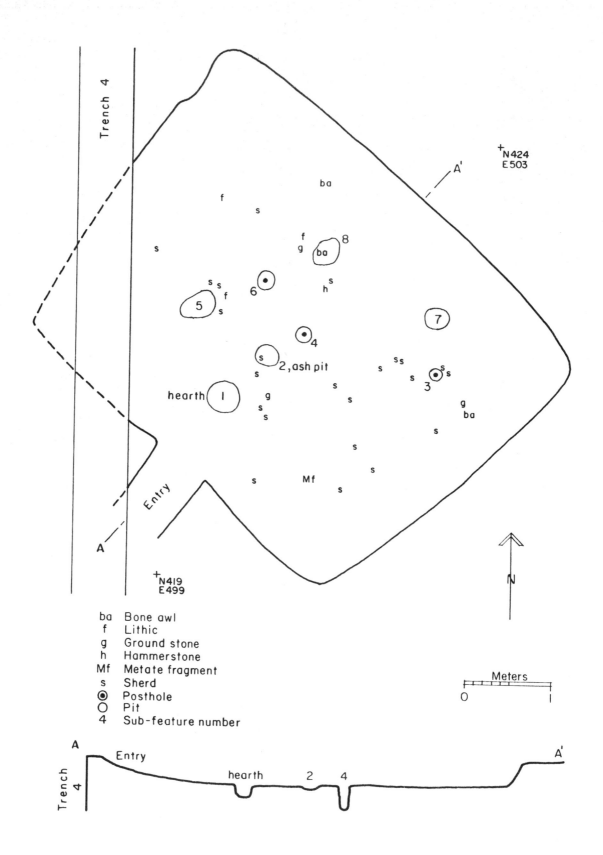

Figure 3.5. Plan and profile, Feature 19, pit house.

Figure 3.6. View of Feature 19, pit house, looking southwest.

This stratum, which contained some ash and charcoal, was defined as primarily architectural debris with differential burning.

Fill Artifacts: 1 worked Laevicardium fragment, 4 Glycymeris shell bracelet fragments, 2 unworked Anodonta shell fragments, 1 Spondylus shell bead fragment, 1 unworked Anodonta shell fragment; 1 hammerstone, 1 abrader, 1 mano fragment, 3 metate fragments, 1 unidentified ground stone fragment; 105 flakes, 2 cores, 4 unifaces; 1 bifaces, 6 utilized flakes, 3 hammerstones; 1 figurine fragment; 1,387 sherds (1,135 plain ware, 136 unidentified, 108 decorated, 8 worked); 3 reconstructible whole vessels; 169 animal bones, 3 bone awl fragments

Floor: The floor of this feature was unprepared, compacted, sterile Stratum 60. It was orange-brown in color and had some burned areas. A total of 19.6 square meters of floor surface was exposed.

Floor Artifacts:	1 unworked <u>Anodonta</u> shell fragment; 1 grinding slab fragment, 1 trough metate fragment, 1 pestle-hammerstone; 5 flakes, 1 uniface; 55 sherds (25 plain ware, 23 unidentified, 6 decorated, 1 worked); 4 animal bone fragments, 1 complete bone awl and 2 fragments
Floor Features:	Feature 19 included a hearth, an associated ash pit, three postholes, and three pits.
	Feature 19.1, a hearth, was badly eroded but did exhibit some plastered surfaces along the sides. It was 28 cm in diameter and 12 cm deep. The fill consisted of a 5-cm-thick layer of fine white-gray ash mixed with orangish silt that was overlain by orange, black, and brown mottled roof fall.
	Feature 19.2, an ash pit, was rather irregularly shaped and was located approximately 40 cm northeast of Feature 19.1. It measured 15 cm by 20 cm by 5 cm deep, and was filled with fine, whitish gray ash.
	Feature 19.5 may have functioned as a storage pit. It had a diameter of approximately 35 cm and a depth of 15 cm. Fill was a soft gray-brown silt with some pockets of sand.
	Feature 19.7 was a shallow (6 cm) oval-shaped (13 cm by 25 cm) pit; its function was not determined. Fill consisted of fine, gray ashy silt.
	Feature 19.8 was a poorly defined pit that measured approximately 25 cm in diameter by 7 cm deep. Presence of fire-cracked rock and ash suggests that it may have served some cooking function.
Postholes:	The three roughly cylindrical postholes contained a brown silty sand fill with charcoal flecks.
	19.3, 7 cm diameter by 20 cm deep 19.4, 15 cm diameter by 29 cm deep 19.6, 17 cm diameter by 15 cm deep
Floor Feature Artifacts:	19.4, mesquite charcoal 19.5, 1 flake; sherds: 1 plain ware, 5 unidentified, 1 Rillito Red-on-brown; 2 animal bones 19.8, 1 plain ware sherd; 1 animal bone
Comments:	Feature 19 is one of the few excavated structures with a southwest-facing entry. The structure appears to have been partially burned.

Sampling: A control unit (N421.00–423.00 E498.65–500.65) was excavated from present ground surface down to the floor surface in 20-cm levels. All material from this unit was screened and collected. Surrounding sediment was stripped by backhoe down to the prehistoric occupation surface. The remaining excavation units were dug in two strata. Stratum 1 was not screened; however, all observed artifacts were collected. Stratum 2 was troweled down to the floor and all material was screened.

Samples: Flotation--14 samples collected, 3 samples analyzed (hearth F.19.1, pits F.19.2 and F.19.8); none contained charred macroplant remains
Pollen--10 samples collected, 1 sample analyzed (composite pinches from 7 different samples)
Archaeomagnetic--1 sample, datable
Charcoal--9 samples collected, 1 analyzed (posthole F.19.4)

Feature 20

Feature Type: Pit house (Figs. 3.7 and 3.8)

Provenience: TT9; N411.35–415.85 E457.55–461.80

Stratigraphic Location: Originates in Stratum 50 at 3.38 MBD
Terminates in Stratum 60 at 3.78 MBD

Shape-Dimensions: Square; 4.0 m northwest-southeast, 3.9 m northeast-southwest

Entry: The entry opened to the southeast (115 degrees east of north) and measured approximately 80 cm long by 60 cm wide. It was extremely well defined as it sloped gradually up from the central floor surface and terminated with a step approximately 10 cm high.

Walls: In part because this feature had burned, the pit walls were well defined. They were unplastered, sterile Stratum 60, nearly vertical (with a slight slope where they met the floor surface), and varied in height from 30 cm to 40 cm. Sections of burned beams and upright posts found in the structure were the only evidence of a superstructure.

Roof: Three postholes, which are assumed to represent primary support posts, were found in the house floor. It seems likely that a fourth such feature

64

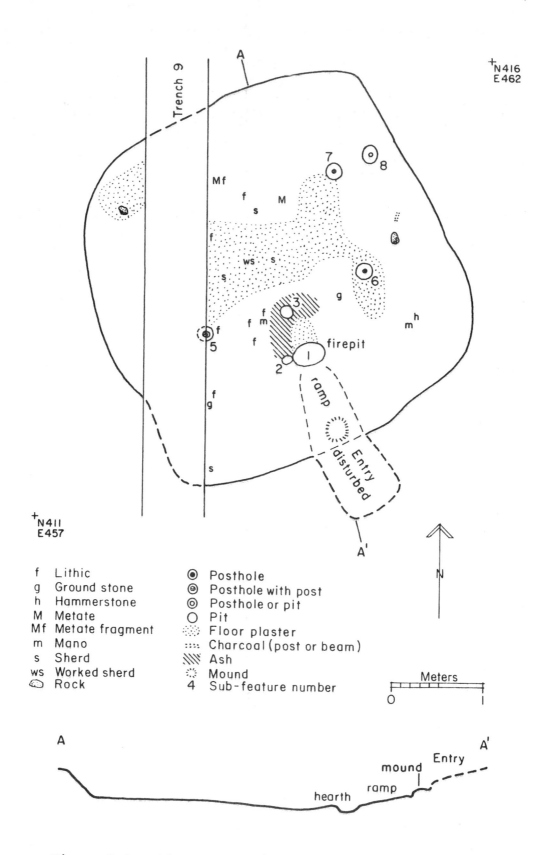

f   Lithic
g   Ground stone
h   Hammerstone
M   Metate
Mf   Metate fragment
m   Mano
s   Sherd
ws   Worked sherd
⬮   Rock

⊙   Posthole
◉   Posthole with post
◎   Posthole or pit
○   Pit
⣿   Floor plaster
⫶⫶⫶ Charcoal (post or beam)
▨   Ash
○   Mound
4   Sub-feature number

Meters
0   1

Figure 3.7. Plan and profile, Feature 20, pit house.

Figure 3.8. View from above of Feature 20, pit house.

was removed during backhoe trenching. Roof fall--
burned and unburned daub and charred beam fragments
--was found in the feature fill (Stratum 2).

Fill: The fill was divided into three separate strata.
               Stratum 1 consisted of a loose brownish orange,
               silty sand with few artifacts. This soil was
               naturally deposited sometime after the house had
               collapsed. Stratum 2 was primarily roof-wall fall
               mixed with tan-orange silty, gravelly sand. This
               deposit also contained burned beam fragments.
               Stratum 2 sloped inward from the edge of the house
               walls toward the center of the feature. Stratum 3,
               a compact tan-orange silty sand, is floor fill that
               may have accumulated after abandonment of the
               structure.

Fill Artifacts:	1 unworked <u>Anodonta</u> shell fragment; 10 flakes, 1 utilized flake, 2 hammerstones; 1 grinding stone fragment, 1 hammerstone, 1 mano fragment; 61 sherds (54 plain ware, 4 unidentified, 3 decorated); mesquite and saguaro charcoal
Floor Fill Artifacts:	1 hammerstone; 5 plain ware sherds; saguaro charcoal
Floor:	Oxidized, unprepared, sterile Stratum 60 with rodent disturbance covering an area of 13.4 square meters excluding the entry.
Floor Artifacts:	13 flakes, 2 utilized flakes, 1 hammerstone; 1 complete metate, 1 metate fragment, 1 complete hammerstone-anvil, 2 or 3 mano fragments, 1 handstone fragment; 8 sherds (7 plain ware, 1 indeterminate Colonial period decorated)
Floor Features:	Feature 20 had 8 floor features, including 4 postholes.
	Feature 20.1 was an unprepared, highly oxidized firepit measuring 31 cm by 35 cm by 7 cm deep. The fill was a loose white-gray ash.
	Feature 20.2 was a small, irregularly shaped depression at the edge of Feature 20.1. This probable ash pit measured 8 cm by 12 cm by 3 cm deep and contained white-gray ash.
	Feature 20.3 was a shallow, irregular depression that measured 14 cm by 15 cm by 1 cm deep and contained white-gray ash.
	Feature 20.4 was an oval-shaped pit of unknown function that measured 65 cm by 45 cm by 18 cm deep. The sides of the feature were oxidized and the fill consisted of white-gray ash with charcoal.
Postholes:	All four postholes were roughly circular and contained loose, silty, gravelly sand. Feature 20.5 contained a section of a burned upright beam.
	20.5, 18 cm in diameter by 28 cm deep 20.6, 16 cm in diameter by 36 cm deep 20.7, 20 cm in diameter by 22 cm deep 20.8, 25 cm in diameter by 12 cm deep

Floor Feature Artifacts:	20.1--charred macroplant remains: cheno-am seeds, horse purslane, drop seed grass, prickly pear, tidestromia
	20.4--1 utilized flake; 2 plain ware sherds
Comments:	Excavators noted that this house may have burned some time after it ceased to be used as a living structure, based on the presence of 3 cm to 13 cm of relatively sterile fill (Stratum 3) over the house floor.
Sampling:	A control unit (N412.00-414.00 E458.90-461.00) was excavated in 20-cm levels from the present ground surface down to the floor of the feature. All materials in this unit were screened and all artifacts collected. The sterile overburden was removed by machine from the rest of the feature, revealing the burned structure outline. Stratum 1 was excavated by hand; it was not screened, but all observed artifacts were collected. Strata 2 and 3 were completely excavated using horizontal control units and screened.
Samples:	Flotation--13 samples collected, 3 samples analyzed (hearth F.20.1, and ash pits F.20.2 and F.20.3); F20.2 and F.20.3 contained no macroplant remains Pollen--8 samples collected, 2 samples analyzed (hearth and from floor beneath metate) Archaeomagnetic--1 sample, datable Charcoal--14 samples collected, 3 analyzed

Feature 25

Feature Type:	Pit house (Figs. 3.9 and 3.10)
Provenience:	TT6; N411.24-417.23 E486.64-492.20
Stratigraphic Location:	Originates in Stratum 50 at 2.98 MBD Terminates in Stratum 60 and Stratum 1 of Feature 55 at 3.18 MBD
Shape-Dimensions:	Subrectangular; 5.0 m northwest-southeast, 4.7 m northeast-southwest
Entry:	The entry opened to the southeast (139 degrees east of north) and measured approximately 85 cm wide by 120 cm long. It sloped gently downward into the house and may have had a shallow step at its midpoint.

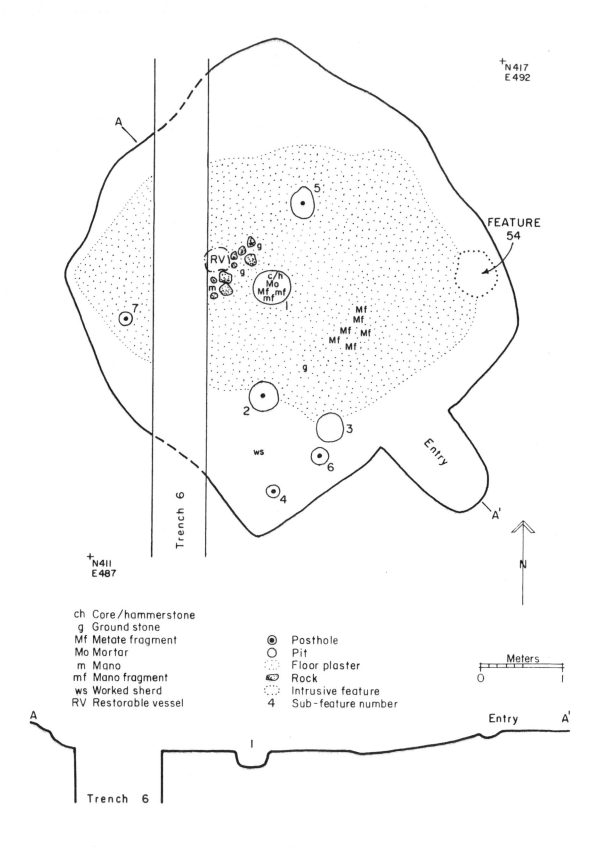

Figure 3.9. Plan and profile, Feature 25, pit house.

Figure 3.10. View of Feature 25, pit house, looking northeast.

Walls: The pit walls were unprepared sterile Stratum 60,
                    and they varied from slightly sloped to near
                    vertical. Wall height varied from 25 cm to 35 cm.

Roof: Evidence of roof construction consisted of a
                    compacted, mottled, tan-gray sandy, silty daub with
                    charcoal flecking and some gravels. It was unburned
                    and appeared to have simply collapsed and "melted"
                    into the center of the structure.

Fill: The fill consisted of two distinct strata. Stratum
                    1 was a loose, grayish brown sandy silt with
                    charcoal inclusions. This material overlay the
                    structure's roof-wall fall and probably represents
                    later trash deposits. Stratum 2 was predominantly
                    mottled tan-gray, sandy, silty roof-wall fall with
                    charcoal inclusions. A very thin (1 cm to 2 cm)
                    lens of ash separated Stratum 2 from the floor.
                    This ash may have been on the floor surface during
                    occupation.

Fill Artifacts:	Stratum 1--1 unworked <u>Glycymeris</u> shell bracelet fragment; 1 metate fragment; 108 flakes, 7 unifaces, 2 bifaces (1 hand axe), 11 utilized flakes, 3 hammerstones; 605 sherds (507 plain ware, 69 unidentified, 23 decorated, 6 worked); 48 animal bones
	Stratum 2--1 unworked <u>Anodonta</u> shell fragment; 2 complete manos and 1 mano fragment; 133 flakes, 3 unifaces, 1 biface, 9 utilized flakes, 1 hammerstone; 591 sherds (481 plain ware, 56 unidentified, 42 decorated, 2 possible red wares, 10 worked); 41 animal bones
Floor:	The profile of Test Trench 6 revealed that Feature 25 was actually superimposed over another pit house (Feature 55). A plastered surface of gray, silty clay had been placed over the fill of Feature 55, which created the floor surface for Feature 25. Feature 25 was somewhat larger than the earlier feature, extending 10 cm to 50 cm beyond it on all sides. The floor surface was not plastered beyond the limits of Feature 55 but is sterile Stratum 60. This suggests that the plastering was done only to cover the fill of that feature. The total usable floor surface was 20.4 square meters.
Floor Artifacts:	1 abrader, 1 grinding slab; 20 flakes, 2 unifaces, 1 biface, 1 utilized flake; 119 sherds (92 plain ware, 16 unidentified, 8 decorated, 2 worked); 1 reconstructible Cañada del Oro Red-on-brown bowl; 1 complete pregnant female figurine; 7 animal bones
Floor Features:	Feature 25.1 was a floor pit measuring approximately 45 cm in diameter by 18 cm deep. It contained a large mortar, the top of which was flush with the floor surface. The fill around this mortar consisted of gray, ashy silt intermixed with 15 small stones (including ground stone fragments) that were apparently used to level and steady the mortar.
	Feature 25.3, a floor pit of unknown function, measured 33 cm by 36 cm by 22 cm deep. This pit had clearly been intentionally filled with gray clay or adobe. Furthermore, the very compact nature of the adobe suggested that the feature was filled with wet clay. It is suggested that this feature fell into disuse and was filled during the occupation of Feature 25.

Postholes:	Five postholes were associated with the floor of Feature 25. The fill was generally a loose, ashy, grayish brown silt with some charcoal. The features were not always well defined, in part because they all intruded the cultural fill of Feature 55.

25.2, 34 cm in diameter by 11 cm deep
25.4, 16 cm in diameter by 6 cm deep
25.5, 32 cm in diameter by 5 cm deep(?)
25.6, 20 cm in diameter by 7 cm deep(?)
25.7, 19 cm in diameter by 26 cm deep

Floor Feature Artifacts:	25.1--1 boulder mortar, 2 mano fragments, 1 handstone, 1 abrader, 1 hammerstone; 2 plain ware sherds; charred macroplant remains: cheno-am, corn, grass 25.2--1 flake; 4 plain ware and 4 decorated sherds 25.4--1 plain ware sherd 25.7--2 flakes; 4 plain ware sherds
Comments:	Feature 54, a roasting pit, intruded the fill of Feature 25 along its east wall.
Sampling:	A 2-m by 2-m control unit (N414.00-416.00 E488.45-490.45) was excavated in cultural strata. All levels were screened, and flotation samples were collected. The remainder of the sterile overburden (Stratum 50) was then removed both by hand and by machine. With the exception of the control unit, all of Stratum 1 was only grab sampled; all of Stratum 2 was screened.
Samples:	Flotation--11 samples collected, 1 analyzed (mortar pit F.25.1) Pollen--11 samples collected, 2 analyzed (composite pinches of 2 floor samples and mortar pit F.25.1) Archaeomagnetic--no samples taken Charcoal--4 samples collected, none analyzed

Feature 55

Feature Type:	Pit house (Figs. 3.11 and 3.12)
Provenience:	TT6; N411.65-416.98 E486.75-492.00
Stratigraphic Location:	Originates in Stratum 60 at 3.10 MBD Terminates in Stratum 60 at 3.40 MBD
Shape-Dimensions:	Square; 4.0 m northwest-southeast, 4.0 m northeast-southwest

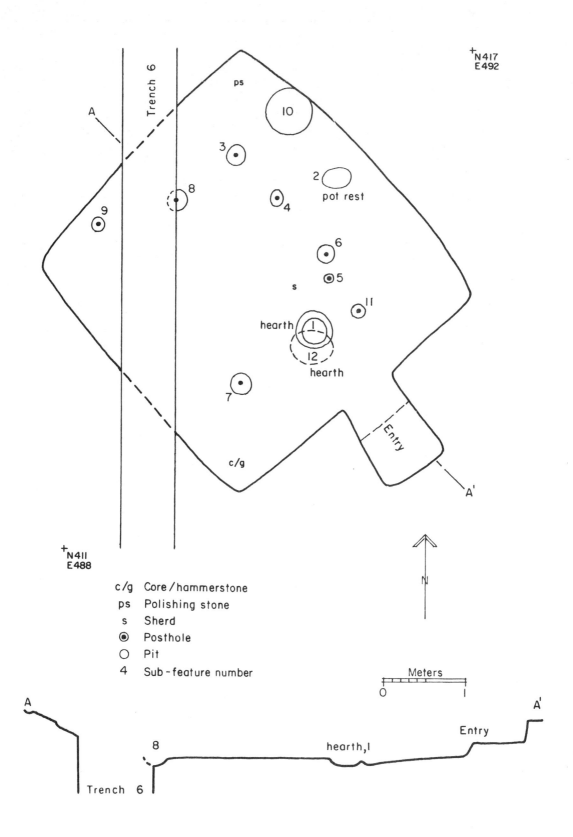

Figure 3.11. Plan and profile, Feature 55, pit house.

Figure 3.12.   View of Feature 55, pit house, looking northwest.

Entry: The entryway was in essentially the same location
                (144 degrees east of north) as that of the
                superimposed pit house (Feature 25). It measured 90
                cm at its widest point and 1.1 m in length. A 15-
                cm-high step was located near the midpoint of the
                entry; it then sloped upward to the prehistoric
                occupation surface.

Walls: The pit walls, which were virtually vertical,
                averaged approximately 25 cm in height and exhibited
                evidence of a thin layer of unburned plaster. All
                of the pit walls may have been plastered during
                occupation.

Roof: The only evidence of roof construction was the
                presence of probable "roof fall" in the fill. This
                appeared as a very compacted, partially oxidized,
                mottled, tan-orange sandy silt intermixed with trash
                deposits (see Fill description). A series of
                postholes found in the floor probably represents the
                roof support system.

Fill:	The fill was fairly homogeneous and consisted of a mottled, tan-orange sandy silt intermixed with gray sandy silt with charcoal chunks and flecks. Stratum 1 appears to be a mixture of architectural debris and trash deposits.
Fill Artifacts:	8 Glycymeris shell bracelet fragments (2 decorated, 6 unworked), 3 Anodonta shell fragments (1 worked); 138 flakes, 4 unifaces, 4 utilized flakes, 1 hammerstone; 1 palette fragment, 1 mano, 2 mano fragments, 2 abrader fragments, 2 metate fragments, 2 pebble polishers; 694 sherds (565 plain ware, 75 unidentified, 54 decorated); 25 figurine fragments, 1 complete miniature scoop; 108 animal bones, 1 complete bone awl and 3 awl fragments
Floor:	The floor of Feature 55 appears to have been prepared or smoothed out with a thin layer of light-tan, compacted, clayey silt. This material was placed over the sandy, gravelly, sterile substrate (Stratum 60). The total floor area was 15.3 square meters.
Floor Artifacts:	1 Glycymeris shell fragment, 2 unworked Anodonta shell fragments; 19 flakes, 2 unifaces, 1 utilized flake; 1 metate fragment, 2 pebble polishers, 1 unknown ground stone; 38 sherds (29 plain ware, 2 unidentified, 2 decorated, 5 worked); miscellaneous figurine fragments, 1 miniature bowl, 1 miniature scoop
Floor Features:	A total of 12 floor features was found, including 8 postholes.

Feature 55.1 was one of two hearths; the other, Feature 55.12, was found under and slightly offset from Feature 55.1. The upper hearth had an oxidized soil collar and a diameter of approximately 40 cm. It was filled with white ash to a depth of 12 cm.

Feature 55.2 was an oval-shaped (25 cm by 30 cm) feature that may have functioned as a potrest. It was shallow (7 cm) and somewhat basin shaped, and its fill consisted of loose, gray-brown sandy loam with some charcoal flecks.

Feature 55.10 was a pit found abutting the northeast wall; it may have been an internal storage pit. It had a diameter of approximately 60 cm and a depth of 40 cm. The bottom was oxidized, and the fill consisted of loose, gray-brown sandy silt with charcoal chunks and flecks. |

Feature 55.12 was found beneath Feature 55.1. This lower hearth was an unprepared cylindrical basin that measured approximately 45 cm in diameter by 10 cm deep. The fill was a loose whitish gray ash.

Postholes:

55.3, 21 cm in diameter by 10 cm deep
55.4, 18 cm in diameter by 23 cm deep
55.5, 11 cm in diameter by 4 cm deep
55.6, 22 cm in diameter by 33 cm deep
55.7, 25 cm in diameter by 25 cm deep
55.8, 24 cm in diameter by 9 cm deep
55.9, 18 cm in diameter by 12 cm deep
55.11, 15 cm in diameter by 9 cm deep

The fill of Features 55.8 and 55.11 consisted of a loose tan, sandy silt with some charcoal flecking. All other fill was a tannish gray silt with charcoal chunks and flecks.

Floor Feature Artifacts:

55.1 and 12--1 unworked Anodonta shell fragment; 1 flake, 1 uniface; 1 figurine fragment; charred macroplant remains: cheno-am, saguaro
55.4--1 flake
55.8--1 utilized flake
55.10--4 flakes, 2 utilized flakes, 1 biface; 1 figurine fragment; 5 animal bones; charred macroplant remains: drop seed, grass

Comments:

Feature 54, a roasting pit, intruded the fill.

Sampling:

Because this feature was entirely sealed by the prepared floor of Feature 25, it was decided to excavate, screen, and sample all of the fill in the structure. The last 5 cm was arbitrarily designated floor fill and was excavated separately.

Samples:

Flotation--5 samples collected, 2 analyzed (hearths F.55.1 and F.12, and pit F.55.10)
Pollen--5 samples collected, 2 analyzed (hearths F.55.1 and F.12 and floor)
Archaeomagnetic--1 sample, datable
Charcoal--5 samples collected, none analyzed

House Group 2

Feature 7

Feature Type:

Pit house (Fig. 3.13)

Provenience:

TT19; N408.10-412.80 E394.65-396.70

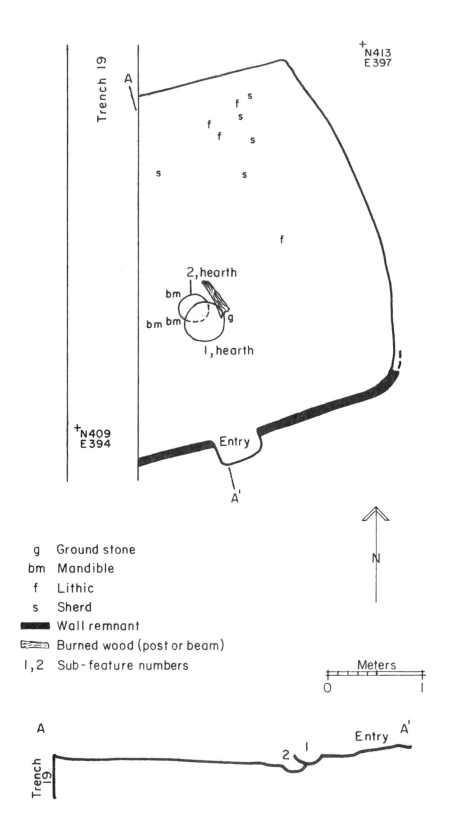

Figure 3.13.   Plan and profile, Feature 7, pit house.

Stratigraphic Location:	Originates in Stratum 60 at 4.50 MBD Terminates in Stratum 60 at 4.85 MBD
Shape-Dimensions:	Subrectangular; 3.6 m northwest-southeast, 4.0 m northeast-southwest (estimate based on the excavation of approximately 70% of the feature)
Entry:	The entry was oriented 163 degrees east of north and measured 45 cm wide by approximately 30 cm deep. It was slightly ramped and may have been prepared with a tan, compacted silt.
Walls:	The pit walls of Feature 7 were somewhat variable. The north and east walls were vertical, sterile Stratum 60, averaging 25 cm in height. The south side of the feature had been excavated into a loosely compacted gravel deposit, possibly a prehistoric stream channel. Presumably to prevent these gravels from collapsing inward, a small adobe retaining wall was built inside the pit wall. It was 10 cm to 15 cm thick, 25 cm to 35 cm high, and was made of tan clayey silt.
Roof:	No evidence
Fill:	Two separate strata were defined within the fill. Stratum 1 was a tannish orange silty sand with some charcoal flecks; it appeared to be naturally deposited and exhibited evidence of root, rodent, and insect disturbance. Stratum 2 (floor fill) was similar in character to Stratum 1, but had a higher percentage of ash and charcoal and was much more compacted.
Fill Artifacts:	1 pebble polisher; 26 flakes, 1 biface; 25 sherds (19 plain ware, 3 unidentified, 3 decorated); 1 animal bone
Floor Fill Artifacts:	1 unworked Anodonta shell fragment; 1 pebble scraper; 34 flakes; 34 sherds (28 plain ware, 5 unidentified, 1 Rillito Red-on-brown); 1 probable human figurine leg fragment; 1 animal bone
Floor:	The floor surface consisted of sterile (Stratum 60) gray-brown soil intermixed with small- to medium-sized gravels. Differential oxidation observed in some sections of the floor suggested that the structure may have burned. Floor area for the excavated portion of the house is 8.31 square meters.

Floor Artifacts:	1 complete pestle, 1 complete maul-mano; 5 flakes, 3 utilized flakes; 4 animal bones, 1 bone tube fragment
Floor Features:	The only two floor features located were hearths.

Feature 7.1 was a well-prepared, plastered hearth roughly 44 cm in diameter and 9 cm deep. The fill consisted of oxidized, tannish orange, gravelly silt with very little ash or charcoal. This feature was later found to be superimposed upon and slightly offset from Feature 7.2, another hearth.

Feature 7.2 was an unprepared hearth that measured approximately 35 cm in diameter and 12 cm in depth. The sides of the feature were oxidized, and it was filled with loose, white-gray ash.

Floor Feature Artifacts:	7.1--1 plain ware sherd; charred macroplant remains: cheno-am seeds
Comments:	Stratigraphically, Feature 7 was from 40 cm to 70 cm lower than two nearby houses, Features 26 and 29. It seems possible that, when the builders of Feature 7 encountered the gravel deposit, they attempted to dig through it to a deeper, more stable stratum. When this failed on the south side of the house, they then built an adobe retaining wall to keep out collapsing gravel deposits.
Sampling:	Seventy percent of the structure was excavated; the remainder was removed by excavation of the backhoe trench. A 2-m by 2-m control unit (N408.00-410.00 E394.65-396.65) was excavated in 20-cm levels within each stratum. All fill was screened and artifacts were collected. The overburden was stripped by machine from the remainder of the feature. The remainder of Stratum 1 was not screened, although all observed artifacts were collected. All remaining Stratum 2 (floor fill) was screened.
Samples:	Flotation--5 samples collected, 2 analyzed (hearths F.7.1 and F.7.2); F.7.2 contained no macroplant remains
	Pollen--6 samples collected, 2 analyzed (1 from hearth F.7.1, and a composite pinch from 5 floor samples)
	Archaeomagnetic--1 sample, datable
	Charcoal--none taken

Feature 26
_____

Feature Type: Pit house (Fig. 3.14)

Provenience: TT20; N412.05–417.10 E385.65–391.10

Stratigraphic   Originates in Stratum 60 at 4.14 MBD
Location: Terminates in Stratum 60 at 4.47 MBD

Shape-Dimensions: Square; 4.9 m east-west, 4.8 m north-south

Entry: The entry was not well defined, but appeared to open
                         to the east (106 degrees east of north). It was
                         approximately 80 cm wide by 50 cm in length and
                         sloped up from the interior of the feature to the
                         prehistoric surface.

Walls: Pit walls consisted of loose sand and gravel, and
                         were very difficult to delineate, but were
                         approximately 25 cm high.

Roof: No evidence

Fill: The fill was a single mottled, disturbed stratum.
                         It consisted of ashy, gray, silty sand with some
                         areas of gravel deposits and pockets of dark ash.
                         Much of it may be architectural debris mixed with
                         intrusive trash from Feature 59. Floor fill was
                         provenienced as Stratum 1, Level 2.

Fill Artifacts: 2 unworked Glycymeris shell bracelet fragments, 1
                         worked unidentified marine shell fragment; 60
                         flakes, 2 cores, 7 unifaces, 1 biface, 5 utilized
                         flakes, 1 hammerstone; metate fragment; 312 sherds
                         (246 plain ware, 18 unidentified, 45 decorated, 3
                         worked)

Floor Fill   52 flakes, 3 cores, 1 uniface, 2 utilized flakes
Artifacts: (Sherds and other artifacts lumped under "Fill.")

Floor: The floor surface in the central portion of the
                         house (Fig. 3.14) was prepared, compacted silt.
                         The remainder of the floor was difficult to define
                         because, like the pit walls, it consisted
                         predominantly of sand and gravels. Floor surface
                         area was 20.7 square meters.

Floor Artifacts: 1 unworked unidentified marine shell fragment;
                         4 flakes; 11 sherds (8 plain ware, 1 unidentified,
                         2 worked)

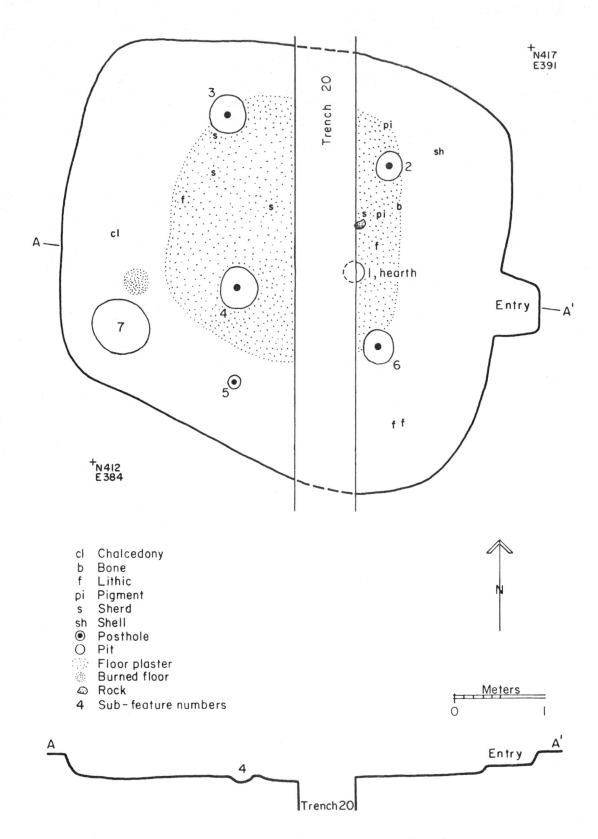

cl   Chalcedony
b   Bone
f   Lithic
pi   Pigment
s   Sherd
sh   Shell
⦿   Posthole
○   Pit
    Floor plaster
    Burned floor
    Rock
4   Sub-feature numbers

Figure 3.14.   Plan and profile, Feature 26, pit house.

Floor Features:	Most of the hearth, Feature 26.1, was removed by Test Trench 20. All that remained was remnant oxidation on the floor surface at the edge of the trench and directly in line with the entry.
	Feature 26.7 was an irregularly shaped pit of unknown function that measured 60 cm by 65 cm by 10 cm deep. Its fill was a brownish white sandy silt.
Postholes:	Feature 26 contained five identifiable postholes filled with loosely compacted, ashy, gray silt with some sand and charcoal flecks.

26.2, 31 cm by 26 cm by 14 cm deep
26.3, 40 cm by 35 cm by 11 cm deep
26.4, 40 cm by 35 cm by 10 cm deep
26.5, 10 cm in diameter by 10 cm deep
26.6, 33 cm in diameter by 12 cm deep

Floor Feature Artifacts:	26.2--1 flake; 1 plain ware sherd 26.3--1 plain ware sherd 26.7--1 flake
Comments:	The walls of this feature were so poorly defined that the actual pit size and floor surface area may be smaller than shown in Figure 3.14. This feature was overlain by Feature 59, which was recorded as a trash-filled pit, and labeled Stratum 30 during excavation. Feature 59 was later identified as a trash midden located above Feature 26.
Sampling:	Initially, a 2-m by 2-m control unit (N413.10-415.10 E386.30-388.30) was excavated in the structure, using 20-cm levels. This unit included overlying sterile sands (Stratum 50) and trash deposits (later identified as Feature 59). Fill from the control unit was screened. The remaining Stratum 50 and Stratum 30 deposits were mechanically stripped to reveal the feature outline. All remaining fill was excavated by hand, and only grab samples were taken (except from floor fill). All floor fill (Stratum 1, Level 2) was screened and all artifacts collected.
Stratum 30 (Feature 59) Artifacts:	1 unworked Laevicardium shell fragment; 408 flakes, 14 cores, 13 unifaces, 9 bifaces, 18 utilized flakes, 4 hammerstones; 2 miscellaneous ground stone fragments, 1 pebble polisher, 3 mano fragments, 1 metate fragment, 1 complete pebble pounder; 1,115 sherds (938 plain ware, 64 unidentified, 101 decorated, 12 worked); 2 figurine fragments

Samples:	Flotation--22 samples collected, none analyzed
	Pollen--6 samples collected, none analyzed
	Archaeomagnetic--none taken
	Charcoal--6 samples collected, none analyzed

Feature 29

Feature Type:	Pit house (Fig. 3.15)
Provenience:	TT18; N414.90-419.90 E394.20-398.40
Stratigraphic Location:	Originates in Stratum 60 at 3.88 MBD
	Terminates in Stratum 60 at 4.38 MBD
Shape-Dimensions:	Subrectangular; 4.3 m northwest-southeast, 4.7 m northeast-southwest (estimate based on the excavation of approximately 80% of the feature)
Entry:	The entryway faced southeast (172 degrees east of north) and measured 80 cm wide by 65 cm long. It was not sloped, but terminated at a step approximately 30 cm high.
Walls:	Pit walls were unprepared, sterile Stratum 60 and measured from 40 cm to 50 cm in height.
Roof:	No evidence
Fill:	The fill was overlain by a trash midden deposit (Stratum 30) and may include some of this material. Stratum 1 was predominantly a mottled, reddish brown, sandy silt with gravels and artifacts. This stratum probably represents refuse and architectural debris. The last 10 cm of Stratum 1 (Level 2) above the floor surface was called floor fill and was excavated as a separate unit.
Fill Artifacts:	1 unworked Glycymeris shell bracelet fragment; 36 flakes, 2 cores, 3 utilized flakes, 3 hammerstones; 1 mano, 1 mano fragment; 309 sherds (265 plain ware, 13 unidentified, 28 decorated, 3 worked); 1 figurine fragment; 46 animal bones, 2 bone tube fragments
Floor Fill Artifacts:	4 unworked Glycymeris shell bracelet fragments, 1 unidentified marine bivalve shell pendant fragment, 1 fragment of Laevicardium shell manufacturing debris, 1 worked Pecten shell fragment, 1 worked Haliotis shell fragment; 130 flakes, 3 cores, 1 biface, 5 utilized flakes, 1 hammerstone; 1 tabular abrader, effigy pendant (Sherds and animal bone, if any, are lumped with "Fill.")

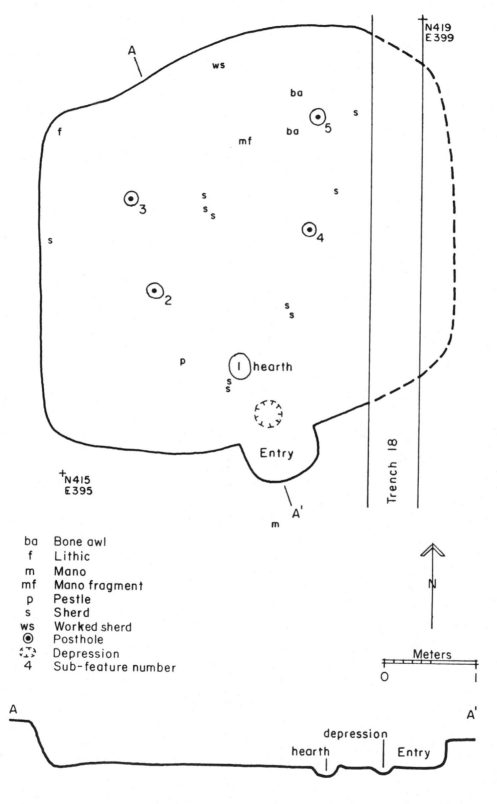

Figure 3.15. Plan and profile, Feature 29, pit house.

Floor: Although most of the floor surface was found to be only unprepared, sterile Stratum 60, some areas (particularly around the hearth) exhibited possible evidence of plastering in the form of a thin layer of tan, sandy silt. Floor surface covered an area of 18.2 square meters.

Floor Artifacts: 4 flakes; 1 mano fragment, 1 pestle, worked argillite preform (?); 32 sherds (25 plain ware, 2 unidentified, 1 decorated, 4 worked); 3 animal bones, 1 complete bone awl, 1 awl fragment, 1 bone tube fragment; charred macroplant remains: agave, cheno-am

Floor Features: Feature 29.1 was a well-defined, well-plastered hearth that measured 33 cm by 26 cm by 15 cm deep. The fill was a light gray ash mottled with pieces of possible roof-wall fall.

Postholes: Four postholes were found in the floor, and the pattern created by these features suggests that they represent the primary roof support posts. The fill was a brown, sandy silt.

29.2, 19 cm by 15 cm by 13 cm deep
29.3, 16 cm in diameter by 13 cm deep
29.4, 15 cm by 10 cm by 8 cm deep
29.5, 18 cm by 15 cm by 8 cm deep

Floor Feature Artifacts: 29.1--2 plain ware sherds; charred macroplant remains: cheno-am, drop seed, globe mallow, mesquite, salt bush
29.2--1 flake

Comments: Approximately 80 percent of this pit house was excavated, and there was evidence of substantial root and rodent disturbance throughout the structure. The shallow (5 cm deep) depression between the hearth and entry was not assigned a feature number; it may or may not be of cultural origin. Its location immediately inside the entryway suggests that it is not cultural.

Sampling: A control unit (N416.00-418.00 E396.30-398.30) was excavated from the present ground surface, with all identified strata (Strata 50, 30, and 1) excavated in 20-cm (maximum) levels. Fill was screened and all artifacts collected. The remainder of Strata 50 and 30 was removed by backhoe. Only the floor fill, the last 10 cm of Stratum 1, was screened and artifacts collected. All other fill was excavated by hand and a grab sample of artifacts taken.

Midden Artifacts:	39 flakes, 2 cores, 7 unifaces, 2 bifaces, 5 utilized flakes, 2 hammerstones; 209 sherds (184 plain ware, 9 unidentified, 12 decorated, 4 worked)
Samples:	Flotation--15 samples collected, 5 analyzed (hearth F.29.1 and 4 from floor contact) Pollen--5 samples collected, 1 analyzed (composite pinches from 5 floor samples) Archaeomagnetic--1 sample, datable Charcoal--none taken

House Group 3

Feature 27

Feature Type:	Pit house (Figs. 3.16 and 3.17)
Provenience:	TT6; N351.70-357.55 E406.50-411.95
Stratigraphic Location:	Originates in Stratum 60 at 4.05 MBD Terminates in Stratum 60 at 4.58 MBD
Shape-Dimensions:	Subrectangular; 4.0 m northwest-southeast, 4.8 m northeast-southwest
Entry:	The entry was opened to the southeast (130 degrees east of north) and measured 1.70 m long and 80 cm wide. It sloped up from the floor surface to a step that was 25 cm high. From the top of this step the entry extended 1.1 m upward at a gradual slope to the prehistoric occupation surface. The entryway was plastered with a light tan silt and a posthole was found on either side of the opening (Fig. 3.16; Features 27.5 and 27.6).
Walls:	The burned pit walls were extremely well defined, with areas throughout the structure showing evidence of remnant plaster. The walls were virtually vertical in some locations and slightly sloping in others. They varied in height from 50 cm to 60 cm.
Roof:	The only direct evidence was the presence of mixed architectural debris in the fill (Stratum 1). The roof was likely supported by four posts.
Fill:	Feature 27 was overlain by trash fill (Stratum 30). The fill of the structure was divided into two distinct strata. Stratum 1 was a compacted, tan sandy silt intermixed with ash that probably represents architectural debris (roof-wall fall).

86

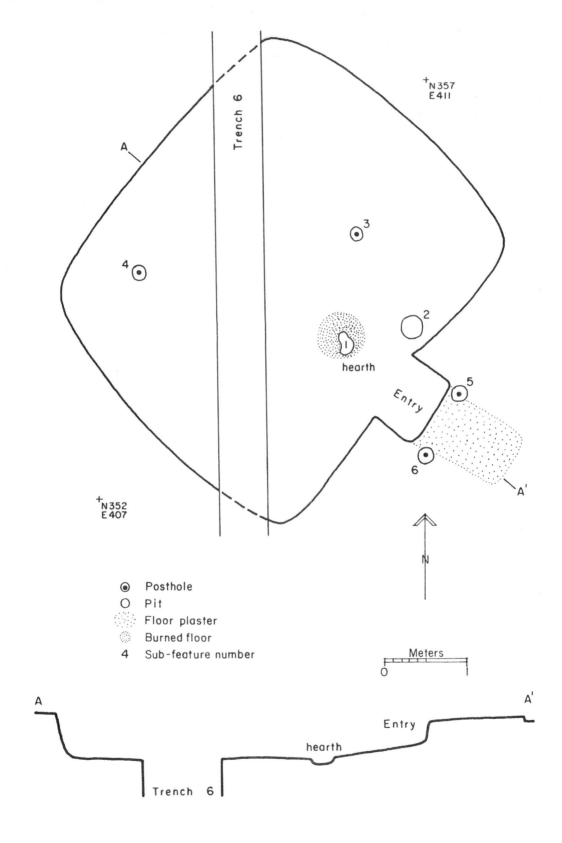

Figure 3.16. Plan and profile, Feature 27, pit house.

Figure 3.17. View of Feature 27, pit house, looking northwest.

Stratum 2 (floor fill) was a black, sandy silt with ash and charcoal. This layer, which was easily distinguished from Stratum 1, may represent some of the burned organic constituents of the interior architecture.

Midden Artifacts:	1 unworked Glycymeris shell bracelet fragment; 1 complete mano; 74 flakes, 2 cores, 13 unifaces, 8 utilized flakes, 3 hammerstones; 349 sherds (301 plain ware, 15 unidentified, 28 decorated, 5 worked), 1 whole Rillito Red-on-brown bowl
Fill Artifacts:	1 pebble pounder; 34 flakes, 6 utilized flakes; 101 sherds (87 plain ware, 3 unidentified, 9 decorated, 2 worked); mesquite charcoal
Floor Fill Artifacts:	1 pebble polisher; 69 flakes, 2 unifaces, 1 biface, 7 flakes, 2 hammerstones; 43 sherds (35 plain ware, 1 unidentified, 4 decorated, 3 worked); charred macroplant remains: corn, grass, saguaro

Floor:	The floor was prepared with a brown-tan, compacted, silty plaster approximately 2 cm to 3 cm thick. There were 18.5 square meters of floor space not including the entryway.
Floor Artifacts:	1 Cañada del Oro Red-on-brown sherd, 1 plain ware sherd
Floor Features:	Feature 27.1 was an irregularly shaped hearth. This small, highly oxidized pit measured 28 cm by 17 cm by 5 cm deep. Its fill was a fine-grained, dark gray, ashy, sandy silt. The floor surface around the hearth was oxidized and covered with a thin layer of white ash.
	Feature 27.2 was a small circular pit that may have been used for storage. It measured 22 cm in diameter by 25 cm deep and was filled with brown silty sand and gravels. This relatively clean fill was overlain by the black Stratum 2 and may have been intentionally filled during the occupation of the structure.
Postholes:	Four postholes were found. Features 27.3 and 27.4 represent primary roof-support posts; other postholes were probably removed by the backhoe. The fill of these features was a dark, gray-brown, ashy, sandy silt intermixed with charcoal and gravel.
	Two postholes, Features 27.5 and 27.6, were found on either side of the entry. Their fill was a light brown, sandy silt with gravel.
	27.3, 12 cm in diameter by 26 cm deep
	27.4, 18 cm in diameter by 18 cm deep
	27.5, 16 cm in diameter by 8 cm deep
	27.6, 17 cm by 14 cm by 15 cm deep
Floor Feature Artifacts:	27.1--charred mesquite seeds
	27.6--1 flake
Comments:	The virtual absence of floor artifacts suggests that the structure may have been abandoned prior to burning.
Sampling:	A control unit (N354.00-356.00 E409.10-411.10) was excavated by hand in 20-cm levels through all strata (Strata 50, 30, 1, and 2) down to the floor surface. All fill was screened and all artifacts collected. The remaining Strata 50 and 30 deposits were removed by backhoe. Stratum 1 was excavated by hand, but only a grab sample of artifacts was taken. All of

Stratum 2 (floor fill) was troweled and screened and all artifacts were collected.

Samples: Flotation--18 samples collected, 6 analyzed (hearth F.27.1, pit F.27.2, 4 from floor); F.27.2 contained no charred macroplant remains
Pollen--7 samples collected, 2 analyzed (pit F.27.2 and a composite pinch sample from 6 floor samples)
Archaeomagnetic--1 sample, datable
Charcoal--7 samples collected, 1 analyzed

Feature 33

Feature Type: Pit house (Fig. 3.18)

Provenience: TT12; N363.10-368.00 E428.80-431.85

Stratigraphic Location: Originates in Stratum 50 at 3.74 MBD
Terminates in Stratum 60 at 4.05 MBD

Shape-Dimensions: Subrectangular; 3.6 m northwest-southeast, 3.9 m northeast-southwest (estimate based on excavation of approximately 60% of the feature)

Entry: The entry, which was partially destroyed during the excavation of Test Trench 12, appeared to be gently ramped and opened to the southwest (195 degrees west of north).

Walls: The poorly defined pit walls were nearly vertical, sloping slightly to meet the floor surface. They were unprepared, sterile Stratum 60 and varied from 20 cm to 35 cm in height. The subtle differences between some of the house fill and the surrounding Stratum 60, coupled with extensive root, rodent, and insect disturbance, made wall definition extremely difficult.

Roof: No evidence

Fill: The fill was divided into two distinct strata. Stratum 1 was a light- to medium-brown sandy silt with gravel and some charcoals. Although this soil contained some charcoal-stained sediment and gray ash, it was cleaner than Stratum 2 and more closely resembled Stratum 60. Stratum 1 probably represents the natural deposition of eroding soil. Stratum 2, which includes floor fill, was predominantly architectural debris mixed with artifacts. It was a light brown-gray, hard-packed sediment mixed with gray ash, charcoal, and oxidized soil.

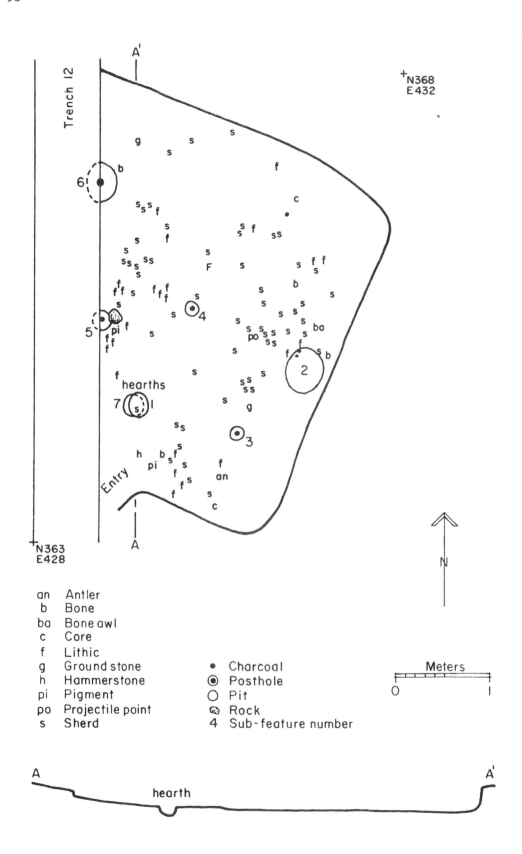

an   Antler
b   Bone
ba   Bone awl
c   Core
f   Lithic
g   Ground stone
h   Hammerstone
pi   Pigment
po   Projectile point
s   Sherd

•   Charcoal
◉   Posthole
○   Pit
☒   Rock
4   Sub-feature number

Meters

Figure 3.18.   Plan and profile, Feature 33, pit house.

Fill Artifacts:	1 unworked <u>Anodonta</u> shell fragment; 27 flakes, 1 biface, 4 utilized flakes; 127 sherds (107 plain ware, 6 unidentified, 13 decorated, 1 worked); 9 animal bones
Floor Fill Artifacts:	1 unworked <u>Glycymeris</u> shell bracelet fragment, 1 worked <u>Pecten</u> shell fragment, 1 unworked <u>Laevicardium</u> shell fragment, 1 complete shell pendant; 130 flakes, 9 unifaces, 4 bifaces, 7 utilized flakes; 1 hammerstone; 325 sherds (267 plain ware, 24 unidentified, 31 decorated, 3 worked); 31 animal bones
Floor:	Unprepared, hard-packed, sterile Stratum 60 burned in some areas. Minimum floor area is 10.6 square meters.
Floor Artifacts:	21 flakes, 1 core, 1 uniface, 1 biface, 4 utilized flakes, 1 hammerstone; 1 ground stone fragment; 91 sherds (58 plain ware, 1 unidentified, 31 decorated, 1 worked); 1 human figurine; 8 animal bones, 1 complete bone awl-needle
Floor Features:	Seven floor features were located, including four postholes.

Feature 33.1 was an unprepared, irregularly shaped hearth measuring 25 cm by 19 cm by 4 cm deep. It was well oxidized and filled with loose gray ash.

Feature 33.2 was a slightly oval (40 cm by 45 cm) shaped pit of unknown function. It was 10 cm deep and contained tannish brown fill with charcoal flecks.

Another hearth, Feature 33.7, was found underneath and slightly offset from Feature 33.1 while sampling that feature. It too was unprepared and irregular in shape. It measured 25 cm by 8 cm and contained gray-white ash.

Postholes:	33.3, 15 cm in diameter by 5 cm deep
	33.4, 16 cm in diameter by 5 cm deep
	33.5, 20 cm in diameter by 11 cm deep
	33.6, 20 cm in diameter by 14 cm deep (feature partially destroyed by Test Trench 12)

The fill in these four features was fairly consistently a loose, tan-orange silty sand.

Floor Feature Artifacts:	33.1--4 flakes; 21 plain ware and 2 unidentified sherds; 2 animal bones; charred macroplant remains: cotton, drop seed, grass 33.4--1 animal bone, 1 complete bone awl 33.5--1 flake; 2 plain ware sherds 33.6--1 unworked <u>Laevicardium</u> shell fragment; 1 unidentified sherd, 1 worked sherd; 5 animal bones 33.7--charred macroplant remains: cheno-am, mesquite, tansy mustard
Comments:	This feature was partially excavated (60%). It may have burned while in use, thus accounting for the relatively extensive floor assemblage.
Sampling:	A control unit (N364.00-366.00 E428.80-431.00) was excavated according to observed strata (Strata 50, 1, and 2), using 20-cm (maximum) levels. All soil from this unit was screened and materials collected. A backhoe removed the remaining postabandonment deposition (Stratum 50). All of the remaining Stratum 1 was excavated by hand, taking only grab samples of artifacts. All of Stratum 2 (floor fill) was troweled to floor, screened, and all artifacts collected.
Samples:	Flotation-14 samples collected, 2 analyzed (hearths F.33.1 and F.33.7) Pollen--4 samples collected, 2 analyzed (hearth F.33.1 and composite pinches from 2 floor samples) Archaeomagnetic--none taken Charcoal--7 samples collected, none analyzed

Feature 35

Feature Type:	Pit house
Provenience:	TT10; N379.35-382.00 E448.31-451.50 (This feature was sampled; complete provenience information and feature size were not determined.)
Stratigraphic Location:	Originates in Stratum 60 at 3.67 MBD Terminates in Stratum 60 at 4.03 MBD
Shape-Dimension:	Unknown
Entry:	Not located
Walls:	Approximately 2 linear meters of the pit wall were identified. The curvature of this section of wall suggests that it represents the southwest corner of

the structure. The wall averaged 10 cm to 20 cm in height and consisted of unprepared, sterile Stratum 60.

Roof: No evidence

Fill: As observed in the test trench profile, fill consisted of one homogeneous stratum overlain by approximately 60 cm of sterile alluvial deposit (Stratum 50). Fill was a mottled brownish orange, compacted sandy silt intermixed with pockets of charcoal and ash.

Fill Artifacts: 19 flakes, 2 cores, 2 unifaces, 1 utilized flake, 1 hammerstone; 175 sherds (128 plain ware, 28 unidentified, 18 decorated, 1 worked); 101 animal bones

Floor: The floor was predominantly hard-packed, sterile Stratum 60 that had been burned in some areas. A small area (25 cm by 25 cm) adjacent to the hearth (Feature 35.1) had some remnant plaster.

Floor Artifacts: 4 plain ware sherds and 1 Rillito Red-on-brown sherd

Floor Features: Feature 35.1 was an informal, oxidized hearth with a diameter of 20 cm and a depth of only 3 cm. Its fill consisted of gray-white ash.

                 Feature 35.2 was a rather amorphous (pit?) feature partially exposed in the corner of one 2-m by 2-m excavation unit. It was roughly oval in shape, measuring at least 75 cm by 85 cm, with a maximum depth of 18 cm. Fill was predominantly mixed sands and gravels with some charcoal and fire-cracked rock. It may be an intrusive roasting pit rather than a floor feature.

                 Feature 35.3 was a pit measuring 75 cm by 82 cm by 12 cm deep. Its fill was a mottled, gravelly sand mixed with charcoal, ash, and a few pieces of fire-cracked rock. Its function is unknown.

                 Feature 35.4 was a posthole with a diameter of 10 cm and a depth of 8 cm. The fill consisted of brown silty sand with some small pieces of charcoal.

Floor Feature   35.2--50 sherds (46 plain ware, 3 unidentified, 1
Artifacts: decorated); 4 animal bones

Comments: Despite limited testing, the presence of a pit wall
                     and floor indicate that this feature does represent
                     a pit house.

Sampling: Two 2-m by 2-m grid units (N379.00-381.00 E446.80-
                     448.80 and N380.00-382.00 E449.50-451.50) were
                     excavated from the present ground surface to the
                     floor of the feature. These were excavated in 20-cm
                     levels (maximum) in Strata 50 and 1, with the fill
                     screened and all artifacts collected.

Samples: Flotation--4 samples collected, 1 analyzed (hearth
                     F.35.1); it contained no macroplant remains
                     Pollen--2 samples collected, none analyzed
                     Archaeomagnetic--1 sample, datable
                     Charcoal--3 samples collected, none analyzed

Feature 36

Feature Type: Pit house (Fig. 3.19)

Provenience: TT9; N371.70-374.50 E458.98-460.90 (This feature was
                     sampled; complete provenience information and
                     feature size were not determined.)

Stratigraphic   Originates in Stratum 60 at 3.44 MBD
Location: Terminates in Stratum 60 at 3.69 MBD

Shape-Dimensions: Subrectangular(?); 3.89 m north-south, 3.5 m east-
                     west (estimate)

Entry: Not located

Walls: The walls were unprepared, sterile Stratum 60. They
                     averaged 18 cm to 23 cm in height and sloped gently
                     to meet the floor surface.

Roof: No evidence

Fill: Fill consisted of gray, ashy, sandy silt (Stratum 1)
                     overlain by sterile alluvium (Stratum 50).
                     Artifacts were abundant in Stratum 1, which appeared
                     to be intentionally deposited trash.

Fill Artifacts: 1 mano; 19 flakes, 1 core, 1 utilized flake, 2
                     hammerstones; 145 sherds (119 plain ware, 6
                     unidentified, 18 decorated, 2 worked); 10 animal
                     bones

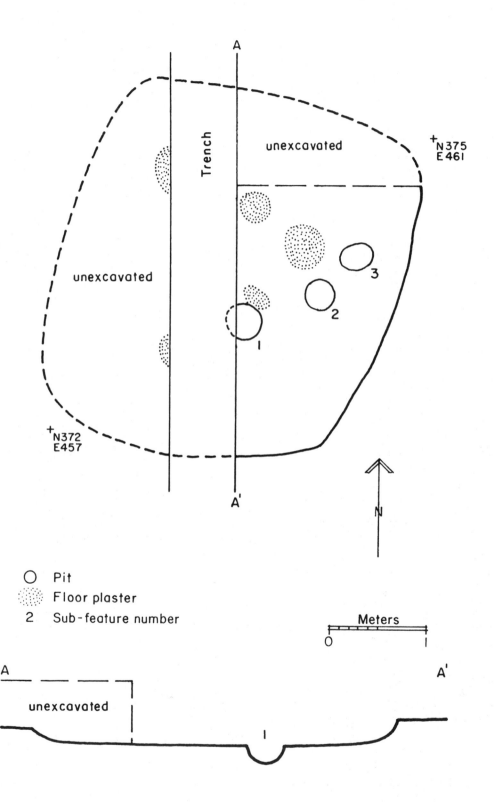

Figure 3.19. Plan and profile, Feature 36, pit house.

Floor:

Unprepared, sterile Stratum 60 with some oxidized patches; the floor area could not be determined.

Floor Artifacts:

None

Floor Features:

Three pits of unknown function were found in the small portion of floor that was exposed.

Feature 36.1 was a pit 35 cm in diameter by 22 cm deep. Its fill consisted of dark brown sandy silt with some charcoal and gravel.

Feature 36.2 was a pit, 33 cm in diameter by 14 cm deep, filled with dark brown silty sand with some charcoal flecks.

Feature 36.3 was a pit measuring 40 cm by 22 cm by 18 cm deep. Its fill consisted of brown sandy silt with some pebble and charcoal inclusions.

Floor Feature
Artifacts:

36.1--charred macroplant remains: cheno-am, hedgehog cactus

Comments:

Feature 36 appears to have been an unburned house that was abandoned and subsequently filled with trash deposits.

Sampling:

Initially a 2-m by 2-m grid unit (N372.50-374.50 E459.00-461.00) was excavated from the present ground surface down to the floor. An additional 1-m by 1-m unit was excavated in a successful attempt to locate a corner of the structure. All materials in the larger unit were excavated in 20-cm levels, screened, and artifacts collected. The smaller unit was only grab sampled during excavation.

Samples:

Flotation--5 samples collected, 1 analyzed (pit F.36.1)
Pollen--15 samples collected, none analyzed
Archaeomagnetic--1 sample, datable
Charcoal--none taken

Feature 44

Feature Type:

Pit house/structure (Fig. 3.20)

Provenience:

TT7; N348.00-349.52 E478.95-480.50 (This feature was sampled; complete provenience information and feature size were not determined.)

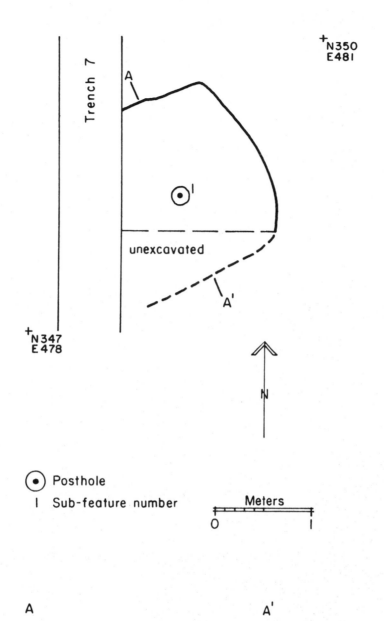

Figure 3.20. Plan and profile, Feature 44, pit house.

Stratigraphic
Location: Originates in Stratum 60 at 3.38 MBD
                   Terminates in Stratum 60 at 3.65 MBD

Shape-Dimensions: Subrectangular(?); 1.6 m northeast-southwest, 1.8 m
                   northwest-southeast (estimate)

Entry: Not located

Walls:	The walls were unburned, unprepared, sterile Stratum 60, averaging 20 cm to 25 cm high and sloping slightly to meet the floor surface.
Roof:	No evidence
Fill:	Stratum 1 was a tannish gray, compacted silt with some charcoal. This stratum was overlain by what may be a trash midden (Stratum 30) that varied from it slightly in color, texture, and composition. This trash deposit was a brown sandy silt with abundant artifacts.
Fill Artifacts:	25 flakes, 1 utilized flake, 1 hammerstone; 96 sherds (80 plain ware, 5 unidentified, 10 decorated, 1 worked); 1 figurine fragment; 5 animal bones
Floor:	The floor was not plastered; however, it was extremely smooth and compacted, giving the appearance of a prepared surface. The entire surface was oxidized, sterile Stratum 60.
Floor Artifacts:	1 abrader; 17 sherds (9 plain ware, 1 unidentified, 6 decorated, 1 worked); 1 figurine fragment
Floor Features:	Only one floor feature (F.44.1) was encountered during test excavation, and it appeared to be a centrally located posthole. It was well defined and measured 19 cm in diameter by 7 cm deep. The fill was a tannish brown silt with some gravel and charcoal flecking.
Floor Feature Artifacts:	None
Comments:	Feature 44 is small in comparison to the other structures and may have been used for storage or some function other than habitation. Feature 44.1 may be a posthole for a central roof-support post.
Midden Artifacts: (Stratum 30)	1 unworked Glycymeris shell bracelet fragment; 1 mano fragment; 367 sherds (251 plain ware, 90 unidentified, 21 decorated, 5 worked)

Sampling: A 2-m by 2-m grid unit (N348.00-350.00 E479.00-481.00) was excavated in 20-cm levels from the present ground surface down to the feature floor. This was excavated through Stratum 30 and Stratum 1. All material was screened and artifacts collected. After excavating 30 cm, an outline of the feature was clearly visible in plan view. It is estimated that approximately 50 percent of the feature was excavated.

Samples: Flotation--5 samples collected, none analyzed
Pollen--3 samples collected, 1 analyzed (floor)
Archaeomagnetic--none taken
Charcoal--none taken

Feature 53

Feature Type: Pit house (Figs. 3.21 and 3.22)

Provenience: TT26; N350.85-355.90 E416.00-421.60

Stratigraphic   Originates in Stratum 50 at 4.17 MBD
Location: Terminates in Stratum 60 at 4.70 MBD

Shape-Dimensions: Square; 4.8 m north-south, 4.7 m east-west

Entry: The entryway was well defined and was oriented 93 degrees east of north. It measured approximately 75 cm wide by 95 cm long. The ramp sloped up slightly from the house floor to a step at its midpoint and again to a step out onto the prehistoric occupation surface. This final step was about 10 cm high (Fig. 3.21).

Walls: The walls were essentially vertical, well defined, and varied in height from 40 cm to 55 cm. The structure had burned entirely, and this burning episode was reflected in the presence of highly oxidized walls as well as large areas of remnant plaster. It is assumed that all walls of this feature were plastered during occupation.

Roof: This house is assumed to have had a four post roof-support pattern even though only two postholes were located. The other two postholes were probably removed by excavation of the backhoe trench. The only other evidence of roof construction was the presence of some daub and charcoal in the fill of the feature.

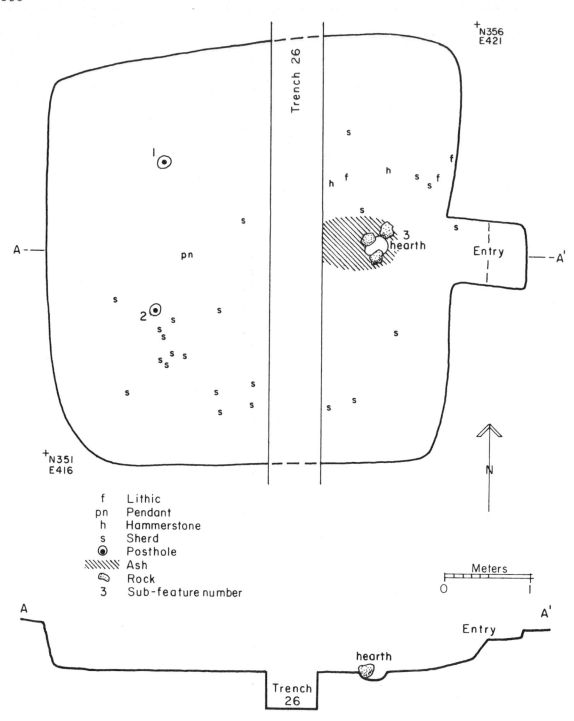

Figure 3.21. Plan and profile, Feature 53, pit house.

Fill: Fill was defined as two separate and distinct
                          strata. Stratum 1 consisted of a brown silty sand
                          with some pebbles, charcoal, and artifacts. Stratum
                          1 probably represents natural deposition. Stratum 2

Figure 3.22.   View of Feature 53, pit house, looking west.

	is architectural debris (Level 1) and floor fill (Level 2). It was made up of compacted silty sand with vitrified soil, charcoal, and small pebbles.
Fill Artifacts:	1 Glycymeris shell ring fragment; 217 sherds (198 plain ware, 7 unidentified, 8 decorated, 4 worked); 39 animal bones; 25 flakes, 6 unifaces, 1 utilized flake, 1 hammerstone
Floor Fill Artifacts:	(Note: Because Stratum 2, Levels 1 and 2 were not always differentiated, totals from both levels are reported here.) 331 sherds (268 plain ware, 34 unidentified, 23 decorated, 6 worked); 75 animal bones; 72 flakes, 3 cores, 3 unifaces, 1 biface, 2 utilized flakes; charred macroplant remains: saguaro
Floor:	The floor surface was simply a compacted, sterile Stratum 60 with patches of vitrified soil

throughout. Total floor area was 21.7 square meters.

Floor Artifacts: 1 stone pendant, 2 handstones, 1 pebble pounder; 39 sherds (24 plain ware, 13 Rillito-Red-on brown, 2 worked); 7 flakes

Floor Features: Feature 53.3 was a formal, well-plastered, basin-shaped hearth with a 25-cm diameter and a maximum depth of 11 cm. Associated with this feature was a series of three ground-stone artifact fragments that had been used as trivets or as a tripod to hold a vessel over the hearth for cooking or heating. In addition to this potrest, the fill of the feature consisted of gray ash intermixed with charcoal, lithics, and some burned bone. The hearth and the floor surface adjacent to it were highly oxidized.

Postholes: Two postholes in the floor probably represent primary roof-support posts. They contained loosely compacted, dark brown sandy silt.

                   53.1, 18 cm in diameter by 25 cm deep
                   53.2, 15 cm in diameter by 23 cm deep

Floor Feature   53.3--1 metate fragment; charred macroplant remains:
Artifacts: cheno-am, corn

Comments: Feature 53 was located immediately east of another pit house, Feature 27. Architecturally, these features were nearly identical; moreover, both were intensively burned and they may have been occupied contemporaneously.

Sampling: A 2-m by 2-m control unit (N352.00-354.00 E419.70-421.70) was excavated in 20-cm levels through all strata (Strata 50, 1, and 2). All fill from this unit was screened and the artifacts were collected. After the control unit was excavated, all the overlying Stratum 50 was removed by backhoe, revealing the feature outline. Stratum 1 was removed by hand, unscreened, by units, with all observed artifacts collected. Stratum 2, which includes floor fill, was completely screened and collected.

Samples: Flotation--19 samples collected, 4 analyzed (hearth F.53.3, 3 floor contact samples)
                   Pollen--6 samples collected, 1 analyzed (composite pinches from 5 floor samples)
                   Archaeomagnetic--1 sample, datable
                   Charcoal--none taken

House Group 4

Feature 58

Feature Type:	Pit house (Figs. 3.23 and 3.24)
Provenience:	TT29, N302.60-309.35 E338.25-343.95
Stratigraphic Location:	Originates in Stratum 60 at 5.02 MBD Terminates in Stratum 60 at 5.56 MBD
Shape-Dimensions:	Subrectangular; 4.6 m northwest-southeast, 5.1 m northeast-southwest

Entry: This house was entered from the southeast (159 degrees east of north) through a slightly ramped, stepped, and grooved entryway (Fig. 3.23). The entry sloped up from the hearth (F.58.1) to meet a 30-cm high step that had a narrow groove in front of it. Presumably, this groove held some sort of sill, possibly of wood. From that point the entry continued another 90 cm where it terminated in another groove (sill?). The entry also had parallel grooves along its margins and was undoubtedly covered by a superstructure of some sort.

Walls: The pit walls were nearly vertical and averaged 50 cm to 60 cm in height. Remnant wall plaster was found throughout the structure. Walls were highly oxidized due to an intense fire that had burned the entire structure.

Roof: In addition to primary support posts, several sections of burned beams and sticks representing roof-wall construction materials were identified.

Fill: The fill of Feature 58 was observed in profile as two distinct strata. Stratum 1 was a compact, light tan silt with some sand and gravel. This stratum was mixed with some dark gray ashy silt and is believed to represent a combination of architectural debris and prehistoric refuse. Stratum 2 (floor fill) consisted primarily of gray-black vitrified material, the remains of burned construction material. In some areas, the contact between Stratum 1 and Stratum 2 was difficult to discern.

Fill Artifacts: 61 flakes, 1 core, 1 uniface, 2 bifaces, 1 utilized flake; 95 sherds (78 plain ware, 3 unidentified, 13 decorated, 1 worked); 135 animal bones, 1 complete bone awl

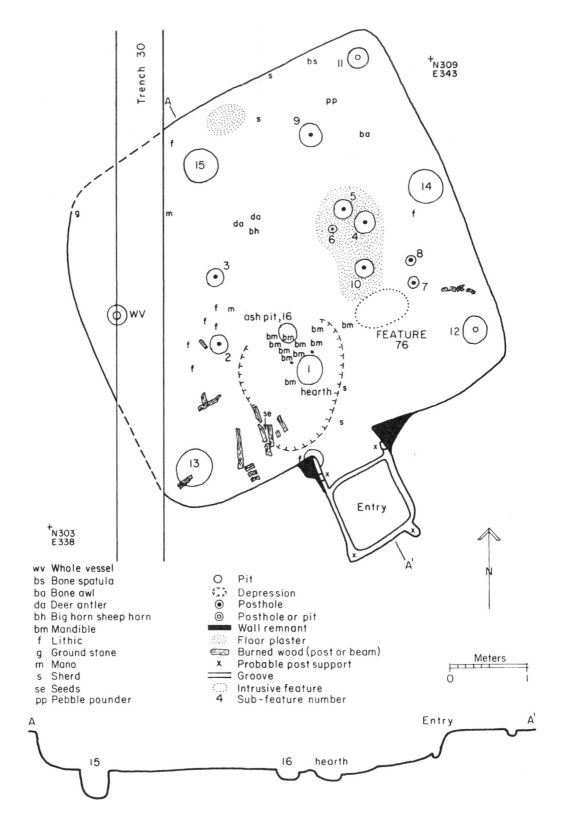

wv Whole vessel
bs Bone spatula
ba Bone awl
da Deer antler
bh Big horn sheep horn
bm Mandible
 f Lithic
 g Ground stone
 m Mano
 s Sherd
se Seeds
pp Pebble pounder

○ Pit
⊞ Depression
⊙ Posthole
◎ Posthole or pit
▬ Wall remnant
⋯ Floor plaster
⬬ Burned wood (post or beam)
x Probable post support
═ Groove
⋮ Intrusive feature
4 Sub-feature number

Meters
0   1

Figure 3.23. Plan and profile, Feature 58, pit house.

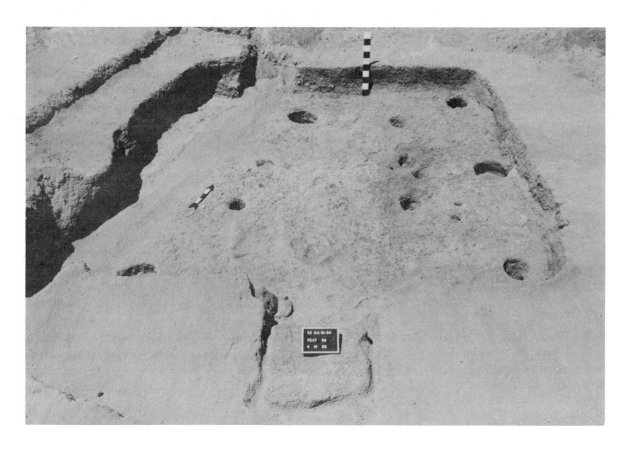

Figure 3.24. View of Feature 58, pit house, looking north.

Floor Fill
Artifacts: 1 unidentified marine shell pendant fragment,
                  1 Glycymeris shell bracelet fragment; 80 flakes,
                  2 unifaces, 1 biface, 5 utilized flakes, 1
                  hammerstone; 1 handstone, 1 turquoise pendant; 116
                  sherds (97 plain ware, 5 unidentified, 11 decorated,
                  3 worked); 134 animal bones, 2 bone awl fragments, 1
                  bone spatula fragment, 1 almost complete bone awl;
                  saguaro charcoal

Floor: The floor surface was a highly oxidized, unprepared
                  Stratum 60 of mixed silty sand with a high
                  percentage of gravel; it covered 22.2 square meters.

Floor Artifacts: 6 flakes, 2 unifaces, 1 biface, 2 utilized flakes;
                  1 pestle, 2 manos; 5 sherds (3 plain ware, 2
                  decorated), 1 reconstructible plain ware jar;
                  18 animal bones, 1 complete bone awl, 1 bone awl
                  fragment; charred macroplant remains: agave,
                  saguaro, grass; saguaro charcoal

Floor Features: A total of 16 floor features was identified within Feature 58, including 11 postholes.

Feature 58.1, the hearth, was oval shaped (32 cm by 38 cm), with remnants of a plaster collar. It was 10 cm deep and contained two separate strata. Stratum 1 consisted of dark gray, ashy silt with some sand. Stratum 2 was a compacted white ash.

Feature 58.13 was a probable storage pit, which was 47 cm in diameter, 29 cm deep, and contained reddish brown sandy silt with some gravel and charcoal.

Feature 58.14, a roughly circular pit approximately 45 cm in diameter and 26 cm deep, probably functioned as a storage pit. The fill was mottled gray-brown, orangish silty sand with gravel and some charcoal flecks. Mixed with the fill were some small burned seeds, sherds, lithics, and a possible pigment stone.

Feature 58.15 was a probable storage pit that measured 48 cm by 40 cm and had a depth of 32 cm. Two distinct strata were identified: Stratum 1 was a gray-brown, sandy silt with some gravels and a high percentage of charcoal and artifacts, and Stratum 2 consisted of light brown sandy silt with some gravels and charcoal.

Feature 58.16, an ash pit associated with Feature 58.1 (hearth), measured 26 cm by 20 cm by 11 cm deep and was filled with gray sandy silt with gravels.

Postholes: 58.2, 20 cm in diameter by 28 cm deep
58.3, 22 cm in diameter by 11 cm deep
58.4, 20 cm by 25 cm by 21 cm deep
58.5, 26 cm in diameter by 18 cm deep
58.6, 8 cm in diameter by 9 cm deep
58.7, 11 cm in diameter by 11 cm deep
58.8, 8 cm in diameter by 10 cm deep
58.9, 30 cm in diameter by 34 cm deep
58.10, 25 cm in diameter by 25 cm deep
58.11, 30 cm in diameter by 25 cm deep (may also be a floor pit)
58.12, 30 cm by 36 cm by 29 cm deep (may also be a possible floor pit)

The fill of these postholes was generally loose, charcoal-stained, silty sand. Features 58.2, 58.9, and 58.10 are probably the primary roof-support posts (a fourth may have been destroyed in the backhoe trench).

Floor Feature Artifacts:	58.1--charred macroplant remains: cheno-am, cotton, grass, salt bush, spurge, mesquite 58.4--3 plain ware sherds 58.10--1 animal bone 58.11--1 animal bone 58.12--6 plain ware, 2 decorated sherds 58.13--3 plain ware sherds 58.14--5 flakes; 11 animal bones 58.15--30 flakes, 1 hammerstone; 2 plain ware sherds; 2 animal bones
Comments:	Feature 76, an isolated hearth, intruded into the fill of Feature 58. The recovery of a large and varied floor assemblage from this feature, particularly the mule deer and bighorn sheep remains, suggests some important function(s) for this structure.
Sampling:	A control unit (N304.00-306.00 E339.50-342.00) was originally excavated, by observed strata, from the present ground surface down to the floor of the structure. All materials in this unit were screened and everything collected. All other excavation units were grab sampled only down to an arbitrary surface 10 cm above the floor of the feature. Below that level the soil was troweled, screened, and all artifacts collected.
Samples:	Flotation--35 samples collected, 8 analyzed (hearth F.58.1; 2 samples, pit F.58.14; pit F.58.16; 4 samples floor contact); F.58.14 and F.58.16 contained no charred macroplant remains Pollen--12 samples collected, 3 analyzed (hearth F.58.1; composite pinches from 5 floor samples; mano wash) Archaeomagnetic--1 sample, not datable Charcoal--49 samples collected, 9 analyzed

Feature 61

Feature Type:	Pit house (Fig. 3.25)
Provenience:	TT29, N312.85-318.00 E339.60-342.25
Stratigraphic Location:	Originates in Stratum 60 at 4.77 MBD Terminates in Stratum 60 at 5.04 MBD
Shape-Dimensions:	Subrectangular(?); 4.0 m northwest-southeast, 4.4 m northeast-southwest (estimated)

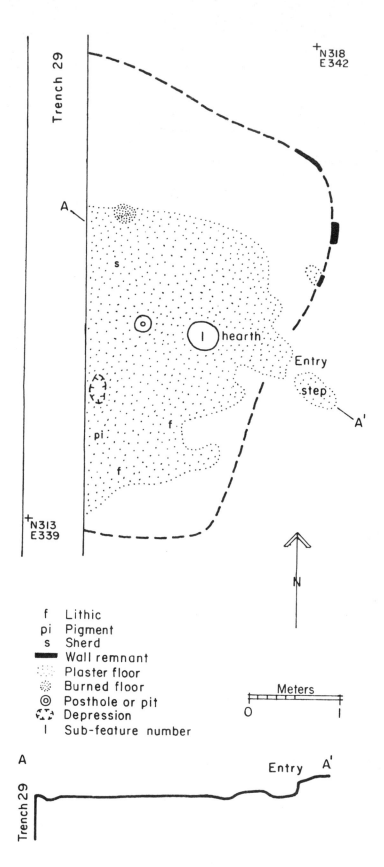

Figure 3.25. Plan and profile, Feature 61, pit house.

Entry:	The entryway faced southeast (112 degrees east of north) and measured approximately 50 cm wide by 1 m long. It was prepared by laying down a thick (5 cm to 10 cm) layer of tannish gray silt over the coarse, loose gravel deposits that occur naturally in this area. It was slightly ramped and may have been stepped during occupation.
Walls:	The pit walls were very poorly defined and in some cases impossible to discern due in part to the location of Feature 61 in a very loose gravel deposit. The wall, indicated by a dashed line in Figure 3.25, is projected based on the compaction of the floor.
Roof:	No evidence
Fill:	The fill was divided into two separate strata. Both were loosely compacted gray-brown silty sand intermixed with artifacts, charcoal, and gravel. Stratum 2 was distinguished from Stratum 1 by the presence of some possible architectural debris-- chunks of compacted mottled gray-brown clayey material. This stratum was in direct contact with the floor.
Fill Artifacts:	1 _Glycymeris_ shell bracelet fragment; 66 flakes, 2 cores, 1 uniface, 2 bifaces; 201 sherds (152 plain ware, 14 unidentified, 34 decorated, 1 worked); 82 animal bones
Floor Fill Artifacts:	1 whole _Pecten_ shell pendant fragment, 1 _Laevicardium_ shell fragment, 1 unworked _Anodonta_ shell fragment; 13 flakes, 3 bifaces, 1 flake, 1 hammerstone; 1 handstone-hammerstone, 1 possible stone bead; 68 sherds (57 plain ware, 4 unidentified, 5 Rillito Red-on-brown, 2 worked); 76 animal bones
Floor:	A large portion of the floor surface was a compacted tannish gray silt overlying the loose gravel substrate. It was probably not a prepared surface. Some areas of the house floor were not definable. Only a portion of the house was excavated, and its minimum floor area is 9.16 square meters.
Floor Artifacts:	1 biface, 1 utilized flake; 1 plain ware sherd
Floor Features:	The only floor feature (F.61.1) was an unprepared, oval-shaped (28 cm by 33 cm) hearth. The feature was highly oxidized and filled with 10 cm of fine white-gray ash.

Floor Feature Artifacts:	61.1--charred macroplant remains: cheno-am, cotton, grass, mesquite
Comments:	Feature 61 was discovered immediately north of Feature 58. The considerable architectural differences between these structures suggest that they were either functionally or temporally different.
Sampling:	Originally a 2-m by 2-m control unit (N313.00-315.00 E339.60-341.60) was used to test all strata (Strata 50, 1, and 2) in maximum 20-cm levels. All material from this test grid was screened and all artifacts collected; subsequently the rest of Stratum 50 was stripped by machine. All remaining Stratum 1 was grab sampled, and Stratum 2 (floor fill) was screened and collected. Approximately 60 percent of the house was excavated.
Samples:	Flotation--9 samples collected, 1 analyzed (hearth F61.1) Pollen--2 samples collected, none analyzed Archaeomagnetic--none taken Charcoal--1 sample collected, not analyzed

House Group 5

Feature 78

Feature Type:	Pit house
Provenience:	TT45; N365.95-371.20 E184.00-190.00 (estimated)
Stratigraphic Location:	Originates in Stratum 60 at 7.38 MBD Terminates in Stratum 60 at 7.51 MBD
Shape-Dimensions:	Unknown
Entry:	Not located
Walls:	No pit walls were encountered in the test grid, but the profile indicated that the pit walls were simply unprepared, sterile Stratum 60.
Roof:	Except for the presence of some possible roof fall in the fill, no evidence of roof construction was recovered.
Fill:	The fill was a highly compacted, tannish brown, sandy silt with charcoal flecks, gravels, and chunks

of silty clay that may represent collapsed architectural debris.

Fill Artifacts:	12 flakes, 1 core, 1 utilized flake; 1 mano; 68 sherds (50 plain ware, 14 unidentified, 4 decorated); 1 ceramic jar stopper; 18 animal bones
Floor Fill Artifacts:	None
Floor:	Stratum 20 was a hard, compact, grayish tan sandy silt that contained gravel, pebbles, and some charcoal flecks. Evidence of possible plaster was noted in the test unit, suggesting that the floor may have been plastered. The floor was oxidized from burning.
Floor Artifacts:	1 possible mano preform; 9 sherds (4 plain ware, 1 unidentified, 2 decorated, 2 worked); 1 ceramic jar stopper
Floor Features:	Only one floor feature was identified. Feature 78.1 was a hearth that was partially removed by the backhoe trench. It was approximately 35 cm in diameter and 16 cm deep. Some highly oxidized plaster remained. It was filled with gray-white ash.
Floor Feature Artifacts:	78.1--charred macroplant remains: cheno-am
Comments:	The trench profile revealed a highly oxidized floor surface; however, there was little evidence in the fill to suggest that the structure had burned. This feature was only tested in an attempt to gain chronologic information.
Sampling:	A single control unit (N367.00-369.00 E186.00-188.30) was excavated in 20-cm levels in observed strata (Strata 50 and 1). All material was screened and all artifacts collected.
Samples:	Flotation--3 samples collected, 1 analyzed (hearth F.78.1) Pollen--2 samples collected, 1 analyzed (mano wash) Archeomagnetic--none taken Charcoal--none taken

Feature 79

Feature Type:	Pit house
Provenience:	TT44; N388.70-392.15 E198.00-200.00 (estimated)
Stratigraphic Location:	Originates in Stratum 60 at 6.36 MBD Terminates in Stratum 60 at 7.05 MBD
Shape-Dimensions:	Unknown
Entry:	None located
Walls:	No pit walls were encountered during the test excavation; however, the walls revealed in the profile of Test Trench 44 were simply unprepared, sterile Stratum 60.
Roof:	No evidence
Fill:	The fill was divided into two strata. Stratum 1 was a gray-brown sandy silt with some pockets of gray ash and some gravels intermixed. This deposit appeared to be naturally deposited sheet trash. Stratum 2 (floor fill) was predominantly a dark- to medium-gray ashy silt with charcoal flecks.
Fill Artifacts:	1 unworked Laevicardium shell fragment; 18 flakes; 145 sherds (107 plain ware, 17 unidentified, 19 decorated, 2 worked); 11 animal bones, 1 bone awl fragment
Floor Fill Artifacts:	3 Glycymeris shell bracelet fragments, 2 unworked Anodonta shell and 1 unworked Laevicardium shell fragments; 63 flakes, 3 unifaces, 1 biface, utilized flakes; 323 sherds (232 plain ware, 60 unidentified, 29 decorated, 2 worked); 124 animal bones, 2 complete bone tubes
Floor:	The floor surface of Feature 79 consisted of red sandy silt with patches of oxidized soil that may be remnant plaster.
Floor Artifacts:	1 complete bone awl
Floor Features:	A single posthole measuring 23 cm in diameter by 17 cm deep was located in the test area. The fill consisted of ashy gray-brown silty sand.
Floor Feature Artifacts:	None

Comments: This feature was tested with one control unit.

Sampling: A 2-m by 2-m (N389.00-391.00 E198.50-200.50) control
                    unit was excavated in 20-cm levels through all
                    strata identified in Test Trench 44. All material
                    was screened and sampled.

Samples: Flotation--4 samples collected; 2 (fill samples)
                    analyzed; no remains
                    Pollen--1 sample collected and analyzed (floor)
                    Archaeomagnetic--1 sample, datable
                    Charcoal--1 sample collected, not analyzed

Feature 110

Feature Type: Pit house

Provenience: N374.50-379.80 E199.70-204.50

Stratigraphic   Originates in Stratum 60 at 6.70 MBD
Location: Terminates in Stratum 60 at 7.09 MBD

Shape-Dimensions: Square; 4.2 m northeast-southwest, 4.1 m northwest-
                    southeast (estimate)

Entry: The entry was not excavated, but was well defined in
                    plan view after stripping over the feature. It
                    opened to the northeast (39 degrees east of north)
                    and measured approximately 90 cm wide by 80 cm long.

Walls: The walls of the pit were unburned, unprepared,
                    sterile Stratum 60, averaging 35 cm to 40 cm high
                    and sloping slightly to meet the floor surface.

Roof: No evidence

Fill: The fill consisted of reddish orange sandy soil
                    intermixed with charcoal, pebbles, and cobbles
                    (Stratum 2). This material, which probably
                    represents primarily fallen architectural debris,
                    was overlain by gray-brown silty ash with some
                    charcoal, pebbles, and cobbles (Stratum 1). Stratum
                    1 appeared to be intentionally deposited trash.

Fill Artifacts: 116 sherds (22 decorated, 86 plain ware, 8
                    unidentified); flaked stone; mano fragment,
                    hammerstone; animal bones

Floor: The floor was unplastered, but was found to be
                    extremely smooth and compacted.

Floor Artifacts:	2 decorated sherds
Floor Features:	One floor feature (F.110.1), a posthole, was found during the test excavation. The feature measured 25 cm in diameter by 14 cm deep. The fill was a brown silt with charcoal flecks.
Comments:	Feature 110 was observed in plan view as a square ash stain while stripping the nearby cremation area. The temporal relationship between this structure and these cremations is unknown.
Sampling:	One 2-m by 2-m grid unit (N376.00-378.00 E202.00-204.00) was excavated in 20-cm levels into the feature and all material was screened and collected.
Samples:	Flotation--5 samples collected, none analyzed Pollen--2 samples collected, none analyzed Archaeomagnetic--none taken Charcoal--none taken

House Group 6

Feature 66

Feature Type:	Specialized activity area/possible ramada
Provenience:	TT16; N272.00-274.00 E406.85-408.85
Stratigraphic Location:	Originates in Stratum 60 at 4.63 MBD Terminates in Stratum 60 at 4.84 MBD
Shape-Dimensions:	Unknown
Entry:	No evidence
Walls:	No evidence
Roof:	Stratum 2 of the fill contained possible roof fall in the form of clumps of mottled, burned red-brown-yellow daub mixed with chunks of charcoal.
Fill:	The fill was divided into two strata. Stratum 1 was a medium brown, silty loam mixed with charcoal, ash, some gravels, and artifacts. Stratum 2 (floor fill) was a mottled gray silty loam with areas of red sandy clay and daub (see roof description).
Fill Artifacts:	14 flakes; 53 sherds (43 plain ware, 2 unidentified, 8 decorated); 141 animal bones

Floor Fill Artifacts:	1 unworked <u>Laevicardium</u> shell fragment; 27 flakes, 1 uniface; <u>118</u> sherds (89 plain ware, 8 unidentified, 20 decorated, 1 worked); 47 animal bones
Floor:	The floor of this feature was a compacted, red-brown silty sand (sterile Stratum 60).
Floor Artifacts:	None
Floor Features:	None
Floor Feature Artifacts:	None
Comments:	The fill and floor surface of this feature were quite similar to those of Features 67 and 68 in the same area. These features were not positively identified as pit houses; they may have been used as special activity areas. These were the only features at the site with these physical characteristics; that all three were found immediately southwest of the ballcourt may have some significance.
Sampling:	One 2-m by 2-m grid unit was excavated in the feature and all strata (Strata 50, 1, and 2) were screened and collected.
Samples:	Flotation--5 samples collected, none analyzed Pollen--3 samples collected, none analyzed Archaeomagnetic--none taken Charcoal--4 samples collected, none analyzed

Feature 67

Feature Type:	Specialized work area?
Provenience:	TT21; N278.00-282.00 E389.85-392.00 (estimated)
Stratigraphic Location:	Originates in Stratum 50 at 5.05 MBD Terminates in Stratum 60 at 5.33 MBD
Shape-Dimensions:	Unknown
Entry:	No evidence
Walls:	No evidence
Roof:	No evidence

Fill:	The fill (Stratum 1) consisted of gray-brown silty sand with charcoal and artifacts.
Fill Artifacts:	1 unworked Anodonta shell fragment; 3 mano fragments, 3 metate fragments, 1 ground stone; 648 sherds (405 plain ware, 110 unidentified, 120 decorated, 13 worked); 164 animal bones
Floor Fill Artifacts:	None
Floor:	The floor (occupation) surface (Stratum 10) was a gray-brown hard-packed sediment of sand and gravel that was oxidized in some areas.
Floor Artifacts:	1 plain ware sherd, 7 unidentified sherds
Floor Features:	Only one floor feature was encountered. This pit, (F.67.1) measuring 26 cm in diameter by 13 cm deep, was oxidized and contained loose gray ash mixed with lithics and fragmentary bone.
Floor Feature Artifacts:	67.1--3 animal bones; 2 flakes
Comments:	Like Features 66 and 68, this feature may represent a work area. Because its limits are unknown, and its interpretation uncertain, its origin is given as the top of Stratum 1 as excavated.
Sampling:	Two 2-m by 2-m grid units were excavated in 20-cm levels, screened, and collected in all identifiable strata (Strata 50, 30, and 1). The first test unit (N280.00-282.00 E390.00-392.00), was excavated as a control test; the grid unit to the south (N278.00-280.00 E390.00-392.00) was excavated in an attempt to better define the floor surface.
Midden Artifacts: (Stratum 30)	1 complete, worked Anodonta shell; 353 sherds (255 plain ware, 41 unidentified, 51 decorated, 6 worked)
Samples:	Flotation--none Pollen--2 samples collected, none analyzed Archaeomagnetic--1 sample, not datable Charcoal--none taken

Feature 68

Feature Type:	Specialized work area?
Provenience:	TT18; N269.15-272.98 E399.30-403.90

Stratigraphic Location:	Originates in Stratum 60 at 4.95 MBD Terminates in Stratum 60 at 5.13 MBD
Shape-Dimensions:	Unknown
Entry:	No evidence
Walls:	Although this feature was very difficult to define, a possible pit wall, 10 cm to 15 cm in height, was noted. This unprepared pit edge may have been produced by the compaction of the soil in a work area, leaving a ridge of uncompacted soil around it.
Roof:	No evidence
Fill:	Based upon the test trench profile, the fill of the feature was divided into two separate strata overlain by Stratum 50, the postabandonment silty sand. Stratum 1 was a brown silty sand that was only distinguished from Stratum 50 by the presence of charcoal flecks and artifacts. Stratum 2 (floor fill) was mottled dark gray and reddish brown ashy loam with charcoal and artifacts intermixed.
Fill Artifacts:	1 Glycymeris shell bracelet fragment; 17 flakes, 1 utilized flake; 1 hammerstone, 1 mano fragment; 29 sherds (25 plain ware, 4 decorated); 16 animal bones
Floor Fill Artifacts:	3 Glycymeris shell bracelet fragments; 3 Anodonta shell fragments; 92 flakes, 5 cores, 4 unifaces, 2 bifaces, 3 utilized flakes, 3 hammerstones; 1 polishing pebble, 1 hammerstone, 1 mano fragment; 375 sherds (157 plain ware, 33 unidentified, 177 decorated, 8 worked); 296 animal bones
Floor:	The floor surface was an unprepared, compacted reddish brown silty sand with inclusions of gray silty ash. It may not represent a house floor, but it was certainly some sort of occupation surface.
Floor Artifacts:	4 flakes, 1 uniface, 2 utilized flakes; 1 mano, 1 metate fragment; 14 sherds (2 plain ware, 3 unidentified, 8 decorated, 1 worked); 1 animal bone
Floor Features:	Only one floor feature was discovered. This pit, Feature 68.1, had a diameter of 38 cm and a depth of 9 cm and was filled with gray, ashy sand mixed with gravel and some artifacts. The function of this feature is unknown.
Floor Feature Artifacts:	68.1--2 unifaces; 1 plain ware sherd; 2 animal bones

Sampling: Initially a 2-m by 2-m control unit (N270.00-272.00
              E399.30-401.30) was excavated in 20-cm levels in the
              strata observed in the trench profile (Strata 50, 1,
              and 2). All materials were screened and collected
              before a backhoe removed all of Stratum 50 and
              Stratum 1 in an attempt to locate a feature outline
              in plan view. This stripped area covered 36 square
              meters north, south, and east of the control unit.
              Stratum 2, the floor fill overlying the occupation
              surface, was all excavated by hand and all artifacts
              collected.

Samples: Flotation--14 samples collected, 1 analyzed (pit
              F.68.1)
              Pollen--7 samples collected, none analyzed
              Archaeomagnetic--none taken
              Charcoal--4 samples collected, none analyzed

Unexcavated Pit Houses

R. Thomas Euler

Forty-five structures were identified during the excavations at
Water World, and 21 of these were excavated or tested. The remaining 24
structures were not investigated, but some information about them was
recorded from trench profiles. These features are described in Table
3.2.

Excavated Extramural Features

Martha Hueglin
and
R. Thomas Euler

This chapter describes the 18 extramural features that were
excavated. Included are nine roasting pits, two hearths, a ballcourt
(Feature 13), a midden, a borrow pit, a potbreak, and three
miscellaneous pits. Some of the ash and charcoal lenses (Features 22,
23, 28, 30, 31, 42, 50, 51, 63, 65, 75, 97, 112, 116, 117, 141, and 145)
identified in trench profiles may represent structures, but more
definite identification was impossible. These lenses and the two pits
of undetermined use were not excavated (Table 1.3).

Roasting pits were divided into Types A and B. Type A roasting
pits are well-formed pits that exhibit extensive burning on the sides
and base. Their fills consist of charcoal, ash, gray silt, fire-cracked
rock, tan-brown sandy silt, and gravels. Type B pits also are well

Table 3.2

UNEXCAVATED PIT HOUSES

Feature	Depth BPGS*	Description	Fill	Comments
1	Or. 0.15 m Tm. 0.65 m	An unburned, cobble-walled pit house constructed within a pit.	Str. 1: gray fine-grained sand with gravels and pebbles. Str. 2: gray, ashy soil with pockets of pure ash.	Features 1-16 were located during original testing program in 1983.
2	Or. 0.20 m Tm. 0.62 m	An unburned, basin-shaped pit house.	Str. 1: fine gray-brown soil with gravel and pebbles.	
3	Or. 0.20 m Tm. 0.65 m	A poorly defined, unburned pit house.	Str. 1: light brown, compacted silty sand.	
6	Or. 0.20 m Tm. 0.50 m	A poorly defined, unburned pit house.	Str. 1: mottled gray-brown sandy silt with charcoal flecks and pockets of ash. Str. 2: fine-grained silty sand.	Feature may have been a structure other than a pit house.
14	Or. 0.24 m Tm. 0.42 m	A poorly defined structure; a compacted "floor" surface that may represent a pit house.	Str. 1: fine-grained silty sand with charcoal flecks and lenses of light-gray ash.	
16	Or. 0.40 m Tm. 0.60 m	A shallow pit feature that may represent a pit house.	Str. 1: dark, fine-grained silty sand intermixed with artifactual material.	
24	Or. 0.50 m Tm. 0.80 m	Profile may represent cut corner of a pit house, although walls & floor surface were not well defined.	Str. 1: compacted, coarse sandy silt; possibly roof fall. Stra. 2: compact, ashy, gray, sandy silt.	
34	Or. 0.60 m Tm. 0.90 m	Profile may represent cut corner of a pit house, although walls & floor were not well defined.	Str. 1: loose tan-brown sandy silt with a lens of ashy gray-brown sandy silt.	Portion of feature floor is highly oxidized.
41	Or. 0.35 m Tm. 0.70 m	A possible basin-shaped, unburned pit house.	Str. 1: compacted, gray-brown sand with gravels and some charcoal flecks.	
69	Or. 0.70 m (5.50 MBD) Tm. 1.15 m (5.95 MBD)	A well-defined pit house with vertical walls. The walls and floor are unburned and unprepared.	Str. 1: brown, silty sand with charcoal flecks.	Trench profile indicated hearth may have been partially cut by backhoe trench.

Table 3.2, continued

UNEXCAVATED PIT HOUSES

Feature	Depth BPGS*	Description	Fill	Comments
77	Or. ? Tm. 0.40 m	A poorly defined pit house floor that may instead represent the bottom of a trash midden deposit.	Str. 1: loose gray sandy silt with some charcoal flecks.	
92	Or. 0.30 m (5.30 MBD) Tm. 0.70 m (5.70 MBD)	Profile probably represents corner of a burned pit house. It had a compacted, unprepared, oxidized floor surface.	Str. 1: gray-tan, silty sand with charcoal flecks and gravel; some pockets of gray ash.	
93	Or. 0.40 m (5.28 MBD) Tm. 0.80 m (5.68 MBD)	Probable unburned pit house with poorly defined walls and floor. Plastered hearth found above this floor surface was cut by backhoe.	Str. 1: brown-tan, silty sand with charcoal flecks and gravel.	
100	Or. 0.70 m (8.09 MBD) Tm. 1.20 m (8.59 MBD)	Probable burned house with vertical walls and unprepared floor surface.	Str. 1: light brown-tan compacted sand with gravel and charcoal. Str. 2: mottled gray-black organic material in direct contact with floor surface.	
101	Or. 0.50 m (8.16 MBD) Tm. 0.80 m (8.76 MBD)	Well-defined, burned pit house with slightly sloping walls and unprepared floor surface.	Str. 1: gray-brown hard-packed, silty sand with charcoal and gravel. Sediment also contains large pockets of charcoal and ash that may represent another stratum.	
102	Or. 0.20 m (7.45 MBD) Tm. 0.55 m (7.80 MBD)	Poorly defined basin-shaped pit house.	Str. 1: loose, gray-brown silty sand with pockets of gray ash.	Partially oxidized floor surface suggests feature may have burned.
103	Or. 0.30 m (3.60 MBD) Tm. 0.70 m (4.00 MBD)	Poorly defined basin-shaped feature that may be a pit house.	Str. 1: loose, medium gray sandy silt with some charcoal flecks.	
115	Or. 0.15 m (6.95 MBD) Tm. 0.45 m (7.25 MBD)	Well-defined, unburned pit house with nearly vertical walls. Floors and walls are unprepared, compacted, sterile soil.	Str. 1: tannish brown sandy silt with some gravel and charcoal flecks.	Profile as seen in Trench 53 may only represent a corner of structure.

Table 3.2, continued

UNEXCAVATED PIT HOUSES

Feature	Depth BPGS*	Description	Fill	Comments
121	Or. 0.30 m (4.55 MBD) Tm. 0.50 m (4.95 MBD)	A poorly defined, unburned pit house.	Str. 1: powdery silty sand mixed with gray ash and some artifactual material.	Feature appears in both trench walls.
123	Or. 0.30 m (5.05 MBD) Tm. 0.75 m (5.50 MBD)	A basin-shaped pit house that may have burned.	Str. 1: medium gray ash mixed with patches of oxidized soil, charcoal, and artifactual material.	Feature appears in both trench walls. The hearth appears to have been left intact by the backhoe.
124	Or. 0.20 m (5.18 MBD) Tm. 0.50 m (5.48 BMD)	A possible basin-shaped, unburned pit house.	Str. 1: grayish brown silts mixed with ash and gravels.	Feature occurs in both trench walls.
125	Or. 0.40 m (5.16 MBD) Tm. 0.70 m (5.46 MBD)	A shallow pit house with a prepared, oxidized floor surface and a possible hearth visible in profile.	Str. 1: compact, reddish-brown sandy silt mixed with gravel. Str. 2: pale gray, powdery ash mixed with charcoal.	Feature occurs in both trench walls. The structure may have burned.
127	Or. 0.30 m (4.65 MBD) Tm. 0.70 m (5.05 MBD)	A poorly defined, unburned pit house(?).	Str. 1: light gray-brown sandy silt mixed with charcoal and artifactual materials. Str. 2: dark gray ash mixed with some charcoal.	Feature was observed in both trench walls and does not have a well-defined floor surface.
133	Or. 0.65 m (5.06 MBD) Tm. 0.90 m (5.31 MBD)	Profile may represent cut corner of a pit house, although walls and floor surface were not well defined.	Str. 1: dark gray, ashy silt intermixed with some fire-cracked rock and some charcoal flecks.	Feature occurs only in east trench face. The feature may represent a roasting pit or a pit house(?).

* All originate and terminate in Stratum 60
BPGS = Below present ground surface
MBD = Meters below datum
Or = Originates
Tm = Terminates
Aper = Aperture
Str = Stratum

formed, but lack the oxidized sides and base. They are identified primarily on the basis of their fill, which consists of fire-cracked rocks and charcoal in an ashy matrix.

Undoubtedly, both types of pits were used for food preparation; however, they may represent different methods of cooking. The lack of oxidation in Type B roasting pits, despite the ashy fill and fire-cracked rocks, indicates either that fires built in these pits were not in direct contact with their edges, or that heat from the fires built in these pits was less intense than in Type A pits.

Type B pits may represent a method of cooking in which rocks heated elsewhere are placed in the pit, followed by the food, which is then covered by earth, creating a moderately hot oven. This method differs somewhat from that described by Fulton and Tuthill (1940: 20-25). Type A roasting pits, however, exhibit evidence of intense heating that most likely resulted from a fire having been built within them. Whether the fire was maintained in the pit during cooking is unclear.

These two types of pits may represent different stages in a single process rather than two discrete and unrelated cooking procedures. Flotation samples from the three excavated Type A roasting pits yielded evidence of possible food preparation. Feature 54 contained three mesquite seeds and one mesquite pod, which may represent either the remains of seeds and pods that were being cooked or intrusive trash. Feature 56 contained corn cupules and grass, both of which were probably used for fuel; the grass also could have been used to line the pit. Finally, one terminal stem from an agave leaf was found in Feature 86, indicating that agave leaves may have been prepared in the pit. Of the five excavated Type B roasting pits (Features 95, 138, 139, 143, and 148), only one produced macroplant remains; mesquite charcoal was recovered from Feature 138. The mesquite charcoal may be trash that was either accidentally or intentionally introduced. Flotation analyses can shed little light on the function of the Type B pits.

Feature Descriptions

Feature 54

Feature Type:	Type A roasting pit
Provenience:	N414.14-414.71 E491.44-491.95
Stratigraphic Location:	Originates above roof fall material (Stratum 2) in Feature 25, a pit house; terminates at 3.18 MBD beneath the floor in the fill of another underlying pit house, Feature 55

Description: This irregularly shaped pit measured 0.50 m (east-
                 west) by 0.57 m (north-south) at the house (Feature
                 25) floor. The upper portion of the pit was removed
                 during excavation of the house fill. The remaining
                 pit was 0.09 m deep, but its original depth is
                 estimated at 0.24 m. The sides sloped inward to
                 meet a slightly concave base, all of which were
                 defined by an oxidized sandy silt. The heavily
                 oxidized eastern edge of the pit corresponded to the
                 pit house wall (Feature 55).

Fill: At the house floor level, the fill consisted of
                 pieces of charcoal in a light gray ash matrix with
                 some gravels.

Fill Artifacts: Charred macroplant remains: mesquite

Comments: A large concentration of black ash, charcoal, and
                 rock was encountered 0.40 m south of the pit. This
                 appears to represent at least one episode of
                 cleaning and dumping of feature fill.

Excavation   Feature 54 was identified as the pit house floor was
Method: exposed. Once the feature was defined, the fill was
                 removed as one level, retaining most of it for
                 flotation samples.

Samples: Flotation--1 sample collected and analyzed
                 Pollen--none taken
                 Archaeomagnetic--2 samples, not datable
                 Charcoal--none taken

Feature 56

Feature Type: Type A roasting pit

Provenience: N413.46-413.94 E488.58-489.07

Stratigraphic   Originates in the fill of Feature 55, a pit house
Location: (below the floor of Feature 25), and was excavated
                 through the floor into the underlying sterile soil,
                 Stratum 60; terminates at 3.46 MBD

Description: Feature 56 was a roughly circular pit approximately
                 0.48 m in diameter and 0.15 m deep. The upper edges
                 were defined predominantly by reddish orange
                 oxidized silt that graded into a tan silt and clay
                 as it approached the oxidized base. In profile the
                 sides and base formed a shallow bowl shape.

Fill: The feature contained a homogeneous fill of dark
                         black ash, some medium-sized fire-cracked rocks, and
                         large fragments of charcoal. Occasional patches of
                         mottled tan silty sand, ash, and charcoal were also
                         present in the fill.

Fill Artifacts: 1 metate fragment; 31 sherds (30 plain ware, 1
                         unidentified); flaked stone (not analyzed); charred
                         macroplant remains: corn, grass

Comments: Based on stratigraphic information, this feature
                         clearly postdates the occupation of Feature 55 and
                         predates the occupation of the upper pit house,
                         Feature 25. Feature 56 also predates Feature 54,
                         another intrusive roasting pit.

Excavation   The entire feature fill was removed in one level and
Method: flotation samples were taken. In addition, three
                         charcoal samples were collected for C-14 dating and
                         species identification.

Samples: Flotation--2 samples collected, both analyzed
                         Pollen--none taken
                         Archaeomagnetic--1 sample, not datable
                         Charcoal-- 3 samples collected, none analyzed

Feature 86

Feature Type: Type A roasting pit

Provenience: N360.28-361.23 E424.39-425.29

Stratigraphic   The exact level of origin is unknown due to machine
Location: stripping above the feature. It can be assumed that
                         Feature 86 begins at the Stratum 50-Stratum 60
                         contact zone; it terminates in Stratum 60 at 4.28
                         MBD

Description: Feature 86 was a circular pit measuring at least
                         0.90 m (east-west) by 0.95 m (north-south) and at
                         least 0.41 m deep. A concave base curved upward to
                         join nearly vertical and inward curving sides. The
                         sides and base varied in appearance from solid
                         oxidized sediment to intermittent patches of burned
                         red soil and orangish tan sterile sediment. The
                         upper 6 cm of the feature was outlined by a
                         continuous 1-cm to 2-cm thick ring of oxidized soil.

Fill: Two distinct strata were identified. A 0.19-m-thick
                         basal layer consisted of gray ash and ashy silt with
                         some gravel and pebble inclusions. Large chunks of

charcoal were concentrated in the lower portions of the stratum. This stratum was overlain by 0.19 m of gravel, charcoal flecks, and a few small fragments of charcoal in a grayish brown sandy silt matrix.

Fill Artifacts: 8 plain ware sherds and 1 unidentified sherd; charred macroplant remains: agave

Excavation Method: The feature was sectioned and excavated according to cultural strata. Pollen and flotation samples were collected from both strata, and radiocarbon and charcoal samples were taken exclusively from the basal stratum.

Samples: Flotation—4 samples taken and analyzed
Pollen—3 samples taken, 1 sample analyzed (composite pinches from 2 samples).
Archaeomagnetic—1 sample, not datable
Charcoal—2 samples collected, none analyzed

Feature 95

Feature Type: Possible Type B roasting pit

Provenience: N371.60-372.20 E200.45-201.10

Stratigraphic Location: Originates in Stratum 60 at 6.43 MBD
Terminates in Stratum 60 at 6.58 MBD

Description: An oval-shaped pit roughly 0.60 m (north-south) by 0.75 m (east-west) and 0.15 m deep. Inwardly curving sides converged to form a slightly concave base. The edges of the pit were not clearly defined and the feature fill graded into the surrounding sterile matrix.

Fill: The unstratified fill was a charcoal-stained sandy silt interspersed with chunks of charcoal, a few small rocks, and numerous gravels. Some root disturbance was evident.

Fill Artifacts: None

Excavation Method: The feature was sectioned and excavated. The fill was retained as a flotation sample.

Samples: Flotation—1 sample analyzed; no macroplant material
Pollen—none taken
Archaeomagnetic—none taken
Charcoal—none taken

Feature 76

Feature Type: Extramural hearth

Provenience: N305.56-306.10 E342.00-342.72

Stratigraphic Location: Originates and terminates in the roof fall fill of Feature 58, a pit house

Description: A shallow, roughly oval-shaped pit excavated into the underlying pit house fill. It measured approximately 0.50 m north-south by 0.72 m east-west and 0.40 m deep. In profile, the sides and base were continuous, forming a slightly concave depression with a 0.04-m-thick base of oxidized gravelly silt and sand. The outline of the feature was clearly delineated from the surrounding pit house fill of Feature 58.

Fill: The feature fill consisted of a homogeneous, fine white and light gray ash.

Fill Artifacts: Charred macroplant remains: cheno-am, grass, saguaro

Comments: There was no evidence of naturally deposited sediments underlying the feature, indicating that very little time elapsed between the collapse of the roof of Feature 58 and the subsequent construction of Feature 76. It is possible that a natural depression created by the fallen roof was used for the hearth.

Excavation Method: All of the feature fill was collected for a flotation sample, and the base of the hearth was sampled for pollen.

Samples: Flotation--1 sample taken and analyzed
Pollen--1 sample taken and analyzed
Archaeomagnetic--1 sample, datable
Charcoal--none taken

Feature 18

Feature Type: Borrow pit (Fig. 3.26)

Provenience: N412.90-414.75 E498.50-499.90

Stratigraphic Location: Originates at the contact between Strata 50 and 60 at 2.66 MBD; terminates at the beginning of Stratum 70 at 3.38 MBD

127

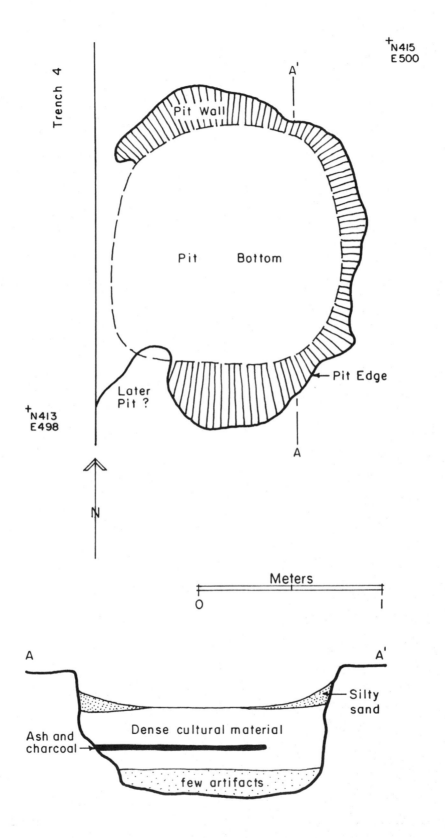

Figure 3.26. Plan and profile, Feature 18, borrow pit.

Description:	An irregularly shaped pit with inward-sloping and stepped sides and a slightly concave base. It measured approximately 1.40 m east-west by 1.85 m north-south at the aperture and narrowed to a nearly circular base, 1.30 m in diameter. The pit was 0.72 m deep. The sides were distinguished by the contact between feature fill and a waterlain gravel and pebble deposit with some sandy silt. Unlike the sides, the base was indicated by a compacted, light tan fine silt referred to as Stratum 70.
Fill:	The feature fill was divided into seven strata (see Excavation Method, below). Ranging from 0.15 m to 0.20 m thick, the basal stratum consisted of charcoal fragments and artifacts in a brown trashy silt deposit. A thin lens of naturally deposited brown silt (Stratum 6) separated Stratum 7 from an overlying, virtually identical trash deposit (Stratum 5). This in turn was topped with a nearly continuous 2-cm thick gray and black ash lens with a moderate amount of charcoal (Stratum 4). The overlying Stratum 3 was comprised of a 0.40-m layer of gray ashy and gravelly silt interspersed with charcoal flecks and rocks, which was partially divided by a naturally deposited charcoal-flecked brown silt sloping inward from the pit edges.
Fill Artifacts:	1 unworked _Anodonta_ shell fragment (Stratum 1); 2 mano fragments, 1 handstone, 1 metate fragment, 1 possible ground stone fragment (all Stratum 50), 1 abrader, 1 mano (both Stratum 1); 58 plain ware, 9 unidentified, and 4 decorated sherds (Stratum 1), 70 plain ware, 13 unidentified, 6 decorated, and 1 worked sherds (Stratum 50); 11 animal bones (Stratum 1); charcoal: mesquite and unidentified nonconiferous wood
Comments:	Based on the stratigraphy, at least four episodes of intentional dumping occurred in the feature, indicating that it functioned as a trash pit at some time. Although the original function of the pit is unclear, it certainly did not serve as a cooking feature; there is no evidence of extensive in situ burning. The few isolated patches of burned sediment exposed on the basal surface may have resulted from the discarding of the heated rocks that were uncovered at the base. Given its size and close proximity to Features 19, 25, and 55 (all pit houses), it is possible that Feature 18 served as a storage pit; however, the unstable condition of the pit edges, due to the surrounding gravel matrix, suggests that it was not constructed for storage.

An alternative, and more convincing, functional interpretation is that it was originally a borrow pit. Generally, borrow pits are made to obtain soils high in calcium carbonate for use in feature construction; however, none was observed in the trenches at Water World. This feature was excavated into a very fine-grained silt (Stratum 70) that resembled the soil used in preparing nearby pit house floors, and Feature 18 may have been the source of that material. The extremely irregular form of this feature may support the latter interpretation. A second pit was tentatively defined during excavation as Feature 18A, but was not definitely identified as cultural.

Excavation Method:	This feature was not excavated according to natural and cultural strata. Instead, it was dug in four arbitrary levels; the upper three levels were 20 cm each and the basal level was from 10 cm to 12 cm thick. Flotation samples were collected from the upper three levels, and pollen samples were taken from the lower two. Additionally, charcoal samples were recovered from all levels for species identification. The basal level yielded one charcoal sample for potential radiocarbon dating.
Samples:	Flotation--8 samples (3 from F.18A), none analyzed Pollen--3 samples collected, none analyzed Archaeomagnetic--none taken Charcoal--10 samples collected, 1 analyzed

Feature 57

Feature Type:	Miscellaneous pit
Provenience:	N417.30-418.10 E396.94-398.10
Stratigraphic Location:	Originates and terminates in the fill of Feature 29, a pit house
Description:	This oval-shaped pit measured 0.80 m north-south by 1.15 m east-west and 0.19 m deep; it had straight and inward-sloping sides and a relatively flat base. Both the sides and the base were defined by the soil contact between feature fill and the surrounding pit house fill. No evidence of burning was observed.
Fill:	The feature fill consisted of a fine gray ash with some sand. Portions of its western and northern edges were disturbed by rodent activity, perhaps resulting in some mixing of the house and pit fills.

Fill Artifacts:	18 sherds (15 plain ware, 1 unidentified, 2 decorated); flaked stone (not analyzed); charred macroplant remains: acacia, hedgehog cactus, mesquite, purslane
Excavation Method:	The fill of Feature 57 was excavated in one level and a small amount retained for flotation and pollen samples.
Samples:	Flotation--2 samples collected, both analyzed Pollen--1 sample collected, analyzed Archaeomagnetic--none taken Charcoal--none taken

Feature 87

Feature Type:	Miscellaneous pit (secondary cremation pit)
Provenience:	N365.10-365.47 E211.06-211.34
Stratigraphic Location:	Originates in Stratum 10 at 6.44 MBD Terminates in Stratum 70 at 6.71 MBD
Description:	Feature 87 was an irregularly shaped pit containing the remains of three cremated individuals (Features 87.1, 88, and 89) and one pile of burned animal bone and bone artifacts (Feature 90). The pit walls and bottom were not oxidized.
Fill:	Brown to reddish brown silt
Fill Artifacts:	1 axe; 10 plain ware sherds
Comments:	The pit was probably dug to bury the remains of at least one of the cremations found in it, and subsequently enlarged to accommodate additional cremations. It is also possible that the cremations and burned animal bone were interred at the same time.
Excavation Method:	The feature was bisected vertically and half was excavated at a time. The feature fill was removed in a single level and collected for flotation. One pollen sample was taken from beneath the sherds.
Samples:	Flotation--2 samples collected, none analyzed Pollen--1 sample collected, not analyzed Archaeomagnetic--none taken Charcoal--none taken

Feature 96

Feature Type:	Miscellaneous pit
Provenience:	N365.70-366.08 E212.73-213.12
Stratigraphic Location:	Originates at the top of Stratum 60 at 6.40 MBD Terminates in Stratum 60 at 6.54 MBD
Description:	Feature 96 was an irregularly shaped pit roughly 0.38 m north-south by 0.40 m east-west and 0.14 m deep. The steeply sloping sides and concave base were defined simply by a soil contact between the feature fill and the sterile matrix.
Fill:	Dark brown sandy loam with some gravels and charcoal
Fill Artifacts:	Reconstructible Rillito Red-on-brown bowl
Excavation Method:	The feature was bisected vertically and half was excavated at a time. The fill was removed in one level and collected for flotation samples. One pollen sample was taken from beneath the sherds.
Samples:	Flotation--2 samples collected, none analyzed Pollen--1 sample collected, not analyzed Archaeomagnetic--none taken Charcoal--none taken

Feature 59

Feature Type:	Pit (This feature was determined to be a midden deposit overlying pit house Feature 26. It was originally recorded as a pit, however, and this description is included to provide additional information on this feature.)
Provenience:	N413.10-415.85 E386.05-389.95
Stratigraphic Location:	Its origin is unknown due to machine stripping directly above the feature. The pit intruded into the fill of Feature 26, a pit house, and appeared to terminate in the roof fall of this house.
Description:	The feature was irregularly shaped in plan view and measured 2.75 m north-south by 3.90 m east-west at the widest point, with a minimum depth of 0.25 m and a maximum of 0.39 m. Although not clearly defined, the inward-curving edges and uneven base combined to form a large depression with a slightly lower

central area. The feature fill filtered into the encompassing pit house fill matrix, resulting in an exceedingly vague feature outline.

Fill: Gray ashy silt and sand interspersed with gravel and pebbles

Fill Artifacts: 5 Glycymeris shell bracelet fragments, Laevicardium shell pendant fragment, complete Laevicardium shell pendant; 1 hammerstone fragment; 73 sherds (62 plain ware, 3 unidentified, 7 decorated, 1 worked); 1 figurine fragment; 13 animal bones (Partial listing for "pit" feature; see description for Feature 26.)

Comments: The overall form, size, and contents of Feature 59 indicate that it represents a trash midden.

Excavation Method: Initially, the feature was excavated in 2-m by 2-m units as part of Feature 26 fill. Once Feature 59 was identified as a separate, intrusive feature, its fill was excavated in two arbitrary levels of varying depths. Flotation and pollen samples were gathered from both levels.

Samples: Flotation--2 samples collected, none analyzed
Pollen--2 samples collected, not analyzed
Archaeomagnetic--none taken
Charcoal--none taken

Feature 13

Feature Type: Ballcourt (Figs. 3.27, 3.28, 3.29, and 3.30)

Provenience: N293.40-302.00 E416.60-436.00

Stratigraphic Location: Originates in Stratum 50 at 4.30 MBD
Terminates in Stratum 60 at 4.78 MBD

Shape-Dimensions: The feature was an oval-shaped depression that measured 17.5 m by 7.8 m. These were interior court measurements and do not include the gravel berms that were once in place outside this surface. The interior surface area, not including the entryways, was 116.5 square meters.

Entry: At both ends of the feature, perpendicular to the short axis of the court, were formal plastered entryways. They were slightly ramped toward the interior of the court and measured approximately 1 m long by 1 m wide (Fig. 3.27).

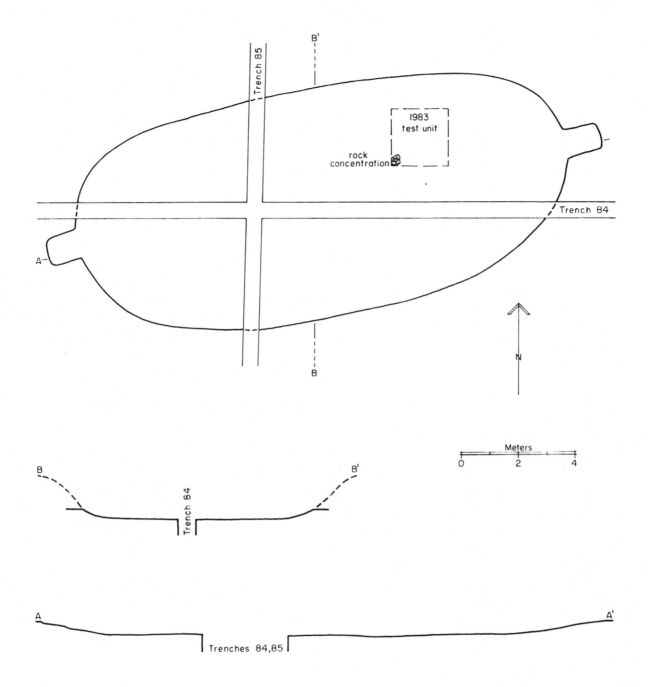

Figure 3.27. Plan and profile, Feature 13, ballcourt.

Walls: The feature was enclosed by an eroded, low, earthen
                      embankment, the remains of the berms that were in
                      place during its use. The lowest sections of the
                      walls, that portion actually dug into the old
                      occupation surface, were found to be extremely
                      compacted and covered with a thin layer of caliche

134

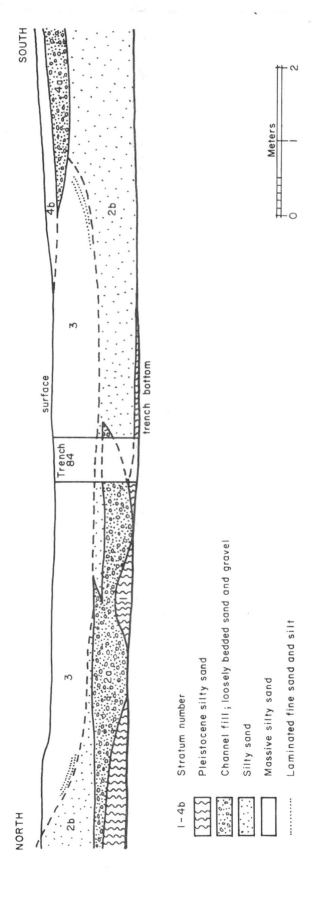

Figure 3.28. Geological profile of the ballcourt.

Figure 3.29. Aerial view of the ballcourt looking southeast (Bureau of Reclamation photograph).

136

Figure 3.30. Excavated ballcourt, Feature 13, showing entryways and plaster remnants (white ring).

plaster. This wall was found to be replastered with identical material in certain areas. The plastered wall was approximately 30 cm high and sloped down to meet the plastered floor.

Fill: The fill of the ballcourt consisted of a tan silty sand mixed with small gravels (Fig. 3.28). The artifact count of this homogeneous soil was relatively low.

Fill Contents: 279 sherds (226 plain ware, 44 decorated, 9 unidentified); mano; flaked stone (not analyzed); animal bones

Floor: Remnant plaster found along the entire length of the floor-wall contact was approximately 0.5 m to 1 m in width (Figs. 3.29 and 3.30). Some very small patches of this plaster were found toward the center of the feature, suggesting that the entire feature had been plastered at one time. The plaster in the interior of the ballcourt may have been worn away through use.

Floor Assemblage: Although some sherds were found in contact with the floor surface, their presence is probably not related to the actual use of the feature.

Floor Features: During initial testing of this feature, a basin-shaped, cobble-filled pit was found extending below the ballcourt floor surface (Downum and others 1986: 91). At the time, this feature was thought to be a "marker" or some other feature related to the use of the ballcourt. The complete excavation of the ballcourt during the 1987 field season suggested that the cobble-filled pit was most likely a later, intrusive, cooking feature. Another feature (F.13.1) was located during excavation. This was a questionable floor feature consisting of a shallow, circular, ash-filled depression that measured 20 cm in diameter by 5 cm in depth.

No exterior or interior postholes were found in association with Feature 13.

Comments: A 10-m wide area was mechanically stripped to the approximate prehistoric occupation surface around the ballcourt. Stripping revealed a large number of extramural features in plan view. Subsequent excavation of a number of these features indicated that most were roasting pits or isolated hearths.

Field Methods: During the Phase B Class III Survey, Feature 13 was observed as a shallow, oval depression enclosed by a low earthen embankment (Downum and others 1986: 90) and was tentatively identified as a prehistoric ballcourt. One 2-m by 2-m test excavation unit was excavated in an attempt to expose the intersection of the court floor with the embankment. Surface appearance proved to be a poor indicator of this contact point although a hard-packed probable floor surface was located. Conclusive evidence for identification of the feature as a ballcourt was not attained by this limited testing.

Toward the end of the 1986 season, two long backhoe trenches (Fig. 3.27) were dug in an attempt to bisect the feature along its north-south (Test Trench 84) and east-west axes (Test Trench 85). These trenches were faced and then cleaned using a gasoline-powered blower. The profiles were studied by both the project geomorphologist and staff archaeologists, but the feature was not positively identified as a ballcourt or other natural or cultural feature. No additional excavation was carried out in 1986 and the ballcourt question remained unresolved.

In late January of 1987 the two trenches were reopened, faced, and reexamined. Thin lines of plaster were observed in the profile curving up from a hard-packed horizontal surface at the east end of Test Trench 85 and the southern end of Test Trench 84. Excavation units were then laid out over these possible intersections of floor and embankment (N296.38-297.35 E432-434 and N293-295 E424.10-426) and the overburden was removed in 20-cm levels and screened. After exposing plastered surfaces in these units, the outline of the top of the surviving ballcourt sides was followed across these units, which were then excavated to the ballcourt floor.

To quickly locate the northern and western edges of the court, which were not discernible in the trench wall profile, and to trace the floor surface, a 30-cm-wide strip was excavated by hand along both sides of each trench. Once its full dimensions were known, the remaining fill was removed by backhoe (and was not screened) to 10 cm above the floor. This last 10 cm was hand excavated using shovels and trowels and was not screened. Artifacts were collected as seen and provenienced by quadrant (created by the bisecting backhoe trenches). The floor surface was cleared using trowels and brushes and the few floor-contact artifacts located were point provenienced and collected.

Samples: Flotation--1 sample collected (F.13.1), not analyzed
Pollen--4 samples collected (floor), none analyzed
Archaeomagnetic--none taken
Charcoal--none taken

Feature 107

Feature Type: Potbreak

Provenience: N371.40-371.70 E210.77-211.15

Stratigraphic
Location: Originates in Stratum 60 at 6.25 MBD
Terminates in Stratum 60 at 6.30 MBD

Description: This feature was a concentration of sherds that appeared to be from one vessel.

Fill: Soil in the vicinity of the potbreak was found to be sterile, but was oxidized in some places.

Contents: Reconstructible Rillito Red-on-brown flare-rimmed bowl; 3 decorated, 3 plain ware sherds

Comments: Feature 107 was located in a cremation area and was originally thought to be a burial marker. It was not associated with an identifiable pit. Excavation around and under the sherds located no bone, ash, or other cultural material. It may have served as a general marker for the cremation area, but not for a specific cremation.

Feature 138

Feature Type: Type B roasting pit

Provenience: N301.05-302.07 E415.35-416.48

Stratigraphic
Location: Originates in Stratum 60 at 4.27 MBD
Terminates in Stratum 60 at 4.57 MBD

Description: The feature was a roughly oval-shaped pit that measured 1.1 m (east-west) by 0.9 m (north-south) and was 0.20 m deep at its maximum. No evidence of oxidation was encountered; however, the presence of large quantities of fire-cracked rock, charcoal, and ash suggested that the feature probably functioned as a roasting pit.

Fill: The fill of the feature consisted of ashy, sandy silt mixed with gravel, fire-cracked rock, and charcoal. Evidence of rodent and insect disturbance was noted throughout the fill.

Fill Artifacts: Reconstructible Rillito Red-on-brown flare-rimmed bowl; 59 sherds (6 decorated, 46 plain ware, 7 unidentified); handstone, sandstone abrader/anvil; bone; charred macroplant remains: grass, mesquite

Comments: Feature 138 was located approximately 4 m northwest of the ballcourt.

Excavation Method: The entire feature was excavated and all soil screened.

Samples: Flotation--2 samples collected, both analyzed
Pollen--none taken
Archaeomagnetic--none taken
Charcoal--none taken

Feature 139

Feature Type: Type B roasting pit

Provenience: N294.88-295.48 E441.76-442.30

Stratigraphic Location: Originates in Stratum 60 at 4.12 MBD
Terminates in Stratum 60 at 4.26 MBD

Description: The feature was a nearly circular, shallow, bowl-shaped pit that measured approximately 60 cm in diameter and 14 cm deep. The area around the edge of the feature was fire blackened.

Fill: The fill was a compacted, dark gray ash with some coarse gravels, charcoal, and fire-cracked rock.

Contents: No artifacts were located, and no macroplant remains were found in flotation samples.

Comments: Feature 139 was located approximately 10 m southeast of Feature 13 (ballcourt).

Excavation Method: The entire feature was excavated and all material was screened.

Samples: Flotation--2 collected, both analyzed
Pollen--none taken
Archaeomagnetic--none taken
Charcoal--none taken

Feature 143

Feature Type:	Type B roasting pit(?)
Provenience:	N293.02-293.40 E430.30-430.76
Stratigraphic Location:	Originates in Stratum 60 at 4.26 MBD Terminates in Stratum 60 at 4.54 MBD
Description:	The feature was a roughly oval-shaped pit that measured approximately 0.50 m by 0.35 m by 0.28 m deep. No oxidation was observed during excavation; however, the ash, charcoal, and fire-cracked rock encountered suggest that the feature was probably used for cooking purposes.
Fill:	The fill consisted of sandy gray-brown ash intermixed with charcoal, fire-cracked rock, and pebbles.
Contents:	No artifacts were observed, and no macroplant remains where found in flotation samples.
Comments:	The location of the feature along the southern edge of the ballcourt suggests that the feature predates the ballcourt; it had been buried by the berm surrounding the court.
Excavation Method:	The entire feature was excavated and all material was screened.
Samples:	Flotation--2 samples collected, both analyzed Pollen--none taken Archaeomagnetic--none taken Charcoal--none taken

Feature 144

Feature Type:	Roasting pit?
Provenience:	N295.00-295.28 E431.48-431.83
Stratigraphic Location:	Originates in Stratum 60 at 4.25 MBD Terminates in Stratum 60 at 4.40 MBD
Description:	The feature was a small, somewhat irregularly shaped pit with a diameter of approximately 25 cm and a depth of 15 cm.

Fill:	Feature fill consisted of silty ash mixed with fire-cracked rock and burned gravel. No charcoal was observed.
Contents:	No artifacts were recovered.
Comments:	The feature intruded the southern edge of, and thus postdates, the ballcourt.
Excavation Method:	The entire feature was excavated.
Samples:	Flotation--1 sample (all the fill) collected, but not analyzed Pollen--none taken Archaeomagnetic--none taken Charcoal--none taken

Feature 147

Feature Type:	Hearth?
Provenience:	N300.70-301.70 E436.80-437.65
Stratigraphic Location:	Originates in Stratum 60 at 4.14 MBD Terminates in Stratum 60 at 4.25 MBD
Description:	The feature was simply a large, somewhat circular, oxidized area covered with ash. No prepared pit was found.
Fill:	Medium gray ash mixed with silty sand and gravel
Contents:	No artifacts were recovered.
Comments:	The feature was located 1 m northeast of the eastern entry of the ballcourt.
Excavation Method:	The feature was completely excavated.
Samples:	Flotation--1 sample (all feature fill) collected, but not analyzed Pollen--none taken Archaeomagnetic--none taken Charcoal--none taken

Feature 148

Feature Type:	Type B roasting pit(?)
Provenience:	N291.00-291.68 E443.93-444.56
Stratigraphic Location:	Originates in Stratum 60 at 4.14 MBD Terminates in Stratum 60 at 4.24 MBD
Description:	This feature was a roughly circular, ash-filled depression that measured approximately 65 cm in diameter by 10 cm deep. The feature was not well defined in the sterile gravel substrate. The presence of ash, charcoal, and fire-cracked rock suggests that the pit was probably some type of cooking feature.
Fill:	Silty ash mixed with charcoal, fire-cracked rock, and gravel
Contents:	No artifacts or macroplant remains were recovered.
Excavation Method:	The entire feature was excavated, and all the fill was screened.
Samples:	Flotation--2 samples collected, both analyzed Pollen--none taken Archaeomagnetic--none taken Charcoal--none taken

Unexcavated Extramural Features

Martha Hueglin

Thirty-four of the extramural features identified during the excavations at Water World were not excavated. These included 3 Type A roasting pits, 8 Type B roasting pits, 6 possible roasting pits, 16 miscellaneous pits, and 1 borrow pit. Specific information about each of these features is given in Table 3.3.

Cremations

Given the size of the site and the potential significance indicated by the presence of a ballcourt, it was anticipated that a large number of cremations might be found at Water World, and that these features would provide information on Colonial period burial practices and populations. Two small clusters of cremations were found, one to the southwest of the ballcourt (Features 5, 60, 137) and another near

Table 3.3

UNEXCAVATED FEATURES EXPOSED IN TRENCH PROFILE OR BY STRIPPING

Fea-ture	Feature Type	Depth	Description	Fill	Comments
32	Type A roasting pit	Or: Str. 31 at 0.15 m BPGS; Tm: Str. 31; 0.35 m deep	Dome shaped with oxidized sides and partially oxidized top. Aper: 0.60 m N-S	Str.1: 0.25 m gray sandy silt with gravels, rocks, and charcoal. Str.2: 0.05-0.10 m charcoal and some silt. Str.3: 0.05 m gray sandy silt with gravels and charcoal flecks.	Not present in east wall profile.
62	Type A roasting pit	Or: Str. 50 at 0.25 m BPGS (5.12 MBD); Tm: Str. 60 (5.87 MBD); 0.75 m deep	Basin-shaped pit with inward curving sides and concave base. Sides and base are oxidized. Original depth poorly defined. Aper: 0.85 m N-S.	Str.1: 0.30 m gray-tan silty sand and gravels. Rock, 1 sherd, and 1 lithic. Str.2: 0.05 m gray-stained silt. Str.3: 0.30 m similar to S1 but less gravels and no artifacts. Str.4: 0.05-0.08 m gray ash.	Not present in west wall profile.
72	Type A roasting pit	Or: Str. 60 at 0.35 m BPGS; Tm: str. 60; 0.13 m deep	Shallow, irregularly shaped pit with oxidized concave base and inward curving sides. Aper: 0.93 m N-S.	Str.1: gray ash with loamy sand, rocks, and charcoal.	Not present in west wall profile.
64	Type B roasting pit	Or: Str. 50-60? at 0.70 m BPGS (5.48 MBD); Tm: Str. 60 (5.68 MBD); 0.20 m deep	Basin-shaped pit. Concave base formed also by sides; some oxidization on base. Aper: 0.90 m N-S.	Str.1: 0.15 m tan silty sand, slightly charcoal and ash stained. Str.2: 0.05-0.20 m dark charcoal-stained sediment with gravels and rocks.	Not present in west wall profile.
70	Type B roasting pit	Or: Str. 50 at 0.30 m BPGS; Tm: Str. 50-60; 0.10-0.15 m deep	Shallow basin-shaped pit with rounded base that forms sides; slightly concave top. Aper: 0.85 m N-S.	Str.1: gray ash with a lot of charcoal. Fill darker at base and lighter at top.	Fill appears to be from actual feature function.
71	Type B roasting pit	Or: Str. 50-60 at 0.10 m BPGS; Tm: Str. 60; 0.42 m deep	Irregularly shaped pit with inward sloping & outward curving sides & flat base. Aper: 0.62 m N-S.	Str.1: gray ash with loamy sand and fire-cracked rocks, charcoal, 1 sherd and 1 ground stone fragment.	Not present in east wall profile.
73	Type B roasting pit	Or: Str. 60 at 0.30 m BPGS; Tm: Str. 60-70; 0.37-0.45 m deep	Irregular pit with concave base. Sides and top disturbed by rodent activity. Aper: 0.52 m N-S.	Str.1: loamy sand and gray ash with gravels, fire-cracked rocks, and 1 ground stone.	Disturbed by pot hunting. Not present in west wall profile.
84	Type B roasting pit	Or: Str. 50? at 0.52 m BPGS; Tm: Str. 60; 0.20 m deep	Basin-shaped pit with rounded base that forms sides. Aper: 0.64 m N-S.	Str.1: 0.10 m gray ashy silt with charcoal flecks. Str.2: 0.10 m gray ashy silt with charcoal flecks and fire-blackened rocks.	Not present in east wall profile.
111	Type B roasting pit	Unknown	Circular, 0.70 m diameter.	Charcoal and ash with fire-cracked rock.	
134	Type B roasting pit	Or: Str. 50 at 0.15 m BPGS; Tm: Str. 50 at 0.32 m BPGS	Small basin-shaped feature.	Str. 1: loosely compacted mottled gray-black ashy silt intermixed with gray-tan sand and pebbles and some charcoal.	Not present in west wall profile.
135	Type B roasting pit	Or: Str. 50 at 0.25 m BPGS; Tm: Str. 50 at 0.45 m BPGS	Basin-shaped pit with a relatively flat bottom.	Str. 1: grayish tan silty sand mixed with charcoal, pebbles, and fire-cracked rock.	Not present in west wall profile. A 0.15-m section of pit base is highly oxidized.
74	Possible roasting pit	Or: Str. 50-60 at 0.15 m BPGS; Tm: Str. 60; 0.45 m deep	Elliptical in profile with partially flat base Max. width: 0.79 m N-S.	Str.1: gray ash with loamy sand and 1 fire-cracked rock.	Disturbed by pot hunting. Not present in west wall profile.
99	Possible roasting pit	Or: Str. 50 at 0.30 m BPGS (8.14 MBD); Tm: Str. 31 (8.50 MBD); 0.36 m deep	Poorly defined basin-shaped pit with irregular base and inward-curving sides. Aper: 0.82 m N-S.	Str.1: brown sediment with gravels and root disturbance; deposited in upper portion of pit. Str.2: 0.10 m central concentration of dark charcoal-stained sediment with large pieces of charcoal and pebbles. Brown sediment with charcoal and pebbles to either side.	Str.1 within feature is same as matrix, which has been deposited throughout site. Not present in west wall profile.

Table 3.3, continued

UNEXCAVATED FEATURES EXPOSED IN TRENCH PROFILE OR BY STRIPPING

Fea-ture	Feature Type	Depth	Description	Fill	Comments
136	Roasting pit(?)	Or: Str. 50 at 0.20 m BPGS; Tm: Str. 50 at 0.70 m BPGS	Basin-shaped pit with a relatively flat bottom.	Str.1: dark gray-ashy charcoal.	Not present in west wall profile.
140	Roasting pit(?)	Unknown	Circular.	Str.1: charcoal and ash with fire-cracked rock.	Seen in plan view during backhoe stripping operations.
142	Roasting pit(?)	Unknown	Circular.	Str.1: charcoal and ash with fire-cracked rock.	Seen in plan view during backhoe stripping operations.
146	Roasting pit(?)	Unknown	Circular.	Str.1: charcoal and ash with fire-cracked rock.	Seen in plan view during backhoe stripping operations.
21	Miscellaneous pit	Or: Str. 60 at 0.30 m BPGS; Tm: Str. 60; 0.40 m deep	Bell shaped with outward sloping wall and convex base. Aper: 0.50 m N-S. Basal diam: 0.62 m N-S.	Str.1: brownish gray sandy silt with gravels; 0.05-0.10-m layer of gray ash covering most of base.	Not present in east wall profile.
28	Miscellaneous pit	Or: Str. 50 at 0.53 m BPGS; Tm: Str. 50-60; 0.15 m deep	Inward-curving sides, rounded base. Aper: 0.30 m N-S.	Str.1: brownish gray gravelly and sandy ash; 1 charcoal fragment.	Not present in east wall profile.
37	Miscellaneous pit	Or: Str. 50-60 at 0.16 m BPGS; Tm: Str. 60; 0.12 m deep	Shallow basin-shaped depression with narrow base. Aper: 0.56 m N-S.	Str.1: 0.10 m mottled gray ashy and brown sandy silt with roots; 1 sherd. Str.2: 0.02 m gray sandy silt with charcoal flecks.	Possibly natural; associated with vegetation. Not present in east wall profile.
38	Miscellaneous pit	Or: Str. 50-60? at 0.04 m BPGS; Tm: Str. 60; 0.26 m deep	Poorly defined basin-shaped pit with inward-curving sides and slightly rounded base. Aper: 0.48 m N-S.	Str.1: 0.14 m gray ashy and sandy silt with gravels and rocks. Str.2: 0.12 m gray ashy sandy silt with gravels and charcoal flecks; 1 sherd.	Probably natural; associated with vegetation. Not present in west wall profile.
39	Miscellaneous pit	Or: Str. 50 at 0.28 m BPGS; Tm: Str. 60; 0.16 m deep	Basin-shaped with inward-sloping and -curving sides and flat base. Rocks concentrated in upper 0.12 m of fill. Aper: 1.0 m N-S.	Str.1: gray ashy and sandy silt with gravels, cobbles, and charcoal.	Not present in east wall profile.
43	Miscellaneous pit	Or: Str. 60 at 0.45 m BPGS; Tm: Str. 70; 0.30 m deep	Basin-shaped pit with inward-sloping sides and flat base. Aper: 0.90 m N-S.	Str.1: brown sandy silt with gravels and 3 isolated lenses of waterlaid gravels. 0.05 m thick ash lens covering part of base.	Not present in west wall profile.
45	Miscellaneous pit	Or: Str. 60 at 0.30 BPGS; Tm: Str. 70 at 0.85 m BPGS	Irregular pit. Vertical north side, gently curving south side. Bottom sloped down to the north. Aper: 2.50 m N-S.	Str.1: brown silt with gravels and pebbles in loose and compact patches. Str.2: similar to Str.1 but sandier. A few very eroded bone fragments. Str.3: loose brown sandy silt with more gravels than Str.2.	Possibly an inhumation, though it was not ascertained if the bone was human.
47	Miscellaneous pit	Or: Str. 50-60 at 0.22 m BPGS; Tm: Str. 60; 0.24 m deep	Truncated cone-shaped pit lined with compacted silt. Aper: 0.20 m N-S.	Str.1: 0.08 m slightly compact sandy silt; 1 sherd. Str.2: 0.02-0.04 m hard light brown silt. Str.3:0.12 m hard brown silt with sand and gravels. Str.4: 0.02 m fine brown silt with sand.	Not present in west wall profile.
48	Miscellaneous pit	Or: Str. 50-60 at 0.32 m BPGS; Tm: Str. 60; 0.36 m deep	Poorly defined with steeply sloping sides and irregular base. Aper: 0.57 m N-S.	Str.1: similar to Str.70. Str.2: 0.02 m sandy silt lining the pit.	Not present in west wall profile.
49	Miscellaneous pit	Or: Str. 50-60 at 0.22 m BPGS; Tm: Str. 70; depth unknown	Amorphous-shaped feature. Poorly defined with slightly concave base. Width: 68 m N-S.	Str.1: gray sandy and gravelly silt. Str.2: slightly gray brown sandy silt with some gravel, charcoal flecks, and patch of ashy silt.	Not present in west wall profile.
52	Miscellaneous pit	Or: Str. 50-60 at 0.08 m BPGS; Tm: Str. 60-70; 0.30 m deep	Inward-sloping and -curving sides and narrow flat base. Aper: 0.50 m N-S. Basal diam: 0.10 m N-S.	Str.1: silty sand with charcoal and roots; rodent disturbed.	Most of feature removed by backhoe trench. Not present in east wall profile.

Table 3.3, continued

NEXCAVATED FEATURES EXPOSED IN TRENCH PROFILE OR BY STRIPPING

Fea.	Feature Type	Depth	Description	Fill	Comments
114	Miscellaneous pit	Or: Str. 60 at 0.78 m BPGS; Tm: Str. 60?; 0.10 m deep	Irregularly shaped pit. Aper: 0.30 m N-S.	Str.1: gray sandy silt with charcoal flecks. Concentration of charcoal in south portion of feature.	
120	Miscellaneous pit	Or: Str. 60 at 0.25 m BPGS; Tm: Str. 60 at 0.45 m BPGS	Irregularly shaped, poorly defined pit.	Str. 1: compact brown silty sand mixed with gray ash, charcoal, and fire-cracked rock.	Not present in west wall profile.
122	Miscellaneous pit	Or: Str. 60 at 0.35 m BPGS; Tm: Str. 60 at 0.75 m BPGS	Basin-shaped pit, poorly defined at Str. 1/60 contact.	Str. 1: gray brown silty sand with ash, gravel, and some artifactual material.	Not present in east wall profile.
128	Miscellaneous pit	Or: Str. 60(?) at 0.10 m BPGS; Tm: Str. 60 at 0.50 m BPGS	Basin-shaped pit with inward-curving sides and concave base.	Str. 1: gray brown sandy silt with charcoal, ash, and gravel.	Seen in both east and west sides of trench. Feature exhibits evidence of rodent disturbance.
130	Miscellaneous pit	Or: Str. 70(?) at 0.55 m BPGS; Tm: Str. 70 at 0.70 m BPGS	Poorly defined, basin-shaped pit.	Str. 1: loose, gray silty sand with ash, charcoal, and some fragments of oxidized soil.	Not present in west wall profile.
132	Borrow pit?	Or: Str. 60 at 0.10 m BPGS; Tm: Str. 70 at 0.80 m BPGS	Large pit feature with poorly defined sides.	Str. 1: loosely compacted, mottled gray-brown silty sand with some gravels and heavy concentration of artifactual material.	Feature occurs in both sides of trench. Large amount of cultural debris in fill of feature suggests intentionally deposited trash.

BPGS = Below present ground surface
MBD = Meters below datum
Or = Originates
Tm = Terminates
Aper = Aperture
Str = Stratum

House Group 3 (Features 40, 46). Neither cluster appeared to represent a major cremation area, although stripping was limited in both areas. The one cremation area identified at Water World was found in House Group 5 and initially seemed to offer the best opportunity for providing important information on Colonial period interment practices. Because this area was located at the close of the 1986 field season, additional funds were received from Reclamation to complete the excavation of this area in 1987. Investigation of the House Group 5 Cremation Area was ultimately disappointing. Only three additional cremations were identified in 1987, bringing the total to 18, including two cremations (Features 85, 119) located north of the main interment area (see Fig. 1.6).

In all, 23 cremations were located at Water World, 22 during the 1986 and 1987 excavations and 1 (Feature 5) during the 1983 testing. Two cremations (Features 5 and 129) were removed during trenching; little information was retrieved from Feature 5, but some bone and associated artifacts were collected from Feature 129, although provenience data were lost. Upon analysis, Feature 90 was found to contain only burned animal bone mixed with artifacts. It was closely associated with three cremations (Features 87.1, 88, and 89), however, and may represent materials that were originally associated with one or more of these cremations.

Data on these 23 features (22 containing cremated human remains, plus Feature 90) are presented in Table 3.4. Features 105 and 108 were primary cremations; in the latter, the cremated bone was covered with a large sherd. The remaining 20 secondary cremations can be separated into five classes: (1) one or more upright urns (usually jars) with an inverted jar cover (Features 40, 87.1, and 137); (2) urns with an inverted bowl cover (Features 5, 88, 104, and 137); (3) cremated bone usually mixed with sherds and other artifacts, but without a covering vessel or sherd (Features 46, 60, 80, 81, 82, 83, 89, 109, and 118); (4) urns without a covering vessel (Features 94, and 129); and (5) cremated bone covered by an inverted bowl (Features 85 and 106). Most cremations were located in pits, but several could not be associated with a definite pit structure. The absence of a definable pit is most likely due to the nature of the soil in which the vessels were buried. One pit (Feature 87) contained three cremations (Features 87.1, 88, and 89) plus the animal bone deposit (Feature 90). Spier (1970: 303) reported that the Yuma Indians placed the cremated remains of an individual into four separate pits. Haury (1976: 164) commented on cremation features at Snaketown that were reminiscent of the Yuma interment practice. Feature 87 may reflect a similar interment practice with the animal bone deposit (Feature 90) intended as an offering for the deceased.

Grave goods were not particularly abundant or especially noteworthy. Features 40, 60, 80, 81, 87.1, 94, 105, 108, and 118 contained artifacts that could be interpreted as grave goods. Several other cremations contained associated sherds only, which may or may not have been grave items. Features 80, 81, 105, 108, and 118 contained the most varied artifact assemblages, including projectile points (Feature 108 had eight projectile points), shell beads, worked sherds, and bone tools; Feature 40 yielded a carved stone bowl. Some of these artifacts probably represent jewelry that the individuals were wearing when cremated, as well as items placed with the cremated remains at interment. None of the cremations contained items suggesting that the cremated remains belonged to an individual of special status or rank; however, Features 80, 105, 108, and 118 contained relatively large numbers of artifacts, which may suggest that these individuals were considered more important than those who were buried with few or no artifacts (such as Features 46, 82, 83, or 89).

With one exception, all the whole or restorable decorated vessels are Rillito Red-on-brown. The exception is a Santa Cruz Red-on-buff jar with a flaring neck, which was recovered from Feature 129. Santa Cruz Red-on-buff sherds were notably lacking in the decorated sherd inventory from the site (see Chapter 4), so the presence of this whole vessel in a burial context may be noteworthy and may represent a vessel that was considered special.

Table 3.4

CREMATION DATA

Fea.	Burial Type	Stra-tum	Depth (MBD)	Grave Facility	#	Age	Gender	Associated Artifacts	Comments
5	Urn with cover, bowl?	–	Unknown	Unknown	–	–	–	1 plain ware jar, 1 plain ware bowl (cover vessel).	Feature was removed by backhoe during original site testing (Downum and others 1986: 84).
40	Urns (with cover vessel?)	60	3.63-3.87	Pit, 0.56 m in diameter	S	I	I	1 carved stone bowl with 2 snake motifs (FN99); 1 reconstructible plain ware flaring-necked jar (FN98); 1 reconstructible plain ware flare-rimmed bowl (FN96); 41 sherds (23 plain ware, 6 unidentified, 4 decorated, 8 worked).	3 flotation and 3 pollen samples were collected, none analyzed.
46	Cremated bone	60	3.52-3.82	Circular pit, 0.40 m in diameter	I	I	I	None.	
60	Cremated bone	60	4.56-4.80	Circular pit, 0.45 m in diameter	S	Adult	I	Flaked stone (not analyzed); 1 mano; 34 sherds (30 plain ware, 4 unidentified; these may not be related to the cremation).	No flotation or pollen samples were collected.
80	Cremated bone	10/60	6.41-6.77	Subrectan-gular pit, 0.40 m N-S, E-W dimen-sion could not be determined	S	Adult	I	3 projectile points (FN 2058, 2063, 2308); 1 palette (Vol. 3, Chap. 6, Fig. 6.5b); sherds: 2 Rillito Red-on-brown, one is reworked into a pendant; 1 bone hairpin fragment (FN2062) fits with frag-ment in Feature 81.	1 pollen sample collected, not analyzed. Pit partially removed by trenching.
81	Cremated Bone	10/60	6.46-6.71	Roughly circular pit, 0.26 m in diameter	S	Adult	I	2 projectile points (FN 2141, 2142); 1 bone hairpin (FN2140) fits with frag-ment in Feature 80.	5 flotation and 1 pollen sample collected, none analyzed.
82	Cremated Bone	10/60	6.49-6.94	Roughly circular pit, 0.40 m in diameter	S	Adult?	I	1 unidentified sherd.	2 flotation and 1 pollen samples collected, none analyzed.
83	Cremated bone	10/60	6.42-6.83	Pit, roughly 0.40 m in diameter	S	Adult	Male	4 plain ware sherds.	9 flotation and 1 pollen samples collected, none analyzed.
85	Inverted bowl	10/60	6.23-6.56	Roughly circular pit, 0.44 m in diameter	S	Adult?	I	1 reconstructible Rillito Red-on-brown flare-rimmed bowl (FN2066); 4 plain ware sherds.	6 flotation and 1 pollen samples collected, none analyzed.
87.1	Urns? with inverted cover jar	10/60	6.45-6.64	Within large pit (F. 87) 1.50 m N-S by 1.20 m E-W, also contain-ing Features 88, 89, 90	S	I	I	Reconstructible vessels: 2 plain ware flaring-necked jars (FN2015-1027, 2020), 1 plain ware hemispherical bowl (FN2018), 1 Rillito Red-on-brown incurved neck-less jar (FN2016, 2025, 2110); 12 sherds (6 plain ware, 2 decorated, 4 worked).	1 flotation and 1 pollen samples collected, pollen (from vessel fill).
88	Urn with inverted cover vessel	10/60	6.50-6.70	Pit, roughly circular, 0.36 m in diameter, in bottom of F. 87	S	I	I	1 complete plain ware up-curved necked jar (FN2010), 1 reconstructible Rillito Red-on-brown with white slip flare-rimmed bowl (FN2011-2014, 2025).	1 flotation, from vessel fill, no pollen samples collected; flotation sample analyzed, no macroplant remains.
89	Cremated bone	10/60	6.64-6.75	Irregularly shaped pit, 0.28 m N-S by 0.36 m E-W, in bottom of F. 87	S	I	I	None.	2 flotation samples collected, not analyzed.
90	Burned bone (nonhuman)	10/60	6.46-6.71	Pit, roughly circular 0.28 m in diameter, in bottom of F. 87	–	–	–	Animal bone: 1 hairpin and 2 fragments, 2 awl fragments, 2 antler-tine tool fragments (FN2100-2104); flaked stone (not analyzed).	Burnt bone in pit proved to be all nonhuman; however, F. 90 is closely associated with crema-tion Features 87.1, 88, and 89.

Table 3.4, continued

CREMATION DATA

Fea.	Burial Type	Stra-tum	Depth (MBD)	Grave Facility	#	Age	Gender	Associated Artifacts	Comments
94	Urns?	10/60	6.40-6.70	Pit, possibly circular, 0.44 m in diameter	S	I	I	Reconstructible vessels: 1 plain ware flaring-neck jar, 1 plain ware rectangular bowl, 1 indet. Colonial Red-on-brown scoop (all in FN 2145); 2 plain ware sherds.	Feature badly disturbed by backhoe so that exact relationship of vessels to pit is unknown. No flotation or pollen samples collected.
104	Urn with cover vessel	10/60	6.39-6.55	Pit, roughly circular, 0.20 m in diameter	S	I	I	Reconstructible vessels: 1 Rillito Red-on-brown flare-rimmed bowl, 1 Rillito Red-on-brown flaring-necked jar (FN2176, 2177).	1 flotation and 1 pollen sample collected; flotation sample analyzed.
105	Primary cremation?	10	6.52-6.73	Pit, roughly circular, 0.40 m in diameter	S	Adult?	I	Shell: 38 Nerita beads and bead fragments; animal bones; bone artifacts: 1 awl (FN2231); hairpin fragments and awl fragments (collected from F. 105/108).	Pit was heavily oxidized, vitrified in places, and bone was in large pieces, suggesting this may have been a primary cremation feature. 2 flotation and 2 pollen samples collected, not analyzed (F. 108).
106	Inverted bowl	10/60	6.48-6.69	Pit, roughly circular, 0.40 m in diameter	S	I	I	1 Rillito Red-on-brown white slipped flare-rimmed bowl (FN2172).	1 pollen sample collected, not analyzed.
108	Primary cremation? (cremated bone with sherd covering)	10/60	6.50-6.74	Pit, roughly circular, 0.35 m in diameter	S	Adult?	I	1 reconstructible plain ware flaring-necked jar (FN2238, 2247); 2 plain ware sherds; animal bones; 1 bone awl fragment (other awl and hairpin fragments collected as from F. 105/108; 8 projectile points (FN2240, 2251, 2253-2255, 2314-2315); 2 others collected as from 105/108 (FN2312-2313).	Feature lay within an oval ashy area together with F. 105. Heavy oxidation of pit walls, suggesting it was a primary cremation feature. 2 flotation and 1 pollen samples collected, not analyzed.
109	Cremated bone	60	6.49-6.87	Oval pit, 0.44 m N-S by 0.56 m E-W	S	Adult	I	2 sherds (1 plain ware, 1 decorated); 1 animal bone.	No flotation or pollen samples collected; pit not well defined.
118	Cremated bone	60	6.55-6.71	Pit, roughly circular, about 0.45 m in diameter	S	Adult	I	4 plain ware sherds; flaked stone (not analyzed): 1 projectile point (FN2343); shell: 25 Nerita beads and bead fragments (13 more from Str. 50 above feature); 1 animal bone, 2 bone hairpin fragments (1 fits with fragments from F. 105 and F. 108).	No flotation or pollen samples collected.
119	Urn with sherd covering	60	6.08-6.31	Pit, roughly circular, 0.22 m in diameter	S	Adult	Female	1 reconstructible plain ware flaring-necked jar (FN2349, 2351); 63 sherds (61 plain ware, 2 unidentified).	No real pit was definable; feature limits were determined by extent of vessel and sherds; no flotation or pollen samples collected.
129	Urn?	-	Unknown	Unknown	S	Child (3-6 years)	I	1 reconstructible Santa Cruz flaring-necked jar (FN 2385); 5 plain ware sherds.	Feature was totally removed by backhoe so provenience is approximate. No flotation or pollen samples collected.
137	Urn with cover vessel	60	4.27-4.62	Pit not discernible; estimated as just larger than vessel at 0.22 m in diameter	S	I	I	1 plain ware flaring-necked jar (FN2390), 1 plain ware incurved jar (FN2388); sherds: 8 plain ware sherds; animal bones.	1 pollen sample collected.

S = Single
I = Indeterminate
MBD = Meters below datum

The small amount and generally poor condition of the recovered burned bone allowed only for the most general interpretations of the age, sex, and health of the individuals. As Fox points out in her analysis of the cremated bone (Volume 5, Appendix G), residue from several incinerated bodies was very likely to be interred in one or more pits, a practice mentioned by Haury (1976: 171) for cremated remains from Snaketown, and the cremations may in fact represent fewer than 22 individuals.

Comparison with Other Colonial Period Cremation Assemblages

Rillito phase cremation assemblages have been documented at two sites in the Tucson Basin. At the southern end of the basin is Punta de Agua (AZ BB:13:16 and AZ BB:13:43; Greenleaf 1975) with 8 Rillito phase cremations; at the northern end is the Hodges Ruin (AZ AA:12:18; Kelly 1978) with 33 late Colonial period interments.

The eight cremations from Punta de Agua are secondary burials. Greenleaf (1975: 102) identified three as Type I cremations that consisted of calcined bone placed in a bowl or jar that was placed in a burial pit. When a jar was used, it was placed upright in the pit and might or might not have a covering vessel. Five are Type II cremations; the calcined bone was put in a bowl, which was then inverted in a pit with a second bowl often placed over the inverted bowl. The Punta de Agua cremations had few personal ornaments or ceramic or stone offerings; in general, they consisted of calcined bone, a container, and usually a covering vessel that was sometimes "killed" by means of a hole punched out of the bottom (Greenleaf 1975: 102).

At the Hodges Ruin, 28 of the 33 Rillito phase cremations reported by Kelly (1978) were sufficiently intact to provide some information. Interments at the Hodges Ruin were more varied and much more elaborate in their grave offerings than those from Punta de Agua; they appear to be more like the cremations from the Gila Basin (for example, Haury 1976). Fourteen interments consisted of calcined bone mixed with sherds or broken pots. Eight others were primary cremations; two more were urn cremations (upright bowls with calcined bone and no covering vessel), and four were inverted bowls or jars placed over residual bone. The use of an inverted vessel or large sherd to serve as a cover over a pile of residual bone and ash apparently first appeared during the Rillito phase (Kelly 1978: 125).

Cremation offerings were plentiful and varied with ceramics usually present in the form of painted, red, and plain ware vessels. Scoops, jars, flare-rimmed bowls, and plates were common forms. Combinations of artifacts--shell beads, pendants, and bracelets; stone palettes and pendants; projectile points; worked bone; and sherds--were also typical.

The cremations from Water World are similar to those from the Hodges Ruin in both the variety of cremation types and the relative abundance and variety of grave offerings. Cremations with and without covering vessels, cremated bone mixed with artifacts but without a covering vessel, an inverted bowl or large sherd covering a residual pile of bone, and primary cremations were present at both sites. The Type I (bone in upright jar) and Type II (bowl or jar inverted over bone) cremations from Punta de Agua also were found at Water World, but as previously noted, grave offerings were not common at Punta de Agua.

Outside the Tucson Basin, five cremations were found at the Picacho Pass Site (NA 18,030) on Phase A of the Tucson Aqueduct (Greenwald and Ciolek-Torrello 1987: 162, 164). Two of these were primary cremations without grave goods that dated to the late Colonial period. The other three secondary cremations were found in small pits. Sherds from one or more vessels were found in the pits, and one cremation had a large inverted cover bowl. No other artifacts were found associated with these cremations, which apparently date to the late Colonial period.

The five cremations from the Picacho Pass Site were interpreted as cemetery plots associated with an individual house cluster (Greenwald and Ciolek-Torrello 1987: 164). The two small groups of cremations found at Water World near the ballcourt and near House Group 3 may likewise have served as cemetery plots for adjacent residential units.

Possible Inhumation

Feature 45 was identified as a pit in a trench wall on the far eastern edge of the site (Fig. 1.6; Table 3.4)). A few pieces of badly eroded bone were recovered when the feature was recorded, but could not be definitely identified as human. Most of the feature was removed by the backhoe, and there is little evidence to positively identify the feature as an inhumation.

Chapter 4

CERAMICS

William L. Deaver

The single most remarkable characteristic of the pottery
collection from Water World is its chronological homogeneity. Without
exception, the identifiable Tucson and Gila Basin Hohokam pottery types
belong to the Colonial period, most representing the contemporaneous
Rillito and Santa Cruz phases. Although pottery assigned to various
indeterminate categories suggests the possibility of slightly earlier
and later occupations, no pottery was positively identified as belonging
to any but the Colonial period. These data confirm the results of
analysis of ceramics from the survey and testing phase: Rillito Red-on-
brown was the dominant ceramic type, and Cañada del Oro Red-on-brown
also occurred (Rankin and Downum 1986: 73-77). Intrusive pottery types
from northern Sonora and southeastern Arizona recovered at Water World
neither support nor contradict this conclusion.

The pottery collection from Water World, plus that from Fastimes
(AZ AA:12:384), provides a unique opportunity to study the Tucson Basin
Colonial period pottery tradition without a significant mixture of older
and younger pottery. Pure deposits of Colonial period pottery are rare,
usually restricted to cremation offerings (Wallace 1985: 93), and no
single-component sites dating to the Colonial period have been reported
until now.

The Ceramic Collection

The 1986 and 1987 archaeological excavations at Water World
(AZ AA:16:94) yielded 15,021 sherds (Table 4.1) and 32 whole or
partially restorable vessels (Table 4.2). All worked sherds were first
classified and counted as bulk sherds and were then categorized
according to the kinds of secondary modifications present. Basic
typological data and analytic methods are presented in Volume 2, Chapter
3 and in Volume 5, Appendix A-1. A detailed discussion of the analytic
methods that guided the ceramic analysis can be found in the Arizona
State Museum (ASM) Library Archives (Deaver 1987).

The following discussion is based on a typological
classification, and references to technological and decorative features

TABLE 4.1

CERAMIC COUNTS BY POTTERY TYPE

Ceramic Types	Count	Percent
Unidentified	1,512	10.07
Decorated		
Indeterminate Tucson-Gila Basin		
Indeterminate Rillito-Santa Cruz	1	0.01
Indeterminate Colonial-Sedentary	1	0.01
Tucson Basin red-on-brown		
Indeterminate	37	0.25
Indeterminate, white slip	8	0.05
Indeterminate Snaketown-Cañada del Oro	1	0.01
Cañada del Oro	23	0.15
Indeterminate Colonial	618	4.11
Indeterminate Colonial, white slip	13	0.09
Rillito	716	4.77
Rillito, white slip	10	0.07
Indeterminate Rillito-Rincon	19	0.13
Crude	2	0.01
Gila Basin red-on-buff		
Indeterminate buff ware	22	0.15
indeterminate red-on-buff	19	0.13
Gila Butte	2	0.01
Santa Cruz	48	0.32
Indeterminate Santa Cruz-Sacaton	11	0.07
Sonoran		
Trincheras Purple-on-red, specular	7	0.05
San Simon red-on-brown		
Dos Cabezas	1	0.01
Red Ware		
Indeterminate	3	0.02
Possible Red Ware	3	0.02
Plain Ware	11,944	79.52
Total	15,021	100.03

of the pottery are based on informal observations made during the typological analysis. Identifiable pottery types are emphasized, and discussions of technology and manufacture, as well as discussions and illustrations of designs, should not be viewed as a systematic

TABLE 4.2

INVENTORY OF RECONSTRUCTIBLE AND WHOLE VESSELS

Vessel Number	Feature	FN	Type	Shape	Sherd Counts Body	Sherd Counts Rim
1	85	2066	Rillito Red-on-brown	Flare-rimmed bowl	1	8
2	104	2176, 2177	Rillito Red-on-brown	Flare-rimmed bowl	26	5
3	104	2176, 2177	Rillito Red-on-brown	Flaring-necked jar	12	5
4	106	2172	Rillito Red-on-brown, white slip	Flare-rimmed bowl	41	9
5	88	2011, 2012, 2013 2014, 2025	Rillito Red-on-brown, white slip	Flare-rimmed bowl	33	17
6	25	71, 107, 121, 181	Cañada del Oro Red-on-brown	Flare-rimmed bowl	107	16
7	27	495	Rillito Red-on-brown	Flare-rimmed bowl	18	3
8	96	2149	Rillito Red-on-brown	Flare-rimmed bowl	36	13
9	19	37	Plain ware (miniature)	Slight-incurve jar	1	2
10	55	848	Plain ware (miniature)	Outcurved bowl	0	2
11	19	307	Plain ware (miniature)	Outcurved bowl	0	3
12	19	26	Plainw are	Scoop	6	6
13	94	2145	Plain ware	Flaring-necked jar	18	6
14	40	96	Plain ware	Flare-rimmed bowl	0	3
15	55	849	Plain ware (miniature)	Scoop	0	1
16	55	852	Plain ware (miniature)	Scoop	0	1
17	87.1	2016, 2017, 2020	Plain ware	Flaring-necked jar	12	6
18	87.1	2018	Plain ware	Hemispherical bowl	0	2
19	108	2238, 2247	Plain ware	Flaring-necked jar	24	4
20	94	2145	Plain ware	Rectangular bowl	0	4
21	94	2145	Indeterminate Colonial Red-on-brown	Scoop	0	2
22	87.1	2015	Plain ware	Flaring-necked jar	0	1
23	88	2010	Plain ware	Upcurved-necked jar	0	1
24	40	98	Plain ware	Flaring-necked jar	0	1
25	58	1258, 1262	Plain ware	Flaring-necked jar	130	5
26	87.1	2016, 2025, 2110	Rillito Red-on-brown	Slightly incurved neckless jar	220	12
27	119	2349, 2351	Plain ware	Flaring-necked jar	1	3
28	137	2390	Plain ware	Flaring necked jar		4
29	129	2385	Santa Cruz Red-on-buff	Flaring-necked jar	35	0
30	137	2388	Plain ware	Pronounced incurved jar	53	13
31	138	2397	Rillito Red-on-brown	Flare-rimmed bowl	65	7
32	107	2321	Rillito Red-on-brown	Flare-rimmed bowl	51	0

representation of the overall collection. The various "indeterminate" categories listed in Table 4.1 are more fully defined in the discussion on analytic methods in the ASM Library Archives and are only briefly mentioned here.

Refitting Study

The excavated features at Water World have been divided into seven house groups and a cremation area (Fig. 1.6; Chapter 2). Each of the house groups and the cremation area were initially assumed to represent discrete loci of activity and trash deposition. This assumption was tested by examining the distribution of decorated pottery sherds that have been refitted (Table 4.3). Matches between several

TABLE 4.3

DECORATED SHERD MATCHES

No.	Type of Mend	Feature	House Group	Stratum	Level	FSN	To Feature	House Group	Stratum	Level	FSN	Phase
1	Definite	33	3	02	01	776	53	3	02	02	805	Rillito
				02	02	888						
				20		787						
				20		790						
				20		792						
				20		959						
				20		1037						
				20		1047						
				20		1145						
2	Definite	25	1	01	01	71	55	1	01	01	578	Rillito
3	Definite	68	6	02	01	1567	27	3	30	01	439	Cañada del Oro
4	Probable	26	2	01	01	1094	Mend Number 3 above					Cañada del Oro
5	Probable	58	4	50	02	1215	67	6	01	01	1531	Rillito
				50	02	1382						
				30	01	1388						
6	Probable	58	4	50	01	1212	67	6	01	01	1531	Rillito
				50	02	1215						
				50	02	1382						
7	Probable	67	6	01	01	1531	68	6	20		1941	Rillito
									20		1944	
									20		1950	
8	Probable	58	4	50	02	1382	67	6	01	01	1531	Rillito
9	Probable	78	5	50	02	2203	79	5	01	01	2078	Rillito
10	Probable	66		01	01	2041	Mends 3 and 4 above					Cañada del Oro
				02	01	2033						

F = Feature
HG = House Group
S = Stratum
L = Level
FSN = Field Specimen Number

house groups indicate that the deposition of ceramics is not discrete within each house group (Table 4.4). This patterning may indicate that the disposal activities from which the pottery collection resulted were more dispersed at Water World than at Fastimes where no refitted ceramics between house groups were noted, and that there is little distinctiveness between house groups. Comparisons between house groups were not made because they did not appear to represent independent deposits.

Decorated Pottery

A total of 1,559 sherds and 13 restorable vessels constitutes the collection of decorated pottery recovered from Water World. Approximately 48 percent of the decorated pottery could not be

TABLE 4.4

SUMMARY OF DECORATED POTTERY MATCHES BY HOUSE GROUP

House Group	to	House Group	Number of Mends
1		1	1
3		3	1
6		3	1
2		6	1
2		3	1
4		6	3
5		5	1
6		6	1

identified to type; however, all but two sherds were identified to specific ware-series representing general regional geographic source areas (Table 4.1).

Tucson Basin Painted Pottery

Tucson Basin red-on-brown sherds were the most common decorated pottery type totaling 1,447 sherds, or 9.63 percent of all sherds and 92.82 percent of all painted sherds. Twelve of the restorable decorated vessels were red-on-brown. Approximately 48 percent of all red-on-brown sherds and one restorable vessel were too badly weathered or broken to be identified to type. Two types were represented among identifiable sherds and vessels: Cañada del Oro Red-on-brown and Rillito Red-on-brown. Most of the indeterminate sherds are classified as Indeterminate Colonial period red-on-brown (Table 4.1), meaning that they could be either Cañada del Oro or Rillito Red-on-brown. Given the preponderance of Rillito phase ceramics, most probably represent Rillito phase vessels. The remaining indeterminate sherds also were probably from Colonial period vessels, again in all likelihood Rillito Red-on-brown.

Cañada Del Oro Red-on-Brown

The Cañada del Oro Red-on-brown collection consists of 23 sherds and 1 partial vessel. These pieces exhibit characteristics and attributes typically accorded to this type (Kelly 1978; Deaver 1984; Wallace 1985; Whittlesey 1986). Rim sherds (Table 4.5) and the single restorable vessel (Table 4.2) indicate that only bowls are present in the collection. The absence of body sherds with decoration on the convex surface supports this interpretation. The absence of jars may

Table 4.5

VESSEL SHAPE BY POTTERY TYPE AND VESSELS FORM FOR RIM SHERDS

Ware or Type	BOWLS							JARS					Total
			Direct-Rimmed					Neckless			Necked		
	Indeterminate Shape	Indeterminate	Indet.	Hemisphere	Out-Curved	Scoop	Flare-Rimmed	Indet.	Slight Incurve	Pronounced Incurve	Flared	Uncurved	
Unidentified	10 (52.6)	1 (5.3)	6 (31.6)	0	0	0	0	0	0	0	2 (10.5)	0	19 (100.0)
Tucson Basin? Red-on-brown	1 (25.0)	0	2 (50.0)	1 (25.0)	0	0	0	0	0	0	0	0	4 (100.0)
Tucson Basin? Red-on-brown white slip	0	0	0	3 (100.0)	0	0	0	0	0	0	0	0	3 (100.0)
Cañada del Oro Red-on-brown	1 (9.1)	0	0	0	1 (9.1)	0	9 (81.8)	0	0	0	0	0	11 (100.0)
Tucson Basin? - Colonial	6 (5.8)	10 (9.7)	4 (3.9)	1 (1.0)	1 (1.0)	0	74 (71.8)	3 (2.9)	1 (1.0)	0	3 (2.9)	0	103 (100.0)
Tucson Basin? - Colonial white slip	0	0	0	0	0	0	2 (100.0)	0	0	0	0	0	2 (100.0)
Rillito Red-on-brown	2 (1.3)	1 (0.6)	4 (2.5)	4 (2.5)	10 (6.3)	2 (1.3)	123 (76.9)	1 (0.6)	5 (3.1)	2 (1.3)	6 (3.8)	0	160 (100.2)
Rillito Red-on-brown white slip	0	0	0	0	0	0	10 (100.0)	0	0	0	0	0	10 (100.0)
?Rillito-Rincon	0	0	0	0	0	0	3 (100.0)	0	0	0	0	0	3 (100.0)
Crude Red-on-brown	0	0	0	0	0	0	0	0	0	0	2 (100.0)	0	2 (100.0)
Santa Cruz Red-on-buff	0	0	0	0	0	0	4 (100.0)	0	0	0	0	0	4 (100.0)
?Santa Cruz - Sacaton	0	0	1 (100.0)	0	0	0	0	0	0	0	0	0	1 (100.0)
Trincheras Purple-on-red	0	0	0	0	4 (100.0)	0	0	0	0	0	0	0	4 (100.0)
Plain Ware	348 (38.7)	10 (1.1)	127 (14.1)	71 (7.9)	63 (7.0)	1 (0.1)	16 (1.8)	7 (0.8)	8 (0.9)	21 (2.3)	216 (24.0)	11 (1.2)	899 (99.9)
	368 (30.0)	22 (1.8)	144 (11.8)	80 (6.5)	79 (6.4)	3 (0.2)	241 (19.7)	11 (0.9)	14 (1.1)	23 (1.9)	229 (18.7)	11 (0.9)	1,225 (99.9)

indicate that the Cañada del Oro phase pottery tradition is not fully represented and that the few sherds of Cañada del Oro Red-on-brown recovered may represent heirloom vessels brought to Water World during the initial settlement. Alternatively, Cañada del Oro Red-on-brown jar sherds may be less easily distinguished from Rillito Red-on-brown jar sherds.

Cañada del Oro Red-on-brown occurs in only six pit houses: Features 7, 19, 25, 26, 33, and 58 (Volume 5, Appendix A-4). The maximum number of sherds from any single feature is 7; this type never accounts for more than 1.1 percent of all sherds recovered from a feature and never more than 9.09 percent of all decorated sherds. In contrast, in all houses where Cañada del Oro Red-on-brown occurs, the frequency of Rillito Red-on-brown ranges from 39 to 66 percent of the decorated sherds.

Figures 4.1 and 4.2 illustrate examples of the decoration present on the single reconstructible vessel and selected sherds, respectively. In all but one case (Fig. 4.2a-a') the primary design field is the interior of the vessel. Interior designs include negative life forms (Fig. 4.2b), negative zigzag (Fig. 4.2d), serration of lines and other elements (Fig. 4.2c, e, g); wavy-line hachure-fill (Fig. 4.2a), and one instance of hachure-filled motifs (Fig. 4.1). Exterior designs consist of wavy-line hachure-filled panels (Fig. 4.2a'), closely spaced trailing lines (Fig. 4.2d', f'), plain hachure-filled triangles pendent from the rim (Fig. 4.2e'), and widely spaced trailing lines (Fig. 4.1).

For the most part the primary field of decoration has stronger similarities to Rillito Red-on-brown than to the late Pioneer type Snaketown Red-on-buff. This suggests that the Cañada del Oro from Water World is stylistically, typologically, and temporally late. The single restorable vessel of this type (Fig. 4.1) is about one-half of a large flare-rimmed bowl found on the floor of pit house Feature 25. The design is badly weathered and cannot be completely discerned, but what is visible indicates a design composed of double interlocking scrolls with serrated, hachure-filled "backs" that are connected to other similar motifs (Fig. 4.1). The use of hachure-fill in the primary design is a carry-over from the late Pioneer period decorative style typical of Snaketown Red-on-buff (Haury 1976: 214-216). The spacing of the hachure and its use in combination with solid-line motifs led to the identification as Cañada del Oro Red-on-brown. The exterior is decorated with several widely spaced trailing lines, an exterior treatment more commonly associated with Rillito Red-on-brown. The remaining sherds of Cañada del Oro Red-on-brown have design motifs similar to those found on the Rillito Red-on-brown sherds, but have exterior design patterns considered characteristic of Cañada del Oro Red-on-brown, such as hachure-filled triangles and panels pendent from the rim and closely spaced trailing lines (Fig. 4.2). The only interior designs in this collection that appear more commonly on Cañada del Oro Red-on-brown than on Rillito Red-on-brown are those shown in Figure 4.2a, f, and g. That many of the other interior design treatments are

VESSEL 6

Figure 4.1. Cañada del Oro Red-on-brown flare-rimmed bowl (Vessel 6) from floor of pit house Feature 25 (diameter is approximately 46 cm).

Figure 4.2.   Cañada Del Oro Red-on-brown interior and exterior design treatments; all sherds from bowls (height of <u>a</u>: 9.6 cm).

similar to Rillito Red-on-brown may explain the apparent absence of Cañada del Oro Red-on-brown jars in the collection. Whereas exterior decoration of bowls is used in part to define this type, there is no such corroborating aid in identifying jars. Without these exterior decorations, many of these bowl sherds would have been classified as Rillito Red-on-brown. Based on the decorative treatment of the Cañada del Oro Red-on-brown pottery pieces, it is tempting to say that the single flare-rimmed bowl is earlier than the miscellaneous sherds; its primary decoration harkens back to late Pioneer period decorative style, whereas the sherds have primary designs strongly resembling Rillito Red-on-brown.

In support of the interpretation that the Cañada del Oro Red-on-brown vessels are perhaps heirlooms, the single restorable vessel found on the floor of Feature 25 is stratigraphically out of place. Pit house Feature 25 overlies an earlier pit house, Feature 55, in which the only identified pottery type is Rillito Red-on-brown. Furthermore, the other Cañada del Oro Red-on-brown sherds occur in midden and house fill deposits where the dominant decorated type is always Rillito Red-on-brown; only a single sherd is recovered from floor contact (Feature 7). Apparently there has been some redeposition of Cañada del Oro sherds: six sherds, probably from a single vessel, occur in three different midden deposits (Features 68, 27, and 26; see also Table 4.3). The maximum distance between features (Features 68 and 26) is 152 m.

No sherds of Cañada del Oro Red-on-brown were identified that have a whitish or cream-colored wash, an absence possibly attributable to the small sample size. Also lacking is any exterior grooving; however, this may generally be rare on Cañada del Oro Red-on-brown when compared to the analogous Gila Basin type, Gila Butte Red-on-buff (Deaver 1984: 289). A cursory inspection of the sherds suggests that this type as represented at Water World is tempered with a mixture of sand and crushed micaceous rock.

Specific aspects of vessel form are identified from 11 sherds (Table 4.5). All rims but one are from bowls, and the single exception is an indeterminate form. The flare-rimmed bowl is the most common form, represented by nine rim sherds and one restorable vessel. Also represented among the rim sherds is a direct-rimmed, outcurving bowl. Although only a few sherds are present, the array of vessel forms is consistent with shapes documented in other Cañada del Oro Red-on-brown collections (Kelly 1978; Deaver 1984; Whittlesey 1986).

Rillito Red-on-Brown

Rillito Red-on-brown is the dominant pottery type (Table 4.1), outnumbering Cañada del Oro by a ratio of approximately 32:1. The collection contains 726 sherds and 10 restorable vessels, constituting 46.57 percent of all decorated sherds and 50.17 percent of all Tucson Basin red-on-brown sherds. The identified Rillito Red-on-brown sherds exhibit aspects of design and form typically attributed to this type

(Kelly 1978; Deaver 1984; Wallace 1985; Whittlesey 1986) and can be considered "classic" Rillito (Figs. 4.3 through 4.10). Unlike Cañada del Oro Red-on-brown, both bowls and jars are represented, with bowls outnumbering jars by 10.3:1. The presence of both classes of vessel shape indicates a fuller expression of the Rillito phase pottery tradition at Water World than was exhibited for the Cañada del Oro Red-on-brown pottery tradition.

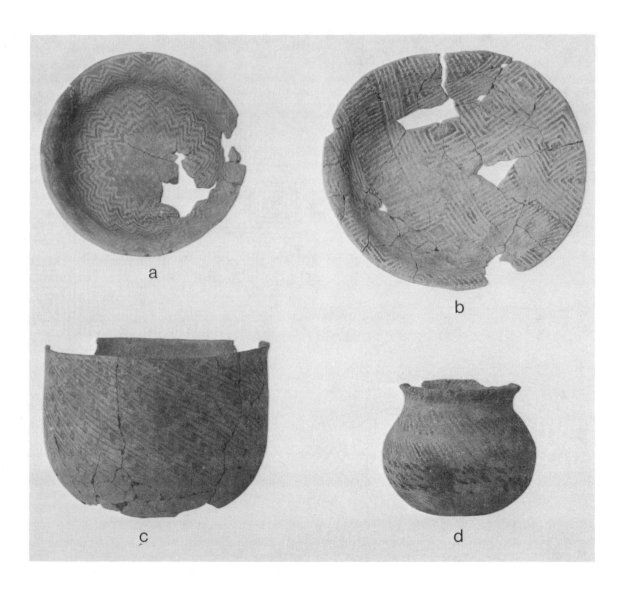

Figure 4.3. Rillito Red-on-brown vessels: a-b, flare-rimmed bowls (Vessel 2, Feature 104 and Vessel 5, Feature 88, respectively); c, incurved jar (Vessel 26, Feature 87.1); d, flaring-necked jar (Vessel 3, Feature 104) (diameter of a: 21.9 cm). Also see Figures 4.5 and 4.6.

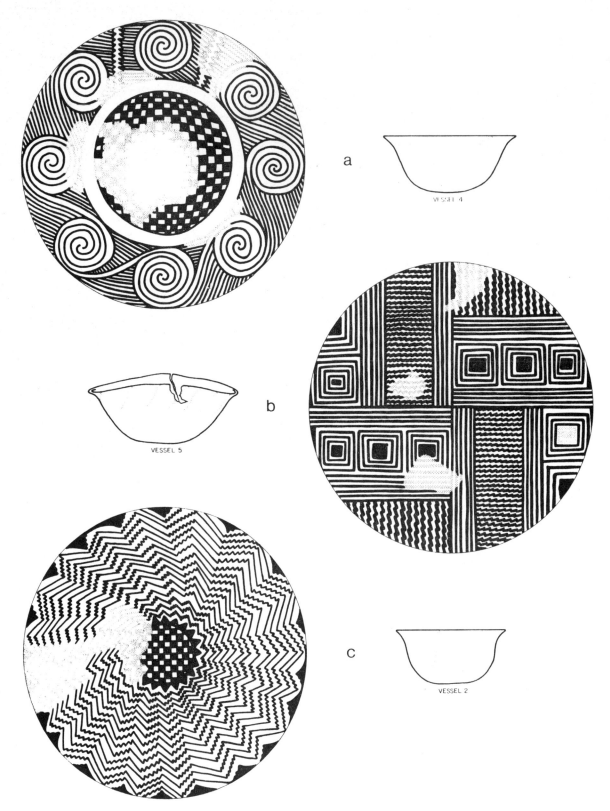

Figure 4.4. Rillito Red-on-brown flare-rimmed bowl designs: <u>a</u>, Vessel 4, Feature 106; <u>b</u>, Vessel 5, Feature 88; <u>c</u>, Vessel 2, Feature 104 (designs shown at arbitrary scales, vessel profiles shown at standardized scale; diameter of <u>a</u>: 25.8 cm).

Figure 4.5.   Rillito Red-on-brown designs: a, flare-rimmed bowl (Vessel 1, Feature 85); b, flaring-necked jar (Vessel 3, Feature 104); c, slight incurve neckless jar (Vessel 26, Feature 87.1) (diameter of c: 23.5 cm).

        Six of the restorable vessels are illustrated in Figures 4.3, 4.4, and 4.5. A sample of sherds representing typical design treatments is illustrated in Figures 4.6, 4.7, 4.8, 4.9, and 4.10. Generally, the primary design field is the interior of the bowls and the exterior of the jars; a few exceptions do occur where the bowl exterior is the primary field. No jars with an interior primary decorative field are present. One feature of the collection is the diversity of decorative

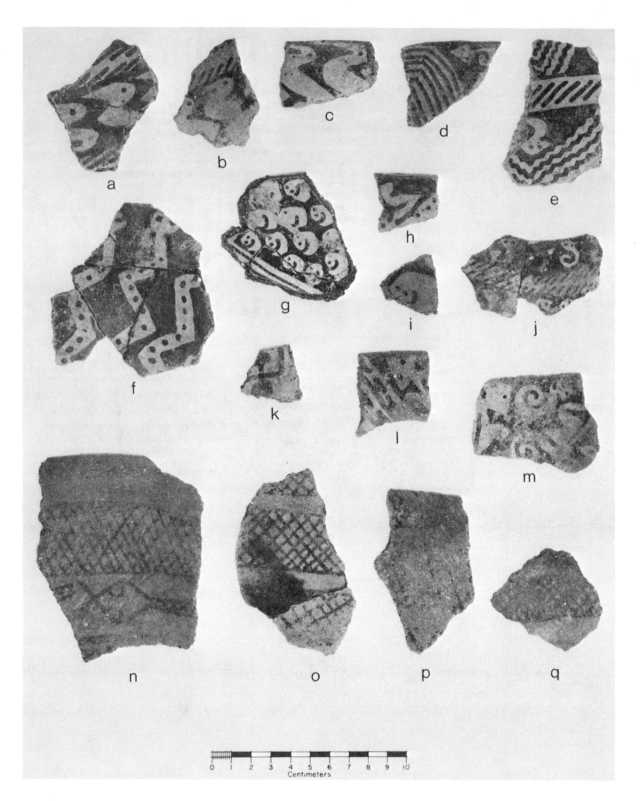

Figure 4.6. Rillito Red-on-brown life forms: a-c, negative birds; d-f, negative snakes; g-i, negative snakes (?); j, positive lizard (?); k-l, negative lizards; m, negative lizards and snakes; n, large-scale positive snakes; o-q, probably same as n (height of n: 10.9 cm).

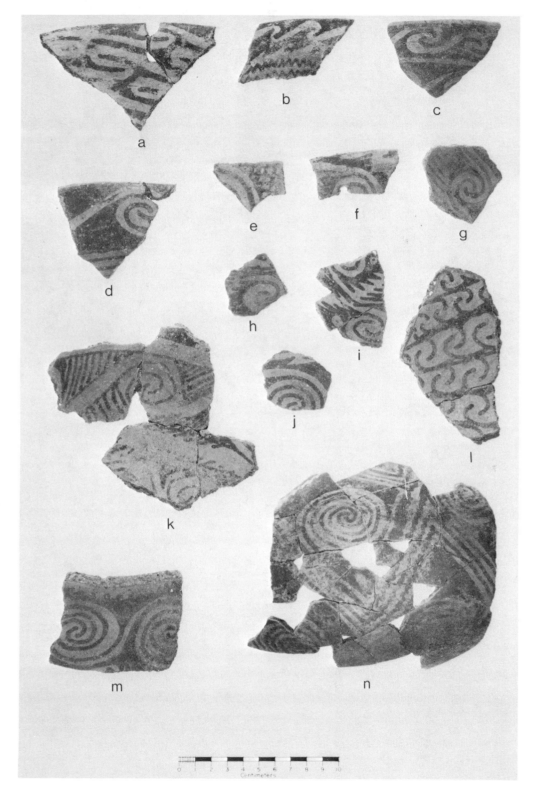

Figure 4.7. Rillito Red-on-brown scrolls: <u>a</u>-<u>d</u>, "running" scrolls; <u>e</u>-<u>k</u>, <u>m</u>-<u>n</u>, scrolls with various edge treatments; <u>l</u>, scroll-derived motif (?) (maximum width of <u>h</u>: 15.8 cm).

Figure 4.8. Rillito Red-on-brown line treatments: a-b, line-and-stagger; c-h, s-t, wavy line hachure; i-m, mixed straight- and wavy-line chevron hachure; n-o, probably mixed chevron hachure; p, plain chevron hachure; q-r, "barred-line" hachure; u, cuneiform hachure (height of u: 12.5 cm).

Figure 4.9. Rillito Red-on-brown miscellaneous design treatments: a, checkerboard; b, cross-hatched; c-d, hachure-filled; e-h, "bull's-eye"; i-m, free fringes; n, fringed-line; o, "L"-fringed line; p-q, free squiggles; r-t, positive "flying birds"; u, negative "flying birds" (width of k: 13.5 cm).

Figure 4.10. Selected Rillito Red-on-brown sherds from the fill of pit house Feature 58: a-t, interior bowl designs; u, interior rim design of flaring-necked jar; v-z, exterior designs, probably from jars (width of z: 16.3 cm).

units. Decorative elements and motifs include positive and negative
life forms (Fig. 4.6); scrolls (Fig. 4.7); various kinds of linework
(Fig. 4.8); small repeated elements (Fig. 4.9); and other miscellaneous
treatments (Fig. 4.9).

Life forms are not common on Rillito Red-on-brown sherds, either
in quantity or in the diversity of figures represented. Only zoomorphic
figures are depicted, the most frequent life form is a snake in both
negative (Fig. 4.6d-f) and positive (Fig. 4.6n) representations. There
is an interesting tadpolelike figure (Fig. 4.6g-j, Fig. 4.10d) that
occurs in several examples and seems to be related to the negative snake
motif (compare these with Fig. 4.6d and e and to Kelly 1978, Fig.
4.19b). An interesting technique for rendering the snake motif is shown
in Figure 4.6n. Although the entire design cannot be postulated from
this single sherd, close inspection indicates that at least two
different snakes are depicted and each band may represent a separate
figure. Other sherds are shown (Fig. 4.6o-q, Fig. 4.10x) that are
probably from similar designs. It is interesting that overall, cross-
hachure is rare for Rillito Red-on-brown, but appears to occur commonly
with this snake motif. This depiction of the snake probably bears more
than a striking resemblance to a Rillito vessel illustrated by Greenleaf
(1975: 47, Fig. 3.2c), and to bird-and-snake motifs on red-on-buff
pottery from Snaketown illustrated by Haury (1976: 232-233, Fig. 12.75).

Only one style of bird figure is depicted and this standardized
form is represented by at least two vessels (Fig. 4.6a-c). Likewise,
three sherds represent lizards rendered in negative (Fig. 4.6h, 1, m)
with triangular heads and probably diamond-shaped bodies (compare Haury
1976: 234-235, and Figs. 12.79-12.81). The life form depicted in Figure
4.6k is problematic and possibly could represent a human figure;
however, it bears more resemblance to simple techniques for depicting
reptiles.

Scrolls usually occur in some variation of an interlocking and
"running" design where one scroll motif is interconnected to another.
This can be a simple interlocking scroll band (Fig. 4.7a-d, i, j, m) or
combined with the mixed wavy-and-straight chevron hachure (Fig. 4.7n).
Figure 4.7 1 depicts a unique design that appears to be a variation of
the simple interlocking scroll. The triangle-shaped base of scrolls are
typically solid (Fig. 4.7a-d, g, m, n), but hachure-fill (Fig. 4.7k),
cross-hachure-fill (Fig. 4.7e), and "bull's-eye" (Fig. 4.7i) also are
present. The edges of the scroll backs are either straight (Fig. 4.7c-
d), serrated (Fig. 4.7b, f, i-k, n), or fringed (Fig. 4.7g, h, k).

Line treatments on the Water World pottery collection also are
typical for Rillito Red-on-brown and include the line-and-stagger motif
(Fig. 4.8a, b, Fig. 4.10p), wavy-line hachure (Fig. 4.8c-h), mixed
straight-and-wavy-line chevron hachure (Fig. 4.7n, Fig. 4.8i-o), plain
chevron hachure (Fig. 4.8p), barred-line hachure (Fig. 4.8q, r), plain
fringed lines (Fig. 4.9n), "T" fringed lines (Fig. 4.6 1), and "L"
fringed lines (Fig. 4.9o). Small repeated elements including fringes
(Fig. 4.9i-m, Fig. 4.10z), free squiggles (Fig. 4.9p-q, Fig. 4.10j), and

flying bird motifs in positive (Fig. 4.9r-t; Fig. 4.10 m, u, v, z) and negative (Fig. 4.9u) also occur. Use of single motifs within a bull's-eye that generally occurs in a triangle-shaped space (Fig. 4.8m, Fig. 4.9e-h) is another typical motif. A single occurrence of a simple checkerboard design was noted in the collection (Fig. 4.9a).

Vessel form information is derived from the classification of 170 rim sherds (Table 4.5). As with Cañada del Oro Red-on-brown, the flare-rimmed bowl is the most common form. There is a greater variety in vessel forms represented, however, undoubtedly due to the larger sample size. Direct-rimmed bowls include hemispherical, outcurving, and scoop varieties. Jar forms are not strongly represented (8.24%), but both neckless, incurved forms as well as necked, flared forms are present.

A variant of Rillito Red-on-brown that has a whitish slip on one or two surfaces is present, represented by 10 sherds (Fig. 4.11b-e) and two restorable vessels (Fig. 4.3b and Fig. 4.4a, b). The white-slipped sherds make up 1.38 percent of all sherds identified as Rillito Red-on-brown and 5.88 percent of rim sherds identified as Rillito Red-on-brown. Although referred to as Rillito Red-on-brown: White-Slipped Variety, the coating is rarely substantial and resembles the wash applied to Gila Basin red-on-buff pottery (Haury 1976). Wiping marks are sometimes evident on the washed surface. Occasionally the surface may be polished after the wash is applied. This variant has been documented at the Rosemont sites where it accounts for 16.2 percent of Rillito rim sherds (Deaver 1984: 299), and at the recent excavations at the Hodges Ruin where this variety constitutes 5.22 percent of Rillito Red-on-brown sherds (Whittlesey 1986: 88, Table 6.15).

The most prevalent tempering material appears to be a mixture of sand and a crushed micaceous rock. Generally, there is good control of the firing atmosphere, and fire clouds usually are small and do not obliterate much of the design. Fire clouds that cover nearly all of the design, such as is typical for early Rincon Red-on-brown (Deaver 1984: 306), are not evident. Figure 4.10 illustrates a collection of Rillito Red-on-brown sherds recovered from Feature 58, showing the range of firing control as well as the diversity of design.

The Rillito Red-on-brown sherds and vessels recovered from Water World represent a typical collection of late Colonial period ceramics. In general there is no direct visual clue to indicate either "early" or "late" Rillito Red-on-brown. It may be possible to sort out a developmental sequence of design attributes with more careful and detailed study and good chronological data. A few sherds identified as Rillito Red-on-brown have decorative characteristics reminiscent of Cañada del Oro Red-on-brown, most obviously the technique of rendering life forms in negative. Other designs that occur more typically on Cañada del Oro than on Rillito are the barred lines (Fig. 4.8q-r), the "L" fringed lines (Fig. 4.9o), the "T" fringed lines (Fig. 4.6 1), and the negative flying bird motif (Fig. 4.9u). All of the sherds that depict these design units lack any kind of exterior decoration that would help to distinguish between Rillito and Cañada del Oro Red-on-brown. Furthermore, none of these designs are duplicated on any sherds that have typical early Colonial exterior design treatments. Serration of double scrolls is given as a diagnostic trait of Cañada del Oro Red-on-brown (Kelly 1978: 24), and those sherds identified as Rillito Red-on-brown with strong serration (Fig. 4.7f, i-k, n) could be classified as Cañada del Oro based on this single characteristic. Although there may be a trend in development from serration on motifs to fringing, it is questionable just how strongly this trait can be used to distinguish Rillito from Cañada del Oro Red-on-brown. Other forms of serration, most notably that which occurs on the border of a triangular unit opposing a squiggle or wavy line (Fig. 4.6e, Fig. 4.7n, Fig. 4.8j, m, o, s, Fig. 4.9c) persist throughout the Rillito phase. Also, in offset quartered layouts where the mixed straight-and-wavy chevron hachure occurs, the margin of the quartering line opposing the wavy part of the hachure is commonly serrated. The tendency to oppose a wavy line with serration is prevalent among Rillito Red-on-brown pottery.

In obvious characteristics Rillito Red-on-brown foreshadows the early Rincon Red-on-brown in that the basic design repertoire used during the early Sedentary is similar to that from the late Colonial. In terms of vessel shape and the execution of design, however, the Water World collection does not strongly resemble early Rincon Red-on-brown (Deaver 1984: 305-322).

"Crude" Red-on-Brown

Two rim sherds come from a single hand-modeled jar with a red painted design (Fig. 4.11a). The examples are sand tempered, and the surfaces are irregular and undulating. By all appearances these sherds seem to represent a painted pinch pot. A similar pottery type was identified in the pottery collection from the Rosemont sites (Deaver 1984: 329-331). At present, little can be said about the occurrence of this kind of pottery.

Intrusive Painted Pottery

Intrusive painted pottery accounts for only 0.73 percent of the collection and 7.06 percent of decorated sherds. One partially restorable vessel of Santa Cruz Red-on-buff was recovered from a cremation during the 1987 field work (Table 4.2, Fig. 4.12). All intrusive sherds are from feature fill (Volume 5, Appendix A-4). This collection is remarkably different from the collection from Fastimes where intrusives account for 3.11 percent of all pottery and 54.05 percent of all painted pottery, as well as seven restorable vessels. Even at the Hodges Ruin, Gila Basin buff wares alone accounted for as much as 40 percent of the decorated pottery in some tests (Kelly

Figure 4.11. Miscellaneous Tucson Basin sherds: a, "crude" red-on-brown; b-e, Rillito Red-on-brown: White-Slipped Variety (height of d: 8.8 cm).

1978: 3). Although intrusive pottery is rare at Water World, the kinds of pottery represented indicate a wide range of contacts.

The dominant intrusive pottery is from the Gila Basin and constitutes 6.54 percent of all decorated pottery and 92.73 percent of all intrusives. Roughly 51 percent of the buff wares could not be identified to type, but of the remaining 49 percent all but two sherds are identified as Santa Cruz Red-on-buff (Fig. 4.13c-i). The final two sherds are identified as Gila Butte Red-on-buff. Only four rim sherds of Santa Cruz Red-on-buff are present, and all are from flare-rimmed bowls (Table 4.5).

Seven sherds from pit house Feature 26 probably represent a single vessel of Trincheras Purple-on-red (Fig. 4.13a). Trincheras pottery is commonly found on Hohokam sites in the Tucson Basin though rarely in any abundance (Deaver 1984: 370). Trincheras pottery is not well dated, but its temporal range includes the Colonial period (Haury 1950; Grebinger 1971; Doyel 1977; Deaver 1984), a fact supported

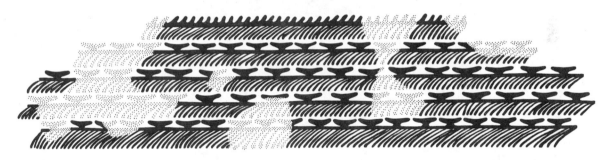

Figure 4.12. Santa Cruz Red-on-buff jar (Vessel 29, Feature 129) and design rendition; maximum width: 16.1 cm.

strongly by this collection. Four rim sherds indicate that the vessel was probably an outcurving bowl (Table 4.5).

A single sherd of Dos Cabezas Red-on-brown (Fig. 4.13b) from the San Simon Series of the Mogollon brown wares (Sayles 1945) was found in the fill of pit house Feature 19. It accounts for only 0.6 percent of the decorated pottery and 0.91 percent of the intrusives. Dos Cabezas Red-on-brown is not firmly dated, but at the Rosemont sites it occurred at only those sites that also yielded Cañada del Oro Red-on-brown, Gila Butte Red-on-buff, and Pioneer period pottery (Deaver 1984: 370). Feature 19 also had a single sherd of Ca~ada del Oro Red-on-brown, although the dominant decorated pottery type was Rillito Red-on-brown. This association confirms the Colonial period date for Dos Cabezas Red-on-brown, even though it cannot be specifically assigned to a phase.

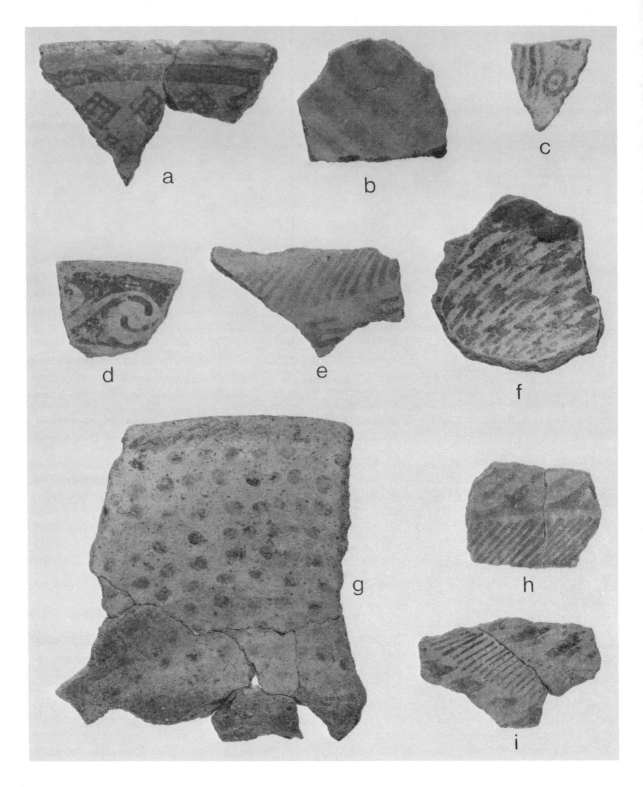

Figure 4.13. Intrusive pottery types: a, Trincheras Purple-on-red; b, Dos Cabezas Red-on-brown; c-i, Santa Cruz Red-on-buff (height of g: 13.2 cm).

Plain Pottery

Undecorated, unslipped pottery constitutes the largest part of the collection: 11,949 sherds and 19 whole or restorable vessels, or 79.52% of all sherds recovered. A cursory inspection of rim sherds indicated that about 72 percent of the plain pottery appeared to be tempered with sand and crushed micaceous rock. These sherds are generally characterized by heavily micaceous surfaces dominated by muscovite mica. The quantity of micaceous rock is variable, however, and some sherds have very little micaceous rock. This group is similar to Type III plain ware identified at the Rosemont sites (Deaver 1984: 348-355), and is probably a local extension of the Gila Basin plain ware tradition typified by Gila Plain. Although crushed micaceous rock seems to have been the dominant tempering material, there is a large number of rim sherds (about 24%) tempered solely with sand that are noticeably less micaceous. Although sherds containing micaceous rock may or may not have a surface sheen, no sand-tempered sherds were found that had a micaceous surface sheen, and phlogopite (gold mica) is the visible micaceous mineral. This group corresponds to Type II plain ware in the Rosemont classification (Deaver 1984: 341-348). Also present is a small quantity (about 3%) of hand-modeled, sand-tempered plain pottery similar to the Type I plain ware identified at the Rosemont sites (Deaver 1984: 335-341). Although the Rosemont Type I plain ware is dominated by small vessels including miniatures, at Water World the hand-modeled plain pottery seems to be exclusively miniatures (Fig. 4.14).

The plain pottery has the widest array of vessel forms of any of the pottery classes and is represented by a sample of 899 rim sherds (Table 4.5). Figures 4.15 and 4.16 illustrate selected reconstructible vessels that represent most of the formal categories. In contrast to the painted pottery, plain rims can be identified to form only on the basis of key shape attributes. Many sherds from vessels with flaring rims have broken in such a way that it is difficult to distinguish between sherds from flare-rimmed bowls and those from flaring-necked jars. Consequently, a large fraction (about 39%) of plain rims are indeterminate in form. Therefore, taking the raw counts at face value, bowls would appear to slightly outnumber jars by 1.09 to 1. Because plain ware flare-rimmed bowls are rare (Table 4.5), it is likely that most Indeterminate Form rim sherds are from jars with flaring necks. When the number of Indeterminate Form flare-rimmed sherds are added to the number of jar rims, then jars outnumber bowls 2.12 to 1. It is clear that the relative ratio of plain ware bowls to jars is greatly dependent on the interpretation of the large class of Indeterminate Form rim sherds.

The most striking characteristic of the array of shapes is the low percentage of flare-rimmed bowls (Table 4.5), which account for only 1.8 percent of all forms and 5.6 percent of bowls. Plain ware flare-rimmed bowls tend to have short, abrupt rims (Fig. 4.15b). Conversely, plain ware direct-rimmed bowls account for 29.03 percent of all forms and 90.6 percent of all bowl forms. This is in contrast to painted

Figure 4.14. Miniature vessels: <u>a-d</u>, bowls; <u>e</u>, scoop (length of <u>e</u>: 9.2 cm).

Figure 4.15. Plain ware bowls: <u>a</u>, outcurved rim, Vessel 18, Feature 87.1; <u>b</u>, flare-rimmed, Vessel 14, Feature 40; <u>c</u>, rectangular, Vessel 20, Feature 94 (height of <u>b</u>: 11.3 cm).

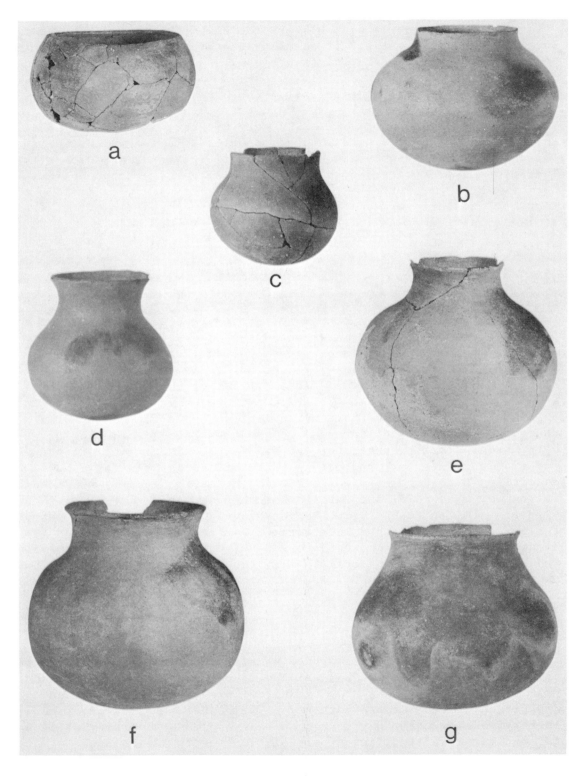

Figure 4.16. Plain ware jars: a, incurved rim, Vessel 30, Feature 137; b-c, upturned neck, Vessels 23, Feature 88 and Vessel 17, Feature 87.1; respectively; d-g, flaring-necked, Vessel 24, Feature 40; Vessel 27, Feature 119; Vessel 28, Feature 137; and Vessel 22, Feature 87.1; respectively (height of f: 23.9 cm).

vessels where flare-rimmed bowls are the dominant form represented.
Based on this information, it seems evident that plain and painted
pottery have different formal traditions.

A single rectangular vessel (Table 4.2; Fig. 4.15c) was
recovered from the cremation area and bears a strong resemblance to
"elongate vessels" identified at Snaketown (Haury 1976: 227). All of
the Snaketown examples have abraded interior bottoms, which led Haury to
the conclusion that they may have been chili graters, or molcajetes.
The specimen from Water World also has an abraded interior bottom. This
form is not represented in the sherd counts because it is difficult to
identify in sherd form unless the sherd represents a corner; otherwise
it is classified as an indeterminate, direct-rimmed bowl.

Red-Slipped Pottery

Because the dominant painted pottery types are identified to the
Colonial period, it is to be expected that red-slipped pottery, if
present, would be rare. The Colonial period is a stage in ceramic
development between the final production of the Pioneer period red-
slipped pottery tradition and the emergence of the Sedentary period red-
slipped pottery tradition. Three red-slipped sherds, accounting for
only 0.02 percent of the pottery collection, occur at Water World. All
three come from a single provenience and may represent a single vessel.
No rim sherds are present, but the pieces are slipped on both the
interior and exterior, indicating that the sherds are from a bowl. It
is difficult to determine whether this pottery is locally produced or
intrusive. The color and softness of the paste and the color of the
slip are similar to San Simon Red-on-brown pottery, but these characteristics also are within the range of variation seen on sherds typed as
Rincon Red. These three sherds may represent intrusive pottery from the
San Simon Mogollon or a local continuation of the Pioneer red-slipped
pottery tradition of the Gila Basin, or even the beginnings of the later
Sedentary red-slipped pottery tradition represented locally by Rincon
Red. Regardless, red-slipped pottery does not constitute a significant
fraction of the pottery collection.

In addition to these three sherds are another three sherds that
have the bright red color and well-polished surface typical of red ware
traditions. But because they lack a definite red slip they cannot be
classified as red-slipped pottery. These sherds may be oxidized plain
pottery, but even if they represent red wares, such pottery still does
not constitute a significant part of the pottery assemblage.

Colonial Period Tucson Basin Pottery Production

The preceding discussion has provided a descriptive summary of
the Water World pottery collection. The basis for studying material

remains is to use the material objects as a foundation upon which to build inferences concerning the nonmaterial aspects of past societies. In order to discuss aspects of Colonial period pottery production for Water World, a conversion must be made from sherds back to the unit of production, a pot. The total number of sherds produced when a vessel breaks is directly proportional to the surface area of the vessel, holding other factors constant such as the kind of breakage (Deaver 1987). This affects not only the number of sherds that can result from the breakage of bowls and jars, but also the relative contribution to the sherd collection of painted, plain, and red-slipped pottery types if each class of pottery has a different range in frequency of bowls or jars, or in vessel sizes. Plain and painted pottery have distinctly different arrays of vessel shapes in terms of both the ratio of bowls to jars and the array of shapes. If jars produce more sherds than bowls, and there is a greater proportion of plain jars than painted, then plain pottery will be more heavily represented in the total sherd count. This fact alone argues that comparisons of the total number of sherds of one class of pottery to another class would not reflect the relative proportion of vessels produced. The intent of this discussion is to interpret from the sherd data the relative level of production of each class of pottery. To do this frequencies of various pottery classes are computed only on the basis of rim sherds. Admittedly rim sherd counts are not the perfect solution to the problem at hand, but this method presents fewer interpretive problems than counts including bulk body sherds (Deaver 1987).

Two facts about the pottery collection emerge immediately from the data. First, the percentage of red-on-brown pottery is high, and second, the percentage of intrusive pottery is low. As noted above, red-on-brown sherds constitute 9.63 percent of all sherds. But when this same calculation is based only on rim sherds, then red-on-brown pottery accounts for 24.33 percent of all sherds. Although this figure is surprisingly high, there are few other Colonial age collections with which to compare. From Colonial period deposits at the Rosemont sites it is estimated that decorated pottery accounts for 5.4 percent of all pottery during the Cañada del Oro phase and 17 percent during the Rillito phase (Deaver 1984: 385, Fig. 4.66). These percentages are based on counts of total sherds, and include both red-on-brown and intrusive decorated pottery. It is possible that the frequencies, if adjusted to rims, could be comparable to those presented here. The only directly comparable site is Fastimes (see Volume 2, Chapter 4), where red-on-brown pottery constitutes only 7.23 percent of the pottery rim collection. Based on this comparison, it seems that the 24.33 percent figure for Water World is unusually high. It also is possible that some of the plain ware at Fastimes is intrusive, and because it is assumed that all plain ware is local, the proportion of locally made pottery that was decorated could be higher at Fastimes and, in fact, compares to the proportion estimated for Water World. As noted, however, there is no base line for comparison, and an average percentage of red-on-brown pottery cannot at present be estimated for the Colonial period.

Another aspect of the pottery assemblage at Water World is the low percentage of intrusive pottery, particularly Gila Basin red-on-buffs. The Trincheras and San Simon pottery from Water World and Fastimes seem to represent one vessel each per site, and therefore these types will not be discussed. Based solely on rim sherds, at Water World red-on-buff pottery accounts for only 1.63 percent of all painted pottery, whereas at Fastimes it accounts for 46.85 percent of all painted pottery. Thus, it would appear that the occupants of Water World imported much less red-on-buff pottery than those at Fastimes. This discrepancy in the frequencies of red-on-buff pottery is highlighted by the cremation assemblages from each site. At Water World all decorated vessels but one from cremations are red-on-browns, whereas all decorated vessels from cremations at Fastimes are red-on-buffs. Sample size may have a major affect on this phenomenon as only one cremation at Fastimes has associated pottery vessels. But the low occurrence of red-on-buff vessels from the eight cremations with pottery vessels at Water World is unexpected. Clearly, there are factors that affect the amount of red-on-buff pottery at each of these sites. One interpretation is that Water World represents a major production locus in the Avra Valley for red-on-brown pottery, whereas Fastimes does not. If all intrusive pottery types are excluded from the calculations and it is assumed that all red-on-brown, plain, red-slipped (including possible red-slipped), and unidentified sherds are locally produced, then red-on-brown pottery at Water World accounts for 24.51 percent of all "local" pottery. At Fastimes, however, red-on-brown pottery constitutes only 7.77 percent of the local rims. The differences in these initial figures lend credence to the possibility that Water World is a locus of substantial red-on-brown pottery production. But this interpretation cannot rest entirely on these figures. These percentages should be treated tenuously, because it is possible that some unknown amount of the plain pottery from Fastimes is imported as well.

If, at Fastimes, some plain ware is imported as well as the red-on-buff pottery, then the relative proportion of red-on-brown pottery at Fastimes would be higher than the raw frequencies presented above would indicate. To explore this I have assumed that the relative proportion of red-on-brown to red-on-buff is indicative of the proportion of locally produced to imported plain wares. When the percentage of plain wares that are thus calculated as possible imports is deleted, the estimated frequency of red-on-brown pottery at Fastimes increases to 24.19 percent of the local pottery (see Volume 2, Chapter 4). This figure is closely analogous to the proportion of red-on-browns of local pottery at Water World, and suggests that the percentage of red-on-brown pottery at Water World may not be inordinately high as is indicated by initial figures. In this vein the Water World collection may represent the relative proportion of red-on-browns (about 24 percent) to locally produced plain wares and that the only significant difference between Fastimes and Water World is the low incidence of imported pottery (both decorated and plain) at this latter site. A preliminary analysis using neutron activation on a small sample of sherds specifically addresses this topic and is discussed in Volume 1, Chapter 10.

Other nonpottery evidence of pottery manufacture at the two sites is rare and consists of polishing stones and chunks of schist or gneiss. There is no significant difference in the percentage of polishing stones at the two sites (Chapter 6, this volume; Volume 2, Chapter 6). Yet, there does seem to be a greater proportion of schist or gneiss chunks at Water World. This material is not native in the vicinity of the site and must be imported. Because a large proportion of both the painted and plain pottery is tempered with a crushed micaceous rock, these chunks may represent temper materials and their larger number at Water World would support the inference that pottery production is more common at this site. This is not, however, convincing evidence that Water World is a major center of pottery production in the Avra Valley. An increased production of red-on-browns may be a response to low accessibility to red-on-buff pottery. If this is so, then this increased production exceeds the percentage of decorated pottery present at Fastimes where access to red-on-buff pottery was higher.

As noted above, red-on-brown pottery accounts for 24.51 percent of what is assumed to be the local indigenous pottery. Plain pottery in turn makes up 73.93 percent. The remaining 1.56 percent consists of sherds that are too eroded to be identified, but in all likelihood are fragments of plain ware vessels. No red-slipped rims occur in the collection, but the three body sherds, if locally produced, indicate that red-slipped pottery may be a very small aspect of pottery production. This information basically confirms the notion that during the Colonial period only two classes of pottery were produced: decorated and plain ware.

The Water World assemblage indicates that there are profound differences in the kinds of painted and plain vessels produced. Overall, for all red-on-brown and plain pottery, the ratio of bowls to jars is 0.86:1 (based on the inference stated above that plain ware and unidentified sherds of Indeterminate Form are in fact from jars). The same ratio for each pottery class is drastically different, however. Painted bowls outnumber jars by a ratio of nearly 12:1, whereas plain bowls are outnumbered by jars approximately 1:2. The proportion of painted bowls to jars at Water World is the same relationship noted at the Rosemont sites (Deaver 1984: 288, 296) and at the recent excavations at the Hodges Ruin (Whittlesey 1986: 94) for Colonial period pottery types, although the ratios vary. Likewise, information from the Rosemont sites indicates a similar relationship in plain pottery vessels, although these figures include "early" Rincon Red-on-brown (Deaver 1984: 386, 387, Table 4.28). It seems evident that during the Colonial period a greater proportion of decorated bowls was produced than jars, and that the reverse is true for the plain pottery.

Differences between painted and plain pottery production are not limited to the proportions of vessel form classes, but are also manifested in the kinds of bowls and jars produced. Tables 4.6, 4.7, and 4.8 present a summary of the vessel form frequencies for all Tucson

TABLE 4.6

COMPARISON OF TUCSON BASIN RED-ON-BROWN AND PLAIN WARE VESSEL FORMS

Vessel Form	Tucson Basin Red-on-Brown		Plain Ware	
Indeterminate shape	10	(3.4)	348	(38.7)
Bowls				
Indeterminate	11	(3.7)	10	(1.1)
Direct-rimmed				
Indeterminate	10	(3.4)	127	(14.1)
Hemisphere	9	(3.0)	71	(7.9)
Outcurved	12	(4.0)	63	(7.0)
Scoop	2	(0.7)	1	(0.1)
Flare-rimmed	221	(74.2)	16	(1.8)
Jars				
Neckless				
Indeterminate	4	(1.3)	7	(0.8)
Slight incurve	6	(2.0)	8	(0.9
Pronounced incurve	2	(0.7)	21	(2.3)
Necked				
Flared	11	(3.7)	216	(24.0)
Upcurved	0		11	(1.2)
Total	298	(100.1)	899	(99.9)

( ) Percent

Basin red-on-brown types and contrast these with the frequencies for array of shapes is similar. The proportions of particular form categories differ dramatically, however. The flare-rimmed bowl form overwhelmingly dominates the painted vessels with sherds comprising 74.2 percent of all decorated rims (Table 4.6) and 83.4 percent of all bowl rims (Table 4.7). In contrast, plain sherds in this category account for only 1.8 percent of all plain rim sherds (Table 4.6) and 5.6 percent of all bowl rims (Table 4.7). Clearly the flare-rimmed bowl is the typical Colonial period painted form. The most common plain form is the direct-rimmed bowl that accounts for 90.7 percent (omitting scoops) of all plain bowl rims (Table 4.7). Scoops are rare among both painted and plain pottery forms.

Differences in jar forms for painted and plain pottery exist though it is more difficult to assess any significance given that only 23 decorated jar rims are present. The upturned-necked jar form does

TABLE 4.7

COMPARISON OF TUCSON BASIN RED-ON-BROWN AND PLAIN WARE BOWL FORMS

Vessel Form	Tucson Basin Red-on-Brown		Plain Ware	
Indeterminate	11	(4.2)	10	(3.5)
Direct-rimmed				
Indeterminate	10	(3.8)	127	(44.1)
Hemisphere	9	(3.4)	71	(24.7)
Outcurved	12	(4.5)	63	(21.9)
Scoop	2	(0.8)	1	(0.3)
Flare-rimmed	221	(83.4)	16	(5.6)
Total	265	(100.1)	288	(100.1)

( ) Percent

TABLE 4.8

COMPARISON OF TUCSON BASIN RED-ON-BROWN AND PLAIN WARE JAR FORMS

Vessel Form	Tucson Basin Red-on-Brown		Plain Ware	
Neckless				
Indeterminate	4	(17.4)	7	(2.7)
Slight incurve	6	(26.1)	8	(3.0)
Pronounced incurve	2	(8.7)	21	(8.0)
Necked				
Flared	11	(47.8)	216*	(82.1)
Upcurved	0		11	(4.2)
Total	23	(100.0)	263	(100.0)

( ) Percent
  * Percentage would be higher if most Indeterminate shape rims were
    from flaring-necked jars

not occur among painted forms although it is noted at the Rosemont sites
(Deaver 1984: 391, Table 4.31). Jars with flaring necks are the most
common form for both painted and plain pottery. The collection suggests
that incurved forms are more common among painted vessels.

     In summary, the data obtained during the typological
classification of the Water World pottery collection indicates that only
two major classes of pottery were produced during the Colonial period:
red-on-brown painted pottery and a plain (undecorated) pottery.
Further, there were pronounced differences in the production of these
two classes in terms of the proportion and kind of pottery vessels
produced. There is yet much information about pottery production during
the Colonial period that needs to be studied, such as the basic nature
of Colonial period pottery production including the level of production,
the unit of production, and the location of the production loci.

Worked Sherds

     In the sherd collection from Water World are 210 sherds that
exhibit some kind of secondary alteration (Volume 5, Appendix A-5). The
kinds of alteration range from edges abraded from use, to repair holes
and cut-off rims that bespeak attempts to refurbish or extend the use
life of a vessel, to large sherds shaped into secondary vessels such as
shallow bowls or plates, and finally, to an array of sherds shaped into
specific geometric forms. By far the most common kind of worked sherd
has abraded or ground edges, but was broken in such a way that it is
impossible to identify the fragments as shaped or utilized sherds. The
next most common kind of worked sherd is the sherd disk. Only 5 of the
89 sherd disks are perforated; the remainder are primarily chipped but
not ground and may be preforms in the manufacture of sherd whorls.
Seven sherds are present that bear single perforations that are in all
probability repair holes for mending cracks to extend the use life of a
vessel. Another kind of refurbishing of pottery containers is
exemplified by three rim sherds that have been horizontally scored and
broken off. This treatment is occasionally noted on some restorable
vessels where the flaring part of the rim is cut off, leaving a neck
similar to the upturned-necked jar. Six sherds fit together to form two
large disks manufactured from large body sherds. These two pieces are
apparently secondary vessels. Eight sherds have a light coating of
ground hematite on one or both surfaces but have no evidence of shaping.
These sherds may have been used as informal palettes to hold pigments.
Two sherds have been shaped by grinding into elliptical forms that have
single perforations in one end and are probably pendants. One was
recovered from cremation Feature 80. The remaining sherds have been
shaped by chipping and grinding into various geometric shapes (Volume 5,
Appendix A-5).

     All basic pottery types in the collection are represented in the
worked sherds, including red-on-brown, red-on-buff, and plain pottery.
It is not possible, given the low incidence of most forms, to determine

whether there may have been a preference to make some items more consistently from one kind of pottery than another. Indeterminate worked sherds and sherd disks are more commonly made from plain sherds, but the frequency of plain pottery within each of these forms approximates the proportion of each pottery type represented by all worked sherd forms.

Figurines and Other Nonpottery Clay Artifacts

In addition to the large collection of pottery artifacts 90 items are present that represent nonpottery clay artifacts (Table 4.9). One clay earspool and six fragments of a modeled lump of clay that may be a jar stopper are present. One nearly complete human figurine was found intact and two others have been pieced together from several fragments. Among the remaining fragments are 5 heads, 11 torsos, and 55 miscellaneous cylindrical or conical pieces of clay that probably represent limbs from human figurines.

The figurine assemblage reflects the common aspects of figurine traditions in the Gila and Tucson basins (Figs. 4.17 and 4.18). Most of the figurines are made of a fine, grayish brown clay with very little nonplastic particles present. One head and several fragments are made of a reddish brown clay with abundant coarse sand. These specimens may represent a single figurine, but the clay is too crumbly to allow complete reconstruction. When sex is determinable, all figurines are female with prominent breasts. A nearly complete specimen represents a pregnant female (Fig. 4.17a). Two of the nearly complete specimens (Fig. 4.17b, c) and all of the torso fragments indicate that they were made using the two-piece method of making figurines that is typical of the Pioneer period at Snaketown (Haury 1976: 255-259) and persists as late as the Rillito phase in the Tucson Basin (Kelly 1978: 79-80). The complete specimen of a pregnant female figure (Fig. 4.17a) is modeled from a single lump of clay. Most of the heads are subrectangular in plan with pinched noses. Eyes occur only on the pregnant female figure where they are depicted by two enclosing concentric incisions for each eye. This specimen also has places on either side of the face where appendages had been attached that may have represented ears or chin ornaments (Haury 1976; Kelly 1978). The remaining bodies vary from nearly cylindrical rods (Fig. 4.18g) to slightly hour-glass shaped (Figs. 4.17c and 4.18d, h). Legs are cylindrical rods of clay slightly pointed on the ends. Arms are represented by nubbins that extend from the shoulders of the torso except in the pregnant figure where the arms are modeled in relief. No evidence of body or facial ornamentation is present except for the possible chin ornaments on Figure 4.17a.

A most curious aspect of the figurine collection is that all but 2 torsos and 12 miscellaneous fragments are from Features 25 and 55, which are superimposed houses. Although two house floors are present, they may represent a single deposit. Other notable aspects of this

TABLE 4.9

INVENTORY OF FIGURINES AND OTHER CERAMIC ARTIFACTS

Feature			FN	Description	Count
7	S2	L1	1907	Cylindrical rod, probably human figure leg	1
19	S2	L1	41	Miscellaneous, unidentified fragment	1
25	S20		84	Whole pregnant female figurine	1
26	S30	L2	752	Earspool with notched edges	1
26	S30	L1	696	Cylindrical rod, probably human figure leg	1
29	S1	L2	993	Fragments to cylindrical rod, probably mend, probably leg	7
33	S2	L1	866	Human figure, torso and leg fragment mend	2
44	S30	L3	1983	Human figure, torso fragment	1
44	S30	L3	1992	Cylindrical rod, probably human figure leg	1
55	S1	L1	587	Human female figure, torso with breasts	2
55	S1	L1	588	Human female figure, missing one breast	2
55	S1	L1	589	Human figure, head with nose	2
55	S1	L1	590	3 leg fragments mend to 594, 1 leg fragment mends to 588, 12 fragments cylindrical rod same clay as 589	16
55	S1	L1	591	Human figure, head with nose	1
55	S1	L1	592	Human female figure, torso with breasts	1
55	S1	L1	593	Cylindrical rod, leg to 588	1
55	S1	L1	594	Human figure, torso fragments, mend	2
55	S1	L1	650	Human figure, head with nose	1
55	S1	L1	841	Human figure, torso fragments	2
55	S1	L1	842	Miscellaneous fragments, human figure, torso and legs?	18
55	S1	L1	851	Miscellaneous fragments, same clay as 589	6
55	S1	L1	853	Human female figure, partially complete	3
55	S1	L1	1486	Human figure, torso fragment	1
55	S1	L1	1487	1 miscellaneous fragment, 2 conical rod fragments, leg/foot	3
55	S1	L1	1494	Human figure, torso	1
55	S1	L1	1495	Human female figure, torso with breast	1
55	S1	L1	1496	Flattened cylindrical rod, probably leg/foot	1
55.1	S1	L1	2028	Fragments cylindrical rod, probably human figure leg	2
55.10	S1	L1	1133	Human figure, head?	1
59	S1		1108	Cylindrical rod, probably human figure leg	1
78	S1	L1	2207	Jar stopper with finger indentations	5
78	S20		2218	Jar stopper same as 2207	1
Total					90

S = Stratum, L = Level

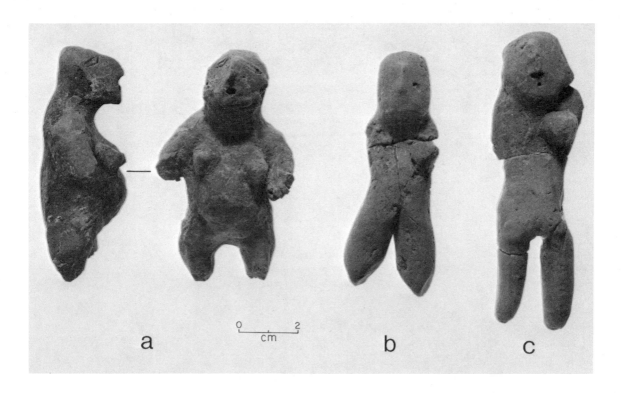

Figure 4.17. Figurines from Water World (height of a: 8.0 cm).

deposit is a single restorable bowl of Cañada del Oro Red-on-brown and three miniature vessels. The concentration of items in this deposit is unique at this site and may be more than coincidental.

A ceramic object illustrated in Figure 4.19a–a' is interpreted as a clay earspool. It resembles a stone artifact identified as an earspool from the early excavations at Snaketown (Gladwin and others 1937, Plate CVIIId). The edges of this specimen are decorated with straight and V-shaped incisions. One surface is flat and the other is concave. A single perforation made when the clay was wet is slightly off center.

The final ceramic artifacts are several pieces of modeled clay from an apparently disk-shaped object (Fig. 4.19b). One surface of the artifact is decorated with indentations apparently made by fingers.

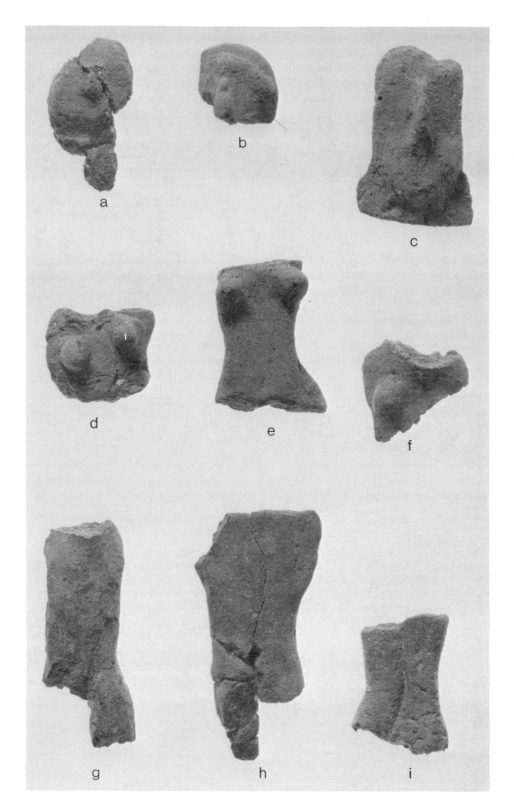

Figure 4.18. Figurine fragments from Water World: a–c, heads; d–h, torsos; i, torso showing weld from two-piece construction (height of h: 5.8 cm).

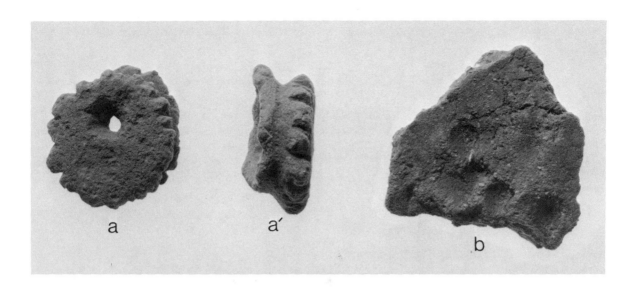

Figure 4.19. Miscellaneous ceramic artifacts: a-a´, earspool; b, possible jar stopper (diameter of a: 2.5 cm).

Chapter 5

FLAKED STONE

Bruce B. Huckell

The largest assemblage of flaked stone from the Phase B sites came from Water World. A total of 4,583 pieces of flaked stone from 20 structures was examined and inventoried, and more than 250 retouched and unretouched implements from five of the structures were studied in detail (see Volume 2, Chapter 5 for a discussion of analytic methods). In addition, all the projectile points recovered from the site were analyzed. In accordance with the analytic priorities for the project (Volume 1, Chapter 2), none of the flaked-stone artifacts recovered from extramural features (except cremations) or general stripping were analyzed. This collection represents the largest Colonial period sample of the Tucson Basin Hohokam flaked-stone industry available to date, and affords an opportunity to study the gross assemblage composition and the range of implement forms in use during a restricted period of time (the Rillito phase).

Summary information for the assemblage is presented in Tables 5.1 and 5.2. As Table 5.1 indicates, the bulk of the assemblage (87.19%) consists of unmodified debitage. Unretouched or utilized flakes are the most abundant single class of implements, making up 4.74 percent of the total assemblage. Unifacially retouched flakes make up 3.54 percent of the assemblage, followed by bifacially retouched implements (1.70%) and hammerstones (1.37%). Unmodified cores make up the final 1.46 percent of the assemblage. This gross assemblage composition is similar to that documented at Fastimes (Volume 2, Chapter 5), the other large Colonial period village investigated on the project. The maximum difference between the two sites in the relative frequencies of any of the six categories is 2.7 percent: at Water World, debitage is 87.2 percent of the assemblage and at Fastimes it is 84.5 percent.

Fourteen material types were recognized in the flaked stone from Water World (Table 5.2). Two materials, silicified sediment and quartzite, make up almost 86 percent of the assemblage. The next most common material is a variegated brown agate, which makes up slightly more than 7 percent of the assemblage. I have been informed by Allen Dart of the Institute for American Research in Tucson that this agate is found in the southern end of the Tucson Mountains, south of Robles Pass (Ajo Way). Chert and limestone are next in relative abundance, each with less than 2 percent, and each of the remaining nine material types

Table 5.1

FLAKED STONE ARTIFACT ASSEMBLAGE COMPOSITION

Feature	Debitage	Core	Unifacially Retouched Piece	Bifacially Retouched Piece	Unretouched Implement	Hammerstones	Total
7	151	2	1	2	7		163
19	315	4	9	6	9	3	346
20	27				6	3	36
25	360		20	5	25	6	416
26	526	19	22	10	26	6	609
27	216	3	15	3	27	5	269
29	238	7	10	5	15	6	281
33	247	3	12	7	19	2	290
35	34	2	3		1	2	42
36	40	2			2	3	47
44	194	2	2	3	8	3	212
53	119	3	10	2	3	1	138
55	163		7	1	8	1	180
58	532	7	18	15	24	6	602
61	104	2	2	6	3	3	120
66	73		3		2	1	79
67	400	4	17	9	20	9	459
68	134	5	7	2	6	3	157
78	41	2	1	1	2		47
79	82		3	1	4		90
Total	3,996	67	162	78	217	63	4,583
%	87.19	1.46	3.54	1.70	4.74	1.37	100.0

Table 5.2

MATERIAL TYPES IN THE FLAKED STONE ASSEMBLAGE

Feature		Material Type													
	Quartzite	Rhyolite	Silicified Sediment	Basalt	Porphyritic Igneous	Chert	Jasper	Chalcedony	Agate	Fine Rhyolite	Limestone	Shale	Quartz	Sandstone	Total
7	57		33			12		1		1		1		1	163
19	128		207	1	1	2		1	57		5			1	346
20	15	1	9			2		1							36
25	192	1	215	1	4	1	1		8		4		1	1	419
26	146	4	220		4	11	3	12	202		10				609
27	112		145		1	2	1	1		1	2				269
29	89		147					1		1	3				281
33	96	2	167			3	2	4	37		4				290
35	12		28			10			5						42
36	30		15			1		1							47
44	123	1	67			9		5	8		9		2		209
53	43		79			1		2	1		2				138
55	76		97			4		6							180
58	221	21	296			15	5	3	17	13	8				602
61	31		82			1	2				1				120
66	19	1	58						1						79
67	193	7	198	1		13		3	6	2	36				459
68	37		114				1		2		3				157
78	18	2	24			1		1		1					47
79	14		75								1				90
Total	1,652	40	2,276	3	10	88	15	42	344	18	88	1	3	3	4,583
%	36.04	0.87	49.66	0.06	0.21	1.92	0.33	0.91	7.5	0.39	1.92	0.02	0.06	0.06	100.00

makes up less than 1 percent of the assemblage. Igneous materials, relatively common at Fastimes (41%), amount to less than 2 percent of the Water World assemblage. It is probable that such differences reflect what material types are available at the southern end of the Tucson Mountains as opposed to the northern end of the range, rather than different cultural preferences. In particular, silicified sediment is abundant from the area around the Arizona-Sonora Desert Museum south to near the end of the range. At Water World almost 50 percent of the flaked-stone artifacts are of this material, whereas at Fastimes its relative abundance drops to nearly 3 percent.

Implement Assemblage

Five structures were chosen as a sample for the detailed analysis of implements. Selection was done on a nonrandom, judgmental basis, using house groups to ensure that the sample was drawn from all excavated parts of the site. Thus, one house was chosen from each of the five house groups of completely excavated houses (House Groups 1, 2, 3, 4, and 6). In each case the house selected was the one in the group with the largest quantity of flaked-stone artifacts, unless it had been disturbed by younger intrusive features. In this case the structure with the second largest quantity of flaked stone was used. The five structures chosen by this process were Features 19, 27, 29, 58, and 67. This sample represents one-quarter of the structures, yet it consists of 44.4 percent of the 520 implements identified in the sorting of the material from the 20 structures. Although not an ideal means of sample selection, this method was justified by assuming that houses with large quantities of material would probably offer the best opportunities to obtain representation of most if not all of the implement types that were made and used at the site. That is, the larger assemblages, particularly from the fills of houses, were interpreted to derive from intentional trash disposal, which offered the opportunity to view the widest range of flaked-stone artifacts.

To augment this sample, projectile points from the cremations at Water World were analyzed. This was done for two reasons. First, these artifacts are known to show stylistic change through time, and it is useful to document the styles associated with a single-period site as potential temporal markers. Second, the cremations at Water World contained 16 of the 27 (59.25%) projectile points recovered from the site and represent a special context in which these particular flaked-stone implements occur.

Projectile Points

Five styles of projectile points were recognized from Water World, and examples of each style are illustrated in Figure 5.1. Two

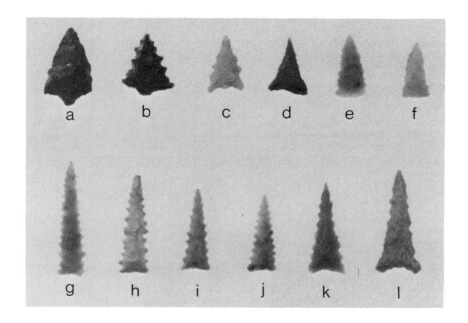

Figure 5.1. Projectile points: a, contracting stem, plain blade; b-c, contracting stem, serrated blade; d, concave base, plain blade; e-f, convex base, serrated blade; g-1, concave base, serrated blade. (Length of g: 29 mm.) Field Numbers: a, 1726; b, 1228; c, 1446; d, 732; e, 1745; f, 1151; g, 1070; h, 2254; i, 2255; j, 2251; k, 2142; 1, 1689.

are stemmed forms, and the other three lack stems. Tables 5.3 and 5.4 present provenience and material data (see also Volume 5, Appendix B-7).

The stemmed points are represented by three specimens. One of these is a simple, short, triangular blade with a short contracting stem (Fig. 5.1a). The other two are similar (Fig. 5.1b and c), but have a serrated blade. All are complete and measure between 14 mm and 21 mm long by 10 mm to 14 mm wide and 3 mm to 5 mm thick. Both styles also were recovered from Hawk's Nest, a late Pioneer-early Colonial site (Volume 4, Part 1). Such styles also are known from other Tucson Basin Hohokam sites in the Rosemont area (Rozen 1984, Fig. 5.11a-m) and the Hodges Ruin (Kelly 1978, Fig. 6.7a-o; Yarborough 1986, Fig. 7.5a-e). Serrated and nonserrated forms are principally Colonial period in age in the Tucson Basin. Outside the basin these styles are known from other Hohokam sites including Tres Alamos (Tuthill 1947, Plate 32, first row third from right) and San Cayetano (Di Peso 1956, Plate 133, row 3). These points are also well represented at Snaketown (Sayles 1937, Plate XCI) in Colonial, principally Santa Cruz, contexts.

The remaining 24 projectile points lack stems. Four of these are best described as simple, triangular points with concave bases as exemplified by Figure 5.1d. Rozen (1984, Fig. 5.12k-m) reports similar forms from the Rosemont area of the Santa Rita Mountains, Doyel (1977:

Table 5.3

PROJECTILE POINT STYLES AND PROVENIENCES

Style	Context Structure Fill	Structure Floor	Cremation	Total
Contracting Stem, Plain Blade	1			1
Contracting Stem, Serrated Blade	2			2
Concave Base, Plain Blade	3		1	4
Concave Base, Serrated Blade	2	1	13	16
Convex Base, Serrated Blade	1	1		2
Unclassifiable Fragments			2	2
Total	9	2	16	27

Rincon site in the middle Santa Cruz Valley, and Yarborough (1986, Fig. 7.5x) illustrates one from a similar temporal position at the Hodges Ruin.

Two other points display slightly convex bases and convex-sided, poorly serrated blades; both are essentially trimmed and shaped flakes (Fig. 5.1e and f). Rozen (1984, Fig. 5.12a-i) illustrates roughly similar, but noticeably more technically refined forms from the Rosemont area.

The final 16 projectile points are long, narrow triangular forms with serrated blade margins; they are presented in Figure 5.1g-l. Bases range from straight or slightly concave (Fig. 5.1g-j) to clearly concave (Fig. 5.1k and l). Length to width ratios also vary on these forms in that the more concave-based specimens are broader relative to the length. It is even possible that two different varieties are represented by these specimens. For these points length ranges from 17 mm to 29 mm, and width varies from 7 mm to 12 mm; they are relatively thick (3.5 mm to 6 mm) and usually diamond-shaped in cross section. Examples of the broader, more concave bases compare favorably with several of Rozen's Type 2 points (Rozen 1984, Fig. 5.11n-aa) and some of

Table 5.4

PROJECTILE POINT STYLES AND MATERIALS

Style	Chert	Chalcedony	Jasper	Agate	Metamorphosed Sediment	Total
Contracting Stem, Plain Blade			1			1
Contracting Stem, Serrated Blade	1				1	2
Concave Base, Plain Blade	3				1	4
Concave Base, Serrated Blade	13	1		1	1	16
Convex Base, Serrated Blade	1				1	2
Unclassifiable Fragments	2					2
Total	20	1	1	1	4	27

Kelly's (1978, Fig. 6.7e and f) and Yarborough's (1986, Fig. 7.5q-v) points from the Hodges Ruin. The more slender specimens with straight to slightly concave bases do not appear to be present in the Rosemont area sites, but have been recovered from the Hodges Ruin (Kelly 1978, Fig. 6.6i; Yarborough 1986, Fig. 7.5f and n). Farther from the Tucson area, Di Peso (1956, Plate 130, row a, Plate 133, b-1) recovered this style from "Upper Piman" (Classic period Hohokam) and Hohokam contexts at San Cayetano and also from Babocomari Village (Di Peso 1951, Plate 58, row a); Tuthill (1947, Plate 32, second row, third through fifth from right) illustrated similar specimens from Tres Alamos; and they also are known from Snaketown (Sayles 1937, Plate LXXXV, group C).

In terms of the temporal association of this style, the Hodges Ruin specimens may be Cañada del Oro (?) (Kelly 1978, Fig. 6.6) or Rillito or Rincon in age (Yarborough 1986: 147). The San Cayetano specimens from Hohokam contexts are most likely Santa Cruz (Rillito) phase in age (Di Peso 1956: 360), but at Snaketown they are overwhelmingly found in Sacaton phase contexts (Sayles 1937, Plate LXXXV, frequency table). The Water World specimens clearly are Rillito

phase in age, however, and their presence in a securely dated Colonial
period site may suggest that the style is somewhat earlier in the Tucson
area than it is at Snaketown. The specimens from Colonial period
Hohokam contexts at San Cayetano may bolster this suggestion, but the
recovery of the same style from Classic period contexts in the middle
Santa Cruz and Babocomari drainages implies that it had a long life.
Another aspect of this style at Water World is that 13 of the 16
specimens were recovered from cremations; except for one specimen, this
was the only style present in cremations. One cremation (Feature 108)
produced eight points of this style. All showed the effects of fire,
but often this amounted only to discoloration.

Finally, two unclassifiable tip fragments were recovered from
one cremation. They had been burned and their bases are missing. Both
are long, slender, serrated blade fragments and most likely represent
the triangular, serrated, straight-to-concave base style. The same
cremation produced three classifiable examples of this style.

Other Retouched Implements

The five structures selected for intensive analysis produced 137
retouched implements, representing 14 different analytical types. Table
5.5 presents the distribution of these types by structure, and Figure
5.2 shows the composition and frequencies of the assemblage. Some
selected implements are illustrated in Figure 5.3.

As discussed in the section on analytic methods (Volume 2,
Chapter 5), these implement types are those defined and illustrated by
Rozen (1984: 456-492). Table 5.5 reveals that 7 of the 14 types are
represented by 6 or fewer examples (each is less than 5% of the total).
These include such uniface forms as notches; irregularly retouched
pieces; discontinuously retouched fragments; and continuous, marginal,
nonextensively retouched pieces. Projectile points, drills, and
projections make up the less common bifacially worked forms.
Continuously retouched uniface fragments are slightly more abundant with
eight specimens, but the most common retouched implements are
continuous, marginal, extensively retouched unifaces; continuous,
invasively retouched unifaces; nonextensively bifacially retouched
pieces; irregular bifaces; projectile point preforms; and hammerstones.

The continuous, marginal, extensively retouched unifaces (Fig.
5.3a and b) and continuous, invasively, retouched pieces (Fig. 5.3d and
e) may be terminologically equated with scrapers. If the continuously
retouched fragments are included as probably representing fragments of
these implements, then the three types account for 32.1 percent of the
assemblage (Table 5.5). Great diversity in edge form, edge angle,
position of retouch, and regularity of retouch is present among these
implements. This diversity frustrated initial efforts to record
attributes of the retouched edges in detail. By the same token, it is
also the reason that Rozen's (1984) system of analytic types makes more

Table 5.5

DISTRIBUTION OF RETOUCHED IMPLEMENT TYPE BY FEATURE

Type	Feature					Total
	19	27	29	58	67	
Notch	0	0	0	0	1 2.7	1 0.73
Irregularly retouched piece	1 5.6*	1 4.3	2 9.5	0	2 5.4	6 4.38
Discontinuously retouched fragment	0	0	3 14.2	1 2.6	0	4 2.92
Continuous, marginal, nonextensively retouched piece	2 11.1	0	1 4.8	0	1 2.7	4 2.92
Continuous, marginal, extensively retouched piece	3 16.6	4 17.4	1 4.8	2 5.3	3 8.1	13 9.49
Continuous, invasively retouched piece	1 5.6	7 30.4	1 4.8	7 18.4	7 18.9	23 16.79
Continuously retouched fragment	0	1 4.3	1 4.8	3 7.9	3 8.1	8 5.84
Nonextensively bifacially retouched piece	2 11.1	1 4.3	1 4.8	4 10.5	2 5.4	10 7.30
Irregular biface	4 22.2	1 4.3	3 14.2	6 15.8	5 13.5	19 13.87
Projectile point preform	1 5.6	0	1 4.8	8 21.0	1 2.7	11 8.03
Projectile point	0	0	0	0	3 8.1	3 2.19
Drill	0	2 8.7	1 4.8	0	0	3 2.19
Projection	1 5.6	1 4.3	0	1 2.6	0	3 2.19
Hammerstone	3 16.6	5 21.7	6 28.5	6 15.8	9 24.3	29 21.17
Total	18	23	21	38	37	137
%	13.14**	16.79	15.33	27.74	27.01	100.00

 * Percent of assemblage from feature
** Percent of analyzed sample

202

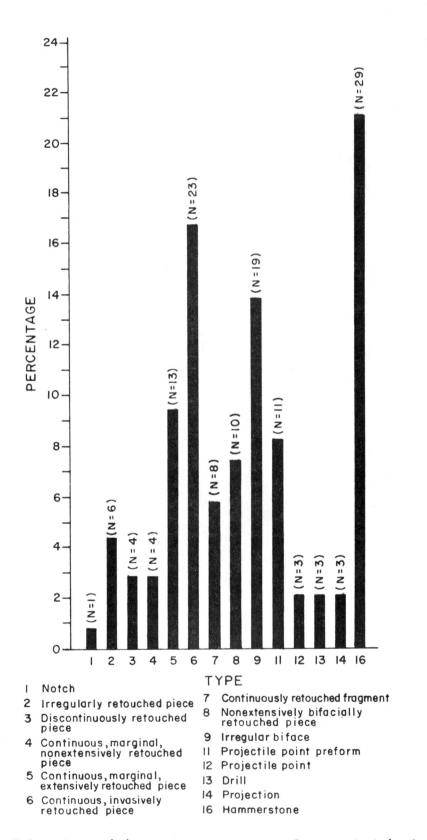

Figure 5.2. Composition and percentages of retouched implements.

Figure 5.3. Retouched implements: a–b, continuous, marginal,
extensively retouched pieces; c, drill; d–e, continuous, invasively
retouched piece; f, irregularly retouched piece; g–h, irregular bifaces.
(Length of a: 67 mm.) Field Numbers: a, 350; b, 305; c, 438; d, 440; e,
440; f, 876; g, 1532; h, 440.

204

sense than most traditional type systems. Why such great variability
exists among these tools is discussed in Volume 1, Chapter 12 (Synthesis
and Interpretations). At this point, however, it is enough to say that
whatever function or functions these implements served, they must have
been undertaken relatively frequently. The general concept of
unifacially retouching a flake in a fairly continuous pattern to produce
a steep-edged, irregular implement seems to constitute an important part
of the retouched implement tradition at Water World.

Bifacially retouched implements also are relatively well
represented in the sample. Nonextensively bifacially retouched pieces
and irregular bifaces comprise 21.1 percent of the total (Table 5.5).
These artifacts, defined in Volume 2, Chapter 5, are just retouched
pieces and not regular, formal bifaces. A nonextensively bifacially
retouched piece may bear only one or two flake scars on each face, and
an irregular biface is simply a tool with slightly more extensive
retouching on both faces (Fig. 5.3g and h). Further, the bifacial
retouch need not be from a common margin. These implements display
great variability in edge configuration, retouch regularity, and working
edge position. It is possible that an occasional flake or flakes might
have been struck from an opposite face of what was a uniface to remove a
prominence or irregularity, or to make the piece easier to hold. In
such cases the retouch on the principal working edge may be unifacial;
however, experience has shown that it is difficult to make consistent
and objective identifications of "principal" working edges. In still
other cases, it is possible that the bifacial retouching of a single
edge represents a last effort to rejuvenate the working edge of a
unifacially retouched piece. Finally, the possibility exists that these
irregularly bifacially retouched pieces are intended to be bifacial
scraping tools, and that the general category of "scraper" in the
Hohokam retouched implement assemblage is even more formally variable
than is suggested by the variability already noted for the continuous,
marginal, extensively retouched pieces and continuous, invasively
retouched unifacial pieces.

Three projectile points were present in the sample from the five
structures (Table 5.5); all came from Feature 67. Two are triangular,
concave-based, plain-bladed forms made on flakes of silicified sediment
by largely unifacially directed retouch. The third point displayed an
abbreviated contracting stem and a short serrated blade. In addition 11
projectile point preforms were analyzed (Table 5.5). All are small
flakes of comparatively fine-grained materials (Table 5.6) that
generally had been broken in manufacture. Some had broken at a
comparatively early stage of reduction, but one tip fragment showed that
it had been broken during the serration process, after one edge was
completely serrated. Their size and configuration, as well as the
presence of pressure flake scars, clearly indicated that they were
intended to become projectile points. Finally, three drills were
recovered; Figure 5.3c presents a typical example.

Hammerstones are the most common single retouched implement,
making up just over 21 percent of the sample (Table 5.5). Without

Table 5.6

RETOUCHED IMPLEMENTS BY MATERIAL TYPE

Material

Implement	Quartzite	Rhyolite	Silicified Sediment	Chert	Chalcedony	Agate	Fine Rhyolite	Limestone	Basalt	Total
Notch	1 2.22*	0	0	0	0	0	0	0	0	1
Irregularly retouched piece	2 4.44	0	3 3.95	0	0	1 50.00	0	0	0	6
Discontinuously retouched fragment	1 2.22	0	2 2.63	0	1 33.33	0	0	0	0	4
Continuous, marginal, nonextensively retouched piece	2 4.44	0	2 2.63	0	0	0	0	0	0	4
Continuous, marginal, extensively retouched piece	4 8.89	0	8 10.53	0	0	1 50.00	0	0	0	13
Continuous, invasively retouched piece	6 13.33	1 100.00	16 21.05	0	0	0	0	0	0	23
Continuously retouched fragment	1 2.22	0	7 9.21	0	0	0	0	0	0	8
Nonextensively bifacially retouched piece	5 11.11	0	5 6.58	0	0	0	0	0	0	10
Irregular biface	4 8.89	0	14 18.42	0	0	0	0	1 50.00	0	19
Projectile point preform	0	0	2 2.63	5 83.33	2 66.67	0	1 100.00	0	1 100.00	11
Projectile point	0	0	2 2.63	1 16.67	0	0	0	0	0	3
Drill	0	0	3 3.95	0	0	0	0	0	0	3
Projection	0	0	3 3.95	0	0	0	0	0	0	3
Hammerstone	19 42.22	0	9 11.84	0	0	0	0	1 50.00	0	29
Total	45	1	76	6	3	2	1	2	1	137
%	32.85**	0.73	55.47	4.38	2.19	1.46	0.73	1.46	0.73	100.00

* Percent of assemblage from feature
** Percent of analyzed sample

exception these specimens are flaked or reused core hammerstones and not
unmodified cobble hammers. They vary considerably in size from very
large to rather small, but all have been extensively flaked. It seems
likely that this retouch was done intentionally to create bifacial edges
or ridges, and to enhance prominences. Furthermore, after the edges
became dulled by battering, additional flaking served to resharpen the
working edge. The presence of flakes in the debitage that bear
battering on their platforms or exterior surfaces testifies to such
rejuvenation. In the five sample structures these flakes ranged from
0.75 to 2.1 percent of the debitage.

Table 5.5 does show some variation in the distribution of
retouched implement types among the five structures. This is to be
expected because most of the implements were recovered from structure
fill and probably represent trash. Some of the differences in implement
frequencies are minor between structures containing approximately equal
numbers of implements. For example, no great differences are seen
between Feature 58 with 38 retouched tools and Feature 67 with 37. If
low numbers of a particular implement type are present in one, then the
same is usually true of the other and vice versa (Table 5.5). Only with
projectile point preforms do the two diverge. Somewhat greater
variability exists between Feature 27 (23 retouched tools) and Feature
29 (21 retouched tools). Feature 29 yielded very few "scrapers"
(continuous, marginal, extensively retouched pieces and continuous,
invasively retouched pieces), whereas Feature 27 produced more (Table
5.5). Considering that feature fills were not subjected to consistent
recovery techniques and that in most cases the variability in
percentages of tools is fewer than three implements of relatively small
sizes, it is suggested that a high degree of homogeneity is present in
retouched implement types. Cases involving larger numerical
discrepancies may reflect particular types of activities within the
house group from which a given sample structure comes.

Table 5.6, which shows the materials that the various tool types
are made from, reveals some interesting trends. First, the major
material types, quartzite and silicified sediment, are represented in
relative amounts almost identical to their proportions in the flaked-
stone assemblage as a whole (see Table 5.2). Quartzite differs by only
3.19 percent, and silicified sediment differs by 5.81 percent. The less
common materials in the total assemblage also are less common among the
retouched tools. This indicates that for most of the implement types
raw material was not a crucial consideration in the selection of flakes
to be retouched. The projectile point preforms depart from this pattern
as might be expected, being dominated by fine-grained siliceous rocks.
Neither do the hammerstones follow the pattern--over twice as many are
quartzite. The quartzites from Water World are consistently coarser in
grain size than the silicified sediments, and it may be that the Hohokam
preferred a material less prone to fracturing for their hammerstones.

Unretouched Implements

One hundred twenty-six unretouched (utilized) flake margins were
present in the sample from five structures. The 126 worn edges occurred
on 97 discrete flakes, indicating that 29 flakes (23%) bore use on two
or more margins. Table 5.7 presents the quantities recovered from each
structure, and Figure 5.4 shows the distribution of working edge shape
and angle. Figure 5.5 illustrates some examples of these implements.

Table 5.7

DISTRIBUTION OF UNRETOUCHED FLAKE MARGINS BY EDGE WEAR
FROM FIVE STRUCTURES AT WATER WORLD

| Feature Number | Edge Ware Type | | | Total |
	Edge Polish	Edge Damage	Edge Damage and Polish	
19	7 (53.85)	4 (30.77)	2 (15.38)	13
27	20 (51.28)	11 (28.21)	8 (20.51)	39
29	7 (38.89)	9 (50.00)	2 (11.11)	18
58	10 (33.33)	14 (46.67)	6 (20.00)	30
67	16 (61.54)	8 (30.77)	2 (7.69)	26
Total	60	46	20	126
Percent	47.62	36.51	15.87	100.00

( ) Percent of type within feature

The general characteristics of these implements deserve brief
description. In terms of edge shape (Fig. 5.4a), the greatest quantity
(N=47) of utilized edges bore evidence of wear on a convex margin (37.3%
of the total; Fig. 5.5a, d, and f). Flakes with wear on points or

208

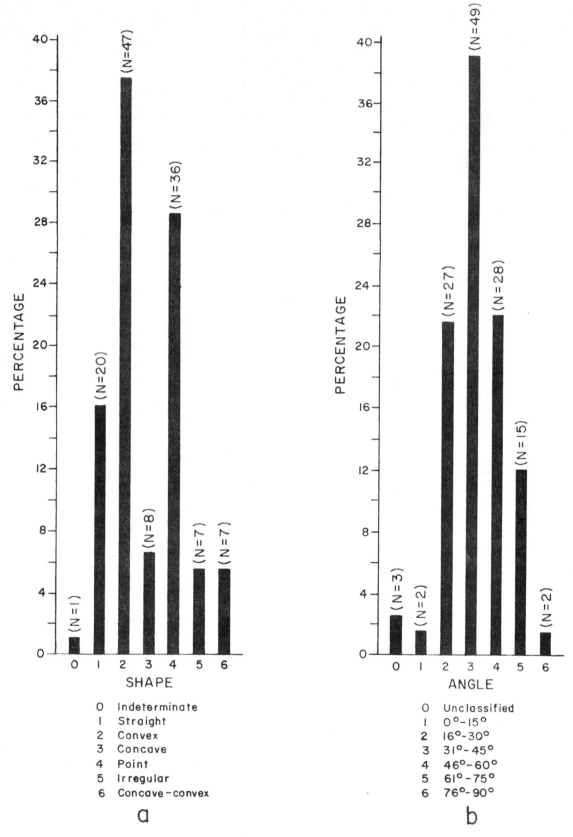

Figure 5.4. Working edge shape and angle frequencies for unretouched (utilized) flakes.

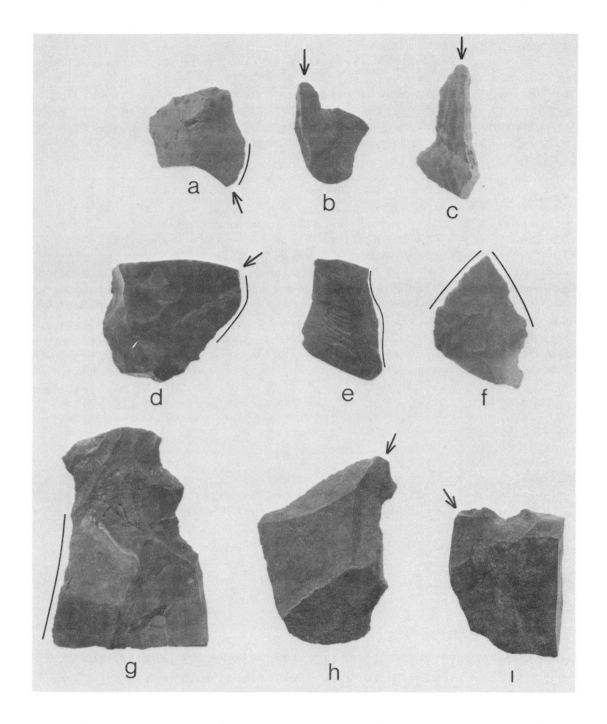

Figure 5.5. Selection of unretouched flake implements: b-c and h-i,
flakes bearing projections with wear on the tip (arrow); a, d, flakes
with wear on a convex edge and a projection; e, flake with wear on a
concave-convex irregular edge; f, flake with wear on two convex edges;
g, flake with wear on a straight edge. (Length of c: 52 mm.) Field
Numbers: a, 638; b, 440; c, 440; d, 381; e, 1214; f, 1214; g, 1635; h,
517; i, 1651.

projections (N=36) were abundant, accounting for 28.6 percent of the total. These flakes either terminated in a point at the distal end, or bore a projection at the striking platform-lateral margin juncture, or had some sort of fortuitous projection at some position on their margins or end. Figure 5.5a-c and h-i illustrates a selection of utilized flake implements bearing wear on such points. Next in abundance are straight working edges (Fig. 5.5g), which make up 15.9 percent of the total (Fig. 5.4a). Less common are working edges that are concave (6.3%), concave-convex (Fig. 5.5e; 5.6%), or irregular in form (5.6%).

Edge angle class frequencies (Fig 5.4b) also are interesting in that they are normally distributed around Angle Class 3 (31 to 45 degrees). The distribution is slightly skewed toward the higher Angle Classes 4 and 5 (46 to 60 degrees and 61 to 75 degrees, respectively); low angle edges (less than 15 degrees) are rare, making up only 4 percent of the sample. Three specimens that bore wear on a flake surface rather than an edge could not be measured. The relative abundance of the modal Angle Class 3 (38.9% of the total) clearly suggests that flakes with this edge angle were usually selected. Flakes in Angle Class 2 or Class 4 also would serve reasonably well, however, for together the specimens in these classes make up 43.6 percent of the sample. These data suggest that edge angle apparently was not a particularly critical consideration in selecting a flake; anything within a range of 16 to 60 degrees was considered usable. Data from the classification of edge shape (Fig. 5.4a) suggest that this attribute was probably the initial concern in selecting a flake.

Material type also seems to have been of comparatively little concern; only four types were represented among the 97 separate flakes. Silicified sediment was most common (51.55% of the total), followed by quartzite (45.36%), and then by rhyolite (2.06%) and basalt (1.03%). The relative abundance of silicified sediment is almost an exact match of its proportion in the general assemblage at 49.66 percent (Table 5.2), but quartzite is nearly 11 percent more abundant among the utilized flakes. This is due in part to the lack of utilized flakes of fine-grained siliceous material, which made up over 10 percent of the materials in the general assemblage. Based on this sample, these finer materials do not seem to have been favored for use as unretouched implements. The same is true among the retouched implement sample discussed previously. When the projectile point preforms and the single projectile point are eliminated, only two other retouched implements remain that were made of these materials. Part of the reason may be that these materials tend to occur in very small pieces that do not produce flakes large enough for easy use. The brown agate, which occurs at the south end of the Tucson Mountains, is an exception; nonetheless, it does not appear to have been commonly used for either retouched or utilized flake implements.

Discussion

The flaked-stone assemblage from Water World is a typical example of the Hohokam lithic repertoire. It contains the same enigmatic suite of irregularly retouched implements of both unifacial and bifacial types, the relatively abundant flaked hammerstones, and the handful of projectile points. Regardless, the assemblage does provide some additional insights into the organization of the flaked-stone implement production system not often available.

One point of note is the relative paucity of cores. Counting only those recovered from the screened 2-m control units from house fills, cores constitute only 1.23 percent of the sample, a flake-to-core ratio of 72.74 to 1 for all structures. The Rosemont area Hohokam sites reported by Rozen (1984, Table 5.1) had a flake-to-core ratio of 46.02 to 1. At Rosemont, lithic raw material is readily available in cobble form within a few hundred meters at most of the Hohokam sites. In contrast, Water World is located on the middle portion of the western bajada of the Tucson Mountains some 4 km from the upper bajada source areas, and nearly the same distance southeast of the investigated quarry site of AZ AA:16:175 (Volume 4, Chapter 20). It is possible that the relatively greater abundance of cores at the Rosemont sites is partially due to the proximity of the source area to the habitation sites--it was easy to pick up a good piece of material and take it back to the habitation site. Water World residents apparently had to travel a longer distance for material, which was conducive to performing the primary reduction away from the site. They may have brought selected flakes or large flakes or chunks back to Water World instead of cobbles, leaving the cores at the quarry loci.

Another point of interest is the proportion of unretouched, utilized flake implements in the assemblage. They make up 4.7 percent of the total assemblage (Table 5.1), and constitute 41.7 percent of the implements. These results can be compared to Rozen's (1984: Table 5.29) findings for the Rosemont area Hohokam sites, where edge-altered flakes from particular proveniences ranged from 0 to 11.3 percent of analyzed flakes. At Water World they averaged 5.15 percent of all flakes, and ranged from 2.46 to 18.18 percent among the features (Table 5.1).

Chapter 6

GROUND STONE

Carl D. Halbirt

One hundred seventy-one pieces of ground stone representing 13 different artifact types were collected from Water World (Table 6.1). Present were manos, metates, pestles, mortars, Types I and II handstones, hammerstones, pebble pounders-polishers, abraders, axes, stone bowls, palettes, beads and pendants, and miscellaneous objects. A definition of each artifact type is given in the overview discussion of ground stone (Volume 1, Chapter 13), and a discussion of the analytic methods is presented in the Fastimes report (Volume 2, Chapter 6).

The implements were collected from a variety of contexts. The majority (105 implements, or just over 61%) was recovered from pit house deposits, which is to be expected given an excavation strategy that focused on these structures. Most of the implements (56%) collected from pit houses were recovered in trash or fill deposits, although a sizable quantity (32%) was recovered from the floors. The remaining 12 percent was found either in overburden or in floor features.

Eighteen excavated or tested structures yielded ground stone; 11 (or 61%) contained floor artifacts, and 7 of these contained three or more floor implements. Pit houses that contained three or more floor implements were Features 19, 20, 25, 29, 53, 55, and 58. The large proportion of houses containing floor artifacts at Water World contrasts with the patterns observed at Fastimes and Hawk's Nest, and may indicate differences in abandonment behavior.

The remaining 64 ground-stone implements were found scattered throughout various contexts: 25 percent were found with occupational surfaces that were probably outdoor work areas or specialized activity areas (Chapter 3); 45 percent were associated with extramural features (roasting pits, pits, and cremations) with 13 implements representing recycled items used in a roasting pit (Feature 8); and 30 percent were found on the ground surface or were collected from trench backdirt piles.

Except for a stone bowl found in the backdirt of Trench 25, the entire ground-stone assemblage was provenienced. Ground stone was recovered from all of the excavated house groups, with quantities differing in respect to the number of houses excavated (Table 6.2).

Table 6.1

DISTRIBUTION OF GROUND STONE ARTIFACTS

	Feature	Stratum	Milling Equipment					Tool Manufacturing				Ceremonial Ornaments				Unidentified	Total
			Manos	Metates	Pestles	Mortars	Hand-stones	Hammer-stones	Pebble P-P	Abraders	Axe	Stone Bowls	Palettes	Beads-Pendants	Unknown		
Surface			6f	5f				1								4f	16
House Group 1	18	50	2f	1f			1f									1f	5
		1	1							1							2
	19	30														1f	1
		1	1f	2f				1		1							5
		2		1f												1f	2
		20		2f	1												3
	20	1		1				1									2
		2	1f														1
		20	2f	1,1f			1f	2									7
	25	30	1f														1
		1		1f													1
		2	2,1f	2f			1f	2		1f						1,1f	11
		20		1						1							2
	25.1	1	2f			1	1			1							5
	55	1	1,2f	2f					2	2f			1f				10
		20		1f					2						1		4
	56		1f					1f									2
Subtotal			4,12f	3,14f	1	1	1,3f	6,1f	4	4,3f			1f		1	1,4f	64
House Group 2	7	1							1								1
		2							1								1
		20				1			1								2
	8	1	1,7f	4f				1		1f							14
	26	30	3f	1f					2						2f		8
		1		1f													1
	29	1	2							1			1				4
		20	1f			1				1							3
	59	1						1f									1
Subtotal			3,11f	6f		2		1f 2,1f	4	2,1f			1			2f	35
House Group 3	27	30	1														1
		1							1								1
		2							1								1
	33	50	1	1f													2
		2						1									1
		20														1f	1
	36	50	1f														1
		1	1														1
	40	1										1					1
	53	20		1f			2							1			5
Subtotal			3,1f	2f		2		1	1			1		1	1f		15
House Group 4	58	50	2f	1f						1f						1f	5
		30		1f										1			2
		2					1										2
		20	2		1								1				3
	61	50											1				1
		2															2
Subtotal			2,2f	2f	1		2			1f			3	1		1f	15
House Group 5	78	1	1														1
		20	1														1
	80	1											1				1
	87a	1									1						1
	110	2	1f														1
		20						1									1
Subtotal			2,1f					1			1		1				6
House Group 6	67	1	2f	3f										1	1f		7
	68	1	1f					1									2
		2	1f						1								2
		20	1	1f											1f		2
Subtotal			1,4f	4f				1	1					1	1f		13
Miscellaneous	44	30	1f					1f									2
	13	1	1														1
	138	1					1			1							2
Unknown																	
Subtotal			1,1f				1	1f		1		1			1		7
Total			16,38f	3,33f	4	1	6,3f	12,2f	12,1f	7,5f	1	2	1,1f	5	4	1,13f	171

f = fragments
P-P = Pounder-polishers

Table 6.2

DISTRIBUTION OF GROUND STONE BY HOUSE GROUP

House Group	Houses	Cremations	Pits	Activity Surfaces	Per House	All Features
			Feature Number		Average # Artifacts	
1	19, 20, 25, 55	--	18, 56	--	11.2	9.4
2	7, 26, 29	--	8*, 59	--	6.7	7.0
3	27, 33, 35*, 36*, 53	40*	--	--	2.8	2.5
4	58, 61	--	--	--	7.5	7.0
5	78*, 79*, 110*	80*, 87*	--	--	1.3	1.2
6	--	--	138*	66*, 67*, 68, 13	--	3.4
Unknown	45	--	--	--	--	--

* Tested only; all other features excavated completely or nearly so.

House Group 3 in particular had a disproportionately low quantity of ground stone despite its five excavated houses. The source of this discrepancy is unclear. Perhaps this house group was early, and the ground-stone implements were recycled by later inhabitants. House Group 5 also had a low density of artifacts; however, houses in this group were tested and not completely excavated. The raw data for the Water World ground-stone assemblage are provided in Volume 5, Appendix C.

Manos

Fifty-six manos, including two hammerstones recycled from mano fragments, were recovered from Water World; 16 are complete and 40 are fragmentary. Except for three small fragments, all of the manos had been shaped through pecking or grinding, or both. Rectangular forms (37 implements) were the dominant style for the 40 implements that could be distinguished to shape (Fig. 6.1a). Two ovoid manos and one oblong mano also were documented. The remaining 16 manos were too fragmentary to determine shape. At least two manos had been recycled from fragments; one from a mano fragment and the other from a metate fragment.

Except for the preference for rectangular shapes, manos from Water World are quite varied in terms of size, motor habits, and raw material. The variation in size is shown by Figures 6.2 and 6.3. The length:width distribution (Fig. 6.2) is continuous with no apparent clustering as is the case with Hawk's Nest (AZ AA:12:484). This distribution was found to be statistically significant using Pearson's r (Fig. 6.2), and may indicate an attempt to keep size in proportion to the degree of pressure exerted during milling. The variation in size also is reflected in mano thickness (Fig. 6.3). Thickness ranges from 2.6 cm to 8.2 cm, with the majority skewed toward thinner manos between 3.5 cm to 4.5 cm. Most of the fragmentary manos are less than 4.5 cm thick, whereas complete manos are equally distributed above and below 4.5 cm.

Unifacial and bifacial manos and mano blanks are present at the site (Table 6.3). When only complete implements are considered, the ratio of unifacial to bifacial manos is almost 2 to 1. If fragments are considered, then the ratio of unifacial to bifacial implements increases to roughly 3 to 1. Why this is true for Water World when other project sites display an essentially equal ratio of unifacial and bifacial manos is unclear. It may be a response to either additional tasks performed with manos, such as percussion implements used in tool manufacturing, or to a milling strategy adapted toward agriculture. In either case, a heavier, thicker implement would be expected that could withstand the crushing or pounding motions produced during these tasks. It should be noted that unifacial manos are thicker and more exhibit batterings on the ends than bifacial manos.

Motor habits are reflected in the grinding surface shape and in the striations or grinding orientation. At Water World, no particular technique was emphasized in the milling process. Instead there is an equal representation between grinding techniques, resulting in either flat (plano) or rocker-shaped (convex) grinding surfaces (Table 6.3). This variability suggests that different milling approaches were used depending on either the type of resources that were processed, the user, or both. The primary grinding orientation was reciprocal (back and forth) with only two instances of a random grinding motion documented.

A variety of raw materials was used to manufacture manos. The materials can be categorized into four basic types: granite (29%), sandstone (24%), vesicular basalt (31%), and porphyritic igneous (16%). When classified into one of two different grain sizes (fine- to medium-grained or medium- to coarse-grained), the raw materials were equally divided. This pattern differs markedly from that documented at other sites where fine-grained material dominates, and may indicate a milling

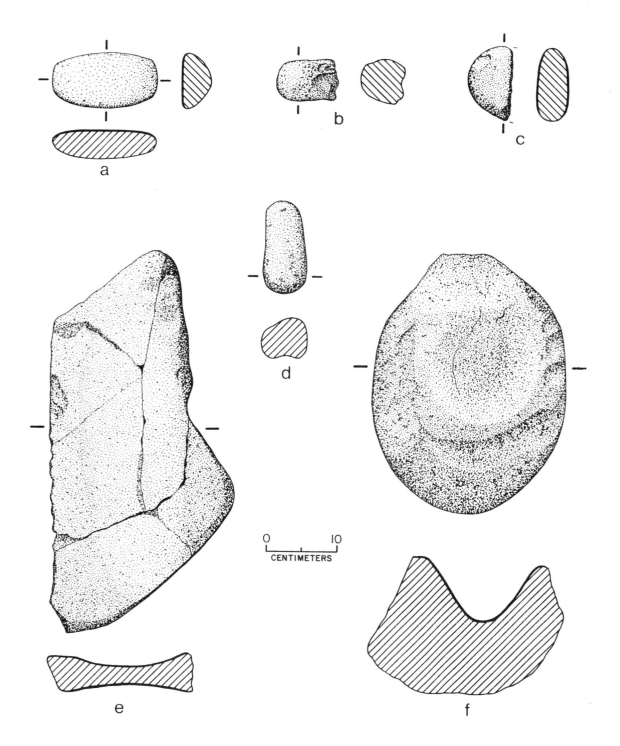

Figure 6.1. Milling equipment: a, mano; b,d, pestles; c, handstone, Type II; e, slab metate; f, mortar.

218

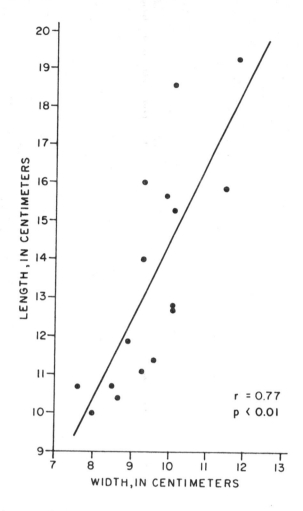

Figure 6.2.   Mano length:width comparison.

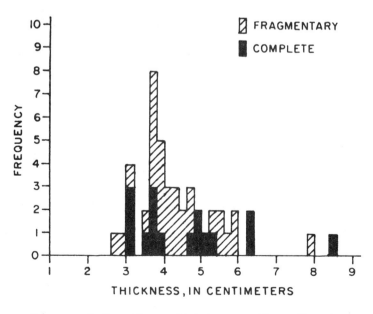

Figure 6.3.   Mano thickness distribution.

Table 6.3

COMPARISON OF MANO GRINDING SURFACE SHAPES
WITH NUMBER OF GRINDING SURFACES

| Surface Shape | Grinding Surfaces | | | | Total |
	0	1	2	Unknown	
Flat		14 (6)	4 (2)	--	18 (8)
Beveled		8 (2)	1 (1)	--	8 (3)
Convex		14 (2)	3 (1)	--	17 (3)
Flat/Convex		--	3 (2)	--	3 (2)
Unknown	1	5	3	1	10
Total	1	41(10)	14 (6)	1	56(16)

( ) Complete implements

although no studies to date have addressed the association between raw materials for manos and processed resources. Conversely, it may signify a two-stage grinding strategy. Puebloan groups are known to have used various grades of raw materials in processing domesticated plants (Bartlett 1933).

In summary, manos from Water World are comparable to the manos from Fastimes and the Type II manos from Hawk's Nest, particularly in terms of size. Most likely these manos were used in conjunction with the larger slab or trough metates (see below), with mano variability reflecting a wide range of applications. Differences that do exist between Water World and other sites, such as the high ratio of unifacial to bifacial implements, and the association between the number of grinding surfaces with thickness, may indicate uses other than milling for manos.

Manos were recovered from a variety of contexts and locations, including the floors of pit house Features 20, 29, 58, 68, and 78. Houses that contained more than one floor mano were Feature 58 (2 complete artifacts) and Feature 20 (2 fragments). In terms of stratigraphic distribution, manos are equally represented in all levels. The majority of manos was found in House Groups 1 and 2, with the former having a slight edge over the latter in complete and fragmentary manos.

Metates

Thirty-six metates, 3 complete and 33 fragments, were recovered from the site. Twenty-two implements could be identified to type: five slab metates (3 complete), two trough metate fragments that were closed at one end (Woodbury 1954: 52), and 15 indeterminate trough metate fragments that could not be identified as to variety. The remaining artifacts (14) were too small to be positively categorized, although five were tentatively labeled as indeterminate trough.

The three complete grinding slab metates are irregular in shape and exhibit little if any modification or shaping. One metate is made from a flat slab of fine-grained quartzite and another from a flat slab of red siltstone. The third is a recycled metate fragment made of a medium-coarse granite. All are unifacial, and exhibit shallow grinding surfaces less than 1 cm deep and a reciprocal grinding orientation.

The slab metate made from the red siltstone (Fig. 6.1e), which outcrops near the Arizona-Sonora Desert Museum 6.4 km north of Water World (Fig. 1.1), is the largest of the three slab metates. It measures 53.6 cm long by 25.6 cm wide and 6 cm thick. The grinding surface area is estimated to have been 550 square centimeters. Two small pecked depressions, measuring 4 cm and 5 cm in diameter, occur toward one end of the grinding surface. The slab metate, broken into six pieces, was found on the floor of pit house Feature 25.

The other two complete slab metates are essentially comparable in size. The recycled granite slab measures 24 cm by 17 cm by 10.5 cm with a grinding surface area estimated at 200 square centimeters. The implement was found in the fill of pit house Feature 20. Pieces of the original metate, from which the recycled metate was made, were found in the fill of pit house Feature 29. The quartzite slab metate measures 23 cm by 29.5 cm by 5.3 cm and was found on the floor of Feature 20. Its grinding surface area is estimated at 200 square centimeters.

The two slab metate fragments are made from fine-grained igneous materials. One was found on the floor of Feature 19, a pit house. It is unifacial and exhibits a reciprocal grinding motion. The metate measures more than 20 cm long, 18 cm wide, and is approximately 10 cm thick. The grinding surface area is more than 300 square centimeters. The second fragment was found in association with Feature 8 and is bifacial, exhibiting a rotary grinding motion.

The 17 trough and indeterminate trough metate fragments are unifacial and exhibit reciprocal grinding motions. The principal raw material used in trough metate manufacture is vesicular basalt (N=10). Other raw materials used are sandstone (N=5), porphyritic igneous, and granite.

Trough metate size can only be considered in terms of ranges for thickness and the grinding surface depth (for example, the degree of

wear evidenced on the grinding surface). The length and width
measurements are essentially unknown, although one fragment from Feature
8 measures more than 21 cm in length and 10 cm in width. Eight of the
16 fragments were recorded for thickness. They range from greater than
5.5 cm to greater than 13.5 cm thick with most (6) occurring from 8 cm
to 13 cm. Grinding surface depth was recorded for all of the fragments.
Ten fragments exhibit a depth greater than 2 cm, and four others are
greater than 3 cm. The actual grinding surface depth was documented for
one fragment from the floor of Feature 53, a pit house, and it measures
6.6 cm.

Based on raw material selection the 14 unidentifiable metate
fragments originate primarily from trough metates. Vesicular basalt is
the principal raw material used (9 cases) in manufacture. Other raw
materials are quartzite, porphyritic igneous, and granite. This
reliance on vesicular basalt closely parallels that documented for the
trough and indeterminate trough metate fragments.

Although it is impossible to estimate the actual number of
metates represented in the current sample of 36 pieces, given the
overwhelming majority of fragments (92%), it can be assumed that trough
variety metates were the dominant type followed by slab metates. This
statement is based on the frequency of metate types present and the
selection of raw materials. Of the 36 pieces recovered, 20 were
vesicular basalt, which was used primarily for trough metates.

Metates were recovered from a variety of contexts, including
nine fragments collected from six pit house floors. In situ metates
were recovered from Features 19, 20, 25, 53, 55, and 68. The majority
of floor metates (N=7) were found in House Group 1 (Features 19, 20, 25,
and 55). One each was found in House Groups 3 (Feature 53) and 6
(Feature 68). Floor metates represent either de facto refuse or
recycled implements, such as the metate fragment used as part of a
hearth trivet in pit house Feature 53. The remaining 21 provenienced
fragments (surface artifacts not included) were found primarily in fill;
the majority of these came from House Group 1.

Pestles

Four pestles, three complete and one fragment, were recovered
from Water World (Fig. 6.1b, d). Each pestle was found on the floor of
a different pit house (Features 7, 19, 29, and 58). All are made of
fine-grained raw materials (either quartzite, metasandstone, or
limestone), and all share similar morphological characteristics. The
implements are subrectangular in plan view and cross section, and range
from 8.8 cm to 14.6 cm long by 6.4 cm to 7.8 cm wide and 6.0 cm to 6.2
cm thick. Both ends on all four pestles exhibit use wear in the form of
battering and grinding. Flaking scars indicate that the pestle from
Feature 19 also may have been used as a hammerstone.

Mortars

One complete boulder mortar (Fig. 6.1f) was recovered from a floor pit (Feature 25.1) in Feature 25, a pit house. The ovoid-shaped boulder measures 36 cm long by 28 cm wide by 29 cm thick, and is made from fine-grained sandstone. The actual mortar cavity measures 15 cm in diameter by 9 cm deep. This is the only in situ mortar found during the Phase B Project. That the implement was found in a floor pit with only the mortar cavity exposed suggests that it was a nonportable object.

Other artifacts were associated with this mortar. A fragmentary Type II handstone (Fig. 6.1c) that exhibits extensive battering was found in the mortar cavity, and was probably part of the tool kit. Three artifacts (2 sherds and 1 piece of ground stone) were found at the base of the mortar and were most likely used as shims to level the implement. Also recovered were two mano fragments and a complete abrader.

Handstones

Nine handstones, six complete and three fragments, were recovered. Five were categorized as Type I handstones based on smooth (nonabraded) surface(s). The other three had ground (abraded) surface(s) and are Type II handstones. All are made from unmodified ovoid or subrectangular fine- to medium-grained river cobbles. Raw materials used are sandstone, quartzite, and granite. All of the handstones exhibit battering on the sides or ends, or both. Most likely, both types of handstone were used for processing foodstuffs, although tool manufacturing or maintenance cannot be overlooked (Woodbury 1954: 93).

Size did not vary significantly between the two types. Measurements for the Type I handstones range from 8.5 cm to 10.7 cm long by 6.4 cm to 9.2 cm wide and 1.5 cm to 5.4 cm thick. The average weight is 522 g.

The nine handstones were found in a variety of contexts. Four were recovered from house floors, one each from Features 20 and 25, and two from Feature 53. The other four were found either in house fill (Features 25, 58, and 61) or in overburden deposits.

Hammerstones

Fourteen hammerstones, 12 complete and 2 fragments, were recovered from Water World. No particular form or type (such as cobble hammerstone) was preferred. Rather, hammerstones took on a variety of forms: five are made from river cobbles, three are large implements with

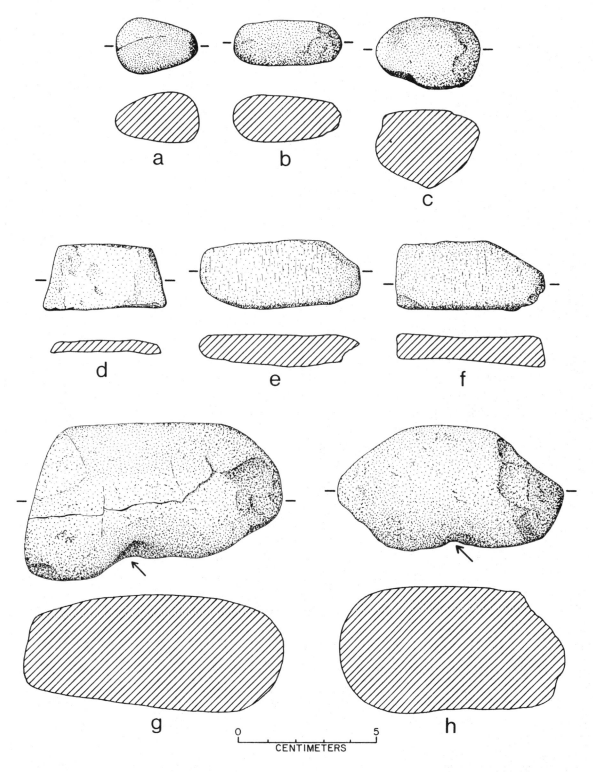

Figure 6.4. Ground stone artifacts indicative of tool manufacturing
(arrows point to finger grips): a-b, pebble polishers; c, g, and h,
hammerstones; d-f, abraders.

finger grips, three implements are multipurpose (for example, tools were not restricted solely to hammering [pounding], but also were used for grinding or polishing), and three implements are recycled from discarded mano or metate fragments.

Four of the five cobble hammerstones are complete and one is fragmentary. All are made from subangular fine- to medium-grained river cobbles (Fig. 6.4c) of basalt (2 implements), limestone, and sandstone. Size ranges from 7.2 cm to 8.9 cm long by 6.2 cm to 6.5 cm wide by 4.0 cm to 5.8 cm thick. Weight averages 342 g. All have been extensively battered on one or more edges. Four of these cobble hammerstones were found in the fill of four features (Features 8, 20, 59, and 68). The fifth was found on the floor of Feature 110, a pit house.

The three large implements with finger grips are complete and were found in House Group 1. The implements are made of igneous materials (gabbro, porphyritic ryholite, and granite) that varies in texture (grain size). Measurements range from 16.6 cm to 19.3 cm long by 9.3 cm to 11 cm wide by 9.5 cm to 11.6 cm thick. The weight averages 2.7 kg. Finger or thumb grips are found along one side on all three implements. Battering or flaking scars are present on one or both ends. Two of the implements (Figs. 6.4g and h) were found in the floor fill of pit house Feature 25. The third was found on the floor of pit house Feature 20.

The three large hammerstones are considered to have been used during the initial manufacturing of manos and metates. Similar large percussion implements weighing approximately 2 kg have been documented as "used for heavy-duty roughing out" of manos and metates by Highland Mayan groups (Hayden and Nelson 1981: 887). Besides weight and size, the implements from Water World share morphological and raw material characteristics with those of the Maya. Parallels are observed with respect to restricted or narrowed ends, resharpening resulting in flaking scars, and the use of dense igneous materials that could withstand the force of impact against a large object (Hayden and Nelson 1981: 887-888). This particular form of hammerstone was only found at Water World.

The three multipurpose hammerstones were found in house fill. Two are rectangular in shape with battered end(s) and minimal abrasion apparent on the surface(s). Raw materials are a fine-grained porphyritic igneous and a siltstone. Size averages 11 cm long by 4.5 cm wide by 3 cm thick; weight averages 270 g. The third implement made from a fine-grained andesite river cobble is a hammerstone-chopper. One end exhibits extensive battering, whereas the other end has been flaked to a blunt edge. This item is subrectangular and measures 9.3 cm by 7.7 cm by 5.7 cm with a weight of 470 g.

The final category of hammerstones, those made from discarded items, is represented by three specimens. Two are reused mano fragments that exhibit extensive battering. They are subrectangular in shape, made from fine-grained sandstone, and weigh 669 g and 1068 g. Each was found on a house floor, one from Feature 7 and one from Feature 20. The third implement was found in the fill of Feature 19, and is recycled from a fine-grained limestone pestle fragment. The broken end exhibits extensive battering. The implement is conical in shape and weighs 337 g.

Pebble Pounder-Polishers

Thirteen pebbles that were used for either pounding or polishing were recovered (Fig. 6.4a and b); 12 are complete and 1 is broken. The implements were found scattered across the site and in various contexts, including three recovered from the floors of Features 53 and 55. All are made from riverworn pebbles of fine- to medium-grained materials: quartzite, sandstone, rhyolite, basalt, and porphyritic igneous. Dimensions range from 4.6 cm to 8.2 cm long, 2.8 cm to 5.8 cm wide, and 1.4 cm to 4.3 cm thick for complete specimens. Weight varies from 29 g to 279 g; the average is 103 g. Generally, the longer implements were used for polishing and pounding, whereas the shorter implements were used for polishing. There appears to be no correlation between raw material types and use-wear on pebbles. One of the implements had been used to grind red ochre (Fig. 6.4a).

Abraders

Twelve abraders, including the two rectangular hammerstones exhibiting abrasion, were recovered from Water World (Fig. 6.4d-f). Seven complete and five fragmentary items are present. The majority (11 implements) are flat abraders (Woodbury 1954: 98-99) with flat grinding surfaces. Striations are both reciprocal and random, indicating varied grinding patterns. Raw materials are fine-grained sandstones, quartzites, igneous stone, and red siltstones (argillite); the last outcrops near the Arizona-Sonora Desert Museum. The flat abraders are primarily rectangular; measurements range from 5.0 cm to 13.4 cm long, 3.9 cm to 8 cm wide, and 1.2 cm to 3.5 cm thick. The other abrader, a fine-grained basalt river cobble, has a concave grinding surface, and is within the size range of the flat abraders.

Axe

A single, three-quarter grooved axe (Fig. 6.5d) was found at Water World. The axe is similar to the Type I variety at Snaketown (Haury 1976: 291) in that the haft groove was flanked by ridges. The axe bit is short (6 cm) and most of the face has been pecked and ground. Only a small area around the poll remains unworked. The edge of the bit is polished. The axe measures 11.3 cm long by 6.2 cm wide and 6.2 cm thick. The weight is 587 g. The axe is made from a fine-grained dense

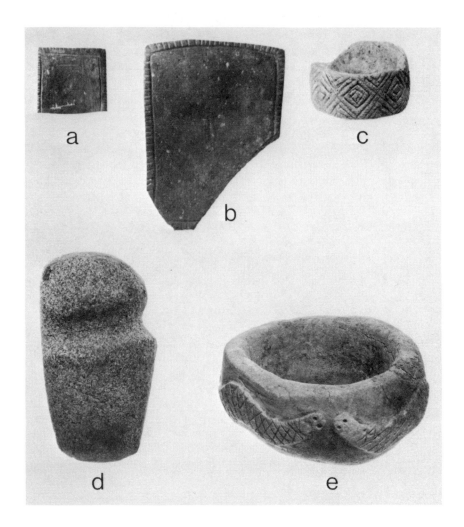

Figure 6.5. Ceremonial worked stone: a,b, palettes; c,e, stone bowls; d, axe (length of d: 11.3 cm).

igneous material. This axe is the only one found during the Phase B excavations, and was recovered in a multiple secondary cremation pit, Feature 87a.

Stone Bowls

Two complete circular stone bowls were recovered from Water World (Fig. 6.5c and e). Both bowls have been carved, one with two facing snake motifs in bas-relief and the other incised with what appears to also have been a snake. The designs encircle the exterior surface of each bowl. The bowls share design similarities to other Hohokam Colonial phase stone bowls (Volume 2, Chapter 6).

The effigy bowl with the two snakes (Fig. 6.5e) measures 10.9 cm in diameter by 5.5 cm thick. The bowl cavity is 2.6 cm deep and exhibits evidence of grinding as well as battering. Striations are evident along the sides of the bowl, and the base is pitted. The snakes resemble rattlesnakes. The heads face one another and the bodies are demarked by a series of cross-hatched incisions. The bowl is made from a fine-grained volcanic tuff. This bowl was found in a secondary cremation pit, Feature 40, and had been fire-blackened.

The incised bowl (Fig. 6.5c) measures 5.4 cm in diameter by 3.4 cm thick. The bowl cavity is 1.6 cm deep and exhibits evidence of grinding and some battering. Striations occur along the sides and base of the bowl. The exterior has been incised with a series of seven diamond motifs that nearly encircle the bowl. This continuous band is thought to represent the body designs of a snake. An open square with two opposed drill holes representing eyes is considered to be the head. The bowl is made from a fine-grained volcanic tuff and was found in the backdirt pile of Trench 25; its context is uncertain.

Palettes

Two fragmentary palettes were recovered from the site (Fig. 6.5a and b). Both are rectangular in plan and tabular in cross section. Each palette has been incised along the raised border, a characteristic diagnostic of the Colonial phase (Volume 2, Chapter 6).

One of the palettes (Fig. 6.5b) was found associated with a secondary cremation pit, Feature 80. The implement had been broken during mechanical trenching. It measures 10.7 cm by 8.1 cm by 0.88 mm. The palette is made from a fine-grained porphyritic igneous material that has been shaped by grinding. Striations are still visible on all surfaces. The item has been fire blackened.

The second palette fragment (Fig. 6.5a) was found in the fill of pit house Feature 55. It measures over 3.8 cm long by 4 cm wide and 6 mm thick. The surface is concave with a red pigment stain present around the edges. The artifact is made from a fine-grained mudstone, and has been shaped through grinding.

Stone Beads and Pendants

Five complete stone beads or pendants were collected from Water World (Fig. 6.6a-e; Table 6.4). Three are manufactured from high-grade turquoise. The other two are made from unidentifiable sources: one is a concretion, the other is a fire-blackened siliceous material (Fig. 6.6e), possibly turquoise, from the floor of pit house Feature 53. The remaining four beads were found in various fill or overburden contexts at three different locations.

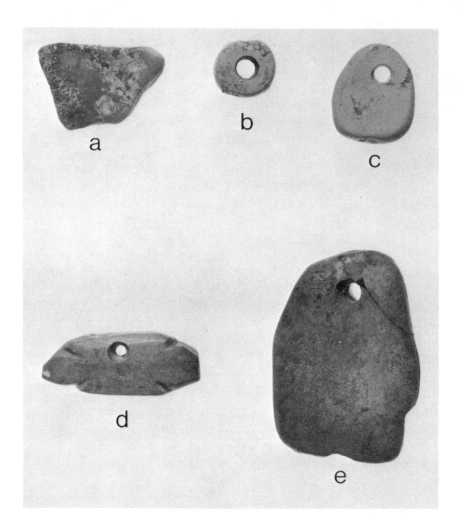

Figure 6.6. Ground stone ornaments: a, worked turquoise; b,c, beads; d,e, pendants (length of e: 2.2 cm).

All of the ornaments have been ground and polished on one or more surfaces. Bead shapes are oval or circular; pendants are either irregular or shaped into effigies. Size is variable (Table 6.4).

Unknown Ground Stone

Four pieces of ground stone were collected that could not be placed into a typological category. One artifact, collected from the fill of Feature 67 (an activity surface), is a subrectangular limestone slab that has flaked edges and one slightly ground surface. Measuring 8.1 cm long by 5.1 cm wide and 1.1 cm thick, it is similar to the artifact category "tabular knives" recovered at other Hohokam sites (Hoffman 1985, Fig. 12.1).

Table 6.4

GROUND STONE ORNAMENTS

Feature	Context	Type	Shape	Weight (g)	Measurements (cm)	Figure	Material
29	Fill	Pendant	Effigy	<1	1.7 x 0.8 x 0.3	6d	Turquoise
53	Floor	Pendant	Irregular	3	2.2 x 1.5 x 0.6	6e	Siliceous
58	Floor fill	Bead	Oval	1	1.1 x 0.9 x 0.3	6c	Turquoise
61	Overburden	Bead	Circular	<1	0.6 diam. x 0.3	6b	Turquoise
61	Floor fill	Bead	Circular	1	0.9 diam. x 0.8	--	Concretion

A chunk of calcite collected from the floor of pit house Feature 55 exhibits extensive grinding at one end and battering at the opposite end. The item is ovoid and measures 8.1 cm long by 6.2 cm wide and 3.5 cm thick. It weighs 255 g. The chunk probably was ground as a mineral resource.

The third object collected from the trash fill of pit house Feature 58 is a thick, cyclindrical block of fine- to medium-grained granite. The object has been shaped through pecking and grinding, and the surfaces are pitted as if used as an anvil. The implement measures 9.8 cm in diameter by 7.2 cm thick. Similar objects have been recovered at Snaketown and the Hodges Ruin, and are referred to as grooved handstones (Gladwin and others 1937, Plate XLV) because of the slight indented curve along the sides, or as shaped stones (Kelly 1978: 95).

The last object is a piece of worked turquoise (Fig. 6.6a). It measures 13 mm long by 9 mm wide by 5 mm thick. All surfaces and sides of this trapezoidal item are smoothed and polished; however, none has been ground. The smoothed, polished appearance may be the result of handling. The provenience of this object is unknown.

Unidentifiable Ground Stone

Fourteen pieces of ground stone could not be identified. Thirteen are small pieces thought to be fragments of manos or metates based on raw material or use-wear attributes, or both. The majority of fragments was collected from the surface or from trash contexts. The other item is complete and represents a rectangular preform; it measures 15.8 cm long by 8.7 cm wide, and 2.2 cm thick. It is made of a fine- to medium-grained porphyritic igneous and exhibits minimal grinding. The item was found in the fill of pit house Feature 25.

Discussion

The ground-stone assemblage from Water World is useful in understanding certain aspects of the systemic context. In particular, general aspects of subsistence and site function can be addressed. The identification of potential activity areas based on the spatial distribution of ground stone, as was done at Fastimes, is tenuous, however. Any patterns observed in the ground-stone assemblage among house groups may be biased due to either prehistoric discard behavior or natural formation processes. This assessment is based on the refitting of both decorated ceramics (Chapter 4, this volume) and ground-stone implements. Both artifact classes had fragments of the same artifact present in features that are widely spaced.

It should be noted that any observed trends in the ground-stone assemblage must be considered tentative given the small sample size

(171 pieces) and the excavation strategy, which focused on houses and cremations. Any trends can be tested with other data sets to determine their validity.

The ground-stone assemblage from Water World, and from Fastimes, contains a variety of tool types and reflects a wide range of activities. Implements used in food processing, tool manufacturing, and for ceremonial and ornamental purposes are present. The most ubiquitous group of implements are items used primarily in food preparation. Manos, metates, pestles, a mortar, and handstones account for approximately 62 percent of all the recognizable ground stone (153 pieces). This apparent abundance of milling stones may be slightly exaggerated given that approximately 71 percent of all documented milling stones, especially manos and metates, were fragments and, therefore, some artifacts may have been counted more than once.

Milling activities at Water World involved various food processing strategies. The use of manos and metates seems to have been the preferred method based on counts (Table 6.1), and the use of mortars and pestles also may have been important. When the number of houses containing floor artifacts is considered (11 structures), nine features contain either manos or metates whereas five contain either pestles or mortars for a ratio of approximately 2 to 1. This figure is in contrast to Fastimes, where the number of houses containing manos or metates, or both, outnumbered those containing pestles by a ratio of approximately 4 to 1. What this implies at Water World is uncertain. It may correlate with the wider use of plants with difficult-to-process pericarps (Goodyear 1975: 167), such as corn. I have noted (Halbirt 1985: 72) that mortars and pestles may have been an important component in the agricultural tool kit based on the large quantities of corn pollen found in mortars.

The possibility that agriculture was an important subsistence component at Water World is supported by two lines of evidence that are not mutually exclusive: (1) the types of metates used at the site, and (2) the raw material selected for metate manufacturing.

Traditionally it has been argued that trough variety metates represent an advanced milling technique associated with an agricultural economy, although some dispute this assumption (Volume 1, Chapter 13). The presence of numerous trough metate fragments, which accounts for 17 of the 22 identifiable metates (77%), indicates an advanced milling technique. This percentage contrasts to that documented for other sites in the Phase B corridor.

Concomitant with the use of trough metates is the selection of coarse-grained materials for tool manufacture. The use of coarse-grained materials has been hypothesized to correlate with the processing of large seeds or kernels such as corn (Ackerly 1979: 326), and has been supported by a study of pollen remains on metate grinding surfaces (Halbirt 1985). Coarse-grained materials, which include vesicular basalt with medium to coarse vesicles (that is, greater than 2 mm in size), were used more often with trough metates than with other types of metates at the site (Table 6.5). When unidentifiable fragments are considered, the importance of coarse-grained materials becomes even more evident in metate manufacturing. Fine-grained raw materials, which are hypothesized to be associated with processing native resources (Halbirt 1985), also were used in trough metate manufacturing, indicating that these implements were not restricted to agricultural products (Halbirt 1985).

Table 6.5

COMPARISON OF METATE TYPES WITH RAW MATERIAL TEXTURE

| Grain Size | Metate Types | | | Total |
	Slab	Trough	Unknown	
Fine-Medium (0-2 mm)	4	8	3	15
Medium-Coarse (2+ mm)	1	9	11	21
Total	5	17	14	36

economy is not negated by the milling tool kit. The presence of slab metates and the use of fine-grained raw material suggests that these resources were processed. What is unique is that equipment that might have been used for processing corn is more prevalent at Water World than at other sites. When the patterns noted for the milling equipment are contrasted with the pollen and flotation data, the association is inconclusive. In both the pollen and flotation data (Chapters 9 and 10, respectively), corn and native resources are present; however, they occur in low frequencies throughout most of the site.

Nonetheless, an interesting aspect of the pollen data may have important ramifications for the interpretation of milling assemblages. This concerns the possibility that Water World was occupied during the winter when residents subsisted primarily on stored resources (Chapter 9). If this was the case, then the milling assemblage may not only have been adapted to certain economic resources, but may also reflect seasonality (Volume 1, Chapter 13). Stored resources would be expected to have hard seed coats (pericarps) because of drying, which necessitates the use of heavier and coarser implements for processing. Clearly, more data must be acquired and more investigation carried out to determine the association between milling equipment and site seasonality.

Other activities reflected by the ground-stone assemblage are tool production, ceremony or ritual, and ornamentation. The majority of implements are related to tool manufacturing. Of the 48 nonmilling artifacts recovered, 39 were manufacturing, 4 were ceremonial or ritual, and 5 were ornamental (Table 6.1). This distribution is in complete contrast to that documented at Fastimes, implying that Water World functioned in a different capacity, possibly as a manufacturing locus for surrounding sites.

Tool manufacturing equipment consisted of three basic artifact classes: hammerstones, pebble pounder-polishers, and abraders. All are represented in roughly the same proportion (Table 6.1). The axe also is included in the category tool production even though at the time of discard it was used in a ceremonial activity as a cremation offering. In addition to these artifacts, manos also may have been used in tool production, based on attribute associations (discussed above), giving further importance to tool manufacturing at the site. Types of manufacturing may have included pottery production, mano and metate production, or shell working.

Ceremonial-ritual and ornamental objects appear to have been a minor component of the ground-stone assemblage. Artifacts included under the heading ceremonial-ritual are stone bowls and palettes; ornamental items are stone beads and pendants. Both categories account for about 6 percent of the total identifiable ground-stone assemblage. This is in contrast to Fastimes where the two categories comprise 17 percent of the total assemblage. Why Water World appears to have few items from either category when it is proposed to have served a specialized function (Volume 1, Chapter 2) is unclear. It may be that production was not oriented toward ceremonial-ritual and ornamental goods, or it may be a result of sampling bias.

In terms of the spatial variability of artifact categories, some patterns are evident. First, when looking at the artifact assemblages from each house group, there does not appear to be specialization at any one house group (Table 6.6). Instead, artifact categories appear to be more or less equally represented throughout the site. Alternatively, when each artifact category is considered as a whole, then House Groups 1 and 2 exhibit greater emphasis on milling equipment and tool production equipment (Table 6.6). Whether this is a function of scattered deposits, as indicated by the refitting of ceramic and ground-stone artifacts, or functional similarities between house groups cannot be determined with the existing ground-stone assemblage. Second, there is a distinct difference between the house groups in terms of ground stone frequencies (Table 6.6). For House Group 1, ground stone frequencies are roughly double that of any other house group. This distribution suggests a more intensive occupation at House Group 1, a supposition supported by the divergence and frequency of economic pollen types for this house group in contrast to the other house groups (Chapter 9). As Fish noted in her discussion of the pollen from House Group 1 (Chapter 9), this divergence in economic pollen types is reflective of a "more comprehensive residency."

Table 6.6

DISTRIBUTION OF GROUND STONE ARTIFACT CATEGORIES BY HOUSE GROUP*

Artifact Category	House Group						Total
	1	2	3	4	5	6	
Milling equipment	39 (61/43)	22 (63/24)	8 (53/09)	9 (60/10)	3 (50/3)	9 (70/10)	90
Tool production	18 (28/49)	10 (29/27)	4 (26/11)	1 (07/03)	2 (33/05)	2 (15/05)	37
Ceremonial	1 (02/33.3)	-	1 (07/33.3)	-	1 (17/33.3)	-	3
Ornamental	-	1 (03/20)	1 (07/20)	3 (20/60)	-	-	5
Unknown	6 (09/46)	2 (06/15)	1 (07/09)	2 (13/15)	-	2 (15/15)	13
Total	64	35	15	15	6	13	148

*Does not consider surface artifacts

(N/n) Column percentage/row percentage. Row percent shows the relative frequency of an artifact category for a particular house group based on the total number of a particular class of artifacts.

The data from Water World are somewhat ambiguous in terms of establishing the relative length of occupation, although a long and intensive occupation is suggested based on three lines of evidence. First, the ratio of fragments to complete implements for milling equipment is approximately 2.5 to 1, indicating a considerable amount of breakage through use. Second, the grinding surface depth for trough metates is greater than 2 cm, with five fragments exhibiting a depth greater than 3 cm. This contrasts with the shallow grinding surfaces documented for trough metates at Hawk's Nest. Third, more artifacts at Water World were found to have been recycled than at the other sites investigated. The information recorded for manos is not in agreement with a long occupation, however. The mano thickness distribution (Fig. 6.3) parallels that at Hawk's Nest, where old manos were not replaced as they were broken, or no longer served efficiently as grinding tools. Part of the problem at Water World is that manos could have been used for other activities, resulting in early breakage. Still, replacement is not apparent. Thus, although three lines of evidence (breakage, metate grinding depth, and recycled artifacts) suggest a long and intensive occupation, the duration of that occupation is not clearly established.

Chapter 7

SHELL ARTIFACTS

Arthur W. Vokes

The excavations at Water World produced 170 shell artifacts and
fragments representing nine genera. The artifact forms include those
commonly recovered from Colonial period Hohokam communities. More than
80 percent of the specimens could be assigned to formal artifact
categories. The remainder of the sample lacked diagnostic attributes,
which precluded categorization. In five cases, specimens exhibited some
degree of modification, but not enough to identify the form from which
the specimen was derived. The remaining fragments were devoid of any
intentional modification.

The methods used in this analysis are the same used to analyze
the shell assemblage from Fastimes. For these and a diagram of the
nomenclature of structural features on molluscan shell, see Volume 2,
Chapter 7.

Genera and Species

Nine genera were identified from the sample recovered from Water
World: eight marine genera and one freshwater genus. Half of the
marine genera and the single freshwater genus could be assigned to the
species level (Table 7.1).

Except for Haliotis, the probable source for the marine material
is the Gulf of California. In some cases, such as with Laevicardium
elatum, the range extends up the California coast for a short distance.
The use of these species by the prehistoric inhabitants of California
seems to have been minimal (Gifford 1947), however. Therefore, with the
exception of Haliotis, it seems unlikely that shell entered the Hohokam
region from California. Haliotis is the only genus that can be
identified as exclusive to the colder coastal waters of California.

The nearest known source of the freshwater pelecypod Anodonta
californensis is the Santa Cruz River. Sites along the river
consistently have produced samples of the species (Vokes 1988, 1987).
Historic use of this shellfish as food has been reported for Tucson's

Table 7.1

SHELL GENERA AND SPECIES

Genus and Species	N of Pieces
Marine Pelecypods	
Glycymeris sp.	45
Glycymeris gigantea (Reeve, 1843)	2
Laevicardium elatum (Sowerby, 1833)	13
Pecten vogdesi Arnold, 1906	3
Argopecten circularis (Sowerby, 1835)	1
Spondylus sp. / Chama sp.	1
Gastropods	
Haliotis sp. (cf. cracherodii Leach, 1814)	1
Columbella sp.	1
Nerita funiculata Menke, 1851	76*
Freshwater Pelecypod	
Anodonta californensis Lea, 1852	24

* Possibly more

Chinese community (Bequaert and Miller 1973: 221). I cannot say that
Anodonta was used as food by the inhabitants of Water World, but it was
used as raw material for jewelry.

Artifacts

A total of 170 pieces of shell was recovered, and of these, 137
pieces were classed as artifacts or identified as manufacturing waste.
The remaining pieces either were too fragmentary or did not exhibit
evidence of intentional modification (Table 7.2). Although many of the
beads were burned and distorted by cremation fires, the rest of the
assemblage was in good shape. A detailed listing of the artifacts,
their condition, and provenience can be found in Volume 5, Appendix D-2.

Table 7.2

SHELL ARTIFACT ASSEMBLAGE

Genus	Beads Whole-shell	Beads Other	Pendants Whole-shell	Pendants Cut Zoomorphic	Pendants Cut Geometric	Bracelets Plain	Bracelets Decorated	Bracelets In process	Rings	Other	Manufacturing Refuse	Shell Fragments Worked (Form Unknown)	Shell Fragments Unworked	Whole Valve	Total
Marine															
Pelecypod															
Glycymeris				1		38	2	1	1	4					47
Laevicardium				1	1						3		7	1	13
Pecten			1									2			3
Argopecten					1										1
Spondylus/Chama		1													1
Gastropods															
Haliotis												1			1
Columbella	1														1
Nerita	76+														76+
Unidentified Genera				1								1	1		3
Freshwater															
Pelecypod															
Anodonta											3	3	18		24
Total	77++	1	1	3	2	38	2	1	1	4	6	7	26	1	170+

+Absolute numbers including fragments probably in excess of this figure
++Nerita beads in two deposits

Beads

Whole-Shell Forms

Two forms of whole-shell beads were recovered during the excavations. The first is represented by a single example recovered from the overburden of Feature 58, a pit house. The specimen consisted of the upper portion of the body whorl and part of the penultimate whorl of a univalve, probably Columbella. It is difficult to determine whether the absence of the spire is intentional because the remaining portion is burned and fractured, which obscures the margins. A definite ground facet is visible on the back of the body whorl in line with the aperture, however, suggesting that the bead was perforated in this manner.

Two cremations, Features 105 and 118, produced all the examples of the second bead form. Forty-eight complete and more than 28 fragmentary beads were recovered from these proveniences. All were burned, and many were calcined. The beads were manufactured from the shells of Nerita funiculata, a small gastropod (Fig. 7.1a). The aperture and contiguous portions of the body whorl were ground on a flat, abrasive surface. Grinding reduced the curvature of the valve and produced a bifurcated perforation with the callus and columellar structure forming the partition. Their presence in two separate, but spatially close cremations raises the question of the relationship between these deposits. Minimally they might represent the limited distribution of a single artisan's craft.

This bead form has previously been reported from an Estrella phase deposit at Snaketown (Haury 1976: 309) and from the excavations at the Gleeson Site (Fulton and Tuthill 1940, Plate XXV). In both cases, however, the species was reported as Theodoxus luteofasciatus, a related species (Nelson 1981: 186; Haury 1976: 313; Fulton and Tuthill 1940: 37).

Other Forms

A fragment of an unusual object was recovered from the roof fall of Feature 19, a pit house. The object is roughly hemicylindrical and was manufactured from the umbo portion of a Chama or Spondylus valve (Fig. 7.1b). The dorsal margin, which would have truncated the arc with a linear plane, is missing, however. A single biconical perforation is visible at the midpoint of the break. All remaining edges are well ground and finished. The perforated face and much of the external sides have been ground and polished, leaving the face nearly vertical to the sides. Segments of the shell are very porous in appearance, evidence of intense parasitic action.

This piece could have fitted over the end of a cord, functioning as a toggle, or it could have been the central element in a necklace.

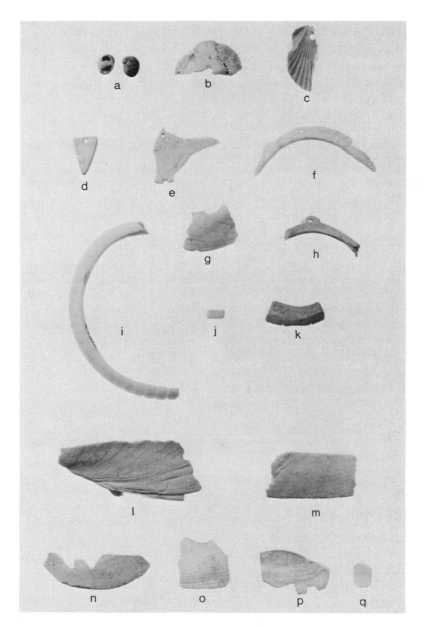

Figure 7.1. Selected shell artifacts: a, whole-shell (Nerita) beads,
Feature 118 (cremation); b, bead, toggle (Spondylus/Chama), Feature 19
(pit house); c, whole-shell (Pecten) pendant, Feature 61 (pit house); d,
geometric pendant (Laevicardium), Feature 59 (pit); e, abstract avian
pendant (Laevicardium), Feature 59 (pit); f, pelican/heron pendant
(Glycymeris), Feature 33 (pit house); g, bracelet (Glycymeris), Feature
29 (pit house); h, plain bracelet, faceted umbo (Glycymeris), Feature 59
(pit); i, decorated bracelet band (Glycymeris), Feature 55 (pit house);
j-k, reworked bracelet fragments (Glycymeris), Feature 58 (pit house);
l-n, manufacturing refuse (Laevicardium), Feature 19.5 (storage pit),
Feature 16 (possible pit house), and Feature 29 (pit house),
respectively; o-p, manufacturing refuse (Anodonta), Feature 68 (activity
surface) and Feature 19 (pit house), respectively; q, worked fragment,
unknown form (Anodonta), Feature 67 (activity surface).

Its classification as a bead is arbitrary. A similar object was recovered from a Rillito phase structure at the Hodges Ruin during recent excavations (Vokes 1986: 211).

Pendants

Six pendants were recovered: one whole-shell form and five cut-ground forms. The whole-shell pendant is represented by approximately half of the left-hand valve of Pecten vogdesi (Fig. 7.1c). A biconical perforation is visible along the break. The side edge and end of the ear have been squared off by light grinding.

The cut forms can be divided into zoomorphic and geometric forms. A triangular pendant, recovered in the fill of pit Feature 59, had been cut from the lower back of a Laevicardium elatum valve (Fig. 7.1d). Two edges are well finished and the third edge is rough from an old break. The perforation is located immediately below the midpoint of this edge. A second geometric pendant was found in the roof fall material of pit house Feature 29. It appears to be part of a reworked fragment of a perforated shell artifact, most likely from an Argopecten circularis valve. It is roughly triangular with a concave arc created by the edge of the central aperture of the original perforated shell artifact. One side is broken, and part of a small perforation is visible along this break. The natural ribbing, which normally would project out from the valve, has been ground down and polished to produce a smooth, flat surface.

A fragment of an abstract bird pendant (Fig. 7.1e) was recovered from the same pit (Feature 59) as one of the geometric forms. It was cut from middle of the back of a Laevicardium valve. One winglike projection and two feet are visible on the remaining fragment. The overall form appears to be a frontal view of a perching bird. The trunk of the body is diamond shaped, and the appendages extend from the corners. The flat interior surface is embellished by a series of incised lines that reflect the diamond shape. A set of crossed lines, which form an X, were cut into the base of the wing. The perforation is located along the incised lines, opposite the feet, which are indicated by two short projections with the talons incised into the bottom margin. Portions of the body, one wing, and the head are missing.

A second zoomorphic form also is on an avian theme; however, it is different in nature. The complete pendant is an example of the pelican or heron form (Fig. 7.1f) described by Haury (1976: 315-316) and discussed by Jernigan (1978: 52) and Ferg (1984: 693-694). This specimen probably was manufactured from a segment of the margin of a Glycymeris bracelet. The eye is indicated by a shallow drilled depression, and the wing and tail feather are depicted by sets of incised lines.

It is difficult to say whether the final pendant is a zoomorphic form because it is very fragmented due to having been burned. The piece has deteriorated along the natural layers in a manner suggesting that the shell medium was of a nacreous material. The projected thickness suggests that the shell was marine, but whether Haliotis, Pteria, or other nacreous genus cannot be determined. The remaining fragments suggest a lozenge shape that might be a bird in flight, with a small tabular projection through which the perforation is located.

Bracelets

Evidence for Manufacturing

A fragment of a Glycymeris valve, recovered in the roof fall of pit house Feature 29, appears to be an example of a bracelet in the early stages of manufacture (Fig. 7.1g). The specimen includes the side and ventral margins of the valve. A ground facet is present along the back edge and several distinct angles are visible. This area also has been chipped to shape.

Plain

A total of 38 discrete segments of plain bracelets was recovered. The artifacts were widely dispersed across the site, and were present in all of the nonmortuary feature clusters. No examples were recovered from the cremation deposits. The specimens are concentrated in House Groups 1 and 2, which together produced 21 of the samples.

The different band segments were recovered in roughly the same proportions as they occur on the band itself. The umbo region is represented by slightly more than 25 percent of the segments. The ventral margin was represented in nearly 40 percent of the sample. These proportions varied widely within the house clusters.

The umbones were often modified; nearly 60 percent were perforated in some manner. Three were drilled and the rest were ground, and in some cases reamed out. In half of the cases the contiguous portions of the band were artificially steepened by grinding the natural margin back to a more vertical face. As a result, the umbones are accentuated and appear faceted (Fig. 7.1h). A pronounced steepening of the profile of the bands occurs on nearly 40 percent of the sample.

Few specimens met the criteria established by Haury (1976: 313) for thin band bracelets. The mean nondorsal band width was 5.5 mm, and several specimens were 8 mm wide. The bands were widely distributed across the site. The absence of thin bracelets contrasts with the material from Snaketown (Haury 1976: 313-314), where this form was well represented in the Colonial period. At present it is difficult to determine if this discrepancy is a sampling bias or an expression of a regional or community bias.

Decorated

Two bracelet fragments, recovered from the roof fall of Feature 55, were embellished with a repetitive decorative element (Fig. 7.1i). The bracelets appear to have been identical in form and probably represent a matched set. Were it not for the overlapping of band sections they would have been ascribed to a single bracelet. The decoration consists of a series of grooves that encircle the band's cross section along the ventral margin. The spacing is carefully placed to coincide with the natural radial rib structure. The cuts were made in a two-step process; the interior and exterior surfaces were done separately. As a result, a number of the grooved lines are slightly misaligned. One specimen reflects only a small portion of band with a groove appearing along the break. The other piece is nearly half of the band and provides evidence for the patterning of the elements. This specimen is estimated to have had an internal diameter of more than 75 mm, which would make it large enough to have been worn on the upper arm.

Rings

A fragment of a Glycymeris ring (or pendant) was recovered from the fill of pit house Feature 53. It is nearly one-half of the band with the entire ventral margin represented. The exterior surface has been artificially steepened to a near vertical face. The function of this artifact form is unclear. Fewkes (1896: 362) reports specimens in burials worn as fingers rings, and Di Peso (1956: 91-92) notes that this form was worn as pendants at San Cayetano del Tumacacori. The provenience of this artifact does not give any information about the way it was used.

Miscellaneous Reworked Fragments

During the course of excavations four articles were recovered that show that bracelet segments were being reworked. One specimen, recovered from the lower fill of pit house Feature 58, is a small block of shell (Fig. 7.1j) made from the dorsal margin, including a portion of the lateral taxadontic teeth. The piece has been carefully ground at both ends, and is rectangular with a slight tapering at one end. This piece is too small to have functioned as a nose plug. A second, larger piece, also from the fill of Feature 58, had been ground at both ends (Fig. 7.1k). One end was finished with an encircling groove reminiscent of the decorated bracelet discussed above. This specimen also has two notches cut into the exterior margins, both of which are spaced roughly equidistant from each end.

The remaining cases involve band segments from the ventral margin that have been rounded at one end by grinding. To what end this recycling was directed is unknown.

Manufacture Refuse

Six pieces of shell, three Laevicardium and three Anodonta, exhibited evidence characteristic of manufacturing. One of the Laevicardium specimens may be manufacturing waste, but the others appear to be pieces still in the process of being shaped.

The Laevicardium specimen is a large portion of the posterior side panel of the valve up by the umbo (Fig. 7.1 1). The edge opposite the natural margin has been chipped and lightly ground. It is possible that this piece is in the early stages of shaping; however, the width of this portion of the valve is highly variable, which might discourage its use.

The other two Laevicardium specimens use portions of the back and side margins (Fig. 7.1m and n). In both cases multiple edges have been ground, and most of the edges do not appear to have been finished. The groove-and-snap technique of shaping is visible along several of the margins.

Many of the Anodonta fragments appear to be unusually robust for this region. Many of the specimens recovered from sites in the Tucson Basin are fragile and difficult to work (Vokes 1987: 263). The Water World specimens average over 1 mm in thickness. Two examples bear direct evidence of the manufacturing process; the third is included here because of its regularity of shape and the straightness of its sides (Fig. 7.1o). One specimen (Fig. 7.1p) was in the process of being carved, with cut and abraded edges present along one margin. The intended form is unclear, but the cut portion is reminiscent of several zoomorphic motifs. A second fragment has several parallel lines scored into the interior surface, possibly the result of an attempt to cut the valve.

Worked Fragments of Unknown Form

Several pieces of shell were recovered that exhibited intentional modifications, but were too fragmentary to allow a determination of form and use. Two pieces were cut from Pecten vogdesi. One small fragment of Haliotis was recovered from Feature 29, a pit house. A worm-eaten fragment of an unidentified marine shell that was ground on one surface was found in the fill of pit house Feature 26.

Two pieces of Anodonta californensis have been crudely fashioned into small subrectangular segments with the cut edges and smoothed by light abrasion (Fig. 7.1q). Both pieces retain considerable portions of the exterior cortex, and the specimens are unusually thick for this species. One specimen exhibits a series of superficial striations on the exterior face paralleling one side. What these represent is unclear, although they are probably too small to have been pendant blanks. A third fragment of Anodonta had been cut and ground along one margin.

Unworked Fragments

Twenty-six shell fragments (18 Anodonta, 7 Laevicardium, 1 unidentified marine shell) were recovered; none exhibited any evidence of cultural modification. All of the Laevicardium specimens were from the ribbed back of the valve. All specimens were quite small; the largest piece weighed 1 g and measured about 2 cm on a side. Although no house groups produced a concentration of material, House Group 1 was notable by the absence of Laevicardium fragments. This is a more surprising because a relatively high density of other material, especially unworked Anodonta fragments, was present in this house group.

Anodonta appears in all of the house groups, but it is concentrated in House Group 1; almost all of the excavated features yielded specimens. The reasons for this are not known. Anodonta is known to have been used historically as a food resource (Bequaert and Miller 1973: 221). It occurs at some prehistoric sites in sufficient quantity to suggest that it was eaten by inhabitants of the region. The proximity of the Santa Cruz River is a possible explanation for its presence at Water World. As noted previously, several fragments exhibit evidence of manufacturing efforts. It is possible that this unworked material represents the by-products of the efforts of a local artisan. There is some circumstantial support for this as two of the three worked specimens also came from House Group 1. The size of the sample does not permit any conclusions to be drawn about these possibilities.

Whole Valve

Stripping around the features in the cremation area yielded a complete Laevicardium valve in association with the prehistoric ground surface. The exterior surface of the valve has eroded and cortex is restricted to the upper back and umbo. The specimen does not appear to have been burned, but is discolored as if it had been in contact with an ashy matrix. This staining is restricted to the remaining cortex, indicating that the exposure occurred prior to the circumstances that led to its eroded condition. In the immediate area are several primary cremations that have an ashy matrix. It is possible that this shell may have been an offering in one of these features.

Discussion

This assemblage appears to have characteristics commonly found in other Colonial period Hohokam sites. Overall the dominant artifact form is the plain shell bracelet. It was recovered from more proveniences than other classes of shell artifacts and, in contrast to bead forms, its dispersed distribution suggests that it was probably worn by many of the inhabitants and was not a marker of social status in the community.

The dominance in absolute terms of whole-shell bead forms is the result of a limited number of cremation deposits having high concentrations of this form.

The presence of Nerita funiculata is unusual. As stated above, the artifact form (bead) has been recovered at a few other sites, but the species is not well known. It was reported at the La Playa Site in northern Sonora (Johnson 1960: 167); however, the artifact form represented is not clear and the chronological placement of the settlement is also a matter of debate. Craig (1982) has suggested that some low-level exchange occurred between the people of northern Sonora and the Hohokam via the Santa Cruz River drainage prior to the Classic period. It is possible that the occurrence of this shell species at Water World is a product of such exchange during the Colonial period. In reviewing the La Playa assemblage it is evident that there was a greater diversity of genera at the site than would be found in a comparable Hohokam settlement, and that gastropods were relatively common in Trincheras assemblages. It must be stressed that this connection is tenuous, however, and that the other genera at Water World are often, and in some cases consistently, recovered from other Hohokam habitation sites and were most likely traded from the north. According to Richard J. Martynec of Northland Research in Flagstaff, Arizona, excavations at the Hind Site (AZ AA:1:62) and Shelltown (AZ AA:1:66) have uncovered evidence of extensive trade and manufacturing activities during the Late Pioneer and Early Colonial periods. The relationships between these regions and the mechanisms involving exchange among the Hohokam are not as yet fully understood.

The presence of Anodonta in a number of deposits at Water World is of interest, especially in light of its near absence at Fastimes. Water World is somewhat farther from a source of this freshwater mussel than Fastimes, although the distance is probably insignificant. Of potentially greater more significance are the efforts of local craftsmen to use this species. This would have provided a market for the shell beyond that of its potential as a source of food. This also might provide an answer to why the recovered pieces seemed to be thicker than many of the specimens recovered from settlements nearer the local source, the Santa Cruz River: suitability for the craftsman might influence the choice of specimens.

The occurrence of several reworked sections of bracelets, as well as evidence of low levels of local manufacturing, indicate that the inhabitants of Water World supplied themselves with some of the desired finished products. Undoubtedly they could not fill the needs of the entire community and the presence of the reworked specimens, along with the fact that Anodonta probably was not the most suitable material for working, indicates that these people were not receiving quantities of raw materials from the coast. Apparently these people were limited, in part, to recycling materials at hand.

In summary, although the occupants of Water World were not totally dependent on outside sources for finished shell materials, they were largely importing finished artifacts from other communities. Whether some of the material entered from the southern (Sonoran) connection cannot be determined. The artifact forms compare well with the samples recovered from settlements of the same period to the north in the Salt-Gila Basin, suggesting that much of the material was derived from that region.

Chapter 8

VERTEBRATE FAUNAL REMAINS

William B. Gillespie

Faunal Assemblage

Excavations at Water World resulted in the recovery of 4,349
specimens of animal bone. Less than half (46%) are identifiable to at
least the family level, and nearly all of these are assigned to genus
and species. A minimum of 21 taxa are represented among the
identifiable remains including 13 mammals, 1 amphibian, 4 reptiles, and
3 birds (Table 8.1). Discussions of the analytic methods used and
comparison with other sites are given in Volume 2, Chapter 8.

As with other Phase B sites, the assemblage is dominated by
remains of Lepus, the genus of jackrabbit (Table 8.2). The 1,850 Lepus
specimens represent 43 percent of all recovered bones and 92 percent of
the identified specimens. Both of the two local species of Lepus are
present in roughly equal amounts: L. californicus (black-tailed
jackrabbit) is slightly more common than L. alleni (antelope
jackrabbit). Sylvilagus (cottontail) is the next most abundant taxon;
the 67 specimens represent 3 percent of the identified remains.

The 133 artiodactyl bones recovered include 50 specimens
referred to Odocoileus hemionus (mule deer), 9 Antilocapra americana
(pronghorn), 3 Ovis canadensis (bighorn), and 71 fragments not
identified to family or genus. Nearly a third of the artiodactyl bones
were recovered from three roasting pits (Features 4, 8, and 9) excavated
during the testing phase described by Downum and others (1986). A major
portion of the remaining artiodactyl remains were special deposits on
the floors of two pit houses, Features 7 and 58, and a cremation pit,
Feature 90. Together these features contain a minimum of 20 mandibles
(16 mule deer and 4 pronghorn). Feature 58 also contained four antler-
horn racks still attached to the posterior portions of skulls (3 deer
and 1 bighorn).

Carnivore, rodent, and nonmammalian taxa are all relatively less
abundant than at Fastimes (Volume 2, Chapter 8) or, especially, Hawk's
Nest (Volume 4, Part 1). Most noteworthy is the relative lack of kit
fox (Vulpes macrotis) elements, which are well represented at these two

Table 8.1

VERTEBRATE TAXA RECOVERED

Taxon	Common Name
Mammals	
Leporidae	
Lepus alleni	Antelope jackrabbit
L. californicus	Black-tailed jackrabbit
L. sp.	Unidentified jackrabbit
Sylvilagus cf. S. audubonii	Desert cottontail
Sciuridae	
Ammospermophilus harrisii or	Unidentified small ground
Spermophilus small sp.	squirrel
Heteromyidae	
Dipodomys cf. D. spectabilis	Banner-tailed kangaroo rat
D. merriami or D. ordii	Small kangaroo rat
Perognathus sp.	Unidentified pocket mouse
Cricetidae	
Neotoma cf. N. albigula	White-throated wood rat
Canidae	
Vulpes macrotis	Kit fox
Mustelidae	
Taxidea taxus	Badger
Cervidae	
Odocoileus hemionus	Mule deer
Bovidae	
Ovis canadensis	Bighorn sheep
Antilocapridae	
Antilocapra americana	Pronghorn
Amphibians	
Pelobatidae	
Scaphiopus couchi	Couch's spadefoot toad
Reptiles	
Testudinidae	
Gopherus agassizi	Desert tortoise
Iguanidae	
Phrynosoma solare	Regal horned lizard
Teiidae	
Cnemidophorus sp.	Whiptail lizard
Colubridae	
Masticophis cf. M. flagellum	Coachwhip

Table 8.1, continued

VERTEBRATE TAXA RECOVERED

Taxon	Common Name
Birds	
Phasianidae	
Callipepla cf. C. gambelii	Gambel's quail
C. cf. C. squamata	Scaled quail
Columbidae	
Zenaida cf. Z. macroura	Mourning dove

more northern sites. Only two V. macrotis elements were recovered from Water World compared to 31 at Hawk's Nest and 26 at Fastimes.

The majority of the unidentified remains are leporid-size small mammals (33% of all specimens) with fewer unidentified artiodactyl-size large mammals (19% of all specimens). Unidentifiable rodents and carnivore-size remains are nearly absent in the collection.

Faunal remains were recovered from 41 numbered features as well as general site proveniences. Table 8.3 gives frequencies of identified and unidentified remains and estimates of the minimum number of individuals (MNI) of each taxon in each of the features. MNI estimates use the feature as the basic unit of aggregation; that is, each feature is assumed to be an independent deposit whereas partitions within features (individual excavation units) are not considered to be independent. Volume 5, Part E-6 shows frequencies for strata and individual floor features in major proveniences.

The majority of the bones from features are from pit house fill. Ten of the structures yielded over 100 specimens and another five contained at least 50 specimens. Bone remains in features other than pit houses are most abundant in roasting pits, in particular three pits excavated during the testing phase (Features 4, 8, and 9). Another concentration of bone debris was found in Feature 90, a cremation pit. Remains in these pit features differ from the assemblages found in pit house fills in that they contain, almost exclusively, the remains of artiodactyls (and unidentified large mammals), nearly all of which are burned. Identifiable lagomorphs, although predominant in the site-wide collection, are completely absent in the four roasting pits and ten cremations that contained animal bones.

One-third of the total number of specimens are from general site proveniences, including some from six house groups (Table 8.3).

Table 8.2

SUMMARY FREQUENCIES OF VERTEBRATE TAXA

Taxon	Number of Specimens	% All Specimens	% ID Specimens
Mammals			
Lepus alleni	546	12.6	27.1
L. californicus	617	14.2	30.6
L. sp.	687	15.8	34.1
All Lepus	1,850	42.5	91.9
Sylvilagus cf. S. audubonii	67	1.5	3.3
small squirrel	2	t	0.1
Dipodomys cf. D. spectabilis	4	0.1	0.2
D. small sp.	1	t	t
Perognathus	1	t	t
Neotoma cf. N. albigula	11	0.3	0.5
Vulpes macrotis	2	t	0.1
Taxidea taxus	3	0.1	0.1
Odocoileus hemionus	50	1.1	2.5
Ovis canadensis	3	0.1	0.1
Antilocapra americana	9	0.2	0.4
Unidentified artiodactyl	71	1.6	–
Amphibians			
Scaphiopus couchi	1	t	t
Reptiles			
Gopherus agassizi	1	t	t
Phrynosoma solare	1	t	t
Cnemidophorus sp.	1	t	t
Masticophis cf. M. flagellum	1	t	t
Birds			
Callipepla cf. C. gambelii	3	0.1	0.1
C. cf. C. squamata	1	t	t
Zenaida cf. Z. macroura	2	t	0.1
Unidentified specimens			
Bird	1	t	–
Small mammal	1,431	32.9	–
Large mammal	832	19.1	–
Totals for site			
Identified specimens	2,014	46.3	99.4
Unidentified specimens	2,335	53.7	
Total specimens	4,349	100.0	

t = Less than 0.001 percent

Table 8.3

NUMBERS OF SPECIMENS AND ESTIMATED MINIMUM NUMBERS OF INDIVIDUALS (MNI)
OF VERTEBRATES IN FEATURES

Feature	Lagomorphs					Rodents				
	Lepus alleni	Lepus californicus	Lepus sp.	All Lepus	Sylvilagus	Small squirrel	Dipodomys spectabilis	Dipodomys small sp.	Perognathus sp.	Neotoma cf. N. albigula
3										
4										
7			1/1	1						
8										
9										
13	1			1						
18			2/1	2						
19	35/3	25/5	33/-	93	14/2					2
20			2/1	2						
25	13/4	15/2	23/-	51	3					
26	10/2	7	16/-	33	1					
27	8/2	4	3/-	15			1			
29	6	12/2	4/-	22	1					
33	12/2	7	6/-	25	2					1
35	23/3	14/2	23/-	60						
36			1/1	1			1			
40						1				
44		1	3/-	4						
53	6/2	17/2	16/-	39	7/2					
55	30/3	21/2	15/-	66	5					
57										
58	51/4	47/4	65/-	163	1		2			5
59	2	3	2/-	7						
61	18/3	22/3	36/-	76	1					
66	13/2	60/4	55/-	128	5					1
67	22/2	33/4	37/-	92	6/2					
68	47/4	75/9	58/-	180	12/2					
78	3		4/-	7						
79	20/2	17/2	27/-	64	1					
80/81										
83									1	
87										
90										
105/108										
109										
110	7	11/2	5/-	23						1
118										
137										
138										

General Site Proveniences

Feature	Lepus alleni	Lepus californicus	Lepus sp.	All Lepus	Sylvilagus	Small squirrel	Dipodomys spectabilis	Dipodomys small sp.	Perognathus sp.	Neotoma cf. N. albigula
House Group 1	4	1	12/-	17						
House Group 2	9/2	8/3	15/-	32	1					1
House Group 3	16	21/5	21/-	58	1					
House Group 4	177/11	175/11	184/-	536	5	1		1		
House Group 5	1	1	2/-	4						
House Group 6	12/2	20/3	16/-	48	1					

Totals

	Lepus alleni	Lepus californicus	Lepus sp.	All Lepus	Sylvilagus	Small squirrel	Dipodomys spectabilis	Dipodomys small sp.	Perognathus sp.	Neotoma cf. N. albigula
N	546	617	687	1,850	67	2	4	1	1	11
MNI	61	72	4	137	21	2	3	1	1	6

Percent N

	Lepus alleni	Lepus californicus	Lepus sp.	All Lepus	Sylvilagus	Small squirrel	Dipodomys spectabilis	Dipodomys small sp.	Perognathus sp.	Neotoma cf. N. albigula
All specimens	12.6	14.2	15.8	42.5	1.5	t	0.1	t	t	0.3
ID specimens	27.1	30.6	34.1	91.9	3.3	0.1	0.2	t	t	0.5

Percent MNI

	Lepus alleni	Lepus californicus	Lepus sp.	All Lepus	Sylvilagus	Small squirrel	Dipodomys spectabilis	Dipodomys small sp.	Perognathus sp.	Neotoma cf. N. albigula
ID specimens	28.8	34	1.9	64.2	9.9	0.9	1.4	0.5	0.5	2.8
MNI/N	0.11	0.12	---	0.07	0.31	1	0.75	1	1	0.55

MNI values given only if greater than 1

Table 8.3, continued

NUMBERS OF SPECIMENS AND ESTIMATED MINIMUM NUMBERS OF INDIVIDUALS (MNI)
OF VERTEBRATES IN FEATURES

Feature	Carnivores			Artiodactyls			Toads	Reptiles			
	Vulpes macrotis	Taxidea taxus	Odocoileus hemionus	Ovis canadensis	Antilocapra americana	Unidentified Artiodactyl	Scaphiopus couchi	Gopherus agassizi	Phrynosoma solare	Cnemidophorus sp.	Masticonhis cf. M. flagellum
3											
4			3			8					
7			1	2		1					
8			4			19					
9			2			6					
13						1					
18			2			1	1				1
19	1		3			4		1			
20											
25	1					1					
26			2								
27						1					
29						3					
33						2					
35			1								
36											
40											
44											
53						2					
55											
57											
58			13/5		3	6					
59											
61											
66											
67											
68						1					
78											
79						4					
80/81											
83											
87						2				1	
90			8/4		3	3					
105/108			1			2					
109											
110		1									
118											
137											
138											
General Site Proveniences											
House Group 1											
House Group 2			6/2		3						
House Group 3		1	1			1					
House Group 4		1	3	1		3			1		
House Group 5											
House Group 6											
Totals											
N	2	3	50	3	9	71	1	1	1	1	1
MNI	2	3	22	1	4	--	1	1	1	1	1
Percent N											
All specimens	t	0.1	1.1	0.1	0.2	1.6	t	t	t	t	t
ID specimens	0.1	0.1	2.5	0.1	0.4	--	t	t	t	t	t
Percent MNI											
ID specimens	0.9	1.4	10.4	0.5	1.9	--	0.5	0.5	0.5	0.5	0.5
MNI/N	1	1	0.44	0.33	0.44	--	1	1	1	1	1

Table 8.3, continued

NUMBERS OF SPECIMENS AND ESTIMATED MINIMUM NUMBERS OF INDIVIDUALS (MNI)
OF VERTEBRATES IN FEATURES

Feature	Birds Callipepla cf. C. gambelli	Callipepla cf. C. squamata	Zenaida cf. Z. macroura	Bird	Unidentified Remains Small Mammal	Large Mammal	NISP	Totals No. Burn	No. Burn
3						1	1	0	0
4					10	21	42	41	98
7						2	7	4	57
8						339	362	359	99
9						51	59	59	100
13							2	0	0
18	1				4		11	3	27
19	1				50	13	182	12	7
20					4	9	15	12	80
25					40		96	4	4
26					16	20	72	15	21
27					15	2	34	11	32
29					22	6	54	1	2
33					25	2	57	10	18
35					43	1	105	16	15
36					12		14	2	14
40							1	0	0
44					1		5	0	0
53					66	2	116	12	10
55					38	4	113	7	6
57					2		2	0	0
58					86	23	302	87	29
59			2		3	6	18	9	50
61					79	2	158	7	4
66	1				53		188	4	2
67					60	9	167	8	5
68	1				118	4	316	9	3
78					11		18	0	0
79					103		172	44	26
80/81						1	1	1	100
83							1	0	0
87					1	10	14	13	93
90					1	112	127	126	99
105/108						14	17	6	35
109					1		1	0	0
110		1		1	23	3	53	9	17
118						1	1	1	100
137					2		2	0	0
138					1	8	9	2	22

General Site Proveniences

House Group 1					24	2	43	15	35
House Group 2					28	68	139	61	44
House Group 3					53	67	182	88	48
House Group 4					363	24	939	593	63
House Group 5					22	3	29	17	59
House Group 6					51	2	102	4	4

Totals

N	3	1	2	1	1,431	832	4,349	1,672	39
MNI	3	1	1	--	--	--	212		

Percent N

All specimens	0.1	t	t	t	32.9	19.1	No.ID	
ID specimens	0.1	t	0.1	--	--	--	2014	

Percent MNI

ID specimens	1.4	0.5	0.5	--	--	--	--	
MNI/N	1	1	0.5	--	--	--	--	

House Group 7 was trenched by backhoe in 1987; no excavation was done and no bone was collected. Remains are especially abundant in overburden and trash deposits (Strata 50 and 30, respectively) overlying Feature 58, a pit house in House Group 4. Nearly a quarter of all bones from the site and over a third of the burned specimens are from this trash deposit.

Previous Work

Nearly 500 specimens were collected during the initial testing phase in 1983 and 1984. These remains were analyzed and are reported in Downum (1986). The specimens have been reexamined and the results are included in this report. Included are remains from three roasting pits (Features 4, 8, and 9) and a small number of bones from other features and general site proveniences.

The reanalysis yields only minor differences in identification and enumeration. Specifically, I am more reluctant to identify fragmentary artiodactyl remains, particularly ribs and vertebrae, to genus, but more willing to assign fragmentary lagomorph limb bones to genus and often species. Thus, the revised tabulations given here include fewer specimens referred to Odocoileus (deer), more listed as unidentified artiodactyl, and more identified as Lepus (L. alleni, L. californicus, or L. sp.). Downum (1986) reports 21 artiodactyl specimens from these features in contrast to the 42 listed here. The primary difference in this discrepancy is that more fragmentary vertebrae are referred to unidentified artiodactyl in this study. This occurs despite using a "minimum number of elements" approach for very fragmentary bones; the actual number of vertebral fragments is even greater.

The vertebrate assemblage recovered during the testing phase is remarkably different from that of the site as a whole, or those of any of the other excavated sites. Artiodactyl remains are much more common than rabbits in the test assemblages. The principal difference is in the unique nature of the three excavated roasting pits (Features 4, 8, and 9). These features contained only artiodactyl and unidentified large mammal bones, nearly all of which are burned. Identifiable small mammal remains are completely missing in these roasting pit assemblages.

The fill from roasting pit Feature 8 contained more than 300 very small fragments of large mammal bone, in addition to at least 23 artiodactyl elements. This represented nearly half of the total number of the unidentified large mammal bones from the site. Despite the large number of specimens, all of these bones may be from a single deer carcass, the bones of which were highly fragmented from burning.

It is clear that the faunal remains from roasting pits are markedly divergent from the more abundant structure fill assemblages.

When pit houses contain abundant vertebrate remains, they nearly always can be characterized as jackrabbit trash with elements of Lepus numerically dominant. Frequency of charring is variable but is usually very low to moderate. Conversely, the few roasting pits from the site almost exclusively contain remains of large mammals, especially deer, when they contain bone remains at all. Charring is evident on nearly all specimens. This suggests that processing of large and small game and the discard of bone remains were performed in different ways, and to a large extent in spatially distinct locations.

It is evident that roasting pits at Water World were used for roasting large game in addition to preparing certain plant resources. Burned large mammal remains were recovered from three of four roasting pits excavated during the testing phase, including the more than 300 bones in Feature 8. In contrast, bones were found in only one (Feature 138) of the eight probable roasting pits investigated during the 1986-1987 excavations. As with the previously excavated roasting pits, this feature contained mostly large mammal remains, although there are relatively few in number (8 specimens), included no identifiable bones, and had a lower percentage of burned specimens (only 2 of 8).

Assemblage Composition

Lagomorphs

As noted above, jackrabbits (Lepus) are by far the most abundant genus at the site, with cottontails (Sylvilagus) much less abundant. Table 8.4 shows the occurrence of the different lagomorphs in each feature and the relative abundances of the two Lepus species and the two genera, Lepus and Sylvilagus. Overall, of the Lepus specimens assigned to species (63% of the total 1,850 Lepus specimens), L. californicus (black-tailed jackrabbit) is slightly more abundant than the larger L. alleni (antelope jackrabbit). For the site as a whole, L. alleni makes up 47 percent and L. californicus 53 percent of the Lepus specifically identified. In individual features, the relative percentage of L. alleni ranges from 18 to 63 percent (with sample sizes greater than 25) and is less abundant than L. californicus in about half (8 of 17) of the collections with adequate sample size.

The two species of jackrabbit presently in the Avra Valley show a substantial difference in habitat preference (Madsen 1974). Antelope jackrabbits (L. alleni) show a clear preference for expansive flat areas nearly devoid of vegetation, including field areas. According to Madsen (1974), this species is nearly limited to the flat valley bottom. Black-tailed jackrabbits (L. californicus) are found mainly on bajada slopes covered by Sonoran desert scrub vegetation. Sylvilagus audubonii is found in the densest vegetation cover, primarily along small washes.

Table 8.4

DISTRIBUTION OF RABBIT REMAINS BY FEATURE

Feature	Type	Lepus alleni	Lepus californicus	Lepus sp.	All Lepus	Sylvilagus	All Leporids	Percent Sylvilagus	% L. alleni of identified Lepus
7	Pit House			1	1		1		
13	Ballcourt	1			1		1		
18	Pit			2	2		2		
19	Pit House	35	25	33	93	14	107	13	58
20	Pit House			2	2		2		
25	Pit House	13	15	23	51	3	54	6	46
26	Pit House	10	7	16	33	1	34	3	59
27	Pit House	8	4	3	15		15		
29	Pit House	6	12	4	22	1	23		
33	Pit House	12	7	6	25	2	27	7	63
35	Pit House	23	14	23	60		60		62
36	Pit House			1	1		1		
44	Pit House?		1	3	4		4		
53	Pit House	6	17	16	39	7	46	15	26
55	Pit House	30	21	15	66	5	71	7	59
58	Pit House	51	47	65	163	1	164	1	52
59	Pit	2	3	2	7		7		
61	Pit House	18	22	36	76	1	77	1	45
66	SWA/PH	13	60	55	128	5	133	4	18
67	SWA/PH	22	33	37	92	6	98	6	40
68	SWA/PH	47	75	58	180	12	192	6	39
78	Pit House	3		4	7		7		
79	Pit House	20	17	27	64	1	65	2	54
110	Pit House	7	11	5	23		23		
Feature Total		327	391	437	1,155	59	1,214	5	46
General Site									
House Group 1		4	1	12	17		17		
House Group 2		9	8	15	32	1	33	3	53
House Group 3		16	21	21	58	1	59	2	43
House Group 4		177	175	184	536	5	541	1	50
House Group 5		1	1	2	4		4		
House Group 6		12	20	16	48	1	49	2	38
Site Totals		546	617	687	1,850	67	1,917	3	47

SWA = specialized work area, PH = pit house
Percentages given only when sample size is greater than 25.

Lepus specimens were recovered from 24 features and more than 50 specimens occur in 10 of the features. They also were recovered from six nonfeature general site proveniences; the greatest number (536) occurs in the unnumbered trash deposit of House Group 4, mainly overlying pit house Feature 58.

All of the 67 Sylvilagus remains presumably are from the desert cottontail, the only species now occurring in the site vicinity. Cottontail remains are scattered in 13 features, but in only two (Feature 19, a pit house, and Feature 68, an activity area,) were more than 10 specimens recovered. Despite the low frequencies, the minimum number of individuals (MNI) is two for four features (Features 19 and 53, pit houses; and Features 67 and 68, activity areas). All other features have an MNI of 1. In only two features (Features 19 and 53) does the number of Sylvilagus specimens exceed 10 percent of the number of Lepus elements.

Table 8.5 gives the frequencies of specimens of different skeletal elements in each feature. A detailed inventory of specimens by portion and side of each element is given in Volume 5, Part E-7. All skeletal parts are represented, although frequencies vary. For the entire assemblage of Lepus elements, most of the variability in relative abundances of skeletal parts appears to be related to taphonomic factors of preservation and recovery rather than processing by humans.

Skeletal part frequencies for the assemblage of cottontail remains differ from the Lepus assemblages in having relatively more major limb elements, especially hind limb bones, and fewer small elements, in particular axial elements (ribs and vertebrae), which are not represented in the small assemblage of cottontail specimens. Again, these differences may be a function of taphonomic processes.

Nearly one-fourth of all the Lepus specimens are burned, but only 7.5 percent of the Sylvilagus bones show any burning (Volume 5, Part E-8). These percentages are strongly influenced by the abundance of charred bones in the unnumbered trash deposit in House Group 4. This deposit contains 76 percent of the burned Lepus specimens and four of the five burned cottontail bones. In feature fills alone, the frequency of burning is only 7 percent for jackrabbits and 2 percent for cottontails.

Different skeletal elements show varying percentages of charring (Volume 5, Part E-8). Percentages range from 4 percent (ribs) to 48 percent (innominates). Axial elements stand out as having much lower frequencies of charring. There is no tendency for more distal elements (foot bones) to have higher frequencies of charring than more proximal elements, as might occur if charring was incurred accidentally during cooking. Instead, it seems more likely that burning occurred with discard into a fire.

Table 8.5

TOTAL NUMBER OF LAGOMORPH SKELETAL ELEMENTS BY FEATURE

Feature	Mandible	Cranium	Vertebra	Rib	Scapula	Humerus	Ulna	Radius	Innominate	Femur	Tibia	Calcaneum	Metatarsal	Metacarpal	Phalanx	Other	
7										1							1
13						1											1
18														2			2
19	8	1	5	11	3	17	4	7	4	6	2	4	9	7	5		93
20				1									1				2
25	3		1	2	3	3		2	2	12	9	5	7		2		51
26	1	1		2	1	4	6	3	2		2	1	7	2	1		33
27					3	4	1	2		2	2		1				15
29	2	1	1		2		2	6		1	2	1	2		2		22
33	1			2	1	1	2	4	1	5	3	2	2	1			25
35	1	2	4	8	5	2	4	4	1	8	3		12	2	3	1	60
36													1				1
44						1	1		1		1						4
53	1		1	1		6	1	5	4	8		2	4	2	4		39
55	4	3	2	4	2	7	5	6	1	4	6	2	12		5	3	66
58	5	3	2	27	11	16	8	13	6	6	10	4	27	10	14	1	163
59		1				1		2		2			1				7
61	3	4	3	15	5	7	2	3	4	3	5	2	13	3	4		76
66	7		5	37	6	10	6	5	7	7	9	4	13	6	5	1	128
67	8	1	3	5	6	3	3	9	4	8	10	2	24	3	3		92
68	7	8	8	22	10	18	16	14	6	30	19	2	8	6	5	1	180
78	1	1			2									3			7
79	1	4	2	6	1	5	4	2	2	6	8		9	9	5		64
110	2			1		4	1	2	1	2	2		1	6	1		23
General Site																	
H.G. 1		2			2	2			1	1	3	1	1	2		2	17
H.G. 2	3	1	1	1	1	4	2	5	1	3	3		4	1	2		32
H.G. 3	4	2		1	5	12	1	2	3	6	4	2	10	2	4		58
H.G. 4	40	20	5	49	48	45	29	43	54	28	68	22	43	15	20	7	536
H.G. 5								1		1		1	1				4
H.G. 6	2	3	2	2	4	4	4	3	2	7	3	2	5	3	1	1	48
Lepus Total	104	58	45	197	121	177	102	143	107	157	174	59	218	85	86	17	1,850
Sylvilagus Total	8	1			3	7	3	2	7	11	9	4	5	4	2	1	67

H.G. = House Group

Rodents

Skeletal remains of rodents are much less abundant at Water World than at either Fastimes or Hawk's Nest. Only 19 specimens from a probable number of 5 species were found (Table 8.3). Two of the rodent specimens (pocket mouse and small ground squirrel lower jaws) were retrieved from flotation samples and the remainder from screened bulk collections.

Most abundant are remains of wood rats, all of which are listed as Neotoma cf. N. albigula, the white-throated wood rat, the only species now occurring in the site area. Eleven wood rat remains were recovered from five features and are most abundant in pit house Feature 58 where five elements were found. Altogether the retrieved elements include four mandibles (all of them left mandibles, obviously from 4 individuals), six hind limb elements (3 femurs, 2 tibiae, 1 innominate), and one fore limb bone (ulna).

All of the Neotoma specimens are yellow-brown, which indicates that they are not recent intrusives. One specimen, a mandible from pit house Feature 33, is burned gray. Considering that only 18 percent of all of the bone specimens from this feature are burned, it is likely that the burning in this case is indicative of human use. Other unburned wood rat specimens also may represent food remains, although this is difficult to demonstrate.

Other rodent remains are from smaller taxa and are much less likely to be present as the result of human exploitation. These include a large and a small species of kangaroo rat. The larger species is probably Dipodomys spectabilis (banner-tailed kangaroo rat), although it is possible that, with a range extension, the comparably sized D. deserti could have been present prehistorically. Four D. cf. D. spectabilis elements were recovered from three pit houses: one each from Features 27 and 36 and two from Feature 58, the feature that also contained the most wood rat specimens. Elements include three partial tibiae and a metatarsal. A single smaller kangaroo rat, either D. merriami or D. ordii, is represented by a distal tibia from a Stratum 30 unit overlying Feature 58. All are light brown in color and are probably intrusive.

A single pocket mouse (Perognathus sp.) specimen, a mandible, was retrieved from the flotation of cremated remains of Feature 83. This unburned specimen is the only nonhuman bone from this cremation and is undoubtedly a postdepositional intrusive.

Two small ground squirrel specimens are probably from round-tailed ground squirrels (Spermophilus tereticaudus), a common inhabitant of the site vicinity, but could be from Harris' antelope squirrel (Ammospermophilus harrisii), which occurs in rougher terrain in the area. Both are fragmentary left mandibles and appear substantially younger than the archaeological bone remains, indicating recent intrusion into the site. One is the single nonhuman bone from cremation Feature 40, and the other is from a Stratum 50 unit overlying pit house Feature 61.

Carnivores

Remains of carnivores are very sparse at Water World. Included are three badger (Taxidea taxus) and two kit fox (Vulpes macrotis) elements. All are from separate proveniences, suggesting that all may be from different individuals.

Badger specimens include a damaged lower jaw (the anterior parts of the fused left and right halves) from a Stratum 50 provenience overlying pit house Feature 27, a whole radius from the Stratum 50 deposit overlying pit house Feature 58, and an ulna shaft from the fill of pit house Feature 110. The mandible is from an adult individual and is burned black, indicating human processing. The other badger elements also are believed to be present in the collection as a result of human use, rather than later intrusion.

Kit fox, which is much more abundant at Fastimes and Hawk's Nest, is represented only by a partial mandible from the fill of pit house Feature 19 and a damaged innominate from the fill of pit house Feature 25. Both elements are from small individuals and both are highly weathered from exposure on the ground surface. There is no clear-cut reason to believe that these fox elements were deposited by the human inhabitants of the site; they could instead be postoccupational additions.

Artiodactyls

A total of 133 specimens recovered from both the testing phase (42 specimens) and main excavation program (91 specimens) are attributed to artiodactyls. In addition, the majority of unidentified large mammal remains also are undoubtedly fragments of artiodactyl bones. Identifiable artiodactyl specimens are dominated by deer (Odocoileus), all of which are the size of mule deer (O. hemionus). Pronghorn (Antilocapra americana) and bighorn sheep (Ovis canadensis) also are present, but in much smaller numbers. Odocoileus is represented by 50 identified specimens, and 9 elements are referred to Antilocapra and 3 to Ovis.

Table 8.6 gives frequencies of different skeletal elements for identified and unidentified artiodactyls. A detailed inventory of all artiodactyl specimens recovered from the site is given in Volume 5, Part E-9.

Artiodactyl remains were recovered from 20 of the 41 excavated features that contained vertebrate specimens. In only four features (Feature 58, a pit house; Features 4 and 8, roasting pits; and Feature 90, a cremation pit) were more than 10 artiodactyl elements recovered. In nearly all other proveniences, the artiodactyl remains are scattered in small numbers, intermingled with much more abundant jackrabbit trash remains. Of the artiodactyl elements, 21 (17 unidentified artiodactyl, 2 deer, and 2 pronghorn) have been modified into artifacts.

The artiodactyl remains at Water World can be divided into three kinds of deposits: special use mandible and antler-horn core deposits; bone artifacts, which were curated items; and food refuse and other discards. Perception of relative abundances of skeletal parts depends on whether these subsets are considered together or separately.

Table 8.6

FREQUENCIES OF DIFFERENT ARTIODACTYL SKELETAL ELEMENTS RECOVERED

Element	Deer (Odocoileus)	Bighorn (Ovis)	Pronghorn (Antilocapra)	Unidentified Artiodactyl	All Artiodactyl
Skull					
Antler/horn core	15			5	20
Skull with antler/ horn core	3	1			4
Cranial fragment				2	2
Mandible	18		5	3	26
Isolated tooth			2	1	3
Axial					
Cervical vertebra				3	3
Thoracic vertebra				6	6
Lumbar vertebra				2	2
Caudal vertebra				3	3
Unknown vertebra				2	2
Sacrum				2	2
Rib				10	10
Front Limb					
Scapula		1		2	3
Humerus distal	2				2
shaft				3	3
Ulna proximal	1			1	2
Radius proximal				3	3
Hind Limb					
Innominate				1	1
Femur distal				2	2
shaft				3	3
Patella	1				1
Tibia shaft				1	1
Foot Bones					
Calcaneum	1			1	2
Carpal	1				1
Metatarsal			1	1	2
Metacarpal	1				1
Unid. metapodial			1	13	14
Phalanx proximal	5				5
medial	1			1	2
distal	1	1			2
Total	50	3	9	71	133

Because of the numerical abundance of the special cranial deposits and artifacts, the overall assemblage cannot be regarded as the result of food resource procurement and processing procedures.

Overall, the artiodactyl remains show a decidedly nonrandom pattern of element frequencies in that mandibles, antlers (and to a lesser extent horn cores), and foot elements (phalanges and metapodials) constitute the bulk of the collection. Major limb elements and axial elements (vertebrae and ribs) are much scarcer (Table 8.6 and Volume 5, Part E-9).

Elements referred to as deer are mainly mandibles, antlers, and foot bone specimens. The only long bones identified as deer are two distal humerus fragments, a proximal ulna, and a metacarpal. Pronghorn specimens include five mandibles, two isolated mandibular teeth, and two distal metapodials used as artifacts. Bighorn sheep is represented by one posterior cranium with its damaged horn cores, a scapula, and a distal phalanx. The larger assemblage of specimens listed as unidentified artiodactyl includes all of the axial specimens and the majority of limb bone fragments from the site.

The only postcranial axial specimens recovered from the site are from the three roasting pits excavated during the testing phase. These may be the only significant deposits of discarded large game food remains found at the site.

The unusual floor deposits are predominantly skull remains, in particular mandibles. Other mandible and antler-horn core specimens could be the remains of similar deposits. It is noteworthy that although there are at least 26 mandibular specimens, 6 back portions of skulls or occipital fragments, and 18 antler-horn core fragments from the site, there are no maxillary or facial region specimens among the recovered bones. This indicates that the mandible and cranial remains found in the pit houses and in cremation pit Feature 90 are not from whole skulls deposited there. Instead, two different and separate items were deposited in the features: mandibles, already separated from skulls, and antler racks or bighorn sheep horns.

Elements used in the manufacture of artifacts are predominantly metapodial elements (metatarsals and metacarpals), which were favored in the production of awls and related tools. In addition, three femur shafts were modified into large tubular beads.

When the special floor deposits and artifacts are excluded, it is evident that few identifiable artiodactyl specimens are simply discarded food refuse. The only notable concentrations are in the few roasting pits investigated during the testing program. Otherwise, only a handful of recognizable artiodactyl elements are scattered throughout the site. Much more abundant are the predominantly small, highly fragmentary unidentified large mammal specimens, which are presumably derived from broken and splintered artiodactyl elements. Despite the occurrence of some 700 such fragments, the relative paucity of identifiable elements suggests that large game was either an infrequently exploited resource, or that bone debris was discarded elsewhere.

Unusual Artiodactyl Bone Deposits

As at Fastimes (Volume 2, Chapter 8), artiodactyl mandibles were recovered from the floor surfaces of two of the excavated pit houses. Three mandibles were recovered from Feature 7, including two damaged pronghorn specimens and one mule deer (see Volume 5, Part E-9 for specimen numbers). The pronghorn lower jaws are a left (Mandible 2) and right (Mandible 1) specimen that are probably from a single adult individual. The former is badly damaged, however, making it difficult to determine whether the two match in terms of size, morphology, and tooth wear. They were found more than 30 cm apart, suggesting deposition as separate mandible halves rather than as a whole mandible. Mandible 3 is from a large adult deer. Mandible 4 was designated in the field, but the collected remains include only small fragments of Mandible 1. All of these remains are charred black.

Remains, including four partial crania, are more abundant on the floor of pit house Feature 58. In this structure, all of the mandibles, at least nine, are of mule deer. Mandibles are from at least five and maybe six individuals. Six of the mandibles represent three definite left-right matches. These include the jaws of a very young adult, about two years of age, a mature adult, and a very old individual. Two other fragmentary mandibles are left and right specimens from young adults, but are not definitely from the same animal. The ninth mandible is represented only by a small portion of the ascending ramus.

The sizes of mandibles are all within the range of modern mule deer (O. hemionus) and are much larger than white-tailed deer (O. virginianus). Better-preserved specimens for which tooth-row length can be measured are all above the mean of 37 modern specimens of O. hemionus from southern Arizona (24 measured personally, 13 given by Hoffmeister 1986). At least three of the individuals present in the floor assemblage (represented by Mandibles 3, 5, and 9, all left sides from three individuals) are very close to the upper size limit of the modern specimens. All three are larger than all but one or two of the measured modern specimens. The only other large specimens examined are three of the mandibles found on pit house floors at Fastimes.

Numbers assigned in the field do not coincide directly with individual mandibles. In some cases, parts of a single mandible were assigned two mandible numbers. In each case the mandibles appear to have been broken after deposition, thus for this study they are considered single specimens. In two cases, portions of two mandibles were collected as single specimens. Two of the nine represented mandibles were not designated as separate mandibles in the field. Table 8.7 shows the left-right matches of mandibles and the correspondence with field numbers.

Table 8.7

LEFT-RIGHT ARTIODACTYL MANDIBLE MATCHES

	Left Mandible	Right Mandible
Individual A Adult	FN1303("Mand. 5") Major portion FN1305 ("Mand. 7") Ascending portion	FN1299 ("Mand. 1") Major portion FN1302 ("Mand. 4") Anterior portion
Individual B Subadult	FN1301 ("Mand. 3") Major portion FN1304 ("Mand. 6") Ascending portion	FN1300 ("Mand. 2") Match is not definite
Individual C Very old adult	FN1306 ("Mand. 8")	FN1308 ("Mand. 10")
Individual D Young adult	FN1307 ("Mand. 9") Match is not definite	Mandible fragments mixed in with "Mand. 9" and "Mand. 10"

Note: The presence of a fifth individual (Individual E) is indicated by the occurrence of two articular processes from the ascending portions of two left mandibles from FN1298 (S20 "Mand. frags"). Only one of the numbered left mandibles ("Mand. 9") is missing this portion. One or more additional mandibles may be included in this floor assemblage as well.

Major cranial remains from pit house Feature 58 include a large bighorn ram specimen and three deer antler racks attached to sections of skull. In each of these cases, only the back portions of the crania are present, indicating that the antlers and horns were the items of interest and not complete skulls.

The Ovis canadensis skull was deposited on the floor with the right side down. Because of this, a major portion of the right horn core (Fig. 8.1) is preserved whereas the left is nearly completely gone. The specimen is from a large, fully adult individual. The outside curve of the right horn core has a preserved length of 29.5 cm, but was initially much longer, probably twice as long or more. Circumference of the base of the right horn core is approximately 34.5 cm. In comparison, Hansen (1980) reports that basal circumferences of adult desert bighorn ram horns (not cores, which are 1 cm to 2 cm smaller) average about 30 cm but may be as large as 37 cm. Russo (1956) gives an average basal circumference of 33.8 cm for ram horns from southwestern

Figure 8.1.   Right horn core of <u>Ovis</u> <u>canadensis</u> from floor of pit house
Feature 58.

Arizona. Kelley (1974) found an archaeological damaged horn core from
Grasshopper Ruin to be 32.5 cm in basal circumference, again smaller
than the Water World bighorn.

Baker and Bradley (1969) measured bighorn skulls from southern
Nevada and found that adult male horn core basal circumferences averaged
32.5 cm with a maximum of 36.4 cm and with a standard deviation of about
1.8 cm. When compared to this population the Water World bighorn is
slightly more than one standard deviation above the mean. Desert
bighorn in southern Arizona may be somewhat larger than those from
Nevada, however. For example, Krausman and others (1979) found basal
horn circumferences for a small sample of sheep from the Santa Catalina
Mountains north of Tucson to average about 40 cm, far larger than other
measured populations.

One of the deer antler racks (FN1627) also appears to be from a
larger-than-average individual. Although the antler tines are damaged,
each antler beam appears to have supported five points, indicating an
old adult male. Maximum preserved beam length is 49 cm and beam

diameter is 3.5 cm. Maximum spread cannot be measured accurately, but is estimated to have been around 80 cm (maximum preserved spread after removal from the ground is 60 cm). In both size and morphology, this specimen is very close to the largest individual described by Clark (1953) for the historic population of mule deer living in the Tucson Mountains.

The other two partial skull and antler racks from Feature 58 are from smaller and presumably younger individuals. One of these (FN1625) was found adjacent to and slightly overlapping the larger specimen (FN1627). The other was too badly damaged to be collected as a discrete specimen in the field, but appears to have been quite similar to the FN1625 specimen. Both have beam diameters of 2.4 cm to 2.6 cm, suggesting young adult deer. This smaller antler size suggests the possibility of white-tailed deer (Odocoileus virginianus) rather than mule deer, but the relatively large size of the preserved part of the cranium is indicative of mule deer.

There are no obvious indications of any functional use of either the mandibles or cranial specimens. Microscopic examination of the mandibles failed to reveal cut marks or scratches attributable to use, but the surfaces of most of the specimens are sufficiently weathered so that marks could be obscured. The mandibles may have had no functional use.

A third concentration of artiodactyl mandibles was recovered from Feature 90, a pit in the cremation area. Included are a minimum of six deer mandibles (4 left, 2 right) and two pronghorn mandibles (1 left, 1 right). These specimens differ from those on the the pit house floors in that they are highly fragmented and burned white or gray from intense heat (no fragment exceeds 4 cm in length). The number of mandibles above is a minimum number based on matching particular, easily recognized parts of the mandible (for example, the condylar and angular processes and anterior and posterior ends of the tooth row). It is not readily apparent that individual mandibles can be reconstructed.

Also present are a large number of roots of lower cheek teeth (premolars and molars). At least 36 teeth are represented by 71 isolated roots, nearly all of which appear to be from deer. Noticeably absent are enamel fragments of tooth crowns. It appears that all teeth were broken off at the sockets prior to burning and deposition. No definite pronghorn tooth fragments are present nor are there any alveolar portions of pronghorn mandibles. The two referred specimens are based on the posterior portions (angular processes and ascending rami) of two mandibles. These may or may not be from a matched pair from a single individual.

Antler and horn core specimens have been found at many southern Arizona archaeological sites. One of the more noteworthy occurrences of bighorn is at Valshni Village (Withers 1941, 1973) where numerous horn core specimens (at least 17 "good specimens") were encountered, several apparently attached to the backs of crania. Partial skulls with horn

cores were found on the floors of two houses, and another probable
structure contained three pairs and seven single horn cores (Withers
1941 gives more information than the 1973 version).

At Babocomari Village, Di Peso (1951) found antler racks,
usually attached to small portions of crania, on the floors of at least
three structures (a pronghorn skull cap was found on the floor of a
fourth house). The antlers all were found in front of the wall opposite
the house entry. Di Peso interprets these to have been house
decorations and cites a personal communication from Ruth Underhill that
such decorations were used by the modern Pima and Papago (O'odham).
Underhill also is credited with the observation that "antlers were
ceremonial objects used by men, and were hung so that neither dogs nor
women could touch and defame them" (Di Peso 1951: 39). At a prehistoric
site near Tumacacori, Di Peso (1956) found antler racks that he thought
were head masks worn to imitate deer.

Nonmammals

Amphibian, reptile, and bird remains are very scarce in the
Water World faunal collection. A single toad bone is a damaged urostyle
of a spadefoot toad (Scaphiopus couchi) from Feature 18, a pit. Feature
18 also contained the only snake element from the site, a weathered
vertebra of a coachwhip (Masticophis cf. M. flagellum). Both bones are
probably postoccupational intrusives.

Desert tortoise (Gopherus agassizi) is represented by a single
small shell fragment from the plastron, which was found in the lower
fill of Feature 19, a pit house. This specimen has the same coloration
and surface condition as accompanying bone specimens, suggesting that it
may be a human discard.

Two genera of lizards are present. Eleven elements of a partial
skeleton of a very small whiptail lizard (Cnemidophorus) were recovered
from flotation of the contents of a cremation vessel, Feature 87, and
are the only nonhuman bones found in this feature. Although the bones
are not recent, this is almost certainly a postdepositional intrusion.
The other lizard specimen is the regal horned lizard (Phrynosoma
solare); its prominent parietal horns were found in the general site
trash deposit in House Group 4.

Two genera of birds are represented. Quail is most abundant
with four elements found in four separate proveniences: pit house
Features 19 and 110 and activity surface Features 66 and 68. Three of
the quail elements (2 coracoids and 1 sternum) are in the size range of
Callipepla gambelii (Gambel's quail) and are tentatively referred to
that species. The fourth element, a distal tibiotarsus from Feature
110, is larger than any compared C. gambelii, but compares well with C.
squamata (scaled quail), and is tentatively assigned to that species.
Callipepla squamata is now characteristically found in better-developed

grasslands at slightly higher elevations than the site location, suggesting the possibility of some degree of vegetational change in the site vicinity. This species also occurs, if not commonly, on the flat valley bottom of the Avra Valley, however, as well as in higher grasslands (Arizona Game and Fish Department 1983).

Modified Bone

Burned Bone

The spatial distribution and taxonomic identification of burned specimens recovered at Water World is given in Volume 5, Part E-10. A breakdown of the frequency of burning noted on different skeletal elements of lagomorphs in different proveniences is presented in Volume 5, Part E-8. Burning as used here includes all degrees of bone discoloration from exposure to fire, including white or gray calcination from intense heat, blackening from charring, dark brown discoloration, and intermediate stages.

Altogether, some 38 percent (N=1,672) of all vertebrate specimens from the site show some burning. Spatially, there are a small number of localities that yielded the majority of burned remains. Elsewhere, frequencies are much lower.

Percentages of burning are higher in general site proveniences than in the majority of feature fill units. Only in House Group 6 are fewer than 35 percent of the specimens burned. Nearly 40 percent of the burned specimens from the site are from the trash deposit in House Group 2 where the majority of bones (mainly jackrabbits and unidentified small mammals) are burned. In all, slightly over half of the burned specimens come from general site proveniences.

In contrast, only in 4 of the 20 features containing at least 25 specimens does the frequency of burning exceed 35 percent. Not surprisingly, these four features include the three roasting pits excavated during the testing phase and Feature 90, the cremation pit with broken artiodactyl mandibles. In each of these pits at least 98 percent of the bone fragments are burned. Remains are most abundant in Feature 8 where all but 3 of a total of 362 counted specimens are burned. Together these four pits contain 35 percent of the burned specimens from the site. This includes 75 percent of the combined burned artiodactyl and unidentified large mammal bones, but only 1 percent of the recovered burned lagomorph and unidentified small mammals.

None of the pit house fills has burning frequencies as high as 35 percent. Among all of the pit house fills, only Features 79 and 58, where there is evidence of postoccupational burning, contained more than 20 burned specimens.

Volume 5, Part E-10 also gives variability in the frequency burning between different taxa. Only a small number of the taxa found at the site have any burned specimens. Other than the lagomorphs and artiodactyls, the only two burned specimens are the mandibles of a wood rat and a badger.

Large mammal remains (including artiodactyls) are charred more frequently than small mammals (including lagomorphs). More than 65 percent of the artiodactyl specimens and 85 percent of the unidentified large mammal bones are charred. These values are inflated by the inclusion of the unique assemblages of the testing phase roasting pits, Feature 90, and the burned floor assemblage in Feature 58. When these proveniences are excluded, the frequency of charring on large mammal remains is much lower.

For small mammals, the frequency of burning is 30 percent for unidentified remains and 24 percent for Lepus, the main small mammal. In this case, the bulk of the burned specimens are from nonfeature proveniences, in particular the House Group 4 trash deposit that yielded 76 percent of all the burned Lepus bones and more than half of the burned unidentified small mammals. Again, exclusion of this unusual deposit would greatly lower the percentage of charring on small mammal bones. In every feature containing at least 25 jackrabbit bones, fewer than 20 percent are burned. By way of comparison, only 7 percent of Lepus specimens from feature proveniences are burned, whereas more than 50 percent of those from general site excavation units are burned.

The frequency of burning is much lower for cottontail remains than for jackrabbits. Only five Sylvilagus specimens (7.5%) are burned; four of these come from the House Group 4 trash deposit.

Bone Artifacts

A total of 61 manufactured bone artifacts was recovered from Water World (Tables 8.8 and 8.9). The majority are from the general category of "awls" or perforating tools, and are fragmentary. Included among the 50 perforating implements are 11 fine-pointed implements: 2 could be classed as needles and 9 as hairpins.

There are five intact and seven slightly damaged awls for which length can be estimated. Awl lengths range from 5.1 cm to 18.2 cm, with a cluster of four short, stocky awls that fall between 5.1 cm and 5.4 cm. There are a number of other, fragmentary awls that also appear to have been comparably short and stocky. Longer awls are more slender and measure from 6.7 cm to 18.2 cm long with no noticeable clusters. Point shapes and cross sections vary considerably, ranging from narrow and round to blunt and flat.

One of the short, stocky awls (Feature 19 floor contact, FN364) has a small deposit of dried black pitch adhering to the broad butt end,

Table 8.8

SUMMARY OF BONE ARTIFACTS

Feature	Awl	Awl/Needle	Awl with Pitch	Hairpin	Spatula	Antler-Tine Tool	Bone Tube	Total
7							1	1
19	5		1					6
20	2							2
25	1							1
26	2							2
27	1	1						2
29	2						3	5
33	1	1						2
55	4							4
58	5				2			7
79	2						2	4
80/81				1				1
90	2			3		2		7
105/108	3			4				7
118				1				1

General Site

House Group 2	4						1	5
House Group 4	4							4
Total	38	2	1	9	2	2	7	61

Taxonomic Category

Odocoileus						2		2
Antilocapra	2							2
Unidentified Artiodactyl	9			3	1		4	17
Unidentified large mammal	27	2	1	6	1		3	40
Total	38	2	1	9	2	2	7	61

Table 8.9

DISTRIBUTION OF BONE ARTIFACTS

Feature	Stratum	FN	Artifact	Taxon	Element	Remarks
7	Floor contact	1913	Bone tube	Unidentified large mammal	Long bone shaft fragment	Small fragment, highly weathered
19	S1L2	16	Awl	Unidentified large mammal	Long bone shaft fragment	Point portion, weathered
19	S1L2	31	Awl	Unidentified large mammal	Long bone shaft fragment	Shaft fragment
19	S2L1	217	Awl	Unidentified large mammal	Long bone shaft fragment	Small intact awl, blunt tip with spatulate butt end; 5.5 cm long
19	Floor N422.97, E502.75	351	Awl	Artiodactyl	Metapodial shaft	Long slender intact artifact, 15.4 cm long
19	Floor N422.55, E500.90	364	Awl with pitch	Unidentified large mammal	Long bone shaft fragment	Damaged awl with burned pitch adhering to butt end
19	Floor N422.80, E500.90	464	Awl	Unidentified large mammal	Long bone shaft fragment	Point portion, slender tipped awl
20	S2L1	262	Awl	Unidentified large mammal	Long bone shaft fragment	Point portion
20	S2L2	273	Awl	Unidentified large mammal	Long bone shaft fragment	Damaged, full length
25	Floor	86	Awl	Artiodactyl	Distal metapodial	Intact, split metapodial awl
26	S1L2	1188	Awl	Unidentified large mammal	Long bone shaft fragment	Small shaft section
26	S1L2	1357	Awl	Unidentified large mammal	Long bone shaft fragment	Shaft section
27	S1L1	484	Awl/needle	Unidentified large mammal	Long bone shaft fragment	Tip fragment
27	S1L1	485	Awl	Unidentified large mammal	Long bone shaft fragment	Point fragment
29	S1L1	905	Bone tube	Artiodactyl	L femur shaft	Small fragment near distal end
29	S1L1	1008	Bone tube	Unidentified large mammal	Long bone shaft fragment	Small fragment
29	Floor N418.75, E397.50	914	Awl	Unidentified large mammal	Long bone shaft fragment	Intact small robust awl, 5.3 cm long
29	Floor N419.17, E397.55	915	Awl	Artiodactyl	Metapodial, distal portion	Robust awl, damaged but with whole length preserved; 5.5. cm long
29	Floor N418.80, E397.55	1062	Bone tube	Artiodactyl	L humerus shaft	Fragment, incised around circumference near midsection, parallel to ends; 6.7 cm long
33	Floor N365.22, E431.03 (main part)	954,956	Awl/needle	Unidentified large mammal	Complete, very thin, shaft fragment	Sharp-pointed artifact, spatulate butt end; 15.6 cm long
33	F.33.4 (posthole)	1120	Awl	Artiodactyl	Metapodial shaft	Intact long slender awl, 11.7 cm long
55	S1L1	649	Awl	Unidentified large mammal	Long bone shaft fragment	Fragment, point portion

Table 8.9, continued

DISTRIBUTION OF BONE ARTIFACTS

Feature	Stratum	FN	Artifact	Taxon	Element	Remarks
55	S1L1	657	Awl	Unidentified large mammal	Long bone shaft fragment	Fragment, shaft portion, highly polished
55	S1L1	1132	Awl?	Unidentified large mammal	Long bone shaft fragment	Intact small, thin artifact with slender point; 6.7 cm long
55	S1L1	1653	Awl?	Unidentified large mammal	Long bone shaft fragment	Fragment, point portion, small hole located 5 mm from tip
58	Backdirt	1424	Awl	Unidentified large mammal	Long bone shaft fragment	Slender artifact, intact except for broken tip; 7.5 cm long
58	S2L1	1298a	Awl	Unidentified large mammal	Long bone shaft fragment	Fragment, shaft section, burned white
58	S2L1	1298a	Spatulate tool	Unidentified large mammal	Long bone shaft fragment	Fragment; broad, beveled tip, burned white
58	S2L1	1591	Awl	Artiodactyl	Metapodial shaft and proximal section	Major portion of long thin awl, at at least 16 cm and probably 20 cm long
58	S2L1	1682	Awl?	Unidentified large mammal	Long bone shaft fragment	Shaft fragment, burned black
58	Floor contact	1690	Awl/ spatula	Artiodactyl	L tibia shaft	Long curving artifact with spatulate blade on one end, point on other; 19.4 cm long
58	Floor contact	1959	Awl	Unidentified large mammal	Long bone shaft fragment	Point portion, robust awl
79	S1L1	2085	Awl	Artiodactyl	Metapodial, distal condyle	Distal portion of robust split metapodial awl
79	S2L1	2093	2 Bone tubes	Artiodactyl	2 R femur shafts	1 intact bone tube, 1 slightly damaged bone tube; damaged tube is small juvenile; larger is 18 mm diameter, 7.1 cm long; smaller is 14 mm diameter, 6.4 cm long
79	Floor contact	2099	Awl	Artiodactyl	Metapodial, shaft and distal portion	Thin intact awl, distal condyle removed at epiphysis; 10.5 cm long
80 & 81	S1L1	2062 & 2140	Hairpin	Unidentified large mammal	Long bone shaft fragment	Complete length but in several pieces in two features; 14.4 cm long, burned white
90	S1L1	2100-2104	Hairpin	Artiodactyl	Proximal L metatarsal	Point and butt portions, initial length at least 10 cm, burned white
			Hairpin	Artiodactyl	Proximal R radius	Complete length 9.4 cm, in two pieces, stocky, burned white
			Hairpin	Unidentified large mammal	Long bone shaft fragment	Point portion, burned white
			Awl?	Unidentified large mammal	Long bone shaft fragment	Shaft fragment, burned white
90	S1L1	2100-2104	Awl?	Antilocapra	Distal metapodial	Near whole butt tip missing, estimated length 6.7 cm, split metapodial, condyle fused and abraded, burned white
			2 Tine tools	Odocoileus	2 antler tines	Two antler-tine fragments with beveled tips, preserved lengths 2 cm and 4 cm, both burned white
105	S1L1	2225	Hairpin	Unidentified large mammal	Long bone shaft fragment	Thin point portion, calcined white, may match one of other artifacts from Fea. 105-118 cremation area

Table 8.9, continued

DISTRIBUTION OF BONE ARTIFACTS

Feature	Stratum	FN	Artifact	Taxon	Element	Remarks
105	S2L1	2231	Flat-point awl	Artiodactyl	Metapodial shaft	Long, flat-pointed artifact, at least 15 cm long
105 & 108	S1L1	2224, 2242, 2243, & 2244	Hairpin	Unidentified large mammal	Long bone shaft fragment	Butt and shaft sections, burned white, pieces from 4 FNs fit together
105	S1L1	2236	Hairpin	Unidentified large mammal	Long bone shaft fragment	Butt and shaft, burned white
			Awl?	Unidentified large mammal	Long bone shaft fragment	Shaft fagment, burned white
105 & 108	S1L1	2239	Flat-point awl	Unidentified large mammal	Long bone shaft fragment	Point portion, similar to FN2231
105,108 & 118	S1L1	2224, 2242, & 2345	Hairpin	Artiodactyl	Proximal R radius	Nearly complete with pieces from three suggested features (105, 105-108, 118); long thin, strongly bowed artifact, length 15.6 cm, burned white
118	S1L1	2341	Hairpin	Unidentified large mammal	Long bone shaft fragment	Point portion, with small constricted tip, burned white

General Site Proveniences

Feature	Stratum	FN	Artifact	Taxon	Element	Remarks
H.G. 2	S30L3 (over F.26)	733a	Awl	Unidentified large mammal	Long bone shaft fragment	Point missing
H.G. 2	S30L3 (over F.26)	733b	Awl	Unidentified large mammal	Long bone shaft fragment	Shaft fragment
H.G. 2	S30L2 (over F.26)	747	Awl	Antilocapra	Distal metatarsal	Split metapodial awl, point missing
H.G. 2	S30L2 (over F.26)	748	Awl	Unidentified large mammal	Long bone shaft fragment	Tip only
H.G. 2	S30L2 (over F.29)	814	Bone tube	Unidentified large mammal	Long bone shaft fragment	Small fragment
H.G. 4	S30L1 (over F.58)	1228	Awl	Unidentified large mammal	Long bone shaft fragment	Shaft fragment
H.G. 4	S30L1 (over F.58)	1470	Awl	Unidentified large mammal	Long bone shaft fragment	Point portion
H.G. 4	S50L3 (over F.58)	1636	Awl	Artiodactyl	Distal metapodial	Split metapodial awl, point missing
H.G. 4	S30L1 (over F.58)	1640	Awl	Unidentified large mammal	Long bone shaft fragment	Slender point fragment, burned black

presumably the result of using the artifact to mix and apply the pitch. Two similar occurrences were noted on the butt ends of artifacts at Fastimes.

One small fragment from the point portion of a thin, flat awl with a rapidly expanding point is perforated by a small hole, 2 mm by 1 mm in size, located along the central axis of the tool, 4.5 mm from the tip. This appears to be a nutrient foramen in the wall of the long bone that was artificially expanded. The tip of the artifact is sharp, but the point flares quickly (4.75 mm by 2.4 mm diameter at the location of the hole) to give a broader artifact than expected for a needle (6.7 mm wide at 1 cm from the tip).

The two possible needles are very slender, elongated perforators with nearly cylindrical shafts. Although broken into pieces, one is a complete tool; it measures 15.6 cm in length and comes from the floor of Feature 33. It was collected in the field as two specimens (FN954 and FN956), but the breakage appears to be recent. The second possible needle is a point portion only, and comes from the fill of pit house Feature 27.

Nine probable hairpins all come from cremation pits (Features 80, 81, 90, 105, 108, and 118) in House Group 5. These are slender, sharp-pointed artifacts with uneven, undulating edges and shafts that are characteristically not straight, but slightly or strongly bowed. All are calcined white or gray from exposure to intense heat. It is likely that burning was incurred during cremation and that the hairpins were in place at the time of cremation.

All of the hairpins are broken, presumably from burning, but three can be sufficiently reconstructed to estimate the original length. These specimens measure 9.4 cm, 14.4 cm, and 15.6 cm long (Table 8.9). Many of the hairpins represented by more than one fragment, including the three measurable specimens, were found in more than one excavation unit and often in more than one designated feature. Single artifacts were found in as many as four excavation units and three designated features. This implies that: (1) the designated features in the cremation area are not discrete units; (2) the artifacts (and probably the associated cremated human bones) were mixed after cremation, but before deposition; or (3) there has been considerable postdepositional mixing and redeposition.

Two spatulate tools include one well-made, multiple-function tool and a fragmentary burned specimen, both from pit house Feature 58. The better-preserved specimen (FN1690), made from the tibia shaft of an unidentified artiodactyl, was found on the floor of the pit house. This is the longest artifact recovered from the site; its estimated length is more than 19 cm. One end is a damaged awl point and the other has a nicely shaped, very thin flat blade with a rounded tip.

Two beveled deer antler tines were found in Feature 90, the cremation pit containing burned and fragmented artiodactyl mandibles as well as three hairpins and two probable awls. Both of the tines are small fragments that measure 2 cm and 4 cm in length.

Six bone tubes from the site include two nearly complete artifacts found together in the fill of pit house Feature 79, and four fragmentary specimens. Three of the fragments are from Feature 29, a pit house, one on floor contact (Stratum 20), two in Stratum 1, and the fourth from Stratum 30 overlying Feature 29. Despite the stratigraphic dispersal, it is possible that all were deposited at the same time.

Both of the specimens from Feature 79 are cut from the shafts of artiodactyl femurs, but one is from an adult and the other from a much smaller juvenile. One of the Feature 29 specimens is also from an artiodactyl femur and another is from the shaft of a humerus. The remaining two specimens are too fragmentary to identify the element.

All of the artifacts are made from large mammal elements, but element and taxon can be determined in only 21 cases. Four specimens are referred to genus: the two deer antler-tine artifacts, and two awls made from distal pronghorn metapodials (1 metatarsal and 1 undetermined metapodial). The other 17 cases are unidentified artiodactyl limb sections including 10 metapodial shafts modified into awls or hairpins, 2 proximal radii made into hairpins, 1 tibia shaft fragment made into the awl-spatula, and 3 femur shafts and 1 humerus shaft from which bone tubes were cut.

Chapter 9

POLLEN ANALYSIS

Suzanne K. Fish

Contexts sampled at Water World include pit house floors, intramural features, extramural features, and artifact surfaces. Composite samples were analyzed from most structure floor levels to efficiently characterize a maximum number of pollen assemblages. Three of the 25 samples failed to yield adequately preserved pollen. Destructive oxidation probably was involved in the cases of these two hearths and a cremation vessel. Results are arranged in Table 9.1 according to house groups, although there may be chronological variation within these spatially localized sets of features. Methods used in the analysis of Water World samples are described in Volume 2, Chapter 9.

Water World Environment

In the modern vegetation communities of the Tucson Mountain bajada environments similar to Water World, the dominant pollen is Ambrosia-type, contributed by bur sage (Hevly and others 1965). The low proportion of this type in Water World samples is evidence of past clearing of natural vegetation in the site vicinity. Grass (Gramineae) frequencies are not similarly reduced, however, and identify the locality as relatively mesic. Water World grass pollen values are among the highest reported from any Tucson-area prehistoric site. Runoff from the western slope of the Tucson Mountains supplements direct rainfall to support a lush facies of an arborescent desert association.

Other local species indicated by pollen include mesquite (Prosopis), palo verde (Cercidium), creosote bush (Larrea), hackberry (Celtis), saguaro (Cereus-type), cholla (Cylindropuntia), and prickly pear (Platyopuntia). Riparian elements are represented by willow (Salix) and cattail (Typha). Willow pollen was recovered in such low frequencies that the source trees may have been at a distance. Cattail pollen is likely to have been culturally introduced into the site.

A series of nonarboreal pollen types is most numerous in Water World samples. Cheno-am (Chenopodiaceae and Amaranthus) values are variable, but often occur above the 10 percent to 20 percent that

279

Table 9.1

POLLEN FREQUENCIES

	Ambrosia-type	Liguliflorae	High-Spine Compositae	Cheno-am	Tidestromia	Gramineae	Boerhaavia-type	Sphaeralcea	Kallstroemia	Onagraceae	Euphorbia-type	Eriogonum	Cruciferae	Cylindropuntia	Platyopuntia	(Cereus-type)	Larrea	Prosopis	cf. Leguminosae	Pinus	Quercus	Salix	Typha	Other	Indeterminate	Zea (# of grains)	Cucurbita (% of grains)
House Group 1																											
F.55 pit house floor	3.5	-	6.5	29*		4.5	40.5	1	6.5	1.5	1.5	1.5				1.5		4.5	3	1				Juniperus, 0.5 Yucca, 0.5	3	+	
F.55.1/55.12 hearth	8	.0	20.5	20.5		8.5	20	2	7	0.5	1.5						0.5	3	3	1	1			Gilia, 0.5	4.5	1	
F.25 pit house floor comp.	9.5	.7	35	35		6	7.5	0.5			0.5	0.5						1.5	1	1				Juniperus, 1.5	3	+	
F.25.1 pit, beneath mortar	3	1	20.5	42.5*		6	12.5	+			1.5	1	2	+	7		0.5	1	2	2.5				Plantago, 0.5 Liliaceae, 1	2.5	+	
F.25.1 pit, mortar cavity	6	3.5*	13.5	37.5		9.5	9.5		0.5	+	0.5	7	0.5	+	0.5		0.5		1.5	1.5			0.5	Cercidium, 0.5	6.5	+	
F.20 pit house floor, under metate	9		20.5	39	4	8	9.5	3		0.5								1		1				Juniperus, 0.5	4		
F.20.01 hearth	11.5		16	26.5*	12.5*	7.5	13.5*	1.5	2		0.5	3.5	6.5	2		1*	0.5	1		1.5	0.5		0.5	Juniperus, 0.5 Cercidium, 0.5 Ephedra, 0.5	5.5	26	
F.19 pit house floor comp.	6.5		8.5	45		6	15*						1	1					0.5	0.5	0.5				0.5	26	
House Group 2																											
F.29 pit house floor comp.	10		29.5*	26		2.5	20	+	+		2	3.5							1	0.5				Artemisia, 0.5	4.5		
F.57 ash pit	16.5		13	32.5		8	11		0.5		1.5	4.5			+		4		1	3	1			Celtis, 0.5	4		
F.7 pit house floor comp.	16.5		8.5	15.5		10.5	22.5		4.5	1	2	9.5			1			3	0.5	0.5	1			Juniperus, 0.5	6.5	2	
F.7.1 hearth	10.5		2	13		30	33				2.5	4								+					0.5	3	
House Group 3																											
F.27 pit house floor comp.	5		5	21	40*	3.5	10.5*		3			4							1	0.5				Cercidium, 2	3	+	
F.27.02 pit	9.5		14.5	31.5	+	5.5	28		+	+	1.5	5.5	1.5						1.5	3			1		1.5	+	
F.33 pit house floor comp.	8	1.5	11.5	33*		8	25			1.5	1	5	0.5			0.5				+				Cercidium, 0.5	3		
F.33.1 hearth					Insufficient	Pollen																					
F.53 pit house floor comp.	5.5		6	40.5		7*	20.5		3	4	4	1.5		0.5				1	1.5	1.5	0.5	0.5			6	1	
F.86 roasting pit comp.	9.5		14.5	25.5*	8	10.5	12		0.5	1.5	1.5	6.5		2.5				4.5	1.5	1	1	0.5			3		
House Group 4																											
F.58 pit house floor comp.	7		17.5	42*	2	4	23.5*	+	1	1			2							+				Solanaceae, 0.5	0.5	1	
F.58.01 hearth	10.5		14	38.5	1.5	11	20	+	+	+	0.5	2							0.5	+					1.5	+	
F.76 hearth					Insufficient	Pollen																					
House Group 5																											
F.79 pit house floor	12.5		16	12.5		16.5	25	1	+	1		8					1	3		0.5	0.5		1	Solanaceae, 1	1.5	1	
House Group 6																											
F.68 pit house floor comp.	17		11.5	19	1.5	5	18.5*		+	1	2	9.5	1.5				0.5	4.5	2	0.5	0.5		1	Solanaceae, 1	4.5	2*	
Other																											
F.87 cremation vessel					Insufficient	Pollen																					
F.44 pit house floor	7.5		12	46.5*	4	5*	10		+		1.5	6.5	1				0.5	1		0.5				Celtis, 0.5	4.5		

Frequencies of noncultigen types are calculated as percentages of a 200-grain standard sum, which excludes cultigen types. Values for corn (Zea) and cucurbits (Cucurbita) are represented as numbers of grains encountered during tabulation of 200 grains of all other types.
* Type observed in aggregates of 6 or more grains.
+ Type observed in scanning of additional material after completion of the standard sum of 200 noncultigen grains.

characterizes the natural vegetation today (Hevly and others 1965). A number of the higher cheno-am values occur in conjunction with pollen grain aggregates, suggesting that the source plants were present in or near the recovery provenience. Chenopods and amaranths are species commonly encouraged by the disturbed and enriched locales of human habitation. Prehistorically elevated pollen frequencies would undoubtedly reflect this kind of increment. Additionally, chenopods and amaranths provided both edible greens and seeds (for example, Russell 1975; Curtin 1984). Charred seeds of these taxa were recovered in flotation samples (see Kwiatkowski and Gasser, Chapter 10, this volume), confirming economic use.

Liguliflorae, a subfamily within the Compositae or sunflower family, has been recovered so consistently in some Hohokam sites as to indicate a source in a ubiquitous weedy species. At Water World, this type is quite restricted among proveniences, fitting an economic rather than natural distribution pattern. In contrast to the Liguliflorae distribution is that of tidestromia (Tidestromia), a member of the amaranth family. Tidestromia occurs in instances of unusual frequencies and aggregates, and its presence is widespread among site proveniences. Although there may be localized evidence for use, this plant also may have been among the disturbance species in the Water World environs. Today, Liguliflorae and Tidestromia pollen are more common in Tucson Mountain upper bajada and mountain slope communities than at lower elevations (Hevly and others 1965); in some cases these types may have been introduced by adhering to upland gathered plants.

A group of pollen types has been identified that has Hohokam agricultural contexts (Fish 1984, 1985). These include spiderling (Boerhaavia-type), globe mallow (Sphaeralcea), Arizona poppy (Kallstroemia), and Onagraceae (evening primrose family). These types are constituents of the pollen spectra from the natural vegetation in which Water World is located, but in significantly lower frequencies than in site samples.

Distributions at Water World are typical in the cases of spiderling, Arizona poppy, and Onagraceae. Globe mallow is usually the second most frequent in this group, and was recovered accordingly at both Fastimes and Hawk's Nest. The comparatively weak representation of globe mallow at Water World is paralleled by substantially lower seed recovery in flotation samples (Kwiatkowski and Gasser, Chapter 10, this volume). Globe mallow is a prominent weed of modern field situations in the area north of Tucson, and its virtual absence at Water World is suggestive of a different pattern of agricultural activity than at either Fastimes or Hawk's Nest.

House Group 1

Feature 55 is an earlier, smaller pit house below Feature 25 in House Group 1. The composite floor sample contains the highest

spiderling and Arizona poppy values at Water World, although
agricultural products are represented by a single grain of tabulated
corn pollen from the hearth. Both floor and hearth samples yielded
Cereus-type cactus pollen, probably in conjunction with the presence of
a charred saguaro seed in the hearth (Kwiatkowski and Gasser, Chapter
10, this volume). Yucca pollen in Feature 55 is unique. Yucca may have
been acquired from the Tucson Mountains or from abundant plants on
bajadas to the west that are at somewhat higher elevations.

The remaining pit houses sampled in House Group 1 are similar
to one another in pollen distributions. They differ from Feature 55 in
exhibiting lower values for spiderling and higher values for both
Compositae with long spines and the cheno-am category. Because Feature
25 clearly postdates Feature 55, it is possible that Features 20 and 19
also were occupied after that structure.

Features 25, 20, and 19 are marked by comparative variety in
resources among the Water World structures. Each contains corn pollen.
For Feature 25, the cultigen was tabulated only in a floor pit
containing a mortar. Multiple instances were recovered from composite
floor samples in the other two pit houses; the highest site value came
from the Feature 20 hearth. Cattail was recovered from Features 20 and
25. Cholla, prickly pear, and saguaro-type are present in Features 19
and 25. Maximal site frequencies are involved for cholla and prickly
pear, as well as saguaro-type in a large aggregate.

Additional pollen types may pertain to resource use. A single
grain of mustard family (Cruciferae) pollen from the cavity of the
mortar in the Feature 25 floor pit is a five-furrowed type, which is
suggested by Gish (1988) to have been of economic significance in the
lower Santa Cruz Basin sites north of Tucson. The probable species is
spectable-pod (Dithyrea), a plant with larger pods than most related
taxa.

Another potential resource is revealed in this structure by
Liguliflorae pollen. This type occurs in each of three samples from
Feature 25, twice in aggregates. A single other site provenience
contains this type. The species and use cannot be identified. In the
Feature 20 hearth, aggregates of tidestromia parallel recovery of a
charred seed. This plant is used medicinally by the Seri (Felger and
Moser 1985).

House Group 2

Pollen assemblages in Features 7 and 29 suggest that these two
pit houses in House Group 2 may have been disjunct in occupational
histories. Differential functions could account for the differences,
but the proximity of the two similarly oriented structures seems
compatible with temporal differences in use. Feature 7 has higher

Compositae frequencies and Feature 29 has higher values for cheno-am pollen.

Resource evidence is limited for the two structures. Feature 29 produced no cultigens. Only two other possible resources were noted. Prickly pear pollen was observed in scanning. Aggregates may indicate the use of a Compositae species. Corn pollen appears in moderate amounts in both Feature 7 samples. Prickly pear also is present. Unusually high grass frequencies in the hearth of this pit house may denote food preparation.

House Group 3

Distributions indicating temporal or functional differences among Features 27, 33, and 53 in House Group 3 are unclear. The predominance of tidestromia pollen in the Feature 27 floor sample constrains representation of remaining types. The spectrum from a pit in the structure falls within the range of values for the other two structures, however.

Features 27 and 53 contain corn pollen in low amounts. Features 33 and 53 yielded low cholla frequencies, with additional identifications of saguaro-type in the Feature 33 floor and prickly pear in that of Feature 53. Cattail was recovered in Feature 27. The abundant tidestromia pollen and aggregates in Feature 27 may indicate plant use.

Feature 86 is a roasting pit; no resources prepared in the feature are revealed by pollen contents. Agave is the single charred plant remain from this pit; pollen would be unusual for agave, which is customarily harvested before flower development.

House Group 4

Pollen was recovered from a single pit house, Feature 58, in House Group 4. Floor composite and hearth samples each contain corn, although identification in the hearth was through scanning after tabulation. Cholla is the only other resource palynologically associated with the structure.

House Group 5

A single pit house was sampled in House Group 5. An instance of cucurbit (Cucurbita) pollen was tabulated in Feature 79. This is the only occurrence of cucurbit at Water World in either the pollen or flotation results.

House Group 6

The floor composite sample from one structure, Feature 68, contains multiple grains of corn pollen and aggregates. Cholla is a second resource indicated here.

Other Proveniences

Feature 44 is a pit house in the vicinity of House Group 3. Its small size suggests some function other than habitation. The pollen assemblage is not distinguished by plentiful economic types, however. A small amount of cholla pollen is the sole resource documented.

Conclusion

The Water World pollen spectra, as a whole, are marked by relatively low representations of cultigens among Tucson-area sites and by limited diversity in gathered resources as well. These patterns occur in association with scarce pollen of globe mallow, a common agricultural weed, in many site proveniences. Further, the ubiquity of charred corn is lowest at Water World among the Phase B sites, and flotation recovery among all samples was low.

The abundance of economic pollen types in a provenience can be related either to absolute quantities of the source plants or to their form with respect to potential for pollen dispersal. Thus, the modest cultigen record and the overall low diversity per structure is not necessarily evidence of restricted access to resources by site residents. Water World is situated conveniently for the gathering of both upland and valley floor resources. Riparian species along Brawley Wash are close at hand. Bajada runoff could supply floodwater fields on nearby alluvial fan surfaces, and diversion of Brawley Wash may have been possible. In view of these beneficial locational characteristics of the site, patterns of low resource evidence are likely linked to the form of resources present.

Pollen should be dispersed most plentifully by plant materials that have not yet been processed. Outer parts such as corn leaves or husks, which may be discarded, would contain large amounts of pollen. Pollen also would tend to be dislodged or destroyed by sequential processing stages of washing, parching, and so forth. More refined resource forms should add relatively smaller increments of pollen to site proveniences than would unprocessed or newly gathered resources. Similarly, the accidental burning that accounts for many charred remains would often occur during initial processing. Therefore, limited processing of crops at Water World and even limited storage of newly

harvested forms is a reasonable conclusion from the quantitatively low
cultigen record, although corn, cucurbits, and cotton were documented.

Two possibilities can be suggested for the general configuration
of resource distributions at Water World. One is that occupants of all
house groups were more or less permanent residents, but much of the
initial crop processing was at fieldside rather than within site
confines. If this was the case, then field houses or shelters might
have been used seasonally away from the site, with the products later
transferred to Water World in more processed states. Pollen evidence
for such locally accessible wild resources as cacti is also low compared
to Phase B and other Tucson area sites, however. Initial processing of
all kinds may have been moderate at the site, commensurate with a bias
toward winter occupation and an emphasis on stored supplies.

The exception to general patterns of resource evidence at Water
World can be found in House Group 1. As a group, these structures
contain a fairly consistent presence of corn pollen and the highest site
values. Pollen of the common agricultural weed, globe mallow, is
virtually restricted to these proveniences. In addition to
distributional factors pertaining to cultivated products, indicators for
gathered resources also are notable. House Group 1 structures account
for the majority of instances of the three cactus taxa as well as the
upper frequencies of each. Two of the three instances of cattail and
the unique record of yucca occur here, along with probable economic
indications of Liguliflorae and tidestromia.

House Group 1 furnished more samples than several other groups,
and resource contrasts can therefore only be made with broad site
patterns. It is possible that additional samples would have identified
a similar configuration in another house group. Nevertheless, the
divergent pattern of House Group 1 suggests more comprehensive residency
for a segment of site inhabitants, including the summer agricultural
season. Such permanency of habitation for at least some residents would
be in keeping with nearby cultivation, probable year-round storage at
the site, and communal investment in a ballcourt.

Chapter 10

MACROFLORAL ANALYSIS

Scott Kwiatkowski
and
Robert E. Gasser

The nature and significance of the charred plant material recovered from 49 flotation samples collected during the excavation of Water World are discussed in this chapter. Charred cheno-am seeds were the most abundant and ubiquitously distributed charred plant taxon. Charred grass grains, mesquite, and maize remains also were well represented. Other economic taxa included tansy mustard, cacti, cotton, and agave. Several pit house hearths contained good evidence that small seeds and grass grains were processed over them.

The flotation report for Fastimes (Volume 2, Chapter 10) contains a discussion of the methods used to process samples, procedures used to sort samples, criteria used in identifying samples, and the quantitative methods used for all the Phase B flotation analyses.

Results

The 49 flotation samples represented 224.5 liters of sediment. Nineteen charred plant taxa were identified (Table 10.1). A total of 306 identifiable charred plant parts were present, not including grass stem fragments, a maize stem fragment, or unknowns (Table 10.2). The Water World flotation samples exhibited a lower productivity rate than samples from either Hawk's Nest or Fastimes. About 60 percent of the samples (29 of 49) contained identifiable charred plant material (Table 10.3). Of the feature types examined, pits in pit houses and Type B roasting pits (those without basal and sidewall oxidation) yielded more unproductive than productive flotation samples.

When multiple samples from the same feature were grouped, the 49 flotation samples were reduced to 28 sample loci, 9 of which (32%) did not contain charred plant remains (Table 10.4). Table 10.4 also documents the abundance of charred plant material in the productive sample loci. One sample locus, unburned pit house Feature 61, contained over 54 percent (43.00 of 79.17 total relative parts) of the total amount of charred plant material recovered from the site, after an

Table 10.1

PLANT TAXA IN THE FLOTATION SAMPLES

Common Name	Scientific Name	Parts Present
Carbonized		
Acacia	Acacia sp.	Seed
Agave	Agave sp.	Fiber, marginal tooth, terminal spine
cf. Cactus	cf. Cactaceae	Spine
Cheno-am	Chenopodiaceae or Amaranthus sp.	Seed
Cotton	Gossypium hirsutum var. punctatum	Seed
Drop seed	Sporobolus sp.	Grain
Globe mallow	Sphaeralcea sp.	Seed
Grass	Gramineae	Grain, stem fragment*
Hedgehog cactus	Echinocereus sp.	Seed
Horse purslane	Trianthema portulacastrum	Seed
Maize	Zea mays	Cupule, stem fragment*
Mesquite	Prosopis velutina	Pod fragment, seed
Prickly pear	Platyopuntia	Seed
Purslane	Portulaca sp.	Seed
Saguaro	Carnegiea gigantea	Seed
Salt bush	Atriplex sp.	Fruiting bractlet
Spurge	Euphorbia sp.	Seed
Tansy mustard	Descurainia sp.	Seed
Tidestromia	Tidestromia sp.	Seed
Unknown		Seed
Uncarbonized		
Angiosperm	Angiospermae	Anther
Borage family	Boraginaceae	Fruit fragment
Brittle bush	Encelia farinosa	Achene
Cheno-am	Chenopodiaceae or Amaranthus sp.	Seed
Creosote	Larrea tridentata	Fruit fragment, leaf
Filaree	Erodium sp.	Fruit fragment
Grass	Gramineae	Grain, spikelet
Plantain	Plantago sp.	Fruit fragment, seed
Saguaro	Carnegiea gigantea	Seed
Spurge	Euphorbia sp.	Seed
Unknown		Flower, leaf

* Stem fragments were not counted as economic plant parts in the quantitative analyses.

Table 10.2

CHARRED PLANT REMAINS IN FLOTATION SAMPLES

				Cultivars		Wild Legumes			Weedy Types						Grasses		Cacti				Others			
Feature Number	FN	Volume (liters)	Provenience	Corn	Cotton	Mesquite	Acacia	Cheno-am	Globe mallow	Horse purslane	Purslane	Salt bush	Tansy mustard	Tidestromia	Drop seed	Grass	Hedgehog	Prickly pear	Saguaro	cf. Cactus	Agave	Spurge	Unknown	Total
7.1	1962	1.9	Hearth in F.7					2																2
20.1	477	3.3	Hearth in F.20					54		1				1	6	3		4					3	72
25.1	230	2.9	Mortar pit in F.20					4								+st			1					5
27	534/5	8.3	Floor fill	1c												1			1					3
27.1	687	0.6	Hearth in F.27			2																		2
29	900/1	8.7	Floor					1																1
29	994/5	8.0	Floor					2													1fi			3
29.1	1009	2.6	Hearth in F.29			1		5	1			1fb			1									9
33.1	1082	2.2	Hearth in F.33		1										1	1								3
33.7	1963	1.9	Hearth in F.33			1		9					5										4	19
36.1	2117	2.1	Pit in F.36					2											1					3
53	670/1	6.0	Floor fill														1							1
53.3	943	2.5	Hearth in F.53	1c				3																4
54	346	2.0	Roasting pit, intrusive into F.25/55			3, 1pf																		4
55.1/.12	2026	4.7	Hearth in F.55					4							1	+st								5
55.10	1126	3.5	Storage pit	5c,+st												+st								1
56	725/6	8.9	Roasting pit								1					+st								5
57	824/5	7.3	Ash pit			1	1				1					+st	1							5
58	1259/60	8.4	In vessel on floor													+st			3					3
58	1659/60	9.8	Floor									2fb				+st*								2
58.1	1694/5	3.8	Hearth in F.58		3			3								5			1		1mt			15
61.1	1764	3.0	Hearth in F.61		1	2		122								4								129
76	1504	3.0	Hearth, intrusive into F.58		1			10								2								13
78.1	2223	0.9	Hearth in F.78					1																1
86	1710/11	9.6	Roasting pit																		1ts			1
104	2275	0.6	Cremation vessel																	1sp				1
138	2406/7	9.9	Roasting pit													1								2
Total				8c	5	12, 1pf	1	222	1	1	1	3fb	5	1	9	17	2	4	8	1sp	1fi, 1mt, 1ts	1	8	314

+ = Present (stem fragments)
* = Estimated 500 stem fragments
c = Cupule
fb = Fruiting bractlet
fi = Fiber
mt = Marginal tooth

pf = Pod fragment
st = Stem fragment
ts = Terminal spine
sp = Spine
Undesignated are all seeds except grasses, which are grains.

Table 10.3

PRODUCTIVITY OF THE FLOTATION SAMPLES

	Productive		Unproductive	
	# of Samples	Feature Number	# of Samples	Feature Number
Cremation vessel fill	1	104	1	88
Hearth (intrusive into pit house)	1	76		
Pit (intrusive into pit house)	1	57		
Pit in ramada or pit house			1	68
Pit house ash stain			1	53
Pit house fill			1	79
Pit house floors	6	27,29,53,58	1	27
Pit house hearths	12	7,20,27,29,33 53,55,58,61,78	3	7,19,35
Pit house pits	3	25,36,55	7	19,20,27,58
Type A roasting pits	3	54,56,86	1	86
Type B roasting pits	1	138	4	95,139,143, 148
Vessel in pit house	1	58	---	
Total	29		20	

adjustment was made for different sample size volumes. This high abundance was due almost exclusively to the presence of 122 charred cheno-am seeds recovered from the hearth of this structure. Similarly, burned pit house Feature 20 contained a high abundance of charred plant material, which also was due primarily to the large number (N=54) of charred cheno-am seeds in a hearth.

Table 10.4

DISTRIBUTION OF CHARRED PLANT PARTS

Provenience	Number Relative Parts	Actual Number Parts
Productive Sample Loci		
Pit house Feature 61	43.00	129
Pit house Feature 20*	15.33	69
Pit house Feature 33**	4.39	18
Hearth Feature 76	4.33	13
Pit containing mortar in pit house Feature 25	1.72	5
Type A roasting pit Feature 54	1.67	4
Cremation vessel Feature 104	1.67	1
Pit house Feature 36	1.43	3
Pit house Feature 78*	1.11	1
Pit house Feature 55	0.73	6
Pit house Feature 29	0.67	13
Type A roasting pit Feature 56	0.56	5
Pit Feature 57	0.55	4
Pit house Feature 53*	0.53	5
Pit house Feature 7**	0.49	2
Pit house Feature 58*	0.49	20
Pit house Feature 27*	0.24	5
Type B roasting pit Feature 138	0.20	2
Type A roasting pit Feature 86	0.05	1
Unproductive Sample Loci		
Cremation vessel Feature 88		
Pit house Feature 19*		
Pit house Feature 35*		
Pit house Feature 79		
Pit in ramada or pit house Feature 68		
Type B roasting pit Feature 95		
Type B roasting pit Feature 139		
Type B roasting pit Feature 143		
Type B roasting pit Feature 148		

 * Burned pit house
** Possible burned pit house

Table 10.5 presents the taxonomic distribution of the charred plant material recovered from Water World, arranged in descending order of presence values. The assemblage, as at Fastimes and Hawk's Nest, was dominated by charred cheno-am seeds. Mesquite seeds, grass grains including drop seed, and saguaro seeds also had relatively high presence values.

Table 10.5

TAXONOMIC DISTRIBUTION OF CHARRED PLANT MATERIAL IN FLOTATION SAMPLES*

Taxon	Presence Value (%)	Relative parts (%)
Cheno-am seed	63.2	80.11
Mesquite seed	42.1	3.25
Grass grain	36.8	4.02
Saguaro seed	26.3	0.89
Drop seed grain	21.1	2.21
Maize cupule	21.1	1.34
Cotton seed	15.8	0.82
Hedgehog cactus seed	10.5	0.77
Salt bush fruiting bractlet	10.5	0.13
cf. Cactus spine	5.3	2.11
Tansy mustard seed	5.3	1.54
Prickly pear seed	5.3	1.12
Mesquite pod fragment	5.3	0.53
Horse purslane seed	5.3	0.28
Tidestromia seed	5.3	0.28
Acacia seed	5.3	0.17
Purslane seed	5.3	0.17
Agave terminal spine	5.3	0.07
Agave fiber	5.3	0.07
Globe mallow seed	5.3	0.07
Agave marginal tooth	5.3	0.03
Spurge seed	5.3	0.03

* Based on 19 productive sample loci containing a total of 79.17 relative parts.

Discussion

Economic Taxa

Domesticates and Cultivars

Maize and cotton were the only domesticated plants represented in the flotation samples. With one exception, the maize remains were cupules, most of which were probably carbonized through the use of cobs as fuel, as was done historically (Castetter and Bell 1942: 181). Single occurrences of charred cupules occurred in three pit houses (Features 25, 27, and 53). Each came from floors except for Feature 53, which was a hearth sample. The charred maize cupules on pit house floors could represent sheet trash or debris carbonized during the destruction of the pit houses. The hearth sample may reflect the use of maize cobs as fuel. Five charred maize cupules were recovered from Type A roasting pit Feature 56, and may represent the use of cobs as fuel in this feature. The other occurrence of maize was a single stem fragment recovered from Feature 56; it also probably represents a fuel remnant. Although no charred maize kernels were found, the relatively high abundance and ubiquity of charred cob fragments (cupules) can be taken as evidence that maize production and consumption were important activities at Water World; it seems unlikely that cobs would be imported to a site solely for use as fuel.

In addition to the use of cotton lint in textile production, cotton seed is edible. Historically, the Pima and Papago (O'odham) either parched and ground the seed, or prepared it much as we do popcorn (Castetter and Bell 1942: 198). Each occurrence of charred cotton seeds at Water World was from a pit house hearth: one charred seed was found in Features 33.1 and 61.1, and three were found in Feature 58.1. Perhaps the occurrences of charred cotton seeds at Water World result from seed "popping" accidents that occurred over pit house hearths.

A final economic plant represented at the site, agave, could have been cultivated. Fish and others (1985: 109) believe that sufficient evidence exists to conclude that several species of agave were cultivated in southern Arizona by the Hohokam. Further, agave hearts and leaves were used as food by many Southwestern aboriginal groups, and agave leaf fibers were an important source of cordage (Castetter and others 1938).

Although Water World yielded more charred agave than either Fastimes or Hawk's Nest, only three agave remnants were present. Each derived from a different part of the plant. One charred fiber was recovered from the floor of pit house Feature 29. This structure was unburned, thus the fiber probably does not represent the use of cordage in house construction. A charred marginal tooth was recovered from the floor of pit house Feature 58, and a charred terminal spine was recovered from a Type A roasting pit, Feature 86. The presence of both a marginal tooth and a terminal spine may represent local procurement because it is unlikely that these low-utility "waste products" would have been transported great distances only to be later discarded (Gasser and Miksicek 1985: 489).

The occurrence of an agave terminal spine in a roasting pit may be significant. Although it is possible that the spine may represent discarded material from leaf processing for cordage, it may be a remnant from cooking agave leaves for food. The Cahuilla considered the leaves of agave (A. deserti) to be an important food resource particularly because the leaves could be consumed during the lean winter months (Bean and Saubel 1972: 33). The lack of any other identifiable charred plant material except for wood charcoal in the 18.9 liters of sediment sampled from Feature 86 seems to minimize the possibility that the terminal spine was trash unrelated to feature function.

Noncultivated Plants

Cheno-am seeds, grass grains including drop seed, and saguaro seeds probably were commonly used subsistence items at Water World because of their frequent occurrence (each was present in at least four sample loci), their at least moderate abundance (each made up at least 0.89% of the total site relative parts), because they are frequently found at other Hohokam sites (Gasser 1982, Table 1; Miksicek 1987, Table 9.8), and because historically each was processed by parching before grinding (Castetter and Underhill 1935: 24; Russell 1975: 68). Parching accidents would result in the incorporation of these seeds into the archaeobotanical record.

Other parts of the saguaro and cheno-ams also might have been consumed. The fruit of the saguaro was an important food and a source of wine to the Pima and Papago (Castetter and Underhill 1935: 20-22; Crosswhite 1980; Curtin 1984: 53-54; Russell 1975: 71-72). Historically, greens from pigweed (Amaranthus spp.) and goose foot (Chenopodium spp.), members of the cheno-ams, were used by the Pima (Curtin 1984: 48, 70), Papago (Castetter and Underhill 1935: 14-16), and other indigenous Southwestern groups.

Mesquite pod mesocarp was traditionally a more important food to indigenous Southwestern groups than its seeds (Felger and Moser 1985: 339). Nonetheless, charred mesquite seeds were far more common at Water World than pod fragments. Mesquite seed was the second most ubiquitously distributed plant taxon, and the third most abundant charred plant taxon at the site (Table 10.5). In contrast, the only charred mesquite pod fragment at the site was recovered from roasting pit Feature 54 (along with three charred mesquite seeds). The extant information makes it difficult to determine how many mesquite seeds at Water World were the discarded and burned remnants of pod processing and how many were the remains of seeds intended for consumption.

Five charred tansy mustard seeds were recovered from pit house hearth Feature 33.7. Tansy mustard seeds were consumed by the Pima (Curtin 1984: 84; Russell 1975: 77) and Papago (Castetter and Underhill 1935: 24). Charred seeds from this genus are common at Hohokam sites (Gasser 1982, Table 1; Miksicek 1987, Table 9.8). Bohrer and others (1969: 3) found a cache of tansy mustard seeds in an olla in a house at AZ BB:13:41 ASM, and Miksicek (1987: 205, Appendix 9.1) found caches of these seeds associated with vessels in pit house Feature 219 at Muchas Casas, Locus A. It seems likely that the five charred seeds in hearth Feature 33.7 represent the accidental burning of seeds intended for consumption. The same hearth also contained nine charred cheno-am seeds, which could be another example of the accidental burning of small seeds intended for consumption.

Four charred prickly pear seeds were recovered from pit house hearth Feature 20.1. They could be refuse from the consumption of prickly pear fruits (Russell [1975: 75] maintained that the Pima threw these seeds away) or these seeds could have been intended for consumption and accidentally became carbonized.

Two charred hedgehog cactus seeds were recovered from pits. One seed came from pit house Feature 36, and the other from Feature 57, a pit that intruded into the fill of pit house Feature 29. Charred hedgehog cactus seeds were less common at Water World when compared to either Fastimes or Hawk's Nest, where they may have been economically important, yet they could represent the remnants of accidentally carbonized seeds intended for consumption. Alternatively, the seeds could represent waste from the consumption of raw hedgehog cactus fruits (Curtin 1984: 57).

Unlike Fastimes, Hawks' Nest, or many other Hohokam sites (Gasser 1982, Table 1; Miksicek 1987, Table 9.8), charred globe mallow seeds were rare. Only one globe mallow seed was recovered from the site, from the hearth in pit house Feature 29. Based on this single occurrence, it is difficult to conclude much about the economic importance of this plant at Water World. Although globe mallow seeds do not appear to be a component of the modern seed rain (Table 10.1), if they were a significant contributor to the prehistoric seed rain, then it would be readily possible for such a seed to become inadvertently carbonized in a hearth. Conversely, the seed originally could have been intended for consumption, but accidentally carbonized. A Navajo informant told Elmore (1944: 63) that the seeds from one species of globe mallow "probably" were eaten. Another possibility, based on numerous ethnographic examples, is that the seed could represent the remains of a medicinal preparation (Curtin 1984: 80-81; Felger and Moser 1985: 346; Russell 1975: 79).

Two other taxa, horse purslane and purslane, were represented at Water World, each by a single charred seed. The horse purslane seed was recovered from pit house hearth Feature 20.1, and the purslane seed was found in intrusive pit Feature 57. Both seed types are common in low numbers at many Hohokam sites (Gasser 1982, Table 1; Miksicek 1987,

Table 9.8). Consumption of both seed types has been documented (Elmore 1944: 47; Felger and Moser 1985: 228), but historically the greens seem to have been the most commonly consumed part of the plant (Whiting 1939: 75; Elmore 1944: 47; Vestal 1952: 26). Therefore, the charred seeds from Water World could have been incorporated into the archaeobotanical record in one of three ways: as accidentally carbonized components of the prehistoric seed rain, as seeds intended for consumption that were accidentally burned, or as charred trash from the consumption of greens. Horse purslane seeds were far less well represented at Water World than at either Fastimes or Hawk's Nest.

Three charred salt bush fruiting bractlets were recovered from two pit house hearths. One was in Feature 29.1, and two were retrieved from Feature 58.1. They could have been intended for consumption (Curtin 1984: 67), or they could have entered the hearth attached to salt bush wood that was burned in the features.

A single charred acacia seed was recovered from pit Feature 57, which intruded into pit house Feature 29. Russell (1975: 76) has reported that "The beans of the cat's-claw [Acacia greggii] were eaten in primitive times, but no one of the present generation knows how they were prepared." The charred seed from Water World, however, did not resemble a cat claw acacia seed. Charred acacia seeds are rare at Hohokam sites; the taxon does not appear in Gasser's (1982, Table 1) synthesis of flotation data from the Salt and Gila river areas, nor in Miksicek's (1987, Table 9.8) study of Tucson Basin flotation data. Perhaps the seed was an inadvertently charred component of the prehistoric seed rain.

A single charred tidestromia seed was recovered from pit house hearth Feature 20.1. This genus also is rare at Hohokam sites. Because the Seri used Tidestromia lanquinosa herbage medicinally (Felger and Moser 1985: 229), perhaps the charred seed represents a medicinal remnant. It also could be a component of the prehistoric seed rain, or an accidentally carbonized seed that was intended for consumption.

A single charred spurge seed was recovered from the hearth in burned pit house Feature 58. It is unlikely that this plant was used for subsistence because it is at least mildly toxic (Curtin 1984: 99-100; Bean and Saubel 1972: 73).

A single charred, possible cactus spine was recovered from the fill of the cremation vessel in Feature 104. Due to its poor taxonomic resolution, it does not constitute conclusive evidence for the use of cactus products, such as joints, buds, or fruits. Table 10.6 summarizes the results of the economic analysis of the flotation data.

Unrepresented Taxa

As discussed in the Fastimes report (Volume 2, Chapter 10), flotation data have many innate sources of bias, and therefore by

Table 10.6

SUMMARY OF THE ECONOMIC ANALYSIS

Plant Taxa Probably Used for Food
    Agave hearts (represented by a fiber, a marginal tooth, and a terminal spine)
    Cheno-am seeds
    Cotton seeds
    Hedgehog cactus fruits and seeds (represented by seeds)
    Grass grains (including dropseed grains)
    Mesquite pod mesocarp
    Maize kernels (represented by cupules)
    Prickly pear fruits (represented by seeds)
    Saguaro fruits and seeds (represented by seeds)

Plant Taxa Possibly Used for Food
    Acacia seeds (represented by a seed)
    Agave leaves
    Cheno-am greens (represented by seeds)
    Globe mallow seeds
    Horse purslane greens and seeds (represented by a seed)
    Mesquite seeds
    Prickly pear seeds
    Purslane greens and seeds (represented by a seed)
    Salt bush fruiting bractlets
    Tidestromia greens or seeds (represented by a seed)
    Cactus joints, buds, or fruit (represented by a possible spine)

Plant Taxa Probably Used for Cordage or Textiles, or Both
    Agave
    Cotton

Plant Taxa Probably Used for Fuel
    Grass stems
    Maize cobs (represented by cupules)
    Maize stems

Plant Taxon Probably Not Used for Food
    Spurge seeds

---

themselves are a poor reflection of prehistoric subsistence practices. Nevertheless, the absence of one charred plant taxon at the site, chia, may be significant. Although chia is found regularly at Hohokam sites in the Tucson Basin (Miksicek 1987, Table 9.8), it is possible that its absence actually reflects the lack of prehistoric use at Water World.

Variability and Economic Activities in Features

Variability

The first kind of feature-type variability to be considered is density of charred plant material per liter (Table 10.7). The total number of liters sampled in Table 10.7 is the sum of the volumes of both the productive and unproductive sample loci. The feature type "intrusive hearth," represented by the analysis of Feature 76, produced the highest density of charred plant material. Pit houses contained an average of about two charred plant parts per liter. Three feature types, cremation vessels, miscellaneous pits, and Type A roasting pits, each had similar densities of about 0.3 charred plant parts per liter. The feature type with the lowest average density of charred plant material was the Type B roasting pit, with 0.05 charred plant parts per liter.

Table 10.7

AVERAGE NUMBER OF CHARRED PLANT PARTS PER LITER FOR
DIFFERENT FEATURE TYPES SAMPLED

Feature Type	Number Charred Plant Parts	Number Liters Sampled	x Charred Plant Parts per Liter
Intrusive hearth (N=1)	13	3.0	4.33
Pit houses (all contexts; N=12)	276	138.9	1.99
Miscellaneous pit (N=1)	4	10.1	0.39
Type A roasting pits (N=3)	10	30.2	0.33
Cremation vessel (N=1)	1	3.5	0.29
Type B roasting pit (N=1)	2	38.8	0.05

N = Number of productive sample loci.

The presence or absence of a particular taxon in a given feature type is the second kind of variability encountered in the flotation data (Table 10.8). Several taxa at Water World were recovered only from a narrow range of feature types. For example, four charred plant taxa of probable economic importance to the inhabitants of Water World, cotton seeds, prickly pear seeds, salt bush fruiting bractlets, and tansy mustard seeds, were recovered only from pit house hearths. Hedgehog cactus seeds were found only in pits.

Table 10.8

PRESENCE VALUE AND RELATIVE PARTS PERCENTAGE DATA
FOR FEATURE TYPES

Taxon*	Pit Houses (All Contexts) p.v. / r.p.	Type A Roasting Pits p.v. / r.p.	Type B Roasting Pits p.v. / r.p.	Miscellaneous Pits p.v. / r.p.	Intrusive Hearth p.v. / r.p.	Cremation Fill p.v. / r.p.
Cheno-am seed	91.67/85.67				100.00/76.92	
All grass grain	58.33/ 5.94				100.00/15.39	
All mesquite	41.67/ 1.54	33.33/73.06	100.00/50.00		100.00/ 7.69	
Saguaro seed	33.33/ 0.53		100.00/50.00	100.00/25.00		
Cotton seed	25.00/ 0.93					
Maize cupule	25.00/ 0.71	33.33/24.63				
Salt bush fruiting bractlet	16.67/ 0.14					
All agave	16.67/ 0.11	33.33/ 2.32				
Tansy mustard seed	8.33/ 1.74					
Prickly pear seed	8.33/ 1.27					
Hedgehog cactus seed	8.33/ 0.68			100.00/25.00		
Horse purslane seed	8.33/ 0.32					
Tidestromia seed	8.33/ 0.32					
Globe mallow seed	8.33/ 0.07					
Spurge seed	8.33/ 0.04			100.00/25.00		
Acacia seed						
Purslane seed				100.00/25.00		
cf. Cactus spine						100.00/100.00
Totals						
No. r.p.	70.14	2.28	0.20	0.55	4.33	1.67
No. Liters Sampled	138.9	30.2	38.8	10.1	3.0	3.5
No. Productive Sample Loci	12 of 15	3 of 3	1 of 5	1 of 2	1 of 1	1 of 2
No. Charred Plant Parts	276	10	2	4	13	1

* Drop seed grains have been combined with grass grains to create the "all grass grain" category. Similarly, mesquite seeds and pod fragments were grouped to create the "all mesquite" category, and an agave fiber, marginal tooth, and a terminal spine were combined to form "all agave."

p.v. = Presence value
r.p. = Relative parts

Although cheno-am seed was both the most ubiquitous and abundant charred plant taxon at the site, its distribution was somewhat restricted. Cheno-ams occurred only in pit houses and in a hearth intruded into a pit house. The absence of charred cheno-am seeds in roasting pits is interesting because some seeds from chenopodiaceous plants that were used to line roasting pits might be expected. Similarly, saguaro seeds were recovered only from pit house contexts and from a hearth intruded into a pit house. There were so few productive flotation samples from feature types other than pit houses that there would be little value in discussing a third kind of feature type variability: the differences in the proportions of the charred plant taxa that comprise different feature types.

Evidence of Economic Activities in Features

Intrusive Hearth

Hearth Feature 76 intruded into the fill of pit house Feature 58. Charred plant material recovered from this hearth included 10 cheno-am seeds, 2 grass grains, and 1 saguaro seed. Historically the seeds of each of these plants (grass grains are considered to be seeds) were parched and ground for use as flour, thus it appears likely that this feature was used at least once to parch or prepare small seeds for consumption. This activity appears to have taken place outdoors, after Feature 58 was abandoned.

Type A Roasting Pits

Although the three Type A roasting pits sampled (Features 54, 56, and 86) were productive, each yielded charred plant material from different taxa. Feature 54 contained three mesquite seeds and a mesquite pod, Feature 56 contained five maize cupules and a maize stem fragment, and Feature 86 contained an agave terminal spine. It already has been suggested that the maize remains in Feature 56 were probably fuel remnants.

The mesquite remains in Feature 54 could derive from the preparation of mesquite seeds or pods in the feature. Mesquite pods were sometimes parched before consumption (Russell 1975: 75). Alternatively, the mesquite seeds could represent debris that was accidentally deposited in the feature.

Based on ethnographic analogy (Castetter and others 1938), the agave terminal spine in Feature 86 could be a remnant of the roasting of an agave leaf for either food or cordage. The spine also could represent waste inadvertently incorporated into the pit from the roasting of an agave heart.

The three Type A roasting pits were distinctive in that they contained charred termite pellets. Charred termite pellets also occurred in numerous pit house contexts; however, Type A roasting pits were the only feature type that produced the pellets in each sample analyzed. This probably indicates that termite-infested wood was used for fuel in each of the Type A roasting pits sampled. The degree of termite infestation may not, however, have been as intense at Water World as it appears to have been at Fastimes (Volume 2, Chapter 10). Termite pellets at Water World, unlike Fastimes, did not appear in great aggregates, and they were never particularly abundant in the flotation samples although they occurred in 19 of the 29 productive flotation samples from the site.

Type B Roasting Pits

The fills of four of the five Type B roasting pits (Features 95, 139, 143, and 148) were devoid of artifacts and charred plant material other than wood charcoal. Feature 138, however, contained bone, a handstone, and a sandstone anvil. In addition, one charred grass grain and one charred mesquite seed were present in a 9.9 liter flotation sample from this feature. It is probably significant that Feature 138 was the only one of these five features that contained both artifacts and charred plant material. This may indicate that the feature was at least partially filled with trash and that the archaeobotanical material recovered from its flotation sample may not be related to the feature's original function. In short, the flotation data can provide no insight into the original function of any of the Type B roasting pits.

Miscellaneous Pits

Two pits were not definitely associated with structures, and were therefore considered as miscellaneous pits for this study: pit Feature 68.1 in Feature 68, and pit Feature 57 in the fill of pit house Feature 29. Feature 68.1 was unproductive; Feature 57 contained charred examples of an acacia seed, a hedgehog cactus seed, a purslane seed, and an unknown seed. Because this pit exhibited no evidence of sidewall burning and contained sherds and lithics, it is likely that the charred plant material derived from trash deposited in this feature.

Cremation Vessels

The fill from two cremation vessels was analyzed. Feature 88 contained no indentifiable charred plant material, and Feature 104 contained a charred possible cactus spine. It cannot be determined from these data whether the spine represents trash unrelated to the vessels, or is the remnant of a cactus that was once contained in the vessel.

Pit Houses

Thirty-four flotation samples were analyzed from various contexts in 15 pit houses. Three contexts contained identifiable charred plant material: pits, floors, and hearths.

Pits in pit houses. Ten samples came from pits in pit houses, and seven of these were unproductive. The three productive samples were from unburned pit houses and yielded low densities of charred plant material. Two of the pits, Features 25.1 and 26.1, contained no evidence of sidewall oxidation, thus the charred plant material in these features probably resulted from trash that was deposited into the pits. The trash could have been deposited as de facto refuse, primary deposition, or as secondary deposition.

The final productive flotation sample from a pit within a pit house was from Feature 55.10, a probable storage pit. The feature exhibited basal oxidation. One charred drop seed grain and several charred grass stem fragments were recovered from the 3.5 liter flotation sample. Although it is possible that these charred plant remains were deposited as trash, it is also possible that they were remnants of fuel used in the fire that created the oxidized soil. Furthermore, the charred grass remains could be accidentally burned remnants of material used to line pits.

Pit house floors. Seven flotation samples were analyzed from floor contexts from four pit houses. Two of the samples were unproductive, and each of the five productive samples yielded low densities of charred plant material. Three of the productive samples were from burned pit houses (Features 27, 53, and 58). Each of these samples contained charred termite pellets and a charred saguaro seed. The sample from Feature 27 also yielded a charred maize cupule and a charred grass grain, and Feature 58 also contained a charred agave marginal tooth. Perhaps the charred termite pellets from these samples derived from structural wood that was infested with termites when the pit houses burned.

The two remaining productive flotation samples from pit house floor contexts were both from unburned pit house Feature 29. One sample contained a charred cheno-am seed, and the other contained two charred cheno-am seeds and a charred agave fiber. Perhaps these are trash remnants; alternatively, the cheno-am seeds could be residue from processing this resource in the structure's hearth. This possibility is discussed further below.

Pit house hearths. Twelve of the 15 flotation samples analyzed from pit house hearths were productive; two samples were from the same hearth (Feature 58.1). Four of the 11 hearths sampled contained charred termite pellets, and none contained charred grass stem fragments.

Virtually all of the productive hearth samples contained charred seeds or grains that could have resulted from the in situ preparation of

foods over the hearths. Three features (Features 20.1, 33.7, and 61.1)
exhibited particularly good evidence that small seeds from cheno-am and
tansy mustard plants, and small gains from grasses, particularly drop
seed, were processed over them. Feature 20.1 contained 54 charred
cheno-am seeds and 9 charred grass or drop seed grains in its 3.3 liter
flotation sample. Feature 33.7 yielded nine charred cheno-am seeds and
five charred tansy mustard seeds in its 1.9 liter flotation sample.
Feature 61.1 contained 122 charred cheno-am seeds in its 3.0 liter
flotation sample. Two other hearths (Features 29.1 and 58.1) also
contained good evidence for small seed and grain processing, although
their charred plant part per liter densities were lower. Feature 29.1
contained five charred cheno-am seeds, a charred drop seed grain, a
charred globe mallow seed, and a salt bush fruiting bractlet in its 2.6
liter flotation sample. Feature 58.1 contained three charred cheno-am
seeds and five charred grass grains in its 3.8 liter flotation sample.

It already has been noted that charred cotton seeds were
recovered only from pit house hearth Features 33.1, 58.1, and 61.1,
which suggests that these seeds may have been the remnants of parching
accidents of seeds intended for consumption. In short, it appears that
at least some, and possibly most or all, of the pit house hearths at
Water World occasionally were used to process small seeds and grains.

During what activities were these seeds and grains likely to
be incorporated into the archaeobotanical record? Ethnographic data
suggest (Castetter and Underhill 1935: 24; Felger and Moser 1985: 91)
that small seeds were parched immediately after collection and prior
to storage to dry them and inhibit mildew. Furthermore, grinding is
facilitated if the seeds are dry. It seems likely that processing would
have taken place outdoors and over larger fires to facilitate the
preparation of large volumes of seeds. Perhaps the charred small seeds
and grains at Water World derived primarily from consumption-related
activities such as cooking gruel that contained incompletely ground
seeds or grains over a pit house hearth. It may be speculated that
these activities occurred during inclement or cold weather, otherwise
the cooking could have taken place outdoors.

Discussion

The Water World flotation samples exhibited lower productivity
than the samples from either Fastimes or Hawk's Nest. Pits in pit
houses and Type B roasting pits were particularly unproductive. Water
World was the only Phase B site to yield charred cotton remains,
although cotton pollen was recovered from Fastimes (Volume 2, Chapter
9). Charred globe mallow, horse purslane, and hedgehog cactus seeds
were less abundant at Water World than at either Fastimes or Hawk's
Nest. None of the analyzed samples from Type B roasting pits yielded
archaeobotanical information suggestive of feature function. A Type A
roasting pit (Feature 54) once may have served to roast agave leaves,
and termite-infested wood may have been used as fuel in each of the Type

A roasting pits sampled. The degree of termite infestation may not, however, have been as intense at Water World as it was at Fastimes. Intrusive hearth Feature 76 and several of the pit house hearths appear to have been used to process small seeds. Similarly, charred cotton seeds were associated only with pit house hearths and may be remnants of parching accidents.

Chapter 11

CONCLUDING THOUGHTS

John C. Ravesloot
and
Jon S. Czaplicki

Survey of the Tucson Aqueduct Phase B alignment (Downum and others 1986) identified two Rillito phase sites, Fastimes (AZ AA:12:384) and Water World (AZ AA:16:94). The major difference between the two sites is that Water World had a ballcourt, the first of two ballcourts so far identified in the Avra Valley. (The second ballcourt is located at the Pig Farm Site [AZ AA:11:12] along Los Robles Wash at the northern end of the Avra Valley near the confluence of Los Robles Wash and the Santa Cruz River.) The function of ballcourts in Hohokam communities and their relationship to local and regional ritual and economic organization has been the subject of considerable speculation. As of 1986, 19 ballcourts have been identified in the Tucson Basin and Avra Valley, and on the basis of their presence or absence, a number of models have been formulated to explain pre-Classic Hohokam organization (Wilcox and Sternberg 1983; Teague 1984; also Volume 1, Chapter 2; Doelle 1985a, 1987; Doelle and Elson 1986). These models are difficult to evaluate, however, because they are based on data acquired mostly through survey. Prior to 1986, only three Tucson Basin ballcourt sites had been partially excavated: the Hodges Ruin (AZ AA:12:18) (Kelly 1978; Layhe 1986), AZ EE:2:105 (Ferg and others 1984), and Dakota Wash (AZ AA:16:49) (Craig 1988).

Water World was selected for excavation because of its ballcourt and the opportunity that presented to increase the amount of data on excavated ballcourt sites. It also would permit a comparative study of what we perceived to represent two different kinds of Rillito phase Hohokam communities: a ballcourt community and the non-ballcourt, farming community of Fastimes (see Volume 1, Chapter 2).

In the previous chapters descriptive as well as interpretative discussions of the results of the excavations have been presented. The intent of this chapter is not to critically evaluate the competing models for the organization of the Hohokam ballcourt regional system. Rather, it is to discuss this ballcourt site based on the various data gleaned from excavations. This chapter considers some aspects of the site not previously discussed or discussed in limited detail, such as sampling problems, pit house artifact assemblage diversity, pit house function, ritual organization, and exchange. Only with data provided through the excavation of sites such as Water World can we begin to build the data base necessary for evaluating the different organizational models.

Water World

Excavations identified at least seven house groups, a ballcourt area, a cremation area, and a probable central plaza. The house groups were defined solely on the basis of how they appeared to cluster, and in fact may not represent actual groups in each case. The groups generally are not as discrete as those defined at Fastimes (Volume 2, Chapter 2). House Groups 5 and 7 are the most discrete and probably represent real groupings. The remaining five house groups are not as clearly delineated; however, all seven groups served as the basis for analytic comparisons.

Like Fastimes, relative and chronometric dating indicate that Water World was built, occupied, and abandoned during the Rillito phase (A.D. 700 to 900; Kelly 1978: 4; see Chapter 2). Abandonment also appears to have been a planned process because very few houses were found with intact floor assemblages. The resolution in dating is too imprecise to permit more than speculation on the developmental sequence of the site (Chapter 2). It is possible that the house groups were occupied at approximately the same time; the refitting of ceramics among several of the house groups suggest some degree of contemporaneity (Chapter 4). It is also possible that the house groups are temporally distinct and that the settlement structure that has been identified was the result of the process of village drift (Chapter 2). The presence of a ballcourt and central plaza may argue against this interpretation, however. Because of these uncertainties, most questions of a processual nature concerning pre-Classic Hohokam society cannot be addressed with this data set.

In some aspects Water World is not significantly different from Fastimes (Volume 2, Chapter 11). Nonetheless, the presence of a ballcourt and a probable central plaza suggest that the structure of Water World was planned and that the site had a specialized function. Geomorphologic assessment of Water World indicates that the lower bajada environment was chosen to exploit the agricultural potential for floodwater farming (Volume 1, Chapter 3). We can see no other logical reason why this area would have been selected for occupation. Yet, pollen and macrofloral studies (Chapters 9 and 10) identified far less evidence for cultigens than would be expected if agriculture was intensively pursued at this locale. These patterns may be a reflection of preservation rather than actual indicators of agricultural importance in prehistoric times. We believe that Water World is a formalized village that was permanently occupied for a relatively short time. This interpretation is based on the virtual absence of trash midden deposits distinct from trash-filled houses and on a single instance of pit house superpositioning.

Why was Water World the site of such a short-term occupation? One possible explanation may be that the agricultural potential of the lower bajada context was never realized. Good evidence for long-term residency and agricultural intensification was found only in House Group 1. Fish (Chapter 9) has suggested that Water World, with the exception of at least House Group 1, may have been occupied primarily during the winter months. This possible scenario is based on the minimal evidence for local agriculture and an implied reliance on stored foodstuffs. Halbirt's analysis (Chapter 6) of the ground-stone assemblage lends some support to this interpretation. The milling assemblages from house groups were represented by the coarser-grained materials that were better suited for grinding the hard pericarps of dried or parched seeds and grains. This scenario does not agree with Fontana's (1983: 131) description of a Papago winter village, however, if indeed that same type of settlement system operated in prehistoric times. Water World's lower bajada setting is more in agreement with the location of a summer village that took advantage of areas where floodwater farming could be practiced. Unfortunately, adequate evidence is absent, and it is impossible to evaluate either of these scenarios.

The planned nature of Water World suggested that the ballcourt probably was constructed in the initial phases of the settlement. Stratigraphic and ceramic refitting offer little additional insight to site development. The surface of the ballcourt was in very poor condition, but remnant patches of plaster and stratigraphic evidence suggest only one episode of plastering. The absence of multiple plastering episodes could indicate that the ballcourt was not intensively used or was not used over a long period of time, or both.

Sampling

Our interpretation of Water World has been influenced by four sampling domains. Prior to and during excavation and analysis, strategies were developed for sampling the site, individual house groups, individual features, and individual artifact classes. Potential biases introduced by sampling may have affected the representativeness of the data set. These sampling biases include: backhoe trenching of multiple artifact class (MAC) areas, differential excavation of house groups, sampling of pit house fill, and selective analysis of artifact classes. The rational for the sampling procedures, with the exception of that used in the excavation of house groups, is outlined in Volume 1, Chapter 2 and is also discussed in the Fastimes report (Volume 2, Chapter 11); it is not repeated here.

Rather than completely excavate a small number of the identified houses, a decision was made to excavate at least one 2-m by 2-m control unit in as many structures as possible, the same sampling strategy that

was used at Fastimes. This allowed for the collection of a comparable
sample of artifacts from 21 structures. These control units were placed
where they would most likely locate the hearth, which could then be
sampled for archaeomagnetic dating. Twelve of the 21 structures were
either completely or partially excavated because of their potential for
providing intact assemblages or architectural details. None of the
house groups was selected for intensive excavation; instead the decision
was made to sample all of them as equally as possible. In contrast to
Fastimes, extramural stripping was not one of the major aims of the
excavations at Water World, thus it was less intensively pursued. With
these potential biases in mind, a discussion of the diversity of the pit
house artifact assemblage and feature function is presented.

Pit House Assemblage Diversity

Floor assemblages, de facto refuse, provide data for discussing
the range and types of activities that may have occurred at a site, as
well as information on feature and site function. In many Hohokam
sites, including Water World, de facto refuse is absent, however. Most
of the 12 houses excavated at Water World had some artifacts on the
floor, although much of this material may represent trash.
Reconstructible vessels recovered from floor contexts are viewed as de
facto refuse by various archaeologists (Reid 1973; Haury 1976; Schiffer
1976, 1987; Seymour and Schiffer 1987). At the Hodges Ruin, only 19 of
84 floors yielded restorable vessels, and most were from the later
Tanque Verde phase (Kelly 1978). At Water World two structures
(Features 25 and 58) had what could be defined as de facto refuse. One
of the structures, Feature 58, had burned. The floor assemblage from
this feature included, in addition to one plain ware vessel, six pieces
of flaked-stone debris, five flaked-stone tools, three ground-stone
implements, five sherds, a complete bone awl and one bone awl fragment,
nine mule deer mandibles, a partial cranium of a large bighorn ram, and
three deer antler racks attached to sections of skull.

The lack of reconstructible vessels on the floor is not
necessarily conclusive evidence of the absence of de facto refuse
because the activities that occurred in the structure may not have
included the use of ceramic vessels. One or more whole ground-stone
implements were recovered from the floors of eight of the pit houses.
Pit house Feature 55 had 1 Glycymeris shell fragment, 2 unworked
Anodonta shell fragments, 19 pieces of flaked-stone debris, 3 flaked-
stone tools, 1 metate fragment, 2 pebble polishers, 33 sherds, 5 worked
sherds, miscellaneous figurine fragments, a miniature bowl and a
miniature scoop, and a single piece of unidentified ground stone.

Because of the paucity of floor assemblages, the artifact
assemblages from pit house fill were used to provide some indication of
the kinds of activities that may have occurred at the site. The 2-m by
2-m control units from each of the 21 pit houses provide comparable
units of analysis with which to study artifact assemblage diversity. In

general the artifact assemblage recovered from Water World is typical of
a Hohokam farming community and is comparable to the assemblage
recovered from Fastimes (Volume 2). The kinds of activities performed
by the inhabitants of Water World probably included tool maintenance and
perhaps tool production, and food processing, preparation, and storage
(Table 11.1).

Surprisingly, very little was recovered in the way of what could
be considered ceremonial and ritual objects. Prior to the excavations,
it was assumed that these types of artifacts would be prevalent because
of the presence of the ballcourt. Wilcox has stated that:

> Quantities of exotic goods at Snaketown increased [in the late
> Colonial period], and the Tucson Basin, Gila Bend, the lower and
> middle Verde, Point of Pines, and the San Pedro areas were
> incorporated in the [ballcourt] network....For the Phoenix Basin
> populations, however, the late Colonial was clearly a period of
> "good times" marked by vigorous artistic expression and notable
> religious innovations. The fact that the same classes of ritual
> paraphernalia found at Snaketown also occur in the ballcourt
> sites both within and outside the Phoenix Basin....implies that
> these religious innovations made a profound impression on
> neighboring groups as well (Wilcox and Sternberg 1983: 235).

The distribution of artifacts presented in Table 11.1 reflects
the actual paucity of the ritual or ceremonial items recovered from the
site as a whole. Items recovered from the excavations that could be
considered for ritual or ceremonial purposes include 2 stone bowls, 1
complete and 1 fragmentary palette, 5 stone beads, 3 clay figurines and
71 miscellaneous figurine fragments, some 70 shell beads, 6 shell
pendants, 42 shell bracelet fragments, the 3 deer antler racks, and the
portion of bighorn sheep cranium and horn core. It can be argued that
many of these items, such as the stone and shell jewelry, represent
articles of personal adornment, and not special ritual or ceremonial
objects. Of the ground-stone assemblage recovered from Water World,
only 6 percent was attributed to possible ritual or ceremonial use
(Chapter 6), whereas at Fastimes 17 percent of the ground-stone
assemblage was attributed to ritual or ceremonial use (Volume 2, Chapter
6). The shell beads came from two cremations and undoubtedly represent
personal jewelry worn by the deceased individuals. The concentration of
ceramic figurines and other items in House Group 1 (Chapter 4) may
represent the possible ritual deposit of artifacts in trash as noted by
Gregory (1984: 81-84) at the Siphon Draw Site. The antler racks from
pit house Feature 58 in House Group 4 may have been used for hunting or
as decorations (Chapter 8).

The data from Water World do not seem to support Wilcox's
inference that ritual and ceremonial paraphernalia were abundant in
all segments of the ballcourt network. Of course, what part perishable
items may have played in ritual and ceremony will never be fully known.
Furthermore, if the site was occupied for a relatively short period of

Table 11.1

PIT HOUSE FILL ARTIFACT ASSEMBLAGES

Artifact Type	House Group 1				House Group 2			House Group 3			House Group 4		House Group 5		House Group 6
	19	20	25	55	7	26	29	33	44	53	58	61	78	79	68
Milling Equipment															
Pestles			1			1	1				1				
Manos		2f										2			1
Metates	1f	1,1f		1f											1f
Handstones		1													
Grinding slabs	1f		1							2					
Manos-mauls															
Miscellaneous ground stone				1	1										
Tool Manufacture															
Hammerstones		1						1							
Pebble-polishers				2											
Abraders		1							1						
Hammerstones-anvils															
Pestles-hammerstones	1														
Ceremonial Figurines				5f				1	1f						
Ornaments															
Sherd bracelet	1f			1											
Andonta shell				2											
Worked argillite(?)							1								
Debitage	5	13	20	19	5	4	4	21			6				4
Cores	1			2				1							1
Unifacial Retouch		2	2					1			2				
Bifacial								1			1	1			
Utilized Implement	2	1	1	1	3			4			2	1			1
Bone Tools															
Awl-needle								1							
Awls	1,2f					1,1f					1,1f			1	
Tubes				1	1	1									
Worked Sherds	1	2						1	1	2					
Miniature Bowls				1	2	4							2		1
Miniature Scoop				1											

f = fragment

time and then abandoned in an orderly fashion, then few of these objects would be expected to be found.

Feature Function

So few structures have de facto refuse that represents floor assemblages that it is difficult to determine the kinds of activities that may have taken place in each structure. As noted in Chapter 3, most of the 12 pit houses excavated (Features 7, 19, 20, 25, 26, 27, 29, 33, 53, 55, 58, and 61) probably were used primarily for habitation. All are greater than 10 square meters in area, even those that were only partially excavated (Features 7, 29, 33, and 61) and for which floor area could be estimated. Houses that measured less than 9 or 10 square meters in area are thought to have been used for activities such as storage or special use, and not for habitation (Haury 1976: 62, 68; Wilcox and others 1981: 159; Sires 1984: 374). All pit houses except Feature 25 contained at least one hearth or firepit located in front of the entryway. The floors of these pit houses generally were free of pits and postholes (other than roof-support postholes), thus providing usable living space.

Charred seeds, including cotton seeds, or grains were found in flotation samples taken from the hearths of five pit houses (Features 20, 29, 33, 58, and 61), suggesting that food was being prepared in the houses. It is possible that many, if not all, of the pit houses at Water World were occupied during winter months when inclement or cold weather was more frequent and cooking activities could not take place outdoors (Chapter 10).

The pollen (Chapter 9) and macrofloral (Chapter 10) data suggest that the processing of native and domesticated products (corn) was limited primarily to House Group 1. Feature 25 probably was not used for habitation, but may have served as a processing and storage structure. In addition to pollen and macrofloral evidence, a pit was found on the floor of this structure that contained a mortar and several fragments of ground-stone milling equipment. Undoubtedly some of the other pit houses also were used to store native and domesticated foodstuffs. It has been speculated (Chapter 9) that for the most part cultivated foods may have been processed away from the site, and the processed staples stored at Water World, perhaps for use during the winter months when farming was not practical.

Pit house Feature 58 may have served some special purpose in addition to habitation. The unusual assemblage of artiodactyl mandibles, a bighorn sheep horn core, and three deer antler racks found on the floor suggest different kinds of activity (Haury 1976: 62). Three artiodactyl mandibles also were found on the floor of pit house Feature 7. Some of these remains are from large animals, the kind sought by modern trophy hunters (Chapter 8). Their size suggests some special use, perhaps for hunting ritual or ceremonial use, although decoration cannot be ruled out as noted by Di Peso (1951: 39) for the modern Pima and Papago (O'odham) (see Chapter 10). Whether Feature 58 was used for special ceremonies cannot definitely be determined, but these unusual items apparently were kept in the house.

Extramural roasting pits and other kinds of pits were present in each of the house groups, indicating that common work areas were defined for the houses. Only a few of these pits were excavated, and macrofloral analysis showed limited evidence for economic use. The corn, mesquite, and agave identified from some roasting pits can be interpreted either as residue from fuel used in the pits (such as corn cobs and mesquite wood), or as products from food preparation. Three roasting pits (Features 4, 8, and 9) contained mostly burned artiodactyl or large mammal remains, suggesting that large game processing was done in some roasting pits. Remains of small game animals such as jackrabbits were confined primarily to pit house fill and not to roasting pits (Chapter 8).

The ballcourt area contained the most extramural features, but habitation or storage structures were absent. Three structures (Features 66, 67, and 68 in House Group 6) were located to the southwest of the ballcourt and have been interpreted as specialized activity areas rather than pit houses. Their association, if any, with the ballcourt is problematic and any relationship is suggested only by their proximity to the ballcourt. Their function remains an enigma.

The ballcourt represents a special area within the site. As previously mentioned, pit houses were not located in the vicinity of the ballcourt (Feature 41 was not definitely identified as a pit house). The court is small, the interior measuring 17.5 m by 7.8 m. Prior to excavation, small earthern berms were present along the northern and southern sides of the court. In comparison, the excavated ballcourt at Dakota Wash (Craig 1988) is estimated to be 21 m long, and the interior dimensions of the ballcourt at AZ EE:2:105 (Ferg and others 1984: 113) are 17.5 m by 7.4 m, remarkably similar the Water World ballcourt. Orientation of the three ballcourts differs: 77 degrees east of north for Water World, 35 degrees east of north for Dakota Wash, and 10 degrees east of north for AZ EE:2:105. The two entryways of the Water World ballcourt were plastered, as was the entire court although only remnant plaster remained, but no other features such as a surrounding palisade, end markers, or floor features (Wilcox and Sternberg 1983) were found. This also was the case for the ballcourt at AZ EE:2:105 (Ferg and others 1984). Whether the associated roasting pits, hearths, and cremations (Features 5, 60, and 137, located outside the ballcourt to the southwest) were related to the functioning of the court is difficult to determine. Stratigraphic placement of two of the pit features indicated that the area was used for extramural activities before the court was built (Feature 143) and perhaps after the court was abandoned (Feature 144) (Chapter 2).

The presence of the central plaza, first recognized by Downum (1986: 209) after the 1983 survey, is still only conjecture, but cannot be ruled out. No stratigraphic evidence was seen that would confirm the plaza, and its presence is based primarily on the general absence of surface artifacts and features in the area bounded by House Groups 2, 3, 4, 6, and the ballcourt area (Figure 1.6 and Chapter 2).

Exchange

As previously mentioned, ballcourt sites have been considered focal points in Hohokam community organization, as well as in local and regional exchange networks. Consequently, a variety of nonlocal artifacts that signal exchange relationships with other areas is expected at these sites.

Shell is relatively abundant at Water World, and there is some evidence to suggest that Anodonta shell from the Santa Cruz River was used for jewelry. Shell beads of Nerita, a species common in sites from northern Sonora and that may have been exchanged by groups living along the Santa Cruz River (Craig 1982), also are present in the shell assemblage (Chapter 7). Limited evidence for shell manufacturing and for recycling manufactured shell jewelry pieces also is present. Nonetheless, it appears that most of the shell at Water World came from other sources, although perhaps not in the quantity or regularity desired, if recycling was being done and local shell was being used. During the pre-Classic, shell manufacturing appears to have occurred in the Papaguería with finished shell items traded to Hohokam groups in the Santa Cruz River Valley as well as in the Gila Bend and Phoenix Basin areas (Huckell 1979; Masse 1980; Teague 1981: McGuire and Schiffer 1982). This may have been the source from which the inhabitants of Water World received some of their shell jewelry.

Only three turquoise artifacts were found during the excavations. Two were of sufficient quality to be submitted for compositional analysis to determine their source (Volume 4, Chapter 22). One specimen (FN1607; TQA042) appears to have come from the Los Aguajes area in New Mexico, whereas the other piece (FN1293; TQA043) is similar to turquoise from the New Blue Gem Mine in Nevada. One piece of turquoise from Fastimes also is from the same Nevada locality. Considerably more research in turquoise sourcing must be done before definite exchange routes can be identified, but these data suggest that turquoise was imported from some distance during the pre-Classic.

Pottery that is indicative of exchange is not common at Water World. In fact, examples of intrusive pottery made up only 0.72 percent of the pottery assemblage and 7.1 percent of all decorated pottery. Most of the intrusive pottery is Gila Basin buff ware, although there also are seven examples of Trincheras Purple-on-red from northern Sonora and a single example to Dos Cabezas Red-on-brown from southeastern Arizona.

Little evidence for on-site pottery production was found other than several pebble polishers that could be used to smooth a vessel prior to firing. Some pottery was undoubtedly manufactured at the household level (most likely utilitarian plain wares), but a certain amount of the Tucson Basin brown ware and plain ware pottery was also probably obtained locally. Limited exchange with more distant groups also occurred. Compositional analysis of selected sherds from the site may provide some insight into the question of local manufacture of buff wares and brown wares (see Volume 1, Chapter 10).

Overall, exchange relationships appear limited and are similar to those assumed to have existed at Fastimes (Volume 2, Chapter 11). This may indicate that the ballcourt at Water World played a greater role in local Hohokam organization, and a limited role or no role at all in regional relationships.

REFERENCES

Ackerly, Neal W.
1979   The Southern Desert Study Area. In "An Archaeological Survey
        of the Cholla-Saguaro Transmission Line Corridor," edited by
        Lynn S. Teague and Linda Mayro. Arizona State Museum
        Archaeological Series 135(1): 267-406. Tucson: University of
        Arizona.

Arizona Game and Fish Department
1983   Final Report for the Biological Resources Inventory: Tucson
        Division--Phase B, Central Arizona Project Aqueduct. MS,
        Arizona Game and Fish, Special Services Division, Phoenix.

Baker, Lee, and W. Glen Bradley
1969   Skull Measurements of Desert Bighorn Sheep from the Desert
        Game Range. Desert Bighorn Council Transactions 13: 70-74.

Bartlett, Katharine
1933   Pueblo Milling Stones of the Flagstaff Region and Their
        Relation to Others in the Southwest. Museum of Northern
        Arizona Bulletin 3. Flagstaff: Northern Arizona Society of
        Science and Art.

Bean, Lowell John, and Katherine Siva Saubel
1972   Temalpakh, Cahuilla Indian Knowledge and Usage of Plants.
        Banning, California: Malki Museum Press, Morongo Indian
        Reservation.

Bequaert, Joseph C., and Walter B. Miller
1973   The Mollusks of the Arid Southwest. Tucson: University of
        Arizona Press.

Bohrer, Vorsila L., Hugh C. Cutler, and Jonathan D. Sauer
1969   Carbonized Plant Remains from Two Hohokam Sites, Arizona
        BB:13:41 and BB:13:50. The Kiva 35(1): 1-10.

Castetter, Edward F., and Willis H. Bell
1942   Pima and Papago Indian Agriculture. Inter-Americana Studies
        1. Albuquerque: University of New Mexico Press.

Castetter, Edward F., and Ruth M. Underhill
1935   Ethnobiological Studies of the American Southwest II. The
        Ethnobiology of the Papago Indians. The University of New
        Mexico Bulletin 275, Biological Series 4(8). Albuquerque:
        University of New Mexico.

315

316

Castetter, Edward F., Willis H. Bell, and Alvin R. Grove
    1938   Ethnobiological Studies of the American Southwest VI. The
            Early Utilization and the Distribution of Agave in the
            American Southwest. The University of New Mexico Bulletin
            335, Biological Series 5(4). Albuquerque: University of New
            Mexico.

Ciolek-Torrello, Richard, editor
    1987   Hohokam Settlement Along the Slopes of the Picacho Mountains:
            The Picacho Area Sites, Tucson Aqueduct Project. Museum of
            Northern Arizona Research Paper 35(3). Flagstaff: Museum of
            Northern Arizona.

Clark, E. Dan
    1953   A Study of the Behavior and Movements of the Tucson Mountain
            Mule Deer. MS, master's thesis, University of Arizona,
            Tucson.

Craig, Douglas B.
    1982   Shell Exchange Along the Middle Santa Cruz Valley During the
            Hohokam Pre-Classic. Paper presented at the Tucson Basin
            Conference, University of Arizona, Tucson. MS, Arizona State
            Museum Library, University of Arizona, Tucson.

    1988   Archaeological Investigations at AZ AA:16:49 (ASM): The
            Dakota Wash Mitigation. Pima Community College
            Archaeological Report 83-22. Tucson: Pima Community College.

Crosswhite, Frank
    1980   The Annual Saguaro Harvest and Crop Cycle of the Papago,
            with Reference to Ecology and Symbolism. Desert Plants 2(1):
            3-61.

Crown, Patricia L.
    1983   Introduction: Field Houses and Farmsteads in South-Central
            Arizona. In "Hohokam Archaeology Along the Salt-Gila
            Aqueduct, Central Arizona Project, Vol. V: Small Habitation
            Sites on Queen Creek," edited by Lynn S. Teague and Patricia
            L. Crown. Arizona State Museum Archaeological Series 150(5):
            3-22. Tucson: University of Arizona.

Curtin, Leonora Scott Muse
    1984   By the Prophet of the Earth, Ethnobotany of the Pima, reprint
            edition. Tucson: University of Arizona Press.

Czaplicki, Jon S., and Carol Ann Heathington
    1986   Intensive Transect Recording: A Reappraisal and Evaluation.
            In "A Class III Archaeological Survey of the Phase B
            Corridor, Tucson Aqueduct, Central Arizona Project," by
            Christian E. Downum, Adrianne G. Rankin, and Jon S.
            Czaplicki. Arizona State Museum Archaeological Series 168:
            33-40. Tucson: University of Arizona.

Czaplicki, Jon S., and John C. Ravesloot
    1987   Determining Subsurface Site Boundaries at Hohokam Sites by
              Intensive Transect Recording. Paper presented at 52nd Annual
              Meeting of the Society for American Archaeology, Toronto.
              MS, Arizona State Museum Library, University of Arizona,
              Tucson.

Dart, Allen
    1987   Archaeological Studies of the Avra Valley, Arizona, for the
              Papago Water Supply Project. Volume 1: Class III
              Archaeological Surveys on the Tohono O'Odham Indian
              Reservation. Institute for American Research Anthropological
              Papers 9. Tucson: Institute for American Research.

Dart, Allen, William H. Doelle, and Thomas R. McGuire
    1985   Papago Water Supply Project: Class III Archaeological Survey
              for Schuk Toak and San Xavier Districts. Technical Report
              85-6. Tucson: Institute for American Research.

Dean, Jeffrey S.
    1988   Thoughts on Hohokam Chronology. Paper presented at the
              Amerind Foundation Hohokam Seminar, Dragoon, Arizona. MS,
              Arizona State Museum Library, University of Arizona, Tucson.

Deaver, William L.
    1983   Excavations at Jones Ruin (AZ U:15:48) Locus A and Locus B:
              A Transitional Sacaton-Soho Occupation. Part 1 of "Hohokam
              Archaeology Along the Salt-Gila Aqueduct, Central Arizona
              Project, Vol. VI: Habitation Sites on the Gila River," edited
              by Lynn S. Teague and Patricia L. Crown. Arizona State
              Museum Archaeological Series 150(6): 1-158. Tucson:
              University of Arizona.

    1984   Pottery. In "Hohokam Habitation Sites in the Northern Santa
              Rita Mountains," by Alan Ferg, Kenneth C. Rozen, William L.
              Deaver, Martyn D. Tagg, David A. Phillips, Jr., and David A.
              Gregory. Arizona State Museum Archaeological Series 147(2):
              237-420. Tucson: University of Arizona.

    1987   The Tucson Aqueduct Phase B Data Recovery Project: Ceramic
              Typological Classification Methodology. MS, Arizona State
              Museum Library Archives, University of Arizona, Tucson.

Di Peso, Charles C.
    1951   The Babocomari Village Site on the Babocomari River,
              Southeastern Arizona. The Amerind Foundation 5. Dragoon,
              Arizona: The Amerind Foundation.

318

Di Peso, Charles C.
    1956   The Upper Pima of San Cayetano del Tumacacori: An
            Archaeohistorical Reconstruction of the Ootam of the Pimeria
            Alta. The Amerind Foundation 7. Dragoon, Arizona: The
            Amerind Foundation.

Doelle, William H.
    1985a   The Southern Tucson Basin Rillito-Rincon Subsistence,
            Settlement, and Community Structure. In "Proceedings of the
            1983 Hohokam Symposium, Part I," edited by Alfred E. Dittert,
            Jr. and Donald E. Dove. Arizona Archaeological Society
            Occasional Paper 2: 183-198. Phoenix: Phoenix Chapter,
            Arizona Archaeological Society.

    1985b   Excavations at the Valencia Site: A Preclassic Hohokam
            village in the Southern Tucson Basin. Institute for American
            Research Anthropological Papers 3. Tucson: Institute for
            American Research.

    1987   A View of the Avra Valley from the Southern Tucson Basin. In
            "Archaeological Studies of the Avra Valley, Arizona, for the
            Papago Water Supply Project," by Allen Dart. Institute for
            American Research Anthropological Papers 9: 321-373. Tucson:
            Institute for American Research.

Doelle, William H., and Mark D. Elson
    1986   An Overview of Changing Community Patterns. Paper presented
            at the Second Tucson Basin Conference, Tucson, Arizona. MS,
            Arizona State Museum Library, University of Arizona, Tucson.

Doelle, William H., and Henry D. Wallace
    1986   Hohokam Settlement Patterns in the San Xavier Project Area,
            Southern Tucson Basin. Institute for American Research
            Technical Report 84-6. Tucson: Institute for American
            Research.

Doelle, William H., Allen Dart, and Henry D. Wallace
    1985   The Southern Tucson Basin Survey: Intensive Survey Along the
            Santa Cruz River. Institute for American Research Technical
            Report 85-3. Tucson: Institute for American Research.

Downum, Christian E.
    1986   Synthesis and Research Recommendations. In "A Class III
            Archaeological Survey of the Phase B Corridor, Tucson
            Aqueduct, Central Arizona Project," by Christian E. Downum,
            Adrianne G. Rankin, and Jon S. Czaplicki. Arizona State
            Museum Archaeological Series 168: 181-222. Tucson:
            University of Arizona.

Downum, Christian E., Adrianne G. Rankin, and Jon S. Czaplicki
    1986   A Class III Archaeological Survey of the Phase B Corridor,
            Tucson Aqueduct, Central Arizona Project. Arizona State
            Museum Archaeological Series 168. Tucson: University of
            Arizona.

Doyel, David E.
    1977   Excavations in the Middle Santa Cruz River Valley,
            Southeastern Arizona. Arizona State Museum Contribution
            to Highway Salvage Archaeology in Arizona 44. Tucson:
            University of Arizona.

Elmore, Francis H.
    1944   Ethnobotany of the Navajo. University of New Mexico
            Bulletin, Monograph Series 1(7). Albuquerque: University of
            New Mexico.

Elson, Mark D.
    1986   Archaeological Investigations at the Tanque Verde Wash Site:
            A Middle Rincon Settlement in the Eastern Tucson Basin.
            Institute for American Research Anthropological Papers 7.
            Tucson: Institute for American Research.

Ezell, Paul H.
    1961   The Hispanic Acculturation of the Gila River Pimas. American
            Anthropologist Memoir 90, Vol. 63(5), Pt. 2.

Felger, Richard S., and Mary Beck Moser
    1985   People of the Desert and Sea, Ethnobotany of the Seri
            Indians. Tucson: University of Arizona Press.

Ferg, Alan
    1984   Shell. In "Hohokam Habitation Sites in the Northern Santa
            Rita Mountains," by Alan Ferg, Kenneth C. Rozen, William L.
            Deaver, Martyn D. Tagg, David A. Phillips, Jr., and David A.
            Gregory. Arizona State Museum Archaeological Series 147(2):
            687-700. Tucson: University of Arizona.

Ferg, Alan, Kenneth C. Rozen, William L. Deaver, Martyn D. Tagg,
David A. Phillips, Jr., and David A. Gregory
    1984   Hohokam Habitation Sites in the Northern Santa Rita
            Mountains. Arizona State Museum Archaeological Series
            147(2). Tucson: University of Arizona.

Fewkes, Jesse W.
    1896   Pacific Coast Shell from Prehistoric Tusayan Pueblos.
            American Anthropologist (Old Series) 9: 359-367.

320

Fish, Suzanne K.
    1984   The Modified Environment of the Salt-Gila Aqueduct Sites: A
            Palynological Perspective. In "Hohokam Archaeology Along the
            Salt-Gila Aqueduct, Central Arizona Project, Vol. VII:
            Environment and Subsistence," edited by Lynn S. Teague and
            Patricia L. Crown. Arizona State Museum Archaeological
            Series 150(7): 39-52. Tucson: University of Arizona.

    1985   Prehistoric Disturbance Floras of the Lower Sonoran Desert
            and Their Implications. In "Late Quaternary Vegetation and
            Climates of the American Southwest," edited by B. Jacobs,
            P. Fall, and O. Davis. American Association of Stratigraphic
            Palynologists Contribution Series 16.

Fish, Suzanne K., Paul R. Fish, Charles H. Miksicek, and John Madsen
    1985   Prehistoric Agave Cultivation in Southern Arizona. Desert
            Plants 7(2): 107-112.

Fontana, Bernard L.
    1983   Pima and Papago Introduction. In Handbook of North American
            Indians, Volume 10, Southwest, edited by Alfonso Ortiz, pp.
            125-136. Washington: Smithsonian Institution.

Fulton, William Shirley, and Carr Tuthill
    1940   An Archaeological Site near Gleeson, Arizona. Amerind
            Foundation 1. Dragoon, Arizona: The Amerind Foundation.

Gasser, Robert E.
    1982   Hohokam Use of Desert Plant Foods. Desert Plants 3(4):
            216-235.

    1985   Trash Pits and Floor Features: Don't Believe Everything.
            Paper presented at the 50th Annual Meeting of the Society for
            American Archaeology, Denver. MS, Arizona State Museum
            Library, University of Arizona, Tucson.

Gasser, Robert E., and Charles H. Miksicek
    1985   The Specialists: A Reappraisal of Hohokam Exchange and the
            Archaeobotanical Record. In "Proceedings of the 1983 Hohokam
            Symposium, Part II," edited by Alfred E. Dittert, Jr. and
            Donald E. Dove. Occasional Paper 2: 483-498. Phoenix:
            Arizona Archaeological Society.

Gifford, Edward W.
    1947   Californian Shell Artifacts. Anthropological Records 1(9):
            1-132. Berkeley and Los Angeles: University of California
            Press.

Gish, Jannifer W.
    1988   Current Trends, Recent Discoveries, and Future Directions in
            Hohokam Palynology. Paper presented at the 53rd Annual
            Meeting of the Society for American Archaeology, Phoenix.
            MS, Arizona State Museum Library, University of Arizona,
            Tucson.

Gladwin, Harold S., Emil W. Haury, E. B. Sayles, and Nora Gladwin
    1937   Excavations at Snaketown: Material Culture. Medallion Papers
            25. Globe, Arizona: Gila Pueblo.

Goodyear, Albert C., III
    1975   Hecla II and III, An Interpretive Study of Archaeological
            Remains from the Lakeshore Project, Papago Reservation, South
            Central Arizona. Arizona State University Anthropological
            Research Papers 9. Tempe: Arizona State University.

Grebinger, Paul F.
    1971   The Potrero Creek Site: Activity Structure. The Kiva 37(1):
            30-53.

Greenleaf, J. Cameron
    1975   Excavations at Punta de Agua in the Santa Cruz River Basin,
            Southeastern Arizona. Anthropological Papers of the
            University of Arizona 26. Tucson: University of Arizona.

Greenwald, David H., and Richard Ciolek-Torrello
    1987   Picacho Pass Site, NA18,030. In "Hohokam Settlement Along
            the Slopes of the Picacho Mountains: The Picacho Pass Area
            Sites, Tucson Aqueduct Project," edited by Richard Ciolek-
            Torrello. Museum of Northern Arizona Research Paper 35(3):
            130-216. Flagstaff: Museum of Northern Arizona.

Gregory, David A.
    1984   Excavations at the Siphon Draw Site. In "Hohokam Archaeology
            Along the Salt-Gila Aqueduct Central Arizona Project, Vol.
            IV, Part I," edited by Lynn S. Teague and Patricia L. Crown.
            Arizona State Museum Archaeological Series 150(4): 17-215.
            Tucson: University of Arizona.

Halbirt, Carl D.
    1985   Pollen Analysis of Metate Wash Samples: Evaluating Techniques
            for Determining Metate Function. MS, master's thesis,
            Department of Anthropology, Northern Arizona University,
            Flagstaff.

Hansen, Charles G.
    1980   Physical Characteristics. In The Desert Bighorn: Its Life
            History, Ecology, and Management, edited by G. Monson and
            L. Sumner, pp. 52-63. Tucson: University of Arizona Press.

Haury, Emil W.
 1950   The Stratigraphy and Archaeology of Ventana Cave. Tucson:
        University of Arizona Press and Albuquerque: University of
        New Mexico Press.

 1976   The Hohokam: Desert Farmers & Craftsmen. Tucson: University
        of Arizona Press.

Hayden, Brian, and Margaret Nelson
 1981   The Use of Chipped Lithic Material in the Contemporary Maya
        Highlands. American Antiquity 46: 885-898.

Henderson, T. Kathleen
 1987   Ceramics, Dates, and the Growth of the Marana Community. In
        "Studies in the Hohokam Community of Marana," edited by Glen
        E. Rice. Anthropological Field Studies 15: 49-78. Tempe:
        Arizona State University.

Hevly, Richard H., Peter J. Mehringer, Jr., and H. G. Yocum
 1965   Studies of the Modern Pollen Rain in the Sonoran Desert.
        Journal of the Arizona Academy of Science 3: 123-135.

Hoffman, Teresa L.
 1985   Pecked and Ground Stone Artifacts. In "Hohokam Settlement
        and Economic Systems in the Central New River Drainage,
        Arizona," edited by David E. Doyel and Mark D. Elson. Soil
        Systems Publications in Archaeology 4: 565-592. Phoenix:
        Soil Systems.

Hoffmeister, Donald F.
 1986   Mammals of Arizona. Tucson: University of Arizona Press and
        the Arizona Game and Fish Department.

Huckell, Bruce B.
 1979   The Coronet Real Project: Archaeological Investigations on
        the Luke Range, Southwestern Arizona. Arizona State Museum
        Archaeological Series 129. Tucson: University of Arizona.

Jernigan, E. Wesley
 1978   Jewelry of the Prehistoric Southwest. Santa Fe: School of
        American Research and Albuquerque: University of New Mexico
        Press.

Johnson, Alfred E.
 1960   The Place of the Trincheras Culture of Northern Sonora in
        Southwestern Archaeology. MS, master's thesis, Department of
        Anthropology, University of Arizona, Tucson.

Kelley, James E.
 1974   Bighorn Sheep at Grasshopper Ruin: Precautions in Analysis.
        The Kiva 40: 71-79.

Kelly, Isabel T.
      1978   The Hodges Ruin: A Hohokam Community in the Tucson Basin.
              Anthropological Papers of the University of Arizona 30.
              Tucson: University of Arizona Press.

Krausman, Paul R., William W. Shaw, and John L. Stair
      1979   Bighorn Sheep in the Pusch Ridge Wilderness Area, Arizona.
              Desert Bighorn Council Transactions, pp. 40-46.

Layhe, Robert W., editor
      1986   The 1985 Excavations at the Hodges Site, Pima County,
              Arizona. Arizona State Museum Archaeological Series 170.
              Tucson: University of Arizona.

Madsen, Rees L.
      1974   The Influence of Rainfall on the Reproduction of Sonoran
              Desert Lagomorphs. MS, master's thesis, University of
              Arizona, Tucson.

McGuire, Randall H., and Michael B. Schiffer, editors
      1982   Hohokam and Patayan: Prehistory of Southwestern Arizona. New
              York: Academic Press.

Masse, W. Bruce
      1980   Excavations at Gu Achi: A Reappraisal of Hohokam Settlement
              and Subsistence in the Arizona Papaguería. Western
              Archeological Center Publications in Anthropology 12.
              Tucson: National Park Service.

Miksicek, Charles H.
      1987   Late Sedentary-Early Classic Period Hohokam Agriculture:
              Plant Remains from the Marana Community Complex. In "Studies
              in the Hohokam Community of Marana," edited by Glen E. Rice.
              Anthropological Field Studies 15: 197-216. Tempe: Arizona
              State University.

Nelson, Richard S.
      1981   The Role of the Puchtecha System in Hohokam Exchange. MS,
              doctoral dissertation, Department of Anthropology, New York
              University, New York.

Plog, Fred
      1980   Explaining Culture Change in the Hohokam Preclassic. In
              "Current Issues in Hohokam Prehistory: Proceedings of a
              Symposium," edited by David E. Doyel and Fred Plog. Arizona
              State University Anthropological Papers 23: 4-22. Tempe:
              Arizona State University.

Rankin, Adrianne G., and Christian E. Downum
    1986   Site Descriptions. In "A Class III Archaeological Survey of
            the Phase B Corridor, Tucson Aqueduct, Central Arizona
            Project," by Christian E. Downum, Adrianne G. Rankin, and Jon
            S. Czaplicki. Arizona State Museum Archaeological Series
            168: 41-180. Tucson: University of Arizona.

Ravesloot, John C., editor
    1987   The Archaeology of the San Xavier Bridge Site (AZ BB:13:14),
            Tucson Basin, Southern Arizona. Arizona State Museum
            Archaeological Series 171. Tucson: University of Arizona.

Reid, J. Jefferson
    1973   Growth and Response to Stress at Grasshopper Pueblo, Arizona.
            Doctoral dissertation, University of Arizona, Tucson. Ann
            Arbor: University Microfilms.

    1978   Response to Stress at Grasshopper Pueblo, Arizona. In
            Discovering Past Behavior: Experiments in the Archaeology of
            the American Southwest, edited by P. Grebinger, pp. 195-213.
            New York: Gordon and Breach.

Rice, Glen E.
    1985   A Research Design for the Investigation of the Marana
            Community Complex. Arizona State University Anthropological
            Field Studies 10. Tempe: Arizona State University.

Rice, Glen E., editor
    1987   Studies in the Hohokam Community of Marana. Anthropological
            Field Studies 15. Tempe: Arizona State University.

Rice, Glen E., T. Kathleen Henderson, Jeanne Swarthout, and
Suzanne K. Fish
    1984   A Proposal for the Investigation of the Marana Archaeological
            Complex. MS, Arizona State Museum Library, University of
            Arizona, Tucson.

Rozen, Kenneth C.
    1984   Flaked Stone. In "Hohokam Habitation Sites in the Northern
            Santa Rita Mountains," by Alan Ferg, Kenneth C. Rozen,
            William L. Deaver, Martyn D. Tagg, David A. Phillips, Jr.,
            and David A. Gregory. Arizona State Museum Archaeological
            Series 147(2): 421-604.

Russell, Frank
    1975   The Pima Indians, reprint edition. Tucson: University of
            Arizona Press.

Russo, J. P.
    1956   The Desert Bighorn Sheep in Arizona. Wildlife Bulletin 1.
            Phoenix: Arizona Game and Fish Department.

Sayles, E. B.
    1937   Stone: Implements and Bowls. In "Excavations at Snaketown:
            Material Culture," by Harold S. Gladwin, Emil W. Haury, E. B.
            Sayles, and Nora Gladwin. Medallion Papers 25: 101-120.
            Globe, Arizona: Gila Pueblo.

    1945   The San Simon Branch Excavations at Cave Creek and in the San
            Simon Valley I: Material Culture. Medallion Papers 34.
            Globe, Arizona: Gila Pueblo.

Schiffer, Michael B.
    1976   Behavioral Archaeology. New York: Academic Press.

    1987   Formation Processes of the Archaeological Record.
            Albuquerque: University of New Mexico Press.

Schuster, Janette H., and G. Robert Brackenridge
    1986   Late Quaternary Geology and Geomorphology Along the Phase B
            Corridor. In "A Class III Archaeology Survey of the Phase B
            Corridor, Tucson Aqueduct, Central Arizona Project," by
            Christian E. Downum, Adrianne G. Rankin, and Jon S.
            Czaplicki. Arizona State Museum Archaeological Series 168:
            12-28. Tucson: University of Arizona.

Seymour, Deni J., and Michael B. Schiffer
    1987   A Preliminary Analysis of Pit House Assemblages from
            Snaketown, Arizona. In Method and Theory for Activity Area
            Research, An Ethnoarchaeological Approach, edited by Susan
            Kent, pp. 549-603. New York: Columbia University Press.

Sires, Earl W., Jr.
    1984   Hohokam Architecture and Site Structure. Part 2 of "Hohokam
            Archaeology Along the Salt-Gila Aqueduct, Central Arizona
            Project, Vol. IX: Synthesis and Conclusions," edited by Lynn
            S. Teague and Patricia L. Crown. Arizona State Museum
            Archaeological Series 150(9). Tucson: University of Arizona.

Spier, Leslie
    1970   Yuman Tribes of the Gila River, reissue. New York: Cooper
            Square.

Teague, Lynn S.
    1981   Test Excavations at Painted Rock Reservoir: Sites AZ Z:1:7,
            AZ Z:1:8, and AZ S:16:36. Arizona State Museum
            Archaeological Series 143. Tucson: University of Arizona.

    1984   The Organization of Hohokam Economy. In "Hohokam Archaeology
            Along the Salt-Gila Aqueduct, Central Arizona Project, Vol.
            IX: Synthesis and Conclusions," edited by Lynn S. Teague and
            Patricia L. Crown. Arizona State Museum Archaeological
            Series 150(9): 187-250. Tucson: University of Arizona.

Teague, Lynn S., and Patricia L. Crown, editors
1983- Hohokam Archaeology Along the Salt-Gila Aqueduct, Central
1984   Arizona Project. Arizona State Museum Archaeological Series
        150(2-9). Tucson: University of Arizona.

Teague, Lynn S., Susan A. Brew, and Bruce B. Huckell
1982   Arizona State Museum, Cultural Resource Management Division
        Data Recovery Manual. Arizona State Museum Archaeological
        Series 158. Tucson: University of Arizona.

Tuthill, Carr
1947   The Tres Alamos Site on the San Pedro River, Southeastern
        Arizona. The Amerind Foundation 4. Dragoon, Arizona: The
        Amerind Foundation.

Vestal, Paul
1952   Ethnobotany of the Ramah Navajo. Papers of the Peabody
        Museum of American Archaeology and Ethnology 40(4).
        Cambridge: Harvard University.

Vokes, Arthur
1986   The Shell Assemblage. In "The 1985 Excavations at the Hodges
        Ruin, Pima County, Arizona," edited by Robert W. Layhe.
        Arizona State Museum Archaeological Series 170: 207-224.
        Tucson: University Arizona.

1987   Shell Artifacts. In "The Archaeology of the San Xavier
        Bridge Site (AZ BB:13:14 [ASM])," by John C. Ravesloot.
        Arizona State Museum Archaeological Series 171: 251-269.
        Tucson: University of Arizona.

1988   Shell Artifacts. In "The 1982-1984 Excavations at Las
        Colinas: Material Culture," edited by David A. Gregory and
        Carol Ann Heathington. Arizona State Museum Archaeological
        Series 162(4): 319-384. Tucson: University of Arizona.

Wallace, Henry D.
1985   Decorated Ceramics. In "Excavations at the Valencia Site: A
        Preclassic Hohokam Village in the Southern Tucson Basin," by
        William H. Doelle. Institute for American Research
        Anthropological Papers 3: 81-135. Tucson: Institute for
        American Research.

Waters, Michael R., and John J. Field
1986   Geomorphic Analysis of Hohokam Settlement Patterns on
        Alluvial Fans Along the Western Flank of the Tortolita
        Mountains, Arizona. Geoarchaeology: An International Journal
        1: 329-345.

Weaver, Donald E., Jr., Richard Ciolek-Torello, and J. Simon Bruder
1986   Hohokam Settlement Along the Slopes of the Picacho Mountains:
        Research Design, Tucson Aqueduct Project. Museum of Northern
        Arizona Research Paper 35(1). Flagstaff: Museum of Northern
        Arizona.

Whiting, Alfred F.
1939   Ethnobotany of the Hopi. Museum of Northern Arizona Bulletin
        15. Flagstaff: Museum of Northern Arizona.

Whittlesey, Stephanie M.
1986   The Ceramic Assemblage. In "The 1985 Excavations at the
        Hodges Site, Pima County, Arizona," edited by Robert W.
        Layhe. Arizona State Museum Archaeological Series 170:
        61-126. Tucson: University of Arizona.

Wilcox, David R., and Charles Sternberg
1983   Hohokam Ballcourts and Their Interpretation. Arizona State
        Museum Archaeological Series 160. Tucson: University of
        Arizona.

Wilcox, David R., Thomas R. McGuire, and Charles Sternberg
1981   Snaketown Revisited: A Partial Cultural Resource Survey,
        Analysis of Site Structure and an Ethnohistoric Study of the
        Proposed Hohokam-Pima National Monument. Arizona State
        Museum Archaeological Series 155. Tucson: University of
        Arizona.

Withers, Arnold M.
1941   Excavations at Valshni Village, Papago Indian Reservation.
        MS, master's thesis, Department of Anthropology, University
        of Arizona, Tucson.

1973   Excavations at Valshni Village, Arizona. The Arizona
        Archaeologist 7. Phoenix: Arizona Archaeological Society.

Woodbury, Richard B.
1954   Prehistoric Stone Implements of Northeastern Arizona. Papers
        of the Peabody Museum of American Archaeology and Ethnology
        34, Report on the Awatovi Expedition 6. Cambridge: Harvard
        University.

Yarborough, Clare
1986   The Chipped Stone Assemblage. In "The 1985 Excavations at
        the Hodges Site, Pima County, Arizona," edited by Robert W.
        Layhe. Arizona State Museum Archaeological Series 170:
        127-165. Tucson: University of Arizona.